Logos and Life

ANTHEM STUDIES IN WITTGENSTEIN

Anthem Studies in Wittgenstein publishes new and classic works on Wittgenstein and Wittgensteinian philosophy. This book series aims to bring Wittgenstein's thought into the mainstream by highlighting its relevance to 21st century concerns. Titles include original monographs, themed edited volumes, forgotten classics, biographical works and books intended to introduce Wittgenstein to the general public. The series is published in association with the British Wittgenstein Society.

Anthem Studies in Wittgenstein sets out to put in place whatever measures may emerge as necessary in order to carry out the editorial selection process purely on merit and to counter bias on the basis of gender, race, ethnicity, religion, sexual "orientation and other characteristics protected by law. These measures include subscribing to the British Philosophical Association/Society for Women in Philosophy (UK) Good Practice Scheme.

Series Editor
Constantine Sandis – University of Hertfordshire, UK

Forthcoming Titles in the Series
Political Authority: Contract and Critique
Wittgenstein and Popular Culture
Wittgenstein on Other Minds: Strangers in a Strange Land
Kripke's Wittgenstein: Meaning, Rules, and Scepticism
Nightmariners and Wideawakes: The Philosophy of Dreams

Logos and Life

Essays on Mind, Action, Language and Ethics

Roger Teichmann

ANTHEM PRESS

Anthem Press
An imprint of Wimbledon Publishing Company
www.anthempress.com

This edition first published in UK and USA 2025
by ANTHEM PRESS
75–76 Blackfriars Road, London SE1 8HA, UK
or PO Box 9779, London SW19 7ZG, UK
and
244 Madison Ave #116, New York, NY 10016, USA

First published in the UK and USA by Anthem Press in 2022

Copyright © Roger Teichmann 2025

The author asserts the moral right to be identified as the author of this work.

All rights reserved. Without limiting the rights under copyright reserved above, no part of this publication may be reproduced, stored or introduced into a retrieval system, or transmitted, in any form or by any means (electronic, mechanical, photocopying, recording or otherwise), without the prior written permission of both the copyright owner and the above publisher of this book.

British Library Cataloguing-in-Publication Data
A catalogue record for this book is available from the British Library.

Library of Congress Control Number: 2024943704

ISBN-13: 978-1-83999-372-5 (Pbk)
ISBN-10: 1-83999-372-3 (Pbk)

Cover image: Tower of Babel (Babylon), a famous painting by Pieter Brueghel the Elder created in 1563. By jorisvo/Shutterstock.com

This title is also available as an e-book.

CONTENTS

Introduction   1

Part I   Mind

Chapter One	The Functionalist's Inner State	17
Chapter Two	'Not a Something'	27
Chapter Three	Sincerity in Thought	41
Chapter Four	Is Pleasure a Good?	53

Part II   Action

Chapter Five	The Voluntary and the Involuntary: Themes from Anscombe	65
Chapter Six	Rational Choice Theory and Backward-Looking Motives	83
Chapter Seven	Meaning, Understanding and Action	91
Chapter Eight	Why 'Why?'? Action, Reasons and Language	105

Part III   Ethics

Chapter Nine	Ethics and Philosophy: Aristotle and Wittgenstein Compared	123
Chapter Ten	'How Should One Live?' Williams on Practical Deliberation and Reasons for Acting	131
Chapter Eleven	'An Inculcated Caring': Ryle on Moral Knowledge	143
Chapter Twelve	Are There Any Intrinsically Unjust Acts?	151

Part IV Language

Chapter Thirteen	The Identity of a Word	171
Chapter Fourteen	Ryle on Hypotheticals	187
Chapter Fifteen	Metaphysics and Modals	201
Chapter Sixteen	Conceptual Corruption	215

Sources 231

Index 233

INTRODUCTION

I

The essays in this collection were almost all written within the past decade and deal with a range of questions, here brought under the headings 'Mind', 'Action', 'Ethics' and 'Language'. In reality there is so much interconnection and overlap among the themes addressed that this fourfold division is more aesthetic than taxonomic. But it seemed preferable to a dry chronological ordering.

Many of the essays discuss or elaborate on the ideas of Elizabeth Anscombe, and a number discuss or elaborate on those of her friend and teacher Wittgenstein. Both philosophers have sometimes been lumped in with other representatives of something called 'linguistic philosophy', or alternatively 'ordinary language philosophy'. Lazy classifications aside, it is certainly true that the philosophical work of these two thinkers is characterized by an awareness of that tendency to succumb to confusions and pictures (especially of what *must* be the case) which arises out of our intimate and therefore squinting perspective on the workings of our language.

Anscombe's philosophy is explicitly wide-ranging, Wittgenstein's implicitly so – in the sense that he opened up a large arena of potential philosophical investigation. This isn't to say that the problems he explicitly deals with don't cover a lot of ground, for these include problems in philosophy of mind, language, logic, mathematics and epistemology – a broad enough sweep. But out of what he wrote and said many paths lead, and these paths were followed after his death into areas he himself never approached, or into which he ventured only a little way. Anscombe was one of the philosophers to go down some of those paths, as well as exploring the paths off those paths and the paths off those. Her writings on intention and action clearly show the influence of her teacher, picking up some of his discussions where he left off. The same is true of her work in ethics, if only because of the central importance for ethics of intention and action; and this is something worth pointing out, given the great dissimilarity between Anscombe's moral philosophy and Wittgenstein's (such as it is). Here we have an illustration of the 'implicit' philosophical range of Wittgenstein's work to which I've referred.

I mention these two parts of Anscombe's oeuvre, the writings on intention and on ethics, because they have probably attracted the most attention, treatments of *Intention* and of 'Modern Moral Philosophy' tending to dominate 'Anscombe studies'. Even if we restrict ourselves to these two areas within her output, however, the fecundity of her ideas is such as to enable one to travel far with them. Once again, out of what she wrote and said many paths lead.

Take, for example, stopping modals, forcing modals, etc. These are expressions which occur in sentences like 'You *have to* move your king (it's in check)' and 'She *can't* go in there (it's out of bounds)'. Anscombe (1981) introduces the terminology of 'modals' in some articles which would ordinarily be taken to concern ethics (or politics), such as 'On Promising and Its Justice', 'On the Source of the Authority of the State' and 'Rules, Rights and Promises'. But they have a much greater philosophical versatility than that bit of classification might suggest. Indeed, the presence of 'rules' within the title of the third article gives a hint of this, so that it should come as no surprise when Anscombe adverts to stopping/forcing modals in the course of a fourth article, 'The Question of Linguistic Idealism', an investigation of thought, language and reality. It is the 'broader' significance of Anscombean modals which I explore in 'Metaphysics and Modals' (Chapter Fifteen). They also make an appearance in 'Meaning, Understanding and Action' (Chapter Seven), where among other things I invoke them in order to show the incoherence of internalism about reasons for action. A fecund concept is a useful tool.

Another example of such a concept is that of a 'desirability characterization'. Anscombe introduces this in *Intention*: a desirability characterization is the sort of answer to 'Why did you do that? ('Why are you doing that?' etc.) which is apt, in the right sort of (e.g. 'normal') circumstances, to bring iterations of 'Why?' to an end – examples including 'For fun', 'To cure the disease' and 'Because I promised to'. The last sort of answer to 'Why?' expresses what Anscombe calls a backward-looking motive, one that essentially concerns a past fact. Both *desirability characterization* and *backward-looking motive* turn out to be extremely fecund concepts, by no means restricted to the A-B-C-D series in *Intention* with which many a commentator will associate them. The notion of a desirability characterization (along with that of interpretative motives, akin to backward-looking motives) is, I argue in Chapter Four, crucial for an understanding of the concept of pleasure; that of a backward-looking motive allows us to detect a fatal flaw in rational choice theory, and hence in classical economics (Chapter Six); it also lends substance to the idea that the virtue of justice involves rejecting certain kinds of consequentialist calculation (Chapter Twelve).

That many paths can lead out of what a philosopher has said or written mirrors the fact that philosophy itself is a seamless whole, i.e. that getting to grips with a philosophical problem typically involves being able to move around within a network of concepts, thoughts and beliefs without bumping into things or falling down holes. (And there are no 'natural boundaries' separating one network from another.) This picture of philosophy would be rejected by many academic philosophers. For these people, if they turn their minds at all to the nature of the subject they nominally teach and study, philosophy may be a sort of branch of natural science – or a pooling of 'intuitions' concerning various interesting topics – or, if they work in an ethics department, it may be the study of ways of making the world a better place. I touch on the first of these conceptions of philosophy in Chapter Nine, where I sketch (a) how philosophy and science differ, and (b) how the proper aim of philosophy comes much closer than is generally admitted to an overriding aim of any reflective human being, viz. to arrive at an answer, or answers, to the question 'How shall I live?' (NB that two aims are close doesn't mean that they are identical.) This cousinship between philosophy and ethical reflection is further discussed in Chapter Sixteen. It is not the sort of cousinship, by the way, which would justify the approach of those members of ethics departments just mentioned: at any rate, something like Effective Altruism seems to be less of a 'research programme' than an ideology (a utilitarian one).

But, it will be asked, wasn't Anscombe herself an adherent of a well-known ideology, Roman Catholicism? And didn't that pervade her ethics? Is it *bad* to believe in an ideology? – The quick answer to this is that Anscombe's approach to addressing fellow Catholics was quite different from her approach to addressing a more general readership or listenership. There are no Catholic assumptions or presuppositions lying behind the arguments of 'Modern Moral Philosophy' or 'On Being in Good Faith'. But more needs to be said than this. For it is clear that Anscombe would have agreed with the Effective Altruists that there is little point in doing moral philosophy if what you say has no bearing on the practical questions of real life. There certainly are numerous moral philosophers, especially some of those doing 'meta-ethics', whose work you can read without getting even the slightest clue as to what they might actually think is good or bad, right or wrong. (Those four thin moral concepts are the typical pabulum of much meta-ethics.) For such philosophers the conception of philosophy as continuous with science looks untenable: no physicist will be found talking about muons or photons in a spirit of agnosticism. More seriously, the suspicion begins to arise that the real purpose of all this logical geography has more to do with being part of an ongoing discussion than with getting to the bottom of any 'first-order' or 'normative' questions.[1]

But if moral philosophy *is* to be relevant to real life, how can it involve simply 'being able to move around within a network of concepts, thoughts and beliefs'? For that was my rough-and-ready description of the (or an) aim of philosophy, wasn't it? Isn't that 'moving around', or perhaps a description of it, precisely what the arid meta-ethicists are going in for?

The clue here lies in the fact that language and life are interwoven, that what Wittgenstein calls the *use* of signs is not, e.g., the mere uttering of them – not even alongside other signs. Rather, all the various language-games, of calculating, predicting, reporting, brainstorming, warning, greeting, promising, joking, enquiring, commanding, pleading and the rest – all these have, in a necessarily wide sense of 'point', humanly intelligible points. In other words they make sense in the context of human lives with their manifold activities, personal relations, rites of passage, etc. Hence Wittgenstein's talk of a 'form of life' as foundational, and his well-known quotation from Goethe in *On Certainty*: 'In the beginning was the deed.' What I called the network of concepts, thoughts and beliefs around which a person might move, more or less smoothly, is embodied in language, but also in diverse human activities. To be sure, when doing philosophy one's use of concepts is in a certain sense self-conscious, and the activities that anchor them lie well in the background (and of course philosophizing itself can be called a species of activity). But the anchors are there all the same.

If language and life are thus interwoven, and if philosophical problems arise out of 'the bewitchment of our intelligence by means of language',[2] then surely all philosophy, not just moral philosophy, is 'relevant to real life', at least potentially? Won't confusion in word, confusion in thought and confusion in deed all tend to go together? Ditto clarity (in word, thought and deed)? I think this is true. And it helps to explain why Wittgenstein went perhaps further than Anscombe would have when he asked Malcolm, 'What is the use of studying philosophy if all that it does for you is to enable you to talk with some plausibility about some abstruse questions of logic, etc., & if it does not improve your thinking about the important questions of everyday life?'[3]

Those who label the philosophy of the later Wittgenstein (or of Anscombe) 'linguistic' sometimes want to imply that what's going on is a sort of glorified lexicography. What else could all those ruminations about words and signs amount to? I hope that the reflections of the previous paragraphs go some way towards undermining that suspicion. They might also thereby assist in the rejection of the metaphysico-scientific conception of philosophy so often touted as preferable.

The 'anti-linguistic' view of philosophy in any case faces a dilemma. This dilemma takes for its starting point the dichotomy *words vs things*. The anti-linguistic philosopher will, like Ernest Gellner[4] if not with his simplicity, berate Wittgenstein et al. for talking about words, not things. Let's assume the topic is pain. Wittgenstein appears to be talking a great deal about expressions of pain, the teaching of the word 'pain' and so on. Our philosopher, on the other hand, wants to give us a theory about *pain*. Dilemma: either Wittgenstein's remarks are in conflict with the theory or they aren't. If they are, then the two parties can't be talking at cross purposes: there's a real disagreement, and (since the theory is a theory about *pain*) Wittgenstein's remarks must express or entail propositions about *pain*. If, on the other hand, Wittgenstein's remarks are not in conflict with the theory, and he is talking about something else, what is the objection? Why *not* talk about words? Are words so bad?

Perhaps the objection is that Wittgenstein is *purporting* to talk about pain, when in fact he isn't. It would be rather as if he'd said: 'Here's my theory about cows: "cows" is a plural noun.' Let's admit that Wittgenstein is purporting to talk about pain, not just about 'pain'. If he's clearly talking about 'pain' some of the time, it seems he is rejecting the original dichotomy *words vs things*; that's to say, he thinks that in talking about 'pain' he *is* talking about pain. It is certainly possible to do that: e.g. I would manage to talk about Mark's pain by saying, 'One could truly predicate "in pain" of Mark right now – poor fellow.' Our philosopher will have to say that when *Wittgenstein* talks about 'pain', he's not talking about pain. But how show this? Evidently not by repeating the simple dichotomy *words vs things*.

II

The Greek word 'logos' means word, reason, account. A thread running through the essays in this book is the idea that a certain phenomenon is what it is partly (but crucially) in virtue of its connection with reasons, rationality, etc. This will sometimes appear surprising, e.g. if our inclination is to describe the phenomenon in question in terms of its 'intrinsic nature', or of its place in a causal nexus, or of its being the 'best explanation' of some other phenomenon. These are vague words, so let me give some examples.

In Chapter Three I argue that insincerity, in thought, word or deed, cannot be understood merely in terms of a mismatch between a person's overt attitude/belief and their 'real' but hidden attitude/belief. For an important class of cases the charge of insincerity (bad faith, hypocrisy, etc.) relies on the *dubiousness* of the person's attitude/belief, i.e. with its lacking proper grounds or **reasons**, where the criteria indicated by the word 'proper' are objective, not person-relative.

In Chapter Four I argue that to understand the nature of pleasure we should look at such **reasons** – given e.g. in answer to 'Why are you doing that? – as 'For fun' or 'For the pleasure of it'. The intelligibility of such a reason will relate in a certain way to what is humanly natural or normal. Moreover, if you say 'For fun', your statement may be met with a further demand for clarification, 'What's the fun in that?', to which the answer may have to give what I call a rationale, a species of ground or **reason**. If such an answer is lacking, the proper concept to apply might not be pleasure, but e.g. psychological compulsion.

Chapter Five deals with the concept of voluntary action, and it's maintained that more light is thrown on the voluntary/involuntary distinction by considerations concerning actual or possible **reasons** for action than by ones concerning possible-doing-otherwise (or possible prevention), or by ones concerning causal powers, of the agent or of mental states.

In Chapters Seven and Fifteen I emphasize the fact that assertion is a species of action: to assert something is to do something. The rules governing what's assertible or to-be-asserted are thus appropriately understood as rules governing certain human actions; and as Anscombe argued, the basic expression of a rule employs such modals as 'You have to' or 'You may'. The function of these latter bits of language is as part of a certain language-game in which **reasons** are demanded or given. A modal statement can itself be given as a reason, but it in turn is to be backed up by such a **reason** as 'Your king is in check' or 'That would contradict your initial premise' – dubbed by Anscombe a 'logos'.

So what are *reasons*, that they should play such a pervasive role in our conceptual scheme and/or reality? Is what's being put forward some kind of rationalist philosophy?

The disagreements between the early modern Rationalists and Empiricists rested on various agreed assumptions and beliefs. Rationalist and anti-rationalist alike took Reason to be a certain faculty, and reasoning to be a certain (mental) process. The exercise of the faculty involved the doing or undergoing of the process; 'doing or undergoing' points to a notorious dilemma, by the way. Here we have less a *theory* of how things are than a *picture*, I would say, and one which is still far from extinct among philosophers. Whatever the merits of this distinction, the theory/picture typically faces the following question: what is it, if anything, that determines standards of good or bad, logical or illogical, correct or incorrect, in the domain of reasoning? Roughly speaking, the Rationalists invoked some kind of necessity or self-evidence, the Empiricists some kind of psychological regularity (including that of one idea's being 'contained within' another). Neither kind of answer, I think, is ultimately tenable.

For one thing, the shared assumption that such notions as 'reasonable' or 'rational' should be understood by reference to *what went on* in the course of a certain person's cogitation is fatally and demonstrably flawed. As both Wittgenstein and Anscombe in their different ways showed, the reasons behind some action or claim or emotional manifestation of mine will often – if not typically – come out only after the event. Reasons are to be *elicited*; and in giving you my reasons I do not usually consult my memory. (It's not that I'm too lazy to. To look into my inner past would be to look in the wrong place.) To be sure, one can go through some reasoning or calculating in one's head, just as one can do so out loud or on paper. And these are indeed processes. That there are such processes helps to entrench the philosophical picture I'm referring to. But what makes these processes embodiments of *reasoning*? The answer to this, as Frege was perhaps the first to see, cannot be a psychological one.[5]

The reader may already have an inkling of the kind of answer I would propose for the question 'So what are reasons?' The answer would involve describing certain language-games, and their context or contexts within human life.[6] Thus it would not be of the form 'Reasons are Fs', or 'A reason is an F'. One of the main ways in which it seems to me that philosophy has *not* made progress, despite the opportunities, is in the continuing methodological addiction to framing a question in the format 'What is an X?' An answer will then be deemed acceptable only if it takes the form 'An X is a such-and-such'. Two obvious sources of this addiction are: (a) the scientific paradigm, (b) the tendency to think that nouns or noun phrases all work in the same way (enable the same kinds of inference, etc.).

More than a hundred years ago Russell, among others, did a fair bit to open our eyes to the philosophical significance of (b). Someone asserts: 'The average politician has 2.7 children'. As far as surface grammar goes, this is of the same form as 'The oldest politician has 3 children'. So it would be natural for a child to ask, 'What or who is the average politician? And how can you have 2.7 children?' The first step in answering the child's questions is to *avoid* the format 'The average politician is X'. (Similar remarks go for 'An average politician'.) An adequate answer will involve explaining or giving the meaning of the whole sentence in which 'The average politician' appeared, thus: the sentence means (assuming no politician's child has more than one politician parent) 'The number of politicians' children divided by the number of politicians is 2.7'.

It surely *might* be the case that an analogous, if much more complicated, story needs to be told vis-à-vis 'the reason for her action' or 'an intention to eat'. Of course everyday language frequently supplies phrases that are interchangeable (in many contexts) with other phrases, so that one could answer 'What is an intention to eat?' using some such phrase as, 'It's a purpose that one eat'. In the same way, if it weren't for the ambiguity of 'mean', the child's question could be answered thus: 'The average politician is the mean politician.' But the answer would be unhelpful. The same goes for the answer 'An intention to eat is a purpose that one eat': if the first phrase puzzles us, so will the second. Now philosophical answers to 'What is an intention to eat?' do not have such an appearance of emptiness; they include statements like 'It is a belief-desire pair whose typical non-deviant effects include the agent's eating something'. It's to be noted that one might concoct a similarly interesting-sounding answer to 'What's the average politician?' (and indeed I have heard it done): something starting 'It's a function …' or 'It's a ratio …' or 'It's a set of sets which …' Would such an answer assist the child? No.

However, the child is unacquainted with the term 'average', whereas we are acquainted with the term 'intention'. Hence the two species of puzzlement are different. As regards *our* puzzlement a paradox seems to loom, namely Meno's Paradox:[7] if we already know the meaning of 'intention' we shouldn't need to ask what an intention is – moreover, how will we know when we've arrived at a satisfactory answer unless we do already know what an intention is (so that we can recognize the answer as true on finding it)?

The metaphysico-scientific philosopher takes it that there is no paradox here, any more than there is in connection with 'What is the specific gravity of hydrogen?' We know what 'specific gravity' and 'hydrogen' mean, he will say, and so know the sense of 'the specific gravity of hydrogen' – what we don't know is its reference. We need to *find that out*. Similarly, we need to find out the reference of 'Alice's intention to eat'. But how do we do that? Do we investigate Alice?

Let's assume the philosopher answers 'No'. Then the alternative seems to be that we find out the reference of 'Alice's intention to eat' by inspecting something each of us already has: a concept, idea, intuition, universal … The result of our inspection might be the discovery that Alice's intention to eat is in fact a belief-desire pair whose typical non-deviant effects include Alice's eating something. This would be Rationalism all right, Platonic Rationalism. And there is *something* right about it, at least insofar as there is an admission that we don't need to investigate Alice. What is wrong with it is the picture that is associated with, and finds expression in, such terms as 'inspect' and 'find out'. That picture is what impels or encourages us to take for our starting point a particular form of question: 'What is the (or an) X?' If we drop the picture we can do justice to what actually goes on when we tackle the 'philosophical problem of intention'.

Canny readers will know why I used the example of the specific gravity of hydrogen above. In connection with the question 'What is time?' Wittgenstein writes:

> Augustine says in the *Confessions* 'quid est ergo tempus? si nemo ex me quaerat scio; si quaerenti explicare velim, nescio'[8]. This could not be said about a question of natural science ('What is the specific gravity of hydrogen?' for instance). Something that we know when no one asks us, but no longer know when we are supposed to give an account of it, is something that we need to *remind* ourselves of. (And it is obviously something of which for some reason it is difficult to remind oneself.) (1958, 89)

The metaphysico-scientific philosopher will perhaps accuse Augustine of conflating sense and reference. Augustine knows the *sense* of 'time' ('tempus'), what he doesn't know is its *reference*. But what if 'time' has neither a Fregean sense nor reference? Our only reason to think it has a sense and a reference is that, like 'the average politician', it's a grammatical singular term: it's a proper noun, at least as it occurs in sentences like 'Time flies'. The supposition that 'time' has a sense and a reference is really the same as the supposition that the correct answer to Augustine's question must be of the form 'Time is X'.

The sense/reference distinction is most naturally applied to singular terms – to expressions like 'Time' or 'Alice's intention to eat', rather than to ones like 'a dimension' or 'an intention'. I described our quasi-Platonist philosopher as alleging that we need to find out the reference of 'Alice's intention to eat' by inspecting something each of us has. Of course it's part of the picture underlying that line of thought that such 'inspection' is primarily of something *general* – a concept, universal or what have you. In other words, we are primarily asking ourselves 'What is an intention?', not 'What is Alice's current intention to eat?' The sense/reference distinction, or something like it, *might* be invoked in connection with 'What is an intention?'; but one could anticipate difficulties. Another way of proceeding would be to employ Kripke's notion of rigid designation. Perhaps 'intention', like 'lion', is a natural kind term, rigidly designating a kind whose members share some empirically discoverable essence. From Rationalism we veer to Empiricism.

If 'intention' is a natural kind term, then 'Alice's intention to eat' will be akin to 'Alice's hamster', and an empirical investigation of (the nature of) intentions in general and of Alice's in particular will be on the cards. The latter kind of investigation will have priority; after all, the only way to investigate hamsters is by starting on a particular hamster. So there had better be such a thing as an empirical investigation of Alice's intention to eat. Is there?

In Chapter Two I examine this question among others. The answer I give is, in effect, 'There *might* be something that counts as an empirical investigation of (the nature of) Alice's intention to eat – but equally, there might not be.' That this *is* the answer is important, and is enough to throw doubt on a raft of physicalist theories, whether those theories invoke type-identity or token-identity. If 'What is Alice's intention to eat?' is posed as a question asking after some independently describable state of Alice or of anything else, the best answer to that question might in fact be 'There is nothing which *is* her intention to eat.' Or, in other words, 'It's not a something.' In the course of arguing to these conclusions the actual behaviour of the term 'intention' has to be examined and sketched. One result of such a (necessarily never-completed) examination is the recognition that nothing further from a natural kind term à la Kripke can easily be imagined. The same goes for other psychological concepts, like 'pain' (pace Kripke himself[9]).

III

If one thread running through the essays in this book relates to reasons, rationality, etc., a second thread worth mentioning is an emphasis on context and surroundings as providing the clue to some phenomenon's nature or significance. That phrase, 'context and surroundings', is intended in a very broad sense. At one end of the spectrum there is the sort of linguistic context I appealed to when discussing the average politician: the context of the phrase 'the average politician' is the whole sentence in which it occurs ('The average politician has 2.7 children'), and it is by alluding to that context, and ones like it, that we can give a proper explanation of the meaning of the phrase. At the other end of the spectrum there is the context a language-game such as promising has within the life of human beings. A proper account of the nature of that language-game will allude to such things as the kinds of *benefit* which going in for promising brings to the human beings who go in for it, and also to the *connections* which this practice has with other practices and other areas of life. Somewhere in mid-spectrum is the context within an individual's life of particular words or deeds; for example, an assertion like 'It didn't occur to me' might, against a particular biographical background, be expressive of a certain orientation of the will, or ordering of priorities.[10] In each of these three cases, and in many others, the inclination to be resisted is that of *homing in on* the item in question – phrase, practice, utterance or what have you – in the hope of getting clear about it. That inclination is evidently manifested by many philosophers for whom some question of the form 'What is X?' is the paradigm starting point of an enquiry.

I spoke earlier of two sources of the methodological addiction to questions of that form: (a) the scientific paradigm, and (b) the tendency to think that nouns or noun phrases all work in the same way. When it comes to ethics and the philosophy of mind, we can perhaps add a third source, insofar as the methodological addiction embodies an inclination to *home in on* something in the way I've suggested. This third source is a tendency of thought that is as much cultural as philosophical; it is an aspect of our *Zeitgeist*. For want of a better word I will label it 'individualism'.

Individualism, in this sense, is a picture of the human person as in various ways *sovereign*. According to this picture I am an authority, e.g. as to what I feel or think or need; also as to what I mean or understand. For only I have access to these facts about me, and that access is supremely reliable if not infallible. Thoughts, feelings, desires, construed thus, are phenomena whose nature is 'intrinsic': I have but to inwardly home in on one and I can report back what it is. As far as these phenomena go, facts outside me, or opinions outside me, can be ignored, except perhaps in pathological cases (the Freudian subconscious). For another person to *tell* me about myself is liable to be an impertinence – a sort of *lèse-majesté*.

So far, so Cartesian. But the Cartesianism has surely spilled over into areas about which Descartes himself wouldn't have alleged we have the kind of privileged access which we're alleged to have by the individualist. Let me give two examples: feelings and the good.

The concept of *feeling* or *emotion* is a very motley one, but among what are called feelings are ones with a certain ethical import, such as the feeling of offence (or being offended). In Chapter Eight I discuss this concept:

> We often find here a kind of doublethink: there is (a) the recognition that a person really can, in being offended, have just cause for complaint, on account of the reasons behind his taking offence – but on top of this there is (b) a denial of the requirement that taking offence itself be justified by reference to any reasons. Given (b), the only thing to point to as the ground of your complaint is simply the painfulness of the emotion; and so the whole phenomenon is subsumed under a general utilitarian proscription on causing suffering.[11]

Point (a) makes room for the possibility that a person who is offended may challenge, accuse or rail against another person with good reason, while (b) allows the ground of their complaint to rest on first-person authority about what they feel – 'I say I'm offended and no one can gainsay me.' As I argue in the essay, the combination of (a) and (b) is incoherent. But there is a very strong *motivation* for embracing such a form of incoherence. For people like to attack and condemn other people and to think that they're in the right when doing so.

It is (b) of course which is the source of the problem. And (b) is to be countered by pointing out that the criteria determining whether some feeling is offence, as well as the criteria determining whether that feeling is reasonable or unreasonable, are supplied by the socially shared standards of a language-game – not by the *fiat* of an individual. The notion of offence as involving (b) embodies what I call conceptual corruption, a social phenomenon characterized by bad faith and, often, the Will to Power. I discuss conceptual corruption in the essay of that name (Chapter Sixteen).

The sort of motivated doublethink referred to in the above passage crops up in various forms in our society. An example that enjoys a certain notoriety is the way in which 'hate crime' gets defined in the UK:

> The police and the CPS have agreed the following definition for identifying and flagging hate crimes: 'Any criminal offence which is perceived by the victim or any other person, to be motivated by hostility or prejudice, based on … [a list of 'protected characteristics' follows].[12]

Why do I call this doublethink? (After all, it can be called many things.) Because of an incoherent combination: (i) the recognition that a person's grounds for their hostility or aggression can be objectively bad grounds, e.g. the colour of another's skin; (ii) the claim that *what* grounds someone has for their hostility or aggression are simply the grounds they are perceived to have by others. (ii) is not a statement about what counts as good evidence, viz. the perceptions of others, for if that were the case, then conflicting evidences would in principle be possible, and an apparently sincere denial on the defendant's part would probably have to be taken into account. No, (ii) is intended to be, in effect, a definition. But if the concepts of *grounds* and of *motivation* were in the eye of the beholder in this way, (i) would lose its point. And it is (i) which gives prima facie plausibility to the idea that *punishment* might be appropriate.

The absurdity is multilayered. One obvious absurdity is the invocation of first-person authority concerning having been targeted by (e.g.) racial hostility *on top of* the withdrawal of first-person authority concerning whether one harbours any racial hostility. (The defendant's individuality presumably evaporated upon arrest.) But there is more. What if one observer were to say, 'She was motivated by hostility on the ground that P' while another said 'She was in no way motivated by hostility on the ground that P'? Is the concept of a hate crime such that the first kind of perception automatically trumps the second kind? Are negative perceptions necessarily more reliable than positive ones? But 'reliable' suggests evidence, and we don't want to go there. Negative 'perceptions' just are grounds for complaint and potential punishment. And as with the concept of offence, what we seem to be left with is simply a general utilitarian prohibition on causing pain – intentionally *or* unintentionally; though the pain caused to the defendant as a result of an increased gaol sentence might be thought relevant from the point of view of the utilitarian calculus. (In 2021 the Crown Prosecution Service boasted that 'last year, more than half of our requests led to offenders having their sentence increased because it [the crime] was motivated by hate'.[13] Of course, now we know what 'motivated by hate' means.)

Not just doublethink, but *motivated* doublethink. What motives are in play? On the part of members of the public: to attack and condemn other people. On the part of the CPS and the police: to enhance the hit rate and hence their prestige. As for the motivations of the legislators responsible for introducing this bit of conceptual corruption into our lives, these will be as complex and twisty as political motivations so often are, but presumably include: to exhibit credal orthodoxy and to exercise power over what people say or think.[14]

I've dwelt long enough on this particular example. But as Wittgenstein said, what is the use of studying philosophy if it doesn't improve your thinking about the important questions of everyday life? Let me now turn to the second of the two examples of the individualist tendency which I mentioned a while back, namely the individualist view of the good.

I want to look at two individualist lines of thought about the good: the first concerns a person's good – my good or your good, what's good *for* us; the second concerns the general idea of something's being good, as wielded especially by philosophers and among philosophers especially by utilitarians (or consequentialists). As regards the first line of thought, the distinction that is liable to be elided or simply denied by the individualist is that between needs and wants. For what I *want* is plausibly enough thought of as something about which I am an authority, whereas that may be doubted as regards what I *need*. So a philosophy according to which what's good for you has to do with what you need (e.g. in order to flourish qua human being) as opposed to what you want is liable to be suspect for an individualist. That X is or would be good for me is after all meant to supply me with a reason for doing some things and not others; my sovereignty as an individual is obviously at issue, and the question what is good for me must boil down to the question what I want.

Consider internalism about practical reasons, i.e. the view that I have reason to φ if and only if φ-ing would be conducive to my getting or achieving something I want. On this view I have a reason to kill my brother if that would be the best way to hurt my parents and I do want to hurt my parents, while I have an 'all things considered' good reason to kill him if I want to hurt my parents more than I want anything else. The observation that I'd be acting wickedly if I killed my brother can be met with the reply, 'But if I don't *want* to avoid wickedness (whatever that is!) this observation has no bearing on what I've got reason to do.' It is predictably difficult to milk morality out of this kind of position. Internalism about reasons nevertheless remains popular, and this is so, I think, largely on account of the individualist *Zeitgeist*. I criticize internalism in Chapters Seven and Ten.

The second individualist line on the good concerns especially 'good states of affairs'. For a traditional utilitarian, it is a sort of axiom that pleasure is good and pain is bad. That a creature is feeling pleasure is a good state of affairs. This notion is typically connected with a certain picture of pleasure, as a self-intimating episode of consciousness, with a certain duration, typically having a certain intensity, and with an intrinsic 'character' knowable authoritatively by the subject – in short, as a sensation or quasi-sensation. I know that my pleasure is *good* because when I'm feeling it I can home in on it, and can report back 'That's good!' Indeed, it's possible to reduce 'good for me' to 'deemed by me to be good', insofar as the goodness I find in my pleasure is in the (inner) eye of the beholder: about such goodness I cannot be mistaken. And you can tell me, if I ask you, whether your pleasure is good – I presume it is.[15]

Of course there is *something* right about the thought that pleasure is good and pain is bad, however inchoate it is; what that might be is discussed in Chapter Four, where I locate the desirability characterization 'For pleasure' within the context of a language-game and of human life, and so hope among other things to give a sense of why pleasure should be at all important. The *importance* of pleasure is very hard to account for on the view of pleasure as a sensation, despite the fact that the proponents of that view so often wish to present pleasure as supremely important. Anscombe puts the matter thus:

> We might adapt a remark of Wittgenstein's about meaning and say 'Pleasure cannot be an impression; for no impression could have the consequences of pleasure.' They [the British empiricists] were saying that something which they thought of as like a particular tickle or itch was quite obviously the point of doing anything whatsoever. (1963, 77)

Partly because of difficulties faced by the classical utilitarian account of pleasure, latter-day consequentialists have tended to move towards other kinds of 'states of affairs', such as preference-satisfaction, as vehicles or instantiators of goodness. Goodness is still what is to be maximized, however, being (for some reason) supremely important. But one can no longer simply rely on introspection to arrive at 'X is good', as one could with pleasure. So how can I ascertain or know that such-and-such total utility is a good state of affairs? The answer is: by intuition.

Copyright for this manoeuvre must belong to G. E. Moore. Moore felt that he *knew* that friendship was good (as he felt he *knew* that he had hands); and, realizing that the source of this alleged knowledge couldn't be his senses, nor introspection, nor his logical faculty, he invented a faculty, that of intuition. How did he know he had such a faculty? Because he knew he must have *some* faculty yielding the knowledge, since he knew he had the knowledge! Is the position of latter-day users of the concept of intuition markedly different? I don't think so. 'I have an intuition that P' generally appears to mean no more than 'I want to assert that P – don't ask me why'. In Moore's case, the whiff of individualism is detectable in the confidence of the assertion 'I know friendship is good; I have consulted my intuition' – possibly the sort of assertion which so endeared him to the Bloomsburyites. In the case of more recent intuitors of goodness, while the reference to knowledge might be absent, there is still a sort of assumption that Smith's undefended assertion 'X is good' has value simply as *coming from Smith*, just as Smith's vote has value simply as Smith's vote, a value taken very seriously in our culture (and of course endorsed by those who would like to have Smith's vote).

I have been discussing attempts by individualist thinkers to elucidate the concept *good*. Humeans and subjectivists have tried to explain it away in terms of wants. Moore and philosophers like him think that good is an intuitible property of states of affairs. The actual behaviour of the word 'good' (and its equivalents in other languages) is too often ignored, or is taken to be the preserve of ordinary language philosophers and suchlike lexicographers. But there are philosophers who have wanted to investigate that behaviour and do justice to its complexity and contextuality. A notable instance is Philippa Foot, whose *Natural Goodness* (2001) gives us an account of the good which locates it both in our language and in our life.

And here the ethical dimension of a sensitivity to context and surroundings begins to come into view. By attending to those surroundings I not only get a clearer and truer picture of the nature of the phenomenon which interests me, I also engage with the world around me, the people around me; I come face to face with the fact that (as Donne expressed it) 'no man is an island'. A philosophy that embodies the individualist mindset, by contrast, is liable to tend towards moral solipsism.[16] That tendency is perhaps all the more insidious, because apparently deniable, when the official creed is one that extols universal altruism, social justice, etc.

An indication of what I'm talking about is supplied by the picture of rational human behaviour that is presented by the 'science' of economics – a product of Western modernity if ever there was one. At the heart of standard economics is an allegedly neutral account of what people have reason to do, rational choice theory. This theory is explicitly individualist and so suffers from various of the purely conceptual problems one would expect it to; but it also can't help presenting an impoverished picture of human beings and of human life, as I argue in Chapter Six.

Philosophy and philosophers can surely help. Socrates's recommendation to the philosopher to be a gadfly remains a good one. As both Wittgenstein and Anscombe saw, there is much in our *Zeitgeist* worthy of interrogation and critique, as no doubt there is in any *Zeitgeist*. But this negative task is not the only task of philosophy; to present an overview (*übersicht*) of even a portion of human life and language is to achieve something.

Notes

1 In the introduction to her third volume of collected papers Anscombe writes: 'In general, my interest in moral philosophy has been more in particular moral questions than in what is now called "meta-ethics"' (1981, viii.).
2 Wittgenstein (1958, sec. 109).
3 Malcolm (1967, 93).
4 Gellner (1959).
5 It might be objected that I have here prioritized the (first-person) giving of reasons over the (third-person) ascribing of reasons. So I have: I think the former has a logical priority over the latter. See Anscombe (1963, sec. 20); and Chapter Eight of this volume (p. 108).
6 So would *human agreement* determine the standards of good or bad, logical or illogical, reasoning? Yes and no; the question is complex. I discuss it in the final section of Chapter Fifteen.
7 See Plato's dialogue *Meno*.
8 'What then is time? If no one asks me, I know; if I wish to explain to someone, I don't know.'
9 See Kripke (1981, 146–55). See also Chapters One and Two of this volume.
10 See Chapter Five, pp. 76–78.
11 Chapter Eight, p. 113.
12 https://www.cps.gov.uk/crime-info/hate-crime.
13 Ibid.
14 The term 'motivated' doesn't point to consciously embraced purposes, as I explain in Chapter Sixteen.
15 The relevance to this line of thought of Wittgenstein's 'Private Language Argument' is obvious.
16 In a similar vein Richard Gipps argues that the temptations of thought succumbed to by the Private Linguist (the interlocutor targeted in the Private Language Argument) manifest the sort of narcissism which is of interest to psychoanalysts. See Gipps (2020).

References

Anscombe, G. E. M. (1963), *Intention*. Oxford: Blackwell, 2nd ed.
———. (1981), *Collected Papers Vol. III: Ethics, Religion and Politics*. Oxford: Blackwell.
Foot, P. (2001), *Natural Goodness*. Oxford: Oxford University Press.
Gellner, E. (1959), *Words and Things*. London: Victor Gollancz.
Gipps, R. (2020), 'The Narcissism of the Private Linguist', in Maria Balaska (ed.), *Cora Diamond on Ethics*. London: Palgrave Macmillan, pp. 223–46.
Kripke, S. (1981), *Naming and Necessity*. Oxford: Basil Blackwell.
Malcolm, N. (1967), *Ludwig Wittgenstein: A Memoir*. Oxford: Oxford University Press.
Wittgenstein, L. (1958), *Philosophical Investigations*, trans. G. E. M. Anscombe, ed. G. E. M. Anscombe and R. Rhees. Oxford: Basil Blackwell, 2nd ed.

Part I
MIND

Chapter One

THE FUNCTIONALIST'S INNER STATE

Behaviourism and Functionalism

What exactly is the connection between mental states and behaviour? The connection, it seems, is an intimate one; philosophical behaviourism makes it out to be a very intimate one.

There are various forms of behaviourism, more or less extreme. But roughly speaking what they all claim is this: somebody is in pain, or believes that p, or is jealous, or whatever, just in case he or she is behaving in a particular way – *or* just in case he or she is disposed to behave in a particular way. (That 'or' already signifies an important difference of approach.)

Now a certain queasiness about behaviourism has been expressed in the objection: 'But surely pain (or whatever) can't just *be* behaviour, or a behavioural disposition? Isn't the behaviour (or the disposition) *produced by* the pain? And so isn't the pain itself in some sense *inner*?'

The traditional notion of the 'inner', associated with such philosophers as Descartes, has to do with the subject's alleged special and privileged access to his own mental states – and this notion has tended to go with dualism about mind and body. But more recent philosophers have been keen to hang on to the notion of the inner while rejecting traditional dualism – in particular, functionalists.

The main respect in which functionalists differ from behaviourists is in their saying that someone is in pain (or whatever) just in case he or she is in that state which is in fact typically caused by certain things, and which typically produces certain types of behaviour. Again, there are variants of functionalism, but this will do as a broad characterization.

Actually, there are two differences to notice here between functionalism and behaviourism. One is that functionalists mention causes, as well as behaviour; the other is the reference to a state of the subject, productive of that behaviour. It is this state that is typically spoken of as 'realizing', or indeed as 'being identical with', the subject's mental state on a particular occasion; and it is this state that performs the role of an 'inner state' – 'inner' in quite a literal sense, now, since it is usually taken to be a brain state or some such internal state of the creature in question.

A Thought Experiment

Imagine now that a close friend goes for a brain scan. She's been having some headaches, and the doctors think it best to check up. After a few days, the results come through. And it turns out that your friend simply lacks a brain. There's nothing but water in her skull. Perhaps further investigations confirm this, and even reveal the absence of a central nervous system.

Question: How would you respond to these facts?

Now there is of course a sense in which this little story is simply inconceivable.[1] It's inconceivable in the same sort of way as a story would be inconceivable in which it turned out that the first human beings had evolved, over twenty-four hours, out of a dollop of rich mud. The two stories are both inconceivable because they are *so much* in conflict with our scientific knowledge of the world. But there is surely *a* sense in which it is conceivable that human beings should have evolved overnight from mud: at any rate, it would surely be wrong to say that it was part of the concept *human being* that human beings didn't evolve overnight from mud. It's not a conceptual truth that we didn't evolve overnight from mud. And I want to argue, likewise, that it's not a conceptual truth that when someone is, say, in pain, there be any internal state causally responsible for their pain-behaviour.

We need to issue a caveat at this point. Functionalism, it is often said, is a definite improvement on the first theories of mind-brain identity that appeared (in the 1950s) insofar as it allows that different internal states may 'realize' the functional state of pain in different species – perhaps even in different people. David Lewis, in a well-known paper, described the imaginary case of a certain Martian, who exhibits what we would recognize as pain-behaviour, and for what we would recognize as the usual reasons, but in whom the physical causes of that behaviour are 'the inflation of many smallish cavities in his feet' ([1978] 1980, 216).

I shall return to Lewis's thought-experiments later on; at this point, I want merely to admit that functionalism certainly does seem to be more palatable than so-called type-type identity theories when it comes to the possibility of non-human pain. The question I am raising is whether it is even true that someone's pain must be 'realized' by any internal state at all. In the brain-scan story we are not asked to believe that the complexities of pain-behaviour might actually be produced by the water filling your friend's skull; indeed, we're meant to rule out this possibility.

Now to return to our question: How would you respond if you discovered that your friend lacked a brain?

It is, I think, clear that you would *not* think such things as: 'Oh well, Susan is really just like a puppet – it wouldn't matter if I stuck needles into her – when she makes those noises with those facial expressions, she doesn't really mean anything ...', etc., etc. On the contrary, you would probably show a lot of concern and sympathy towards her. (I am assuming that Susan continues to behave like a human being; she is distressed and puzzled by the results of her brain scan, comes to you for advice and so on.)

Somebody might say: Well, even if you can't help treating Susan as you used to treat her, that's simply your conditioning, or your emotions, or something. If you were to reflect on the matter, you'd have to conclude that, yes, she couldn't feel pain, so that, yes, there'd seem to be a sense in which it *wouldn't* in fact matter if you stuck pins into her ...

What's wrong with this way of talking, surely, is that it classes certain natural and spontaneous reactions – reactions of sympathy, etc. – as 'mere emotions', or some such, and thereby makes out that such reactions can have no place in someone's grasp of the concept *pain*. But we might take note of Wittgenstein's remark: 'My attitude towards him is an attitude towards a soul [mind]. I am not of the *opinion* that he has a soul [mind]' (*PI* II, 178).²

Wittgenstein's view of the matter, as expressed by this and other remarks, was that human beings share certain pre-linguistic propensities to react to each other in various ways, and that it was, as it were, on the back of these shared reactions that concepts like 'joy' or 'pain' came into our language. There are other similar cases. We almost all of us happen to react to things that we look at in similar ways: we sort tomatoes with poppies, bananas with lemons and so on. And it is on the back of these shared pre-linguistic reactions that colour-words like 'red' and 'yellow' can get introduced.

Why are these facts (about how concepts come into the language) important? Take colour-concepts. We most of us share the propensity to sort tomatoes together with poppies. This means that the teaching of the word 'red' simply relies on this propensity in the normal infant; and one counts as competent with the word 'red' when one can automatically apply it to the things which the rest of us apply it to, as automatically as one can group poppies with tomatoes. These sorts of facts, together with certain concomitant facts about the practical role the concept *red* plays in our lives, guarantee that the ultimate or paradigm test for whether something is red is whether it is deemed to be red by a normal-sighted person looking at it in normal lighting. This word 'test' should not mislead: it is not as if one first has to ascertain that one is a normal-sighted person, etc., and then see how one responds to the object when looking at it. The important point, for our purposes, is rather of this kind: If after much investigation, the scientific community were to conclude that there was nothing physical common to poppies and tomatoes to account for why we all call them 'red', *this would not matter*. Perhaps it is scarcely possible that there should be nothing physical common to the surfaces of poppies and tomatoes, just as it is scarcely possible that we should have evolved in a few hours out of mud. But if such a scientific discovery *were* made, it would not show that nothing was really red, or that we were somehow mistaken in calling things 'red', or that the concept *red* was not 'objective'. For the life of the concept comes from a certain agreement in responses, and that agreement (I am imagining) would still be there, even if it turned out to be scientifically inexplicable.

Let us return to mental states. In the brain-scan story, it is not our responses and reactions that turn out to be scientifically inexplicable. Our continuing concern and sympathy for Susan may be explained, one supposes, as effects in some sense produced in us by Susan's observable behaviour, demeanour, speech, etc. – a lot of which will be, for us, 'imponderable', in Wittgenstein's phrase. Does Susan's *behaviour*, then, turn out to be inexplicable? Actually, we need not say this either; for the usual sorts of causal explanation will be available, such as 'She is crying because she has just read that poem' or 'She is smiling because she has tasted that lovely cake'. All that is missing is an explanation in terms of an internal state of Susan's.

In other words, if there would not be grounds for saying that poppies weren't red after all, in the eventuality of scientists' finding nothing physical common to red things, then there would be even less reason for saying that people weren't really subjects of pain and other mental states, in the eventuality of scientists' finding only water in people's heads. Why do I say 'even less reason'? – Because of two points:

1. In the colour case, but not in the mental case, our agreement in application of concepts would appear to be inexplicable by reference to independently specifiable common properties. ('Independently specifiable' is meant to exclude *being red*, etc. 'We call them all red because they're all red' might count as an explanation, but not of the sort which is here in question.)
2. In the colour case, but not in the mental case, a thing's being F would itself appear to be in this sense inexplicable: being red would not be explicable, while smiling with joy (or just: being joyful) would, often at least, be explicable in the normal ways.

Madmen and Super-Spartans

Does all this mean that I am arguing for a return to behaviourism? No, it doesn't. It does, however, mean that I don't agree with those who regard functionalism (whatever its other faults) as improving upon behaviourism by referring to an 'inner state'. I have already mentioned why David Lewis thought functionalism an improvement on type-type identity theory; it will be instructive to examine why he thought it an improvement on behaviourism.

As well as 'Martian pain', Lewis imagines a case of 'mad pain'. He describes a human being in whom a certain physiological state can sometimes be detected – namely that which in other human beings is caused by injury, etc., and which (in them) produces pain-behaviour. (The argument is not affected if we substitute 'states' for 'state'.) However, in the 'madman', this physiological state does not produce wincing, aversion, nursing and so on, and it is not caused by injury and the like. It is caused, rather, by 'moderate exercise on an empty stomach'; and as for its effects, it 'turns his mind to mathematics, facilitating concentration on that but distracting him from anything else', it causes the madman to 'cross his legs and snap his fingers' and so on (Lewis [1978] 1980, 216).

Lewis's view is that the human being he describes is one who is in pain on those occasions when the abovementioned physiological state is to be found in him. This is despite the fact that on those occasions he will as likely as not have been out for a brief jog, and will now be sitting cross-legged doing mental arithmetic. Lewis even remarks: 'My opinion that this is a possible case seems pretty firm. If I want a credible theory of mind, I need a theory that does not deny the possibility of mad pain' ([1978] 1980, 216).[3]

It is worth noting that Lewis is not alone in having made this sort of move. Hilary Putnam, who it should be said subsequently came to be dissatisfied with functionalism, imagined (in his paper 'Brains and Behaviour') a race of 'super-spartans':

> Let us suppose that after millions of years they begin to have children who are born fully acculturated. They are born speaking the adult language, knowing the multiplication table, having opinions on political issues, and *inter alia* sharing the dominant spartan beliefs about the importance of not evincing pain (except by way of verbal report, and even that in a tone of voice that suggests indifference). Then there would not *be* any 'unconditioned pain

> responses' in this community [...] Yet there is a clear absurdity to the position that one cannot ascribe to these people a capacity for feeling pain. ([1965] 1975, 333)

My own earlier example, of the person without a brain or central nervous system, I admitted to be 'scarcely conceivable', given our scientific knowledge. The same could of course be said of Lewis's and Putnam's examples. But in Putnam's example we find something more: it is a real question whether what he describes is even 'barely conceivable' – whether, that is, it is a coherent story at all.

Now it was part of Putnam's purpose when he wrote 'Brains and Behaviour' to attack philosophers who ruled out certain accounts of the mind as involving category mistakes, or as being conceptually confused, or as being at root incoherent. He was at this time rather wont to accuse such philosophers of hanging on to a bad old analytic/synthetic distinction. That distinction, however, doesn't seem to be what is at issue, if only for the reason that, even were the coherence of stories about madmen and super-spartans admitted, this would not force anyone to accept Lewis's or Putnam's conclusions about them. Lewis tells us that his opinion that the madman feels pain is 'pretty firm', while Putnam says that to deny that his super-spartans felt pain would be a 'clear absurdity'. Are we to take it that a point has been reached where the data of our enquiry are 'intuitions'? And if so, what if our intuitions disagree?

How to Proceed?

Wittgenstein wrote:

> But can't I imagine that the people around me are automata, lack consciousness, even though they behave in the same way as usual? – If I imagine it now – alone in my room – I see people with fixed looks (as in a trance) going about their business – the idea is perhaps a little uncanny. But just try to keep hold of this idea in the midst of your ordinary intercourse with others, in the street, say! Say to yourself, for example: 'The children over there are mere automata; all their liveliness is mere automatism.' (1958, §420)

It is, of course, *only* in one's room that one can ponder the question whether 'madmen' or 'super-spartans' could feel pain. The injunction 'Don't think – look!' can't be obeyed in the literal way, e.g. by going out into the street. This may explain in part why fantasies about strange creatures feeling pain can grip philosophers more strongly than fantasies about real people being automata. There is also, I think, a tendency to count it an advantage of a philosophical theory of the mind that it is liberal when it comes to doling out the capacity for a mental life. We should not be 'speciesist' about such things after all.

On this latter point, however, we should remember that the functionalist's liberality is not all it seems. For the functionalist must deny that the person without a brain, or any causally relevant internal state, can feel pain. A calm functionalist who decided that Susan lacked the requisite functional state would have to be just as callous as the person who succeeded, for philosophical reasons, in regarding the children in the street as lacking consciousness.

How does Wittgenstein recommend that we approach the question 'Are other people just automata?'? The fact that the question begins to sound hollow if we ask it of real people (not just 'alone in our room') is very important. And this is because the life of a concept like *pain* derives entirely from our actual dealings with others, dealings which involve natural reactions and responses which one cannot just 'think away'. It follows that if one wants to ask a question about an *imaginary* case of putative pain (or whatever), be it that of a brainless person, or a madman, or a super-spartan, then one must really use one's *imagination* – not, as it might be put, one's intellect. For it is the imagination that feeds off those natural reactions and responses. There is at least a strong case that Lewis and Putnam, in their attempts to downgrade the importance of the behavioural criteria for mental states, were suffering from a lack of imagination. Madmen and super-spartans might look like the products of very colourful imaginations; but a vivid and detailed imagination will rule things out as much as in.[4]

Reference, Objectivity, Science

Why *were* Lewis and Putnam so sure about the capacity for pain of creatures with (what they thought of as) the requisite internal states? And, in general, what is the attraction in the functionalist's idea of an inner state?

We find in this reference to an inner state a move of a kind that is made elsewhere in philosophy, and it is made, I think, because the philosopher has got hold of a wrong notion of 'objectivity'. I think it may also be a case in part of succumbing to that old temptation, the temptation to see all linguistic meaning as being on the model of *referring* to things. I'll look at these two issues in reverse order.

Take a genuinely referring term, such as a name 'Socrates', say. Now it does seem to be true that if there were no proper basis for our all largely agreeing (as we do) to such propositions as 'Socrates was Greek', 'Socrates taught Plato', etc., then that would undermine, or at any rate radically change, our use of the name. 'There being no proper basis' would amount, roughly, to 'there being no such person'. The point, it might be said, of a name is to hook up to some particular thing; and if for some reason that hooking-up fails, then the name is liable to be a failure also. And whether it hooks up or not is an empirical matter in rather an obvious sense. We could *discover* that there had been no such person as Socrates.

If one thought that the function of the word 'pain' was similarly to hook up with some particular thing, one would then be inclined to ask such questions as 'Given that it does manage to hook up, what sort of thing is it that it hooks up to, as a matter of fact?' Just as we can find out more and more empirical information about Socrates, we can surely find out more and more empirical information about pain. And this last is of course true: hence the study of the brain, of the central nervous system, of the production of analgesics and so on. But it is *not* true that our word 'pain' might be a failure, in the way in which our word 'Socrates' might be a failure (and in which the word 'phlogiston' was a failure). And this is seen in the fact that straightforward empirical discoveries would not undermine our use of the word 'pain'. If it turned out that many of us had water in our heads, this would not show that no one really felt pain.

What about objectivity? If there is widespread agreement in the use of a predicate, agreement in central cases of whether or not it applies to something, is that enough for us to say that the predicate relates to an 'objective feature of reality'?

The functionalist might say: 'No – for the agreement must be causally explicable, otherwise it would be merely accidental agreement.' Actually, as has been pointed out, we do not need inner states of pain in order to 'causally explain' people's attribution of the predicate 'pain': observed behaviour will do better as an explanation of such attributions.

'But won't that behaviour be inexplicable, if not caused by an inner state – and hence accidental?'

Again, as has been said, this is not strictly so. Someone's behaviour could be explained by what has happened to them, very often. This won't work, admittedly, for spontaneous expressions of mental states – coming to a decision, for example. (At least, it won't work if we allow such a question as 'Why did he come to that decision just *then*?') So the key question is perhaps this: If a regularity, a widespread phenomenon, cannot be explained *by appeal to something else*, will that make it 'accidental'?

Well, even scientific explanations must run out somewhere. 'Why do all quarks consist of just two squarks?' – 'They just do.' We could call it an accident that they do. But would this mean that all regularities at higher levels were accidental regularities? And would this in turn mean that no discourse whatever was really 'objective'? Obviously not.

The search for an explanation of a widespread regularity typifies the activity of science. And it is our science that gives us faith that people in pain are in certain discoverable brain states. It is likewise our science that gives us faith that the first humans did not evolve overnight out of mud. The question 'What makes the application of a predicate objective?' is just a different sort of question. And its answer, in a large class of cases, has to do with agreement in responses.

This means that one should be careful in responding to the assertion that there *must* be something in the head which produces the pain-behaviour. This 'must', it seems to me, *could* have a commonsensical justification; it would amount, roughly, to: 'must, given our knowledge of how things work'. Wittgenstein was very suspicious of assertions about what must be the case, especially in philosophy, and consequently found the idea that there must be something in the head correlated with mental states a mere prejudice, if one can judge from the following remarks from *Zettel*:

> No supposition seems to me more natural than that there is no process in the brain correlated with associating or with thinking. (*Z* §608)

I saw this man years ago: now I have seen him again, I recognize him, I remember his name. And why does there have to be a cause of this remembering in my nervous system? Why must something or other, whatever it may be, be stored up there *in any form*? Why *must* a trace have been left behind? Why should there not be a psychological regularity to which *no* physiological regularity corresponds? If this upsets our concepts of causality then it is high time they were upset. (*Z* §610)

Could Wittgenstein be saying that neurophysiologists really ought not to be at all confident that something in the brain is correlated with one's ability to remember a face (e.g.

because certain specific lesions of the brain have repeatedly been found to impair that ability)? Are the 'concepts of causality' which need upsetting those of the scientist qua scientist?

If Wittgenstein was thinking along such lines, then surely he had swung too far in the other direction. And his comment about the supposition than which 'nothing seemed more natural' would appear to convict him of this fault. On the other hand there is this, a little later:

> Why should there not be a natural law connecting a starting and a finishing state of a system, but not covering the intermediary state? (Z §613)

Here it seems that Wittgenstein is attacking a prejudice about what natural laws there must be – rather than about what must be the case given the actual natural laws. And the remark, construed thus, is one that would be well-directed against certain philosophers, e.g. many functionalists. It is a remark that would be apposite when discussing what sorts of explanation of behaviour would be available in the brainless-person case (see above).

'But can we really imagine the laws of nature to be so different? Won't a vivid and detailed imagination baulk at this task also?' – I would answer 'No' to this last question; but the general issue of imaginability is not my main concern. The crucial point, when it comes to what's wrong with functionalism, has to do with the *source* of the unimaginability (if any) of the brainless-person example. I think it is fairly clear that it is not one's imagined attitude to the brainless person that would come under strain, so much as one's beliefs about human physiology; and it is that 'attitude ' which is important for concepts like *pain*.

Natural Responses

Let me draw a final parallel. In his well-known essay 'Freedom and Resentment', Strawson (1962) posed the question: If causal determinism turned out to be true (or if we all ended up believing it to be true), would we just give up on the idea of freedom, and on the related notions of praise and blame, gratitude and resentment? And if we didn't give up on these notions, would that just show that we were enslaved by our conditioning, or our emotions, or something?

Strawson's answer to both questions was No. The concept of freedom, he argued, has its roots in such shared pre-, or non-, linguistic responses as the resentment of certain actions, objective manipulation in the face of certain others, etc., etc. These responses are not expressions of 'mere emotion'. They are the precondition for acquiring such concepts as 'responsible' and 'blameworthy', in the first place. And they would remain in place whatever metaphysical views we came to adopt concerning causation.

Strawson was in fact attacking two philosophical views: the view that freedom of the will entailed indeterminism about actions, but also the view that freedom of the will entailed determinism about actions. To either side he might, for reasons of persuasion, have said: 'Imagine away the determinism/indeterminism which you believe in; you are still left with gratitude and resentment, praise and blame – and free will.' If either party had said 'I cannot imagine (in)determinism away – that is simply unimaginable', the reply would have come: 'Well, perhaps you can't imagine that, for one reason or another. But the point is really that the issue of (in)determinism is *irrelevant* to the issue of freedom.' This would parallel the encounter with the functionalist who could not imagine someone behaving normally who lacked a brain and central nervous system.

The 'attitudes' which Strawson mentions – resentment, gratitude, etc. – are attitudes in Wittgenstein's sense: 'attitude' as opposed to 'belief' or 'opinion'. And it is not surprising to find them involved in our concept of human freedom, a concept at once moral and psychological. The moral aspect of the broad issue is more evident still in the current debates about the killing, or allowing to die, of foetuses, the newborn, the handicapped, the comatose, the senile. I'll take an extreme example. It has been said that painlessly killing a new-born infant shouldn't produce qualms even in the most sensitive person, unless because of distress caused to other people (such as parents). The proponent of such a view would no doubt think that someone who found it difficult to carry out such an operation was a slave to his conditioning or to mere emotion. But in fact the normal protective responses to a new-born baby play the same sort of role, in connection with the relevant moral concepts, as our responses to others play in connection with psychological concepts. The moral and the psychological are not distinct domains. (The philosopher who succeeded in looking on children in the street as automata would be a danger to society.)

Perhaps the moral to be drawn from these various cases is that we need to beware of a false dichotomy between 'subjectivity' and 'objectivity'. In many cases, the foundation of objectivity resides in those very reactions and responses that get too easily classified as merely subjective.

Notes

1 It should be said that some research suggests that human beings can get by with almost nothing in the way of brains. See, for example, Shewmon (1997).
2 *Philosophical Investigations* is hereafter referred to as '*PI*'. References are to section numbers.
3 It is interesting that Lewis chose the phrase 'mad pain' as a label for his imaginary case; is there perhaps meant to be a subliminal message that *not* to exhibit pain-behaviour when in the relevant physiological state is a sign of madness? A sort of mad stoicism, as it were? But of course one could only regard the 'madman' as crazily stoical if it *were* pain that he was suffering from!
4 As mentioned, Putnam did come round to abandoning functionalism. However, none of the reasons he gave for that abandonment had, as far as I am aware, to do with the issues I am considering in this chapter. (The reasons related more to the 'internalism/externalism' distinction.) In later years Putnam did come to be influenced by the work of Wittgenstein, so it's not impossible that he would have seen problems with functionalism in addition to the ones he had pointed out.

References

Lewis, D. ([1978] 1980), 'Mad Pain and Martian Pain', in N. Block (ed.), *Readings in Philosophy of Psychology*, vol. 1. London: Methuen, pp. 216–22.

Putnam, H. ([1965] 1975), 'Brains and Behaviour', in *Mind, Language and Reality: Philosophical Papers*, vol. 2. Cambridge: CUP, pp. 325–41.

Shewmon, D. A. (1997), 'Recovery from "Brain Death": A Neurologist's Apologia', *The Linacre Quarterly*, 64, no. 1, 30–96.

Strawson, P. F. ([1962] 1974), 'Freedom and Resentment', in *Freedom and Resentment and Other Essays*. London: Methuen, pp. 1–25.

Wittgenstein, L. (1958), *Philosophical Investigations*, 2nd ed., trans. G. E. M. Anscombe, ed. G. E. M. Anscombe and R. Rhees. Oxford: Basil Blackwell.

———. (1981), *Zettel*, 2nd ed., trans. G. E. M. Anscombe, ed. G. E. M. Anscombe and G. H. von Wright. Oxford: Basil Blackwell.

Chapter Two

'NOT A SOMETHING'

'And yet you again and again reach the conclusion that the sensation itself is a *nothing*.' – Not at all. It is not a *something*, but not a *nothing* either! [...] The paradox disappears only if we make a radical break with the idea that language always functions in one way, always serves the same purpose: to convey thoughts – which may be about houses, pains, good and evil, or anything else you please.

(Wittgenstein 1958, 304)[1]

Introduction

Wittgenstein's remarks on sensations and sensation language have typically been discussed in connection with his critique of the notion of privacy, a critique generally thought to reach its apogee in the so-called private language argument. Those commentators who agree that Wittgenstein's position does not fall into (anything that could be called) behaviourism will often be found saying something like the following: Wittgenstein does not deny the *reality* of sensations like pain, a reality that transcends behaviour and behavioural dispositions; he only denies that these psychological states or events are known only to the subject, that one learns a concept like *pain* by some act of inner ostension, that one can only 'infer' that others are in pain, etc. These commentators might well regard the first part of his statement that a sensation 'is not a *something*, but not a *nothing* either' as meaning that a sensation is not a *private* something. For of course pain is real enough – it's *something* – just not anything 'private'.

To forestall the charge of tilting at straw men, I will give some examples of this tendency.

Ernst Konrad Specht writes that 'Wittgenstein is only opposed to an erroneous determination of the naming relation between a sensation word and a sensation, but he does not deny that such a relation exists'. And he goes on: 'Wittgenstein's discussion is also hostile to an ontological misinterpretation of sensation; more precisely to an ontology which interprets sensation on the pattern of an object which is supposed to be internal and private, in contrast to objects that are external and public' (Specht 1969, 94).

Bill Child also speaks of a semantic relation or connection holding between two somethings, the sensation word and the sensation, explaining Wittgenstein's view by saying that a child 'learns to apply the word "pain" to herself in circumstances where she feels pain. That effects a connection between her feelings of pain and her use of the word "pain"' (2011, 167).

John McDowell feels sufficiently uneasy about the wording of *PI* 304 to write that 'Wittgenstein could, and perhaps should, have said something more like this. The sensation (the pain, say) is a perfectly good something – an object, if you like, of concept-involving awareness'. And he goes on to suggest that 'the conceptual content of the episode of consciousness' can 'be parsed in terms of the classification of a something ("the sensation itself": the pain) as the kind of something it is' (McDowell 1989, 289–90).

There are certainly grounds for thinking that part of Wittgenstein's meaning, when he says 'not a something, but not a nothing either', relates to the picture of the private inner object. After all, his next remark is: 'The conclusion was only that a nothing would serve just as well as a something about which nothing could be said', a remark which harks back to his discussion of the 'beetle in the box' (*PI* 293). But of course the conclusion of that discussion was that we should not 'construe the grammar of the expression of sensation on the model of "object and designation" '. Wittgenstein's main aim is evidently to 'reject the *grammar* which tries to force itself on us here' (*PI* 304; my italics).

In this essay I want to argue that 'a sensation is not a something' should not be interpreted as meaning 'a sensation is not a private something'. And the purport of Wittgenstein's remark can only be understood when we have done as he advises: that is, when we have made 'a radical break with the idea that language always functions in one way, always serves the same purpose: to convey thoughts – which may be about houses, pains, good and evil, or anything else you please'.

Context and Constitution

Frege's famous Context Principle urges us never to ask for the meaning of a word in isolation, but only in the context of a proposition. This idea of Frege's surely had a crucial influence upon Wittgenstein, early and late. In his later work, Wittgenstein can be seen as extending the principle beyond the domain of words, to apply – as we might say – to phenomena, such as the phenomena of pointing, or of hope, desire, expectation or belief. Again and again he approaches a question about some phenomenon by locating it in its wider surroundings, or by inviting us to imagine or specify such wider surroundings for ourselves; for by doing so, we gain a better understanding of the significance of the phenomenon. And here the word 'significance' should be taken broadly, so as to connect both with questions about the identity of a phenomenon and with ones about its importance for us.

Wittgenstein's remark that 'an "inner process" stands in need of outward criteria' (*PI* 580) is an instance of the sort of thing I am talking about; for he does not only, or even primarily, mean 'behavioural criteria', as the immediately following remark illustrates: 'An expectation is imbedded in a situation, from which it arises' (*PI* 581). But of course we can include behaviours as *part of* the surroundings of an 'inner process'.

The phrase 'inner process' has scare quotes around it in *PI* 580, and much has already been said by Wittgenstein before this remark concerning the problematic idea of the 'inner'. He has also looked critically at the idea of a 'process', e.g. in the following passage:

> How does the philosophical problem about mental processes and states and about behaviourism arise? – The first step is the one that altogether escapes notice. We talk of processes and states and leave their nature undecided. Sometime perhaps we shall know more about

them – we think. But that is just what commits us to a particular way of looking at the matter. For we have a definite concept of what it means to learn to know a process better. (The decisive movement in the conjuring trick has been made, and it was the very one that we thought quite innocent.) – And now the analogy which was to make us understand our thoughts falls to pieces. So we have to deny the yet uncomprehended process in the yet unexplored medium. And now it looks as if we had denied mental processes. And naturally we don't want to deny them. (*PI* 308)

'We talk of processes and states and leave their nature undecided.' In speaking of remembering, or of intending, or of being in pain, as processes or states we may well already have started down a wrong path, not because a statement like 'Pain is a mental state' is just false, but because the picture that typically accompanies such a statement is liable to lead us into confusion.

A symptom of this sort of confusion is succumbing to false (i.e. bad) analogies. There are a number of sources for the picture of a sensation as a bona fide 'something'. In what follows I want to bring out how one of these sources may be a certain false analogy relating to that very context principle the Wittgensteinian version of which is the beginning of much wisdom. This particular source, in fact, is associated more with an anti-Cartesian stance than with a Cartesian one – to put the matter simply. But regardless of issues to do with philosophical error and its sources, it is illuminating, I think, to come at Wittgenstein's thought ('not a something, but not a nothing') from this direction – from the direction of the context principle.

The word 'rat' only has meaning as it occurs in certain contexts, such as 'There's a rat in the garden'. In the sentence 'Socrates loved Plato' the syllable 'rat' occurs, but not the *word* 'rat'. – This is a perfectly natural way of talking. If we ask, 'What is it that in this case has meaning only in the context of a sentence?' we can reply either 'a word' or 'a syllable'. But for the word 'rat' to occur in a sentence, it is typically necessary that a certain syllable do so, by which is meant a certain sound or shape. The criteria of identity for such sounds and shapes are quite liberal, and are themselves dependent to some extent on context; differing regional accents will yield very different sonic versions of 'rat'. Moreover, we might allow a coded equivalent of 'rat' to count as the word 'rat': a squiggle of a certain shape, say, or the sound *bingle-bongle*.[2] This is why I said that it is only *typically* necessary for a certain syllable to occur for the word 'rat' to occur. But there must in a given instance be *some* description D, different from the description 'the word "rat"', such that D is brute relative to 'the word "rat"', and such that we can say that the occurrence of the word 'rat' consists in the occurrence of something of which D is true (e.g. consists in the occurrence of the squiggle). One could say: a word can't *just occur*; its occurrence must consist in the occurrence of something else. And 'something else' points not to another thing, but to another description of the same thing.[3]

Similar points can be made in connection with many processes, events, actions, etc. Only in a certain context does my pushing a bit of wood count as my checkmating you. Moreover, I can't *just checkmate* you: there must be something I do in virtue of which I checkmate you – which is to say, there must be some description of what I do which is brute relative to the description 'checkmating'.

We might be led to think that wherever some version of the context principle applies, so does a correlative principle about there being some 'more brute' description of the phenomenon in question. That this is not so has been pointed out by Martin Gustafsson (2018) in a paper which discusses the comparison made by Wittgenstein between words and chess pieces. A king is only a king in the context of a chess game and of the rules of chess; but a king need have no embodiment, for, as Gustafsson says, 'there is such a thing as playing chess without any physical pieces or physical board; this is equivalent to both players "playing blindfolded"'. What enables a piece to count as a king as opposed to a pawn in a game of blindfold chess is the knowledge both players have of the starting position. The king's moves are then effected simply by a player's calling out a move. There is no description of the white king which is more brute than 'white king'. To say this is not (by the way) to rule out the thought that the activity of blindfold chess is parasitic, perhaps even conceptually so, on the normal 'embodied' game of chess.

Of course, when in a game of blindfold chess I call out 'king to bishop four', it is my doing so that constitutes the event of my moving my king. So there is a description of the move that is brute relative to 'Roger's moving the white king to bishop four', namely: 'Roger's saying the words "king to bishop four"'. Note how the grammar of the word 'description' is here being determined. (There is not only *one* thing which may be called description.) In this case we are exhibiting what can count as a 'further description of a chess move'.

So far we might say: a king in chess can *just be* a king – but a chess king's moving must also be something else, something more brute. Does this betoken some deep difference between objects and events? – something for the metaphysicians to get their teeth into? Well, inheriting a house only counts as such in a context of laws, legal documents, property and so on, so to that extent the context principle applies; but if in turning eighteen a girl inherits the house left to her in a will, shall we say there must be a description of this event more brute than 'inheriting the house'? Do I give a further *description* of that event by saying, 'She's just turned eighteen'? Or indeed by saying, 'She's just turned eighteen and there's a will which says such-and-such'?[4] If we do speak thus – and why forbid it? – we are evidently adopting a certain, perhaps rather novel, grammar for the expression 'description of an event'.[5] For that matter we could if we wish decide to say that the white king in a game of blindfold chess does have a more brute description, namely: 'the set of utterances by players A or B of the word "king", spoken as part of a move-utterance, and bearing such-and-such relations to other move-utterances made by A or B'.

This last proposal might be objected to on the grounds that you cannot replace 'the white king' by 'the set of utterances, etc.' in the context of a proposition. You can hardly move from 'The white king has taken a black pawn' to 'The set of utterances, etc. has taken a black pawn'. A set of utterances can't take a pawn!deri[6] This objection relies in effect on Leibniz's Law (i.e. 'When $a = b$, everything that is true of a is true of b, and vice versa'). But our notions of being constituted by, and of different descriptions applying to one thing, are too various to be constrained by Leibniz's Law. A credit card can be redescribed as a piece of plastic, but you can't move from 'I've cancelled my credit card' to 'I've cancelled a piece of plastic' – and Napoleon's becoming emperor can be redescribed as his putting a crown on his own head, but you can't move in the opposite direction from

'Napoleon put a crown on his head with both hands' to 'Napoleon became emperor with both hands'.

The point of these remarks is not to make out that all determinations of the grammar of 'describe', in connection with formulating 'descriptions of the same thing', are equally justifiable, or are all on a par, or anything of the sort. It is rather to point to the variety of things that do, and can, count as cases of X's being constituted by Y. Some of these cases are paradigm cases, others more peripheral, others quite stipulative. (When I said above that in blindfold chess there is no more brute description of the white king, I meant that only stipulation could supply such a description.) My overall aim is to prepare us (soften us up) for what ought to be said – or ought not to be said – about sensations, and indeed about other 'mental events'.

'I Was Thinking'

Let us start with some of these other mental events. I want to look specifically at statements involving what are called intentional verbs – verbs like 'want', 'believe', 'think', 'decide', 'regret', 'hope', 'expect'. In connection with statements involving such verbs there is a useful, if rather rough-and-ready, distinction to hand, namely that between disposition-statements and episode-statements. Because our eventual quarry will be sensations, let us focus on the latter.[7] Examples might include 'After investigating the wound for a few seconds, the doctor decided to apply a tourniquet', and 'When I said those words I was thinking of Walt Disney'. In these examples, the deciding and the thinking, we would like to say, take place in real time; some might call the first an event and the second a process. Wittgenstein argues, in ways I won't now rehearse, that such decisions and thinkings can only have the content they do – that is, can only *be* those decisions and thinkings – on account of the wider context, both that of the subject's biography and that of the world more generally (e.g. a world containing Walt Disney, in the second example).[8] To that extent the context principle (in the sense I have been using the phrase) applies to such decisions and thinkings, if Wittgenstein is right. Quite a few philosophers would be happy to agree with this, especially those who endorse 'externalism' about intentional content.

In what did my thinking of Walt Disney *consist*? This is not intended as a question about the nature or essence of thinking, or about the meaning of the expression 'to think of Walt Disney'; we are not here in danger of adopting the strategy described by Wittgenstein at *PI* 316: 'In order to get clear about the meaning of the word "think" we watch ourselves while we think; what we observe will be what the word means!' One can after all note that in a given context the white king was constituted by a bit of balsa wood without being tempted to regard the description 'bit of balsa wood' as helping us in understanding what a white king is, what it is for something to be a white king. Nevertheless, if we look for something in which my thinking of Walt Disney consisted, and if we require that it be something about which I myself could tell you straight off (as I can tell you I was thinking of Walt Disney), then we will either find nothing that satisfies us, or will be faced with one or more of an indefinitely wide range of phenomena, all of which might on different occasions be regarded as constituting my thinking that thought – e.g. imagining his face, saying his name, frowning characteristically, pronouncing certain words with a doleful emphasis, etc. All these phenomena might qualify as things that constitute my thinking of Walt Disney, if we are content to use as our central criterion of 'constitution' the fact of something's going on in or with the subject at the relevant time – which in this example just means the time when I was uttering the words in connection with which I said, 'When I said those words I was thinking of Walt Disney.'

Of course not anything going on in the subject at the time will strike us as a likely candidate for constituting a bit of thinking. The person's fidgeting with his pen will not do so. If we are talking of things about which the person himself could tell us straight off, then it seems that only those things which themselves may be described in terms of the thought will be candidates; thus the doleful emphasis is a candidate because we can hear it as, and describe it as, 'the spoken dolefulness so expressive of his attitude to Walt Disney'.[9] Note that there is little mileage in the idea that any special *connection* exists or gets set up between the expression 'thinks of Walt Disney' and any or all of such assorted phenomena as having an image, frowning, writing, etc.

What of the *criteria* for my having thought of Walt Disney? Such criteria lie elsewhere, in how I respond to questions, how I explain myself and the like. I may of course never be called on to do these things. The temptation now arises to invoke counterfactual conditionals – as, 'If I had been asked what I was up to, I should have said "thinking"; and if I had been asked what I was thinking of, I should have said "Walt Disney"' – and then to say that here we have the *something* in which my thinking of Walt Disney consisted on that occasion. For we seem to have lit on something that existed or subsisted at the relevant time. The counterfactual was true *then*, we want to say; so haven't we got a further description of the thinking, a description more brute than 'NN's thinking of Walt Disney', and which moreover could plausibly be taken as the something with which the description is semantically connected?

As with the case of the stipulative identification of the white king with a set of utterances, there is no reason to *forbid* saying that someone's thinking of Walt Disney consisted in the truth of a counterfactual conditional(s). There is however good reason to discourage it, since the proposer of it is likely to be a philosopher who thinks he has hit upon something substantive and important, something going beyond 'mere criteria'. For present purposes it is enough to note that if my thinking that p did consist in the truth of a counterfactual conditional, we could hardly speak of this thinking as *taking place* – i.e. as being an episode or 'mental process'.

We are considering what a certain alleged process or episode consists in; and if our model or paradigm of this is something like Napoleon's becoming emperor consisting in his putting a crown upon his head, we might end up deciding that, in the case of a person's thinking of Walt Disney, there is nothing in which it consists. Frowns, imaginings and the like seem better candidates than counterfactual conditionals, but there seems no rationale for picking out certain of these phenomena rather than others, in the case where several took place – and taking the thinking to have been constituted by the lot of them looks a bit desperate. Or rather, it seems to be motivated only by the thought that the thinking must consist in *something*.

So perhaps we should allow the possibility that one can *just think of* Walt Disney, in the sense in which a white king in blindfold chess can just be a white king. Such a conclusion might on the face of it be palatable to some of those externalist philosophers who want to say that intentional contents 'aren't in the head'. Externalists who also lean towards functionalism will however resist the idea, preferring to say that a person's thinking of Walt Disney must, on a given occasion, consist in the person's being in some 'intrinsic', probably neurological, state. This position is often called 'token-identity theory', and it has attracted many people. What should be said about such a proposal?

Token-Identity Theory

When I looked at the idea that thinking of Walt Disney might consist in such things as pronouncing words with a doleful emphasis, I noted that we were only considering phenomena about which the person could tell us straight off. Such phenomena do not of course include brain-states and the like. If when you said you were thinking of Walt Disney you were in fact talking about a brain process that had taken place within you, this is not something of which you could ordinarily be aware. But after all, could it not also be said that when you told us you had moved your king you were in fact talking about moving a collection of molecules of such-and-such description, despite the fact that *this* is not something of which you could ordinarily be aware?

But consider: if you are teaching a child how to play chess, using a normal chess set, you will count on the child's being able to take a certain piece of wood (say) as the white king; and it makes good sense to say that the child comes to call that piece of wood 'the white king'. Does the child come to call that collection of molecules 'the white king'?

The sense of the verb 'to call' in which I am here interested is one that concerns a person's mastery of language. What can the child who has cottoned on to our teaching *do*? What do we want to get her to do? – and what will we *take* as her successfully doing it? She needs, for example, to show that she can tell the white king from the white queen; will this be a matter of her telling the difference between this set of molecules and that set of molecules? No – for if it were, we would not be able to *know* by straightforward observation that she had cottoned on to this aspect of the game. We can know, and indeed she can know, that she has distinguished those two pieces on a given occasion, and normally this is because we and she can know that she has distinguished those two pieces of wood or plastic or whatever.

But surely she might not know that she is talking about a piece of wood? (She might not have heard of wood.) Nor need she know that the king is of *such-and-such* a shape – at any rate, if such 'knowledge' is to be articulable. Perhaps then she has some sort of implicit or practical knowledge, that she is talking about and moving a piece of wood and that it is of a certain specific shape?

We do not need to say any of this. She can recognize *this* – that is to say, recognize the white king, say 'This is the white king', etc. When I said that it made good sense to say that the child comes to call that piece of wood 'the white king', that was only because our knowledge that she has successfully and intentionally moved her king is typically articulable using descriptions more brute than 'white king', descriptions like 'that piece of wood'. We can say, and agree, that the child recognizes this piece of wood as the white king. But the possibility of our articulating our knowledge in this way, although typical, is not necessary. We can, in the context of teaching a language, know that a child is able to tell the difference between dim lighting and bright lighting, even though we typically cannot articulate our (or her) knowledge using expressions more brute than 'dimly lit' and 'brightly lit' – cannot specify things in which given cases of being dimly or brightly lit consist.

Does this then open the door to the identity-theorist's claim that when I say I was thinking of Walt Disney I call a certain brain process 'my thinking of Walt Disney', although I *recognize* it only *as* my thinking of Walt Disney? Hardly. For we do not yet have any reason to say that I am talking *about* anything when I utter the words 'I was thinking of …' – unless of course we merely want to recapitulate the surface grammar of the sentence by saying that I am talking about *thinking*. In this sense of 'about' we can talk about unicorns or time travel; 'about' used in this way carries no metaphysical or philosophical weight. To say that I was talking about thinking will then cast no light on what a statement like 'I was thinking of Walt Disney' is doing. In any more robust sense of 'about', the idea that I must be talking about something when I utter the words 'I was thinking of …' is a philosophical prejudice, as Wittgenstein says or implies when he urges us to 'make a radical break with the idea that language always functions in one way, always serves the same purpose: to convey thoughts – which may be about houses, pains, good and evil, or anything else you please'.

One can indeed say that in talking of the white king a child is talking about a piece of wood, or a set of molecules, if by this one means that in that situation the king can in fact be investigated and a description arrived at – e.g. 'piece of wood' – such that it is okay to say that the king is constituted by something of which that description is true – in one of the various possible senses of the expression 'constituted by'. But such an investigation may be impossible, as with Gustafsson's blindfold-chess king. In that case, we can only say things like 'When she said the white king had taken a pawn, she was talking about *the white king*'. In the same way you can, as we saw above, say: when Smith said 'I was thinking of Walt Disney' Smith was talking about *thinking*.

Even where there is such a thing as an investigation of X, and that investigation *does* yield an answer to 'What constitutes X?', so that in talking about X one can be said to talk about Y, this will not in itself enable us to posit any sort of association in thought, or semantic connection, between the idea or expression 'X' (on the one hand) and Y (on the other). In particular this is because there will be no guarantee that the criteria of identity through time of Xs and of Ys will be in harmony. The white king to be found at the end of the game is the *same piece* as the white king to be found at the game's start, but will not be the *same set of molecules*.[10] Hence no semantic or psychological connection *can* have been set up between 'white king' and a given set of molecules.

However, this last point is more of an objection to the views of some of the Wittgenstein commentators I mentioned at the start of this chapter than it is to the views of identity-theorists. An identity-theorist will probably not talk of words or concepts at all, except by way of the assertion that a psychological statement must be about a something, i.e. a psychological state, in some robust sense of 'about'. This state will be what *constitutes* NN's thinking of Walt Disney, for example. In order to home in on this state he adds the assumption that whatever the state is must be something that was 'going on' or subsisting at the relevant time. What is the relevant time? The most obvious answer will be: 'It is the time indicated by the surface grammar of the psychological statement.' So if I say, 'When I uttered those words I was thinking of Walt Disney,' then the brain process in question can be taken – at least as a first shot – as simultaneous with that earlier utterance.

Why a brain process? Indeed, why any process going on in this human being? Surface grammar does not help us in this case, since (as Wittgenstein pointed out[11]) the pronoun 'I' does not pick out a particular human being – at any rate not in a statement like 'I was thinking of Walt Disney'. Of course it is true that it was a human being who was thinking of Walt Disney, since I am a human being and I truthfully uttered those words. Why not then take the process allegedly constituting my thinking of Walt Disney to be a process involving a whole human being? To be sure, we have found that various kinds of damage to the brain hamper or destroy such things as the ability to say 'I was thinking …', and have made other related findings, but since something that happens in or to a human brain ipso facto happens in or to a human being, this can be no objection to claiming that it is a process of the whole human being which constitutes my thinking of Walt Disney. Such a claim would appear to be as respectable as the identity-theorist's claim from the perspective of neurological enquiry, the perspective which is evidently guiding our thought here; for it does not preclude a scientist's going to the relevant *bit* of a human being, her brain.

Be all this as it may, the identity-theorist in fact prefers to identify the thinking (or whatever) with some neurological state or process. Insofar as this homing-in is motivated by the assumption that a psychological statement must be *about* something it is philosophically questionable. And there are further worries, concerning the assumption that the surface grammar of a sentence can guide us to a proper determination of when something happened. In various places Wittgenstein brings out how, and in what sense, a person's subsequent assertions 'make the connection' between an earlier statement and some intentional object, something which if true would suggest that nothing going on at the time of the earlier statement determines that connection. This indeed would not rule out my saying something true when I assert, 'I was thinking of Walt Disney when I said those words,' for the notion of truth need not be tied to the idea of something's *making* the assertion true.[12]

Homing in on brain processes that went on during the time I was saying the words in connection with which I *later* said 'I was thinking of Walt Disney then' may simply be looking in the wrong place altogether – which is not to imply that there is any right place. Analogously, if a court declares a contract made three years ago to be null and void, you would be looking in the wrong place if you investigated what went on at the time when the contract was made in the hope of finding its nullity. The court may base its later decision on facts about what went on then (though it need not), but it is the *decision* which renders the contract null.[13]

Investigation

A key notion in all this is that of investigation. I imagined above someone's investigating a white king and finding, or confirming, that it is a piece of wood of a certain shape, or that it is a set of molecules. It was because such an investigation can yield such answers that it is correct to say that the white king consists of, is constituted by, a piece of wood (or set of molecules), at any rate at the time of the investigation. What counts as investigation in this case is relatively clear. These facts together show that this particular claim about X's being constituted by Y is a non-stipulative one. By contrast, no investigation of the white king in blindfold chess could ever show that it was constituted by the set of utterances by players A and B of the word 'king' made in the context of such-and-such move-utterances; *this* constitution-claim is a stipulation.

There is also a fairly clear sense of 'investigation' applicable to events and processes. Having been invited to attend the ceremony of Napoleon's becoming emperor, you could (in principle) investigate or observe the event with a view to saying, or confirming, what it consisted in – the investigation yielding such an answer as: he put a crown on his head (in certain surroundings). There will evidently be some indeterminacy as to how much of the phenomenon gets investigated, and correlatively as to how compendious our answer is to 'In what did it consist?' These would be matters for stipulation. We can say either that my payment of a debt to you consisted in my writing a cheque and handing it to you, or in these things plus your cashing the cheque – or other things along these lines.[14]

Turning to the position of the token-identity theorist, there will be two questions facing one who adopts such a position: first, whether there is such a thing as an investigation of someone's 'being in mental state S', and second, whether such an investigation yields the sort of answer predicted by the theorist. It is the first question which is likely to be really problematic, in particular in cases where it seems that a 'connection' is made, e.g. between thought and object, by the subject's subsequent statements or actions. But even if we can safely assume, of some mental process, that the surface grammar of the relevant psychological statement(s) is in fact a suitable guide to when it occurred, it is still entirely possible that there is no such thing as an investigation of that process, an investigation of the sort that could tell us what it consisted in.

There is no such thing as an investigation of the white king in blindfold chess, nor of Samantha's inheriting a house on her eighteenth birthday. You can, to be sure, describe the background facts, the surroundings, in virtue of which there is a white king and in virtue of which Samantha inherited the house; but the phrase 'in virtue of', used thus, takes us to criteria and the context principle, rather than to constitution. Using Aristotelian terminology, you could say that this 'in virtue of' indicates a formal cause rather than a material cause. It is true that, quite often, we derive what shall count as a material cause from formal causes: thus, the background facts which together formally (i.e. conventionally) determine that I have given you a book may include my saying, 'Take this; it's yours,' something which in turn can be called the material cause of my giving you the book, i.e. that in which my giving it to you consisted. (For this reason, to talk of *investigating* the event to see what constitutes it, as I did in connection with Napoleon's coronation, is admittedly to use 'investigate' in a rather extended sense.) But when the identity-theorist says of some mental process that it takes place in virtue of the occurrence of a brain process, the phrase 'in virtue of' is intended to signify a material cause *not* simply derivable from formal causes, or criteria for that mental process; the putative material cause is conceived of as discoverable independently of human customs and institutions. And the fact is, there might *be* no material cause of this kind.

The idea that there must be a material cause, a *something* in which the mental process consisted, derives in part, I think, from a species of false analogy, as I mentioned in my introduction. Impressed by the apparent contextuality of many psychological phenomena, by the fact of their necessary dependence on 'external factors', behavioural and non-behavioural, we may fall into the trap of thinking them akin to those phenomena – of which there are many – to which the context principle applies *and* for which more 'brute' descriptions can be found, yielding truths of the form 'X consists in Y'. In many cases, the context principle does only apply because of some convention, custom or what have you, according to which Fs are counted as Gs – e.g. such-and-such shapes all count as the word 'rat'.[15] This means that an F 'by itself' will not be a G, but will only be a G given the right background; which is to say, the Context Principle applies to Fs. Hence, in *these* cases, the application of the Context Principle is tied up with the fact that Gs are constituted by Fs. But the contextuality of my thinking of Walt Disney is not like this, and there is no analogous reason for saying that it must consist in anything at all.

Sensations

But what about sensations? What about pain? Surely there is little temptation to think that it is my subsequent statements or deeds that determine my having been in pain, in any sense of 'determine'? The central status of the first-person, present-tense expression of pain is admitted and even stressed by Wittgenstein himself. This status remains crucial in the face of all those facts to do with behavioural criteria, the learning of the word 'pain', etc. And as Wittgenstein's interlocutor says at *PI* 296: 'Yes, but there is *something* there all the same accompanying my cry of pain. And it is on account of that that I utter it. And this something is what is important – and frightful.' Isn't there a possibility of investigating this something? If it 'accompanies' someone's cry of pain, and if the scientists are right, then won't we be investigating someone's pain if we put them in a brain scanner and observe their brain when they cry out in pain? And if we keep finding the same sort of thing in experiments like that one, won't we have good grounds for saying things like 'A person's migraine will generally consist in such-and-such a brain process'?

The notion of X's consisting of (or in) Y is, as I have argued, flexible, protean even. Cases of constitution include paradigm cases, peripheral cases and stipulative cases, all these cases sitting on a continuum, or on more than one continuum. We should always ask, 'What is achieved by adopting this way of talking? – by saying that X consists in Y?' And we may well find that there is point in saying that Jane's migraine consisted in the electrochemical activity in part of her brain. Saying such a thing does not, after all, rule out other ways of speaking, such as the one sketched earlier, according to which it is changes in Jane, regarded as a unitary subject, which constitute her migraine, or her suffering a migraine.[16] Adoption of such ways of speaking need not betoken succumbing to any philosophical prejudice. But it is a philosophical prejudice to think that there *must be* something that constitutes a person's pain, a something about which that person is talking, in a robust sense of 'about', and to which she is referring when she says 'I have a headache,' or 'That hurts!' – or for that matter 'Ouch!'

And this prejudice is surely false. It is false in the same way as the corresponding prejudice about the white king in chess. A white king can in fact *just be* a white king, for example in a game of blindfold chess. Likewise, a person with water in his head, who talked and acted just as I do and who, on stubbing his toe, cried out 'Ouch! My toe!' would mean just what I mean when I say those words in that sort of situation – and would, consequently, be in pain just as I am. For the brainless person, being in pain, we might say, *just is* being in pain.[17] Of course we do not believe that brainless people who act 'just like us' are biologically possible, and if we read about such a case, we would no doubt discount the story on the grounds that it was too much in conflict with too much of our belief system. But there is nothing conceptually amiss, so to speak, in the hypothesis of the brainless person who is one of us, in the important sense of that phrase.[18]

The philosophical prejudice of thinking that there must be something that constitutes a person's pain is fed by the sort of expostulation Wittgenstein's interlocutor gives us, which I will repeat: 'Yes, but there is *something* there all the same accompanying my cry of pain. And it is on account of that that I utter it. And this something is what is important – and frightful.' Wittgenstein's response to this is very instructive; he does not disagree or demur, but says: 'Only whom are we informing of this? And on what occasion?' (*PI* 296). It is one thing to assure your friend or your doctor that your cry of pain was authentic (not feigned, not hysterical, etc.), to beg them to take it seriously and so on – it is another thing to wield the philosophical picture of a psychological or semantic *connection* between two somethings, viz. pain-language and what pain-language is 'about'.

It is significant that our attempts to express this picture so often take the form of empty statements.

> The very fact that we should so much like to say: '*This* is the important thing' – while we point privately to the sensation – is enough to shew how much we are inclined to say something which gives no information. (*PI* 298)

Part of Wittgenstein's point in this passage relates to the imagined use of the demonstrative 'this' – a futile clutching of air, as it were. But there is more to the point he is making than that. Thus it is empty to assert, as anything other than a protest of sincerity, 'When I said I was in pain, I was really talking about my pain! It was because I *was in pain* that I said I was in pain!' Empty and true, if you like, but empty all the same.[19] It is similarly empty to say, 'When I said my king had taken your pawn, I was really talking about my king!' We can imagine the person who says this trying to give substance to her claim by carrying on: 'Only my king *could* take that pawn – the queen couldn't, for instance. And without the white king the game would fall to the ground, you would be unable to checkmate me, our tactics would be thrown into disarray …' But all this is, after all, compatible with our playing a game of blindfold chess.

Notes

1 *Philosophical Investigations* is hereafter referred to as '*PI*'. References are to section numbers.
2 Wouldn't 'bingle-bongle' just be a (novel) *synonym* of 'rat'? But a code – a secret code, for example – isn't thought of as consisting in a list of synonyms, or of synonym-forming rules. We *could* think of codes thus, but we needn't.
3 The terminology of more or less brute facts is Elizabeth Anscombe's (see Anscombe 1981). She illustrates what she means by the following sort of scenario. Mrs Smith asks the grocer, Mr Jones, for a quarter of potatoes, and the grocer delivers them and sends her a bill for X pounds. These facts make it true that Mrs Smith owes Mr Jones X pounds, and the statement of those facts is brute relative to the 'owes'-statement – though it does not *entail* it. Moreover, it cannot be made to entail it by the addition of clauses ruling out possible defeaters (e.g. 'they are not acting in a film'), since the list of possible defeaters is open-ended.
4 It would be a distraction to start worrying here about what the 'canonical form' of a description ought to be. For present purposes, an event-description (say) might be a sentence, a sentence-nominalization, a gerund or other things.
5 Someone might here invoke Geach's distinction between change proper and 'Cambridge change', in order to deny that someone's inheriting a house can be called an event at all, it not being a case of genuine change. But the move seems to fail; for one thing, if (as is usually said) a Cambridge change supervenes on a 'real change', then on what real change does the girl's turning eighteen supervene? Surely not *Time's passing*?
6 If the black pawn is treated in the same way as the white king, of course, 'the white king has taken a black pawn' will have to be rendered: 'the set of utterances such that p has taken the set of utterances such that q' – which may in turn lead us to replace 'has taken' by some other bit of verbal rigmarole.
7 In starting with a discussion of intentional psychological verbs I am not meaning to suggest that anything that goes for one 'mental concept' goes for them all, if only because it is doubtful whether there is a well-defined notion of *the mental*. But the phrase 'not a something' seems to me to apply in much the same way to thinkings, decidings, etc., as it does to pains and itches. Wittgenstein's net can usefully be cast wider than he happens to cast it in *PI* 304.
8 The sort of contextuality which is at issue is illustrated by the following: 'An intention is embedded in its embedded in its situation, in human customs and institutions. If the technique of the game of chess did not exist, I could not intend to play a game of chess' (*PI* 337).
9 I do not think that this in itself throws doubt on the idea that we could be dealing with descriptions of a phenomenon that are brute relative to the original description (viz. 'NN's thinking of Walt Disney'). A description may be conceptually dependent on the description than which it is 'more brute'. Thus a spoken sound is only a candidate for being that in which the word 'rat' consists on a certain occasion in virtue of our being able to hear it, and take it, as that word. One cannot even in principle assemble all the sounds of a certain (sonic) sort, together with the contexts of their production, and *thereby* determine that they count as utterances of the word 'rat'. See Chapter Thirteen.
10 Indeed, as Gustafsson points out, the white king might be embodied in a succession of different physical items.
11 See e.g. *PI* 404–6.
12 Wittgenstein imagines someone with a headache, who is also enduring some nearby piano-tuning, saying, 'It'll stop soon.'

> 'You said, "It'll stop soon." – Were you thinking of the noise or your pain?' If he answers 'I was thinking of the piano-tuning' – is he observing [verifying, stating] that the connexion existed, or is he making it by means of these words? – Can't I say *both*? If what he said was true, didn't the connexion exist – and is he not for all that making one which did not exist [before]? (*PI* 682)

NB Anscombe's use of 'is observing' to translate '*konstatiert*' may mislead us: she means 'observe' as in 'make an observation', i.e. 'note', not 'notice'.
13 This can be seen in the fact that a legally faulty decision will still be effective and binding so long as it is not *found* to be faulty by a due process, e.g. on appeal.
14 To say that an answer would be stipulative is not to say that it would be arbitrary: when some stipulation is adopted, practical reasons can usually be given in favour of doing so.
15 The phrase 'according to which' is not meant to imply that a convention or rule could be formulated, even in principle, of the form: 'Such-and-such shapes, produced in such-and-such situations, shall count as instances of the word "rat".' See n. 9 above.
16 An analogy might help: one could either say that Emma's crouching consisted in her legs bending a certain way, or in her whole body adopting a certain posture.
17 And the question '*Where* is his pain?' would have a straightforward answer, just as it has in my case – viz. 'In his toe'. – It may be added that the possibility of phantom-limb pain does not force us to 'relocate' people's pains, e.g. into their skulls. This move is not even necessary in the case of those actually suffering from phantom-limb pain.
18 See Wittgenstein (1981, sec. 608–10); also Chapter One of this volume.
19 The protest of sincerity and the empty-true statement both use that 'non-robust' sense of the word 'about' to which I earlier alluded, the use involving a mere recapitulation of surface form. And both statements help us to see the point of the other half of Wittgenstein's phrase: 'not a *nothing* either!'

References

Anscombe, G. E. M. (1981), 'Brute Facts', in G. E. M. Anscombe, *Collected Papers Vol. III: Ethics, Religion and Politics*. Oxford: Blackwell, pp. 22–25.

Child, W. (2011), *Wittgenstein*. London: Routledge.

Gustafsson, M. (2018), 'Wittgenstein, Language and Chess', in E. Bermon and J.-P. Narboux (eds), *Finding One's Way through Wittgenstein's Philosophical Investigations – New Essays on §§1–88*. Dordrecht: Springer, pp. 79–94.

McDowell, J. (1989), 'One Strand in the Private Language Argument', *Grazer Philosophische Studien*, 33, pp. 285–303.

Specht, E. K. (1969), *The Foundations of Wittgenstein's Later Philosophy*. Manchester: Manchester University Press.

Wittgenstein, L. (1958), *Philosophical Investigations*, trans. G. E. M. Anscombe, ed. G. E. M. Anscombe and R. Rhees. Oxford: Basil Blackwell, 2nd ed.

———. (1981), *Zettel*, trans. G. E. M. Anscombe, ed. G. E. M. Anscombe and G. H. von Wright. Oxford: Basil Blackwell, 2nd ed.

Chapter Three

SINCERITY IN THOUGHT

Introduction

A person can be responsible for an outcome, can be held to account for it, despite not having intended it or even foreseen it. The babysitter who brings her Rottweiler along with her and leaves it with the baby while she nips out to buy some cigarettes will be responsible for the baby's injuries. She didn't, let us assume, intend the dog to attack the baby. And she may well not have foreseen this outcome either, if that means foreseeing it as likely, since it might not have been a likely thing to happen, merely something made more likely by her absence. Let us imagine that she is asked, 'Why did you leave the dog with the baby?', and replies: 'I assumed the dog would stay still for the short time I was at the shop.' A question that arises about statements like this is whether they are fully sincere, or bona fide, or genuine.

In her article 'On Being in Good Faith', Elizabeth Anscombe (2008) discusses the phenomenon of insincerity in connection with issues of responsibility, voluntariness and so on. It might be thought that insincerity must attach to statements made to, or behaviour directed towards, other people; but, as Anscombe argues, sincerity and insincerity can be features of thoughts themselves. Indeed, a statement can be insincere on account of its expressing an insincere thought of the speaker, rather than on account of its not expressing the thought the speaker really has. One consequence of this for ethics is that when someone's responsibility for an action or omission depends on the sort of account the person could truthfully give, e.g. in answer to such questions as 'Why didn't you do X?', it is not enough that such possible answers not be *lies* – for the person may not know that her response is false or dubious, and so may not be lying. But in the case of insincerity, 'not knowing' doesn't supply an excuse, as it might in other cases, but is itself a source of culpability.

Insincerity in Thought and Behaviour

It is natural to suppose that the sincerity of an assertion is a matter of the utterance's being an expression of what the person thinks; in some sense, the public and conventional meaning of the utterance, together with the point or purpose of the language-game within which it is made, determine that you should say such-and-such only if you think that p. (Reference to the point of the language-game is needed so as to allow for jokes, play-acting and the like – contexts where you needn't think what you say.) Such a model seems to be inapplicable to thoughts: if a thought can be called insincere, surely this won't mean that it's at odds with some other thought standing behind it? At any rate, if the second thought is meant to be the same sort of thing as the first, it would apparently have to be sincere in its turn, i.e. in line with some thought standing behind it, and so on *ad inf.* So what can the insincerity of a thought consist in?

As Anscombe remarks, 'It need not mean that some feeling of hesitancy or difficulty accompanied the thought. For it depends on the context of the thought whether a feeling of difficulty would be counted as showing that the man did not sincerely think it' (2008, 102). She mentions a man who 'believes in the assurance of a friend that there are no steps to fall down in a dark passage, but who has uneasy feelings as he walks the passage' (103); such a man still quite sincerely thinks that there are no steps to fall down. Of course, the uneasiness that might accompany the babysitter's thought 'The dog is sure to stay put on the sofa' will very likely be a symptom of insincerity, or not full sincerity, and this seems to be because a rational person knowing the facts is unlikely to arrive at such a thought without 'suppressing the knowledge that makes the thought doubtful'. (The phrase is Anscombe's, and we shall be taking a closer look at it later on (see 2008, 103).) In other words, it is the doubtfulness of the thought, given the known facts, that lends a certain character to any feelings of uneasiness or difficulty; and this fact is an indication that it is the doubtfulness of the thought which is the key issue when it comes to the thought's insincerity, in ways we shall see.

We need at this point to make a distinction between thoughts as occurrences and thoughts as more settled states of a person.[1] Anscombe appears to be talking about the first; and someone might object that to the extent that occurrent thoughts are statements made to oneself or occurring inwardly, e.g. as heard with one's 'inner ear', the sincerity or insincerity of *these* will be very like that of external statements. I can, after all, say something to myself I don't believe at all, such as 'The Wykeham Professor has three heads'. What I *believe*, the objector goes on, is in fact something lying behind my occurrent thoughts and with which those thoughts may or may not be in harmony.

But what is the nature of this background belief? If it is said to be a certain disposition of the person, we must ask what manifestations this disposition is supposed to have. A disposition to have occurrent thoughts with a certain content will bring us back to the question whether these occurrent thoughts are sincere or not. For surely I can be disposed to say jokingly to myself, 'The Wykeham Professor has three heads', perhaps even several times a day? And yet I do not believe this, and these inner assertions are not meant sincerely. It is natural at this point to look to the person's non-linguistic behaviour, and to attempt to cast a standing belief as a behavioural disposition, possibly a multi-track one à la Gilbert Ryle. But restricting ourselves to non-linguistic manifestations of a belief, as it seems we must, puts many beliefs out of the range of our analysis; what non-linguistic behaviour could manifest my belief that Hannibal ate meat, for instance? Moreover, non-linguistic behaviour shares with linguistic behaviour the problematic feature that it can be sincere or insincere, genuine or fake.

It is worth pausing to consider this last point. What does the insincerity of a bit of behaviour consist in – a smile, say, or some attentive nodding? It cannot consist simply in a disharmony between the behaviour and an accompanying thought or feeling, if that thought or feeling is an 'inner statement', since that inner statement might itself not be sincere, as we have seen. Perhaps the accompanying thought or feeling is a standing disposition of some sort, such as an attitude of unfriendliness. The insincere smile then counts as insincere because smiling (of that sort) is a sign of friendliness, the contrary of unfriendliness. The smile, in other words, is misleading. Not all misleading signs are insincere, to be sure; the listener who closes her eyes during a lecture may appear to be dozing, and may know that she appears so, and may even relish the thought that she appears so – when in fact she is simply avoiding the strong glare of a lamp on the stage. She is not pretending to doze, for to do that she would have to *mean* to mislead people. And as Anscombe showed us, meaning or intending something can't be equated with inwardly saying something: once again, any such inner sayings would themselves have to be 'meant'.

Is a positive intention to mislead a necessary condition of some behaviour's being insincere? No; for not all insincere behaviour is pretence. An insincere smile can be part of the repertoire of behaviour of someone who is phony, or sycophantic, a repertoire even including behaviours that are involuntary or not fully voluntary, such as laughing or crying. Nevertheless, phony behaviour is insincere – a phony smile is misleading, and not accidentally so. (To say it is misleading is not to say that it does or will mislead, of course; the phoniness might be ineffectual phoniness.)

It should be clear now that to call a smile insincere because it is in conflict with a background behavioural disposition, e.g. unfriendliness, assumes that *this* disposition is a more genuine aspect of the person's character than the disposition embodied in what I called the repertoire of phony behaviour. For evidently insincerity is itself very often a disposition of a person. Smith says and does all these things, indicating friendliness towards his boss – and he also says and does these various other things (we may include inward thoughts here), indicating unfriendliness towards his boss. Which words, deeds and thoughts are genuine? The question does not seem to have to do with any statistical preponderance of friendly or unfriendly behaviour. Throwing up our hands, we may decide that there is just a mess of behaviour, in which two opposing dispositions or tendencies may be discerned, or perhaps as many dispositions or tendencies as we care to pick out, as one picks out shapes and patterns in the bark of a tree.

In fact, of course, we will probably regard the friendliness towards the boss as insincere, given the signs elsewhere of unfriendliness; and this is because there is reason to suck up to your boss. That might suggest that we are simply casting our holistic net wider, so as to include more facts about the person's psychology, such as that he wants to get on in his career. But our thoughts are guided not just by what we 'discover' about the person before us, which is often not very much, but by what is normal and natural for human beings. After all, if we do end up saying that the man wants to get on in his career, it may well be on account of behaviour we have *already* classified as sycophantic, just through observing it. A smile and a bow in a particular social context – e.g. in the presence of the boss – can simply strike us as obviously phony, and our being struck that way is an unmediated reaction, not the forming of a hypothesis. Our propensity to react in that way arises from and develops through experience of life, though it must start off from quite instinctive modes of interpersonal reaction. And although I said that a reaction to some phoniness would not typically have the character of a hypothesis, such a reaction and what one says in expressing it are not free-floating things but point in some directions and not others, can be confirmed or disconfirmed and so on.[2]

I said above that in some cases of insincere behaviour, namely certain kinds of pretending, a person will intend to mislead – but that such an intention isn't a necessary condition of insincerity. Now remember that Anscombe's central criterion of intention is what somebody says, or would say, in answer to the question, 'Why?' (as in 'Why did you do that?'). If we follow Anscombe on this, as I think we should, we shall conclude that someone who intends to mislead by his behaviour would answer the question 'Why?' by saying, 'So as to mislead'; that is, if he answers sincerely, something he is unlikely to do. Evidently we have to assume that the answer to the criterial question 'Why?' is a sincere one. Is this working assumption itself tantamount to the supposition that an answer to 'Why did you give that answer to "Why?"?' would be along the lines of, 'So as to answer truthfully'? We could perhaps say such a thing; though the rule 'Answer truthfully' is as it were built into the language-game, so there is a sense in which 'So as to answer truthfully' could hardly be an informative response.[3] Certainly, the further question 'But why answer my questions truthfully?' would in normal circumstances be frivolous or crazy, not to mention self-undermining.

The Doubtfulness of a Thought

Why did I claim that an intention to mislead isn't a necessary condition of insincerity? After all, even if the sycophant wouldn't answer 'Why did you smile like that?' by saying, 'So as to butter up the boss,' isn't that just because he's insincere? If he were being sincere about it, he surely would give some such reply?

It's worth drawing a distinction here between the cunning hypocrite and what we may call the natural sycophant, or complete sycophant, as in 'compleat angler'. The statement, 'If he were being sincere, he'd admit he was aiming to mislead' applies straightforwardly to the cunning hypocrite; but in the case of the natural sycophant, he is insincere all the way down, and there is a sense in which he *can't* tell us what he's really up to. Some will suggest he has a subconscious intention to mislead, and so is self-deceived. But I think it might be more accurate to say that he lacks self-knowledge: the concept of self-deception typically brings with it some notion of struggle or tension within the person's overall character, and there might not be any of that in the natural sycophant. Perhaps he answers our question, 'Why did you smile like that?' by saying, 'Because I think him a truly wonderful man!' This answer itself would be insincere, but not because of clashing with any belief or attitude of the sycophant himself. What it clashes with is *our* assessment of the situation, as one in which he's merely buttering up the boss. But what has our assessment got going for it that his assessment does not?

It is here that we can turn back to Anscombe's discussion, and also to the question of the sincerity of thoughts. The sycophant, I imagined, tells us that he smiled at the boss like that because he thinks him a truly wonderful man. It is the doubtfulness of this thought that is the issue, as it was the doubtfulness of the babysitter's thought that her dog was sure to stay put. Anscombe puts the matter thus:

> It [the sincerity of one's thoughts] is the purity of one's intentions in thinking these thoughts. By the purity of intention I mean not the ultimate purpose but the immediate purpose in

thinking. The thought is thought, or there is an inclination to think it, because it appears to be the relevant truth on the matter in hand; as opposed to its appearing to be the relevant truth on the matter in hand because it is a convenient or otherwise tempting thought, i.e. because there is an inclination to think it. (2008, 103)

Despite her reference to someone's intentions in thinking something, Anscombe's use of the word 'because' in this passage does not seem to point towards any possible giving of reasons by the subject herself. After all, the sincere person will not say, 'My reason for thinking that p is this: that it seems to me to be true that p.' That is hardly a *reason*.[4] Still less will the insincere person say, 'The reason it seems to me to be true that p is this: that I'm inclined to think that p.' Nevertheless, the sincere person will typically *be in a position* to give reasons for her belief that p; and this is what is usually conveyed by saying, 'It seems to her to be true that p.' By contrast, the explanation by appeal to what it's convenient or otherwise tempting to think is of the nature of a causal explanation, in a broad sense of 'causal'. That we reach for such an explanation shows our assessment of 'p' as being a doubtful or dubious thing to think in those circumstances and given what the person can be expected to have known.[5]

It might seem that we get an idea of what *sort* of causal explanation is at issue from Anscombe's description of the insincere person as 'suppressing the knowledge that makes the thought doubtful'. But in fact what Anscombe's surrounding discussion brings out is not the occurrence of any hypothetical acts of suppressing, so much as certain failures on the part of the person – in particular, the failure to reflect or think properly. The babysitter who thinks to herself 'The dog is sure to stay put' fails to reflect properly on the facts, something which those around her may explain by reference to her desire to go to the shops. And the phrase 'suppression of knowledge' is apt only because we are liable to protest, 'But you *knew* the dog might move!' But as Anscombe says, 'in other cases we say rather "You would have known if you had thought"' (2008, 106) – and it seems clear that the condition of responsibility is in general not knowledge that one's action or the circumstances are of a certain kind, so much as the capacity to think, consider or reflect. Of course this capacity itself presupposes that one have *some* knowledge of relevant facts, if only of a general kind (e.g. concerning dogs).

At the start of this chapter, I imagined the negligent babysitter telling us, 'I assumed the dog would stay put.' This statement could of course be mere pretence, if the babysitter had fully realized the dangers of what she was doing and is now trying to cover things up. But we have been considering the sort of case where what she *thinks*, not just what she *says*, is insincere or not fully sincere; and we seem to have arrived at a point where we can characterize this insincerity. It is not that her thought is in conflict with an occurrent thought standing behind it – nor is it even that her thought directly conflicts with (i.e. contradicts) certain settled beliefs or items of knowledge had by her. It is that she failed to think or reflect properly on the matter when she ought to have done, this failure being naturally explicable as arising from the standing temptation to go and buy some cigarettes, and being such as to enable her to embrace a doubtful thought, namely 'The dog is sure to stay put'.

Insincerity of thought is thus above all a sort of failure, the failure to think properly. And of course that means that many insincere utterances, namely the ones not involving actual pretence, are likewise cases of such failure, being expressions of insincere thoughts. It will now be apparent why it is significant for our discussion that there are forms of outward insincerity not involving actual pretence, such as sycophancy; since if insincerity were tied to pretending, in the sense of having an intention to mislead, then it would be obvious that thoughts could not be insincere. But it is not so tied.

Failure to Think Properly

Now it is natural to say that the reason the failure to think properly is culpable is that if the person had thought properly, she would have realized that such-and-such, and would therefore not have embraced the doubtful thought. And in fact I think this is probably Anscombe's view. But this sort of counterfactual does not seem to be true of my natural sycophant and people like him. It might not be possible to say to the natural sycophant: 'You know the boss is awful, really, don't you?' – nor yet, 'If you'd just think about it a bit, you'd see that he's awful.' The sycophant is insincere all the way down, as I put it. Does he or doesn't he 'really mean' his protestations of adulation? One can reply to this in the manner of Aristotle, saying, 'In one way, yes – in another way, no.' But if one does choose to say, 'No, he doesn't really mean them', this is on account of the inappropriateness of those protestations in the face of the observable character of the boss, and on our consequent interpretation of the sycophant's behaviour as *buttering up*. The psychology of buttering up can be quite complex, and may or may not have to do with possible kick-back benefits to the sycophant; people often adopt a servile stance in the presence of mere worldly success. And even where it is a matter of possible kick-back benefits, we need not posit an *aim*, e.g. subconscious, of getting those benefits. It may be that, like the character Berg in Tolstoy's *War and Peace*, the person just instinctively does and says those things, mixes with those people, etc., which in the long run stand to benefit him – as a bee is attracted to certain flowers. Thus if the boss is unremittingly rude back to him, the sycophant may just take that as part of the natural order of things, and still continue with his habits of sycophancy. He's unlucky in his boss, as a bee can be unlucky in its flower.

Remarks along these lines apply also, it seems to me, to cases of insincere thought. It may on a natural interpretation be false that had Smith thought about it, he would have realized the doubtfulness of what he was thinking, and thus quite probably of what he was doing. I say 'on a natural interpretation'; but there is another, perhaps equally natural, interpretation of the relevant counterfactuals which in effect takes them as saying, 'It was objectively possible to think properly about this matter, and someone thinking properly about it would not, etc. etc.' We are interested in Smith's character, after all, and it may be *part* of his character that he often fails to think properly about certain matters, whether or not there is even a remote chance that he could be brought to see his failures as failures and do something about them.

Relevant here is what Anscombe has to say about invincible ignorance:

> 'Invincible ignorance' is sometimes spoken of as if it were a psychological condition – not necessarily of mental defect or insanity. I am suggesting that it means 'ignorance that the man himself could not overcome'; as appears from the standard example, that the man who has never heard of Christ is invincibly ignorant of Christianity. Here the impossibility is not an impossibility because of the bent of his mind; he simply has not the information available to attend to. (2008, 111)

'Invincible ignorance' is supposed to serve as an excuse. But an impossibility that is due to the bent of your mind will not excuse you, since it is in a sense the bent of your mind that stands accused. And the bent of your mind, e.g. if you are prone to insincere thoughts, may make it hard or impossible for you to think properly about certain matters.

In the end, the fault in thinking insincerely lies in the doubtfulness of the thought. For what counts as 'not thinking properly about a matter'? Surely any thinking which, in those circumstances, leads to the babysitter's concluding that the dog is sure to stay put will prima facie count as not thinking properly. It is a different matter, to be sure, if the babysitter is for some reason ignorant of the habits and capacities of dogs or babies; but if she is an adult of normal experience, then her thinking will be improper *in virtue of* its yielding such conclusions. The case is rather like that of necessary truth in geometry: some measurements that appear to show that the angles of a certain triangle on a flat surface add up to 200° will *thereby* count as flawed, even if we have no inkling which part of the actual measuring procedure was to blame, and indeed even if the whole procedure were captured on film and no flaw could be detected. (The measurements will not throw even a scintilla of doubt on the truths of trigonometry, though if such measurements kept on and on occurring, trigonometry as a practice would eventually be thrown into disarray.) Likewise, in Descartes's *Meditations* it looks as if the clarity and distinctness of your ideas must in the end *consist in* their not producing falsehood – unluckily for Descartes.

If this is right, then the failure of which the insincere person stands accused is what it is only because of the positive fact, if you like, of that person's embracing a dubious thought. This sort of failure is unlike the failure that consists in not doing some necessary thing. In the latter case, the relation between what you fail to do and the outcome of that failure is typically external rather than internal. Externality of relation is relative to description-under-which, to be sure; but even where the only description we can come up with of some failure is 'failure to prevent X's happening' – which is indeed internally related to 'X happened' – still, where the person is deemed *responsible* for the failure, he is ipso facto deemed to have been *able* to prevent X's happening, something which really does depend on there being some independent description of what he could have done to prevent X's happening. Thus, even if we don't know why the soup tastes nasty, it is still the fault of the cook if, and only if, there is some independently specifiable means of preventing this, such as putting salt in, which could be invoked when framing a charge of negligence. By contrast, there often isn't such an independent description of what someone didn't do when he didn't think properly.

Moreover, the sort of 'thinking properly' a person can be blamed for not doing cannot itself be regarded as the adoption of certain mental means towards some goal, e.g. that of arriving at an answer to a practical question. This has been demonstrated by Anselm

Mueller in the course of his arguing that many forms of thinking exhibit what he calls 'unreasoned teleology'. The babysitter who, when considering whether to go to the shops, reflects properly, does so for a purpose, namely – given the circumstances – the purpose of forming any available true judgment of the form *the dog could do such-and-such undesirable thing if I leave it here for 10 minutes*. She succeeds in her purpose if she arrives at the thought *the dog could molest the baby if I leave it here for 10 minutes*. Having this thought is in this sense a means to the end she has set herself in reflecting; if she arrives at the thought she will have achieved her end. But clearly if the babysitter were to *adopt*, as a means, *having the thought that the dog could molest the baby if I leave it here for 10 minutes*, she would already have achieved her end: in just conceiving of her means as a suitable means she would have succeeded in her purpose, for she would be thinking, i.e. judging, 'The dog could molest the baby if I leave it here for 10 minutes.' But this is absurd. The purposiveness of her thinking, in other words, cannot be understood in terms of a practical syllogism. As Mueller puts it, 'You may decide that *this* is the right way to behave and yet not behave this way. But you cannot decide that *this* is the right way to judge concerning a given topic without thereby judging this way' (1992, 178).

Sincerity: Intellectual or Ethical Virtue?

The habit of not thinking properly and the habit of thinking dubious thoughts[6] both sound as if they must be intellectual vices, and we might therefore wonder how they can be objects of ethical blame. The idea that there is a hard-and-fast line between the intellectual and the ethical has in modern times often gone with the idea of a corresponding distinction between the factual and the evaluative, the cognitive and the conative, and so on. One of Anscombe's enduring contributions has been to undermine thoroughly the so-called fact/value distinction and the Humean psychology which is at the root of it. But I'm sure Anscombe would in the main go along with the Aristotelian distinction between intellectual and ethical vices; and we might ask of not thinking properly, and of insincerity in thought, 'Are these vices intellectual or ethical?'

Perhaps the main difference between the two species of vice or defect, for Aristotle, lies in the way the will is involved with each. If you misspell a word by accident, that shows that you're a bad or imperfect speller in a way that your misspelling it on purpose won't; whereas going off with someone else's wallet by accident does not show you to be ethically imperfect (i.e. dishonest) – going off with it on purpose does. To have an ethical virtue means more than being *able* to do a certain good sort of act, it means being inclined to, wanting to; if you accidentally remove someone's wallet, that probably means you didn't want to remove it. To have an intellectual virtue it is typically enough to be able to do whatever it is well; something similar goes for skills.

The intellectually sincere person seems to be someone who wants to say and think the truth, something that shows itself in various ways, including in how the person thinks and in what he ends up thinking. There is also, as we've seen, sincerity in behaviour – in expressions of friendliness, interest, love, indignation and so on. Anscombe might say that such sincerity involves wanting to 'do the truth' (a favourite phrase of hers); and certainly, as we have seen, even the smile of the natural sycophant who harbours no secret intention to mislead is a misleading smile, a smile which 'means something' that is the opposite of the truth.[7] Now it is not that the intellectually insincere person *wants* to embrace falsehoods, and nor need the behaviourally insincere person *want* to embody falsehood in his behaviour. And this is the sort of fact which can lead people to infer that, since the will is not involved, any defect here cannot be an ethical one – for ethical virtues and vices involve the will. But the inference is unsound. This can be shown in two steps: first, by showing that when someone's intentions or wants are relevant to their culpability, this is not typically on account of their wanting to act badly, but rather on account of their wanting to do X, where doing X is acting badly;[8] and second, by showing that in any case, as Anscombe says, 'sin essentially requires, not intention but voluntariness' (2008, 105).

It is the second of these points that is most germane to our discussion. The babysitter in our example doesn't intend the baby to get bitten; and if she thinks to herself, 'The dog is sure to stay put', she doesn't intend to think a false or dubious thought. We do not blame her for her intentional action, i.e. going out to the shops, but for her not securing the dog somehow (given that she was going to the shops); and this failure of hers was not intentional, but voluntary. Likewise, in calling her thought an insincere one, we imply blame for a failure of hers, the failure to think properly, behind which there is likely to be a more general failure, the failure to want to think the truth. Perhaps we should say: the failure to want it enough, for of course in many matters the babysitter will want very much to think what's true. But if how much someone wants to think the truth depends on the subject-matter, we may well have the sort of situation described by Anscombe as one in which something 'appears to be the relevant truth on the matter in hand because it is a convenient or otherwise tempting thought'. The phrase 'otherwise tempting' covers a wide range of cases, and the temptation in question may not be self-interested, in the way in which the temptation to say or think what will excuse your behaviour is self-interested. Thus laziness is in general tempting, and laziness of *thought* often involves the sort of sloppiness or falling into cliché which renders what is thought dubious and also insincere.

It is also tempting to cut a certain sort of figure, in the eyes of others but also in your own eyes, and it is perhaps a bit unclear whether this is a matter of self-interest or not. This temptation can lead to one important species of insincerity, namely hypocrisy. Anscombe discusses the hypocrisy that is outward pretence, taking pretence to be a sort of wanting-to-seem, and writes: 'It is characteristic of this sort of wanting-to-seem that it carries with it an implicit demand for respect for an atmosphere evoked by the pretender, which surrounds not the reality, but the *idea* of such things as being principled, or cultured, or saintly, or rich, or important.'[9] I have argued that intention to mislead is not a necessary condition of insincerity, and Anscombe's 'wanting to seem' is different from 'intending to seem' – so it is possible to extend her account of outward hypocrisy to inward hypocrisy of thought: e.g. a person can be in the habit of thinking deep-seeming thoughts because he in some sense *wants* to seem deep to himself. His thoughts will manifest inward hypocrisy, and will be insincere (or not fully sincere).

Insincerity of thought is evidently a vice that is both intellectual and ethical. On the one hand it concerns thinking and judging, and on the other it concerns a failure of the will in connection with an important human good or goods, namely having and sharing the truth; the virtue of sincerity in thought involves wanting to think the truth. There is a failure of will because of the voluntariness (not intentionalness) that can be ascribed to thoughts. To show more fully than I have here that voluntariness *can* properly be ascribed to thoughts, and also to the *not having* of thoughts, would require further argument.[10] But that is a topic for another occasion.

Notes

1. This distinction is not intended to be either exhaustive or precise, nor do I mean by employing it to be addressing the question 'What sort of *mental state* is thinking/thought?' As Wittgenstein said, 'thinking' is 'a widely ramified concept. A concept that comprises many manifestations of life' (1981, sec. 110); and he advised that we 'look at the word "to think" as a tool' (1958, sec. 360). The distinction between 'occurrent' and 'settled' thoughts is itself merely a tool, whose usefulness is relative to the enquiry.
2. Cf. Wittgenstein (1958, Part ii, 228): 'Imponderable evidence includes subtleties of glance, of gesture, of tone. I may recognize a genuine loving look, distinguish it from a pretended one (and here there can, of course, be a "ponderable" confirmation of my judgment).'
3. This fact helps us to see why no vicious regress is involved in its being necessary that the answer 'So as to answer truthfully' would itself have to be sincere. Sincerity is the default position, and is conceptually prior to insincerity in the way in which a pound coin is conceptually prior to a fake pound coin.
4. Might she instead say, 'I have arrived at the thought that p in order to think the truth about such-and-such'? If 'in order to' points to means-end *reasoning*, this answer would be incoherent, as we shall see later on (pp. 47–8); but it nevertheless makes sense to impute to the person a purpose, *thinking the truth about such-and-such*, such that thinking that p achieves that purpose.
5. This last phrase covers a tangle of issues. A person may end up embracing a thought that happens to be true and reasonable in those circumstances, though doubtful relative to what he believes, and this doubtfulness could render his thought insincere (or rather: warrant the thought's being counted a manifestation of insincerity). But this raises the further question whether his 'beliefs' are themselves sincere – not that this raises any spectre of a vicious regress. – Further, what someone falsely believes is right or wrong, good or bad, etc., will not count as innocent error, in the way in which e.g. falsely believing that the transparent liquid in a bottle is water might be innocent; cf. Anscombe: 'Ignorance of principle is not a cause of involuntariness, but of scoundrelism, according to Aristotle and those who have followed him' (2008, 104). The distinction between matters of principle and matters of fact sounds like, though for various reasons it cannot be equated with, the Humean distinction between values and facts. Elsewhere, Anscombe (1981a) discusses it at length.
6. As has been indicated, this phrase means something like 'thoughts it is dubious to have given what the person can be expected to have known and relative to his actual beliefs'. See the tangle mentioned in n. 5, above.
7. What does the smile mean? One could say it means, 'This is a smile' – i.e. 'This is a real/true/genuine/authentic smile.'
8. The way in which what you want or intend is relevant to blame is parallel to the way in which what you knowingly do is relevant to blame; in both cases, the notion of a 'description under which' is crucial. See Anscombe's discussion of the doctrine that mortal sin requires 'full knowledge': 'This, then, will be the meaning of the condition "full knowledge": given that to do X is gravely wrong, then a man is guilty of wrongdoing in doing what is in fact doing X, only if he knows that he is doing X' (2008, 104).
9. Anscombe (1981b, 93).
10. The topic is discussed in Chapter Five of this volume.

References

Anscombe, G. E. M. (1981a), 'Two Kinds of Error in Action', in *Collected Papers Vol. III: Ethics, Religion and Politics*. Oxford: Blackwell, pp. 3–9.

———. (1981b), 'Pretending', in *Collected Papers Vol. II, Metaphysics and the Philosophy of Mind*. Oxford: Blackwell, pp. 83–93.

———. (2008), 'On Being in Good Faith', in M. Geach and L. Gormally (eds), *Faith in a Hard Ground: Essays on Religion, Philosophy and Ethics by G.E.M. Anscombe*. Exeter: Imprint Academic, pp. 101–12.

Mueller, A. (1992), 'Mental Teleology', *Proceedings of the Aristotelian Society*, 92, part 2, 161–83.

Wittgenstein, L. (1958), *Philosophical Investigations*, trans. G. E. M. Anscombe, ed. G. E. M. Anscombe and R. Rhees. Oxford: Basil Blackwell, 2nd ed.

———. (1981), *Zettel*, trans. G. E. M. Anscombe, ed. G. E. M. Anscombe and G. H. von Wright. Oxford: Basil Blackwell, 2nd ed.

Chapter Four

IS PLEASURE A GOOD?

'Good' and 'the Good'

If someone says 'I want some string', they can be asked what they want it *for*. They might reply, 'I want to tie up this present.' The question 'But why do you want to do *that?*' wouldn't usually be asked by anyone who knows the ways of the world; but it could for all that be informatively answered. That answer might in turn provoke the question, 'And why do you want that?' – and so on and so on. At a certain point we will get an answer to 'Why?' that presents an end as simply desirable in itself. This answer will supply what Elizabeth Anscombe called a desirability characterization. The question 'Why do you want that?', asked of such an end, will be futile, frivolous or uncomprehending.[1]

Given that there are fairly objective criteria for what shall count as a desirability characterization, it seems clear that one example of such a characterization will be: 'X is pleasant.' 'But why do you want what's pleasant?' certainly has the appearance of a silly question. The end presented as thus desirable might be that of drinking another glass of champagne, or of going for a walk on a summer's day. These are examples of activities, but there are also passive pleasures, such as the pleasure of being driven in a fast car.

Now those philosophers who follow Aristotle and Aquinas would say that whatever is desired is desired under the aspect of the good (*'Quidquid appetitur, appetitur sub specie boni'*). A person's goal or end is what they would give as the final answer in a series of answers to the repeated question, 'Why do you want that?' It would thus seem natural for a Thomist to equate the goodness of an end with its desirability, in Anscombe's sense: for a desirability characterization brings an end to such repeated asking of 'Why?' An example of a desirability characterization, as we have noted, is 'X is pleasant'. So it appears that to desire something because it is or would be pleasant, and not as a means to anything further, is to desire that thing under the aspect of the good, and *as* good. But we should at any rate pause before attributing such a claim to Elizabeth Anscombe, despite her adherence to the Thomist view of desire just outlined. Having said that it isn't one of her aims (in *Intention*) to examine the concept of pleasure in any detail, she goes on:

> Nor should an unexamined thesis 'pleasure is good' (whatever that may mean) be ascribed to me. For my present purposes all that is required is that 'It's pleasant' is an adequate answer to 'What's the good of it?' or 'What do you want that for?' (Anscombe 1963, 77–78)

The difficulty we face, and which lurks behind these remarks of Anscombe's, is the following: should we explain the notion of a desirability characterization via that of what is good, or vice versa? In other words, do all answers that terminate a series of 'Why?'

questions by counting as adequate and final manage to count as such because they allude to what is good, or do ends count as good because in citing them as ends one furnishes final and adequate answers to the question 'Why?'? The word 'good' is certainly *capable* of being used in a substantive sense, one that is independent of the notion of a desirability characterization; but it might be argued that if we are to speak of final ends as good, or as desired under the aspect of the good, then we had better tie the sense of 'good', used thus, to that notion. In the case of pleasure, there are certainly problems with the idea that it can be regarded as a substantive good in the sense, say, in which health or virtue or companionship or knowledge are goods. Perhaps the main source of these problems lies in the fact that pleasure is not to be conceived of as a mental accompaniment to those activities, etc. in which we take pleasure; it is rather, as Aristotle saw, conceptually tied to those activities themselves. But of course activities are not as such good. People take pleasure in all sorts of things, good, bad and indifferent; and if an activity is wicked, it appears right to say that pleasure taken in it is wicked also.

No doubt more could be said on this issue.[2] But I want instead to pursue the second line of thought just mentioned. According to this line, to say that 'X is pleasant' presents X under the aspect of the good is simply to say that it supplies a desirability characterization, or, in other words, an adequate answer to 'Why do you want X?', an answer that renders the agent's purposes and behaviour intelligible.

Enjoying and Wanting

If Aristotle, Ryle, Anscombe and others are right that pleasure is not a particular sort of mental experience, not a sensation or quasi-sensation, then what is it? A natural reply is to say that we need to look at such whole phrases as 'take pleasure in'; we can then see that 'Mary takes pleasure in riding' basically means 'Mary enjoys riding'. To enjoy riding is not to do two things simultaneously, riding and enjoying; it is to do one thing (riding) in a certain way, or against the background of a certain set of habits, or something along those lines. Enjoying is conceptually related to preferring, going in for, trying to get, etc. It is in fact a very close cousin of *wanting*.

And this is why there is a problem with the thought that 'X is pleasant' supplies a desirability characterization. Jeremy is asked: 'Why do you want to play pushpin?' He replies: 'Because playing pushpin is pleasant.' But the latter seems in effect to mean, 'Because I like playing pushpin'; and isn't this dangerously close to 'I want to play pushpin'? Our original question surely asked for a description of playing pushpin that would make sense of wanting to go in for it, a description that would render the desire to go in for it intelligible. 'I like playing pushpin' doesn't seem to give information about the activity of playing pushpin, so much as about the agent's propensity to play pushpin – which, it might be said, is the very thing we wanted to be made intelligible.

Of course the concepts of enjoying and of wanting are not the same. You can want to do something you won't at all enjoy, such as unblocking the drains. And while 'These people are pursuing what they desire' has the air of a tautology, 'These people are pursuing pleasure' does not. This is why people who only or largely pursue pleasure form a quite specific class of people, that of hedonists. So 'I am in this instance pursuing pleasure' appears informative as an answer to 'Why?' But what is it to pursue pleasure, over and above pursuing what you want?

It is only in a rather strange sort of case that someone might adduce the pleasantness of an activity as itself a means to some further end. A man following a self-help programme might decide to pursue pleasure so as to reduce his overall stress levels, or so as to indicate to others his right to do things simply for his own sake (assertiveness training) – or for yet more recherché reasons. But by and large, when 'X is pleasant' is given as the answer to 'What do you want that for?', it doesn't characterize X as a means to some further end.

Could the following be true: that in telling us that she finds something pleasant, what a person typically means to tell us is nothing more than that she has no further end in view when she goes in for it? To say that the person aims at pleasure as an 'end in itself' would be a misleading way of putting things; the truth is that she simply pursues the activity *not* with any further end in view. A connection could be made with those theories of art which assert that the essence of the 'aesthetic attitude' is its disinterestedness – the fact that one does *not* view the art object as a means to anything further. Such theories would seem to trade on the basic fact that art is for pleasure, along with the fact that 'X is pleasant' has the character we have just alleged of it. But more importantly for our present discussion, the force of 'X is pleasant' now looks to be very similar to that of another kind of answer to 'Why?' – namely, 'For no particular reason'. This latter kind of statement does not show, if an action is in question, that the action wasn't intentional: the statement does not refuse application to the question 'Why?', in Anscombe's phrase, but it does (of course) indicate that there is no reason for the action, e.g. no further end in view. And indeed sometimes there is not much to choose between the answers (in English) 'No particular reason' and 'Just for fun', if asked 'Why are you doing that?' – for example, when drawing a face in the margin of your essay, or when tapping out the rhythm of Ravel's *Bolero* on the car steering wheel.

If these thoughts were along the right lines, then 'X is pleasant' would in fact appear to be *unsuited* to play the part of a desirability characterization. When given as the answer to 'Why are you doing that?', it would be tantamount to 'No particular reason';[3] and so when given as the answer to 'Why do you want to do that?', it would surely have much the same force. It wouldn't supply one's *reason* for wanting something; it would simply report, or be an expression of, one's wanting that thing, and wanting it not as a means to any further end.

But this account can't be right as it stands. For Jeremy might habitually choose to play pushpin, with no further end in view, and yet get no pleasure out of it. We would perhaps call him 'addicted' to pushpin. So there must be more to finding something pleasant than merely going in for it with no further end in view. The fact that addictive or compulsive behaviour can be utterly devoid of pleasure may help to explain part of the attraction of the old idea of pleasure as a conscious experience. What, after all, is the *difference* between an addiction that gives pleasure and one that doesn't? It's natural to suggest that the difference lies in something going on in the agent in the first, but not in the second, case – especially since nothing in the agent's habits or preferences seems to distinguish the cases.

Moreover, we could cite those possible, if unusual, scenarios which I touched on above, in which the pleasantness of an activity is aimed at as a means to some further end. If 'X is pleasant' were like 'For no reason', surely it could never be given as a reason in a bit of means-end deliberation? – unless, that is, doing something for no particular reason could be aimed at as a means to a further end! And while some of the Existentialists might have made out that this could be attempted, insofar as they thought that the aim of becoming truly Free was to be achieved by acting groundlessly, and so put forward a reason for doing reasonless things, aiming at *pleasure* as a means (to stress reduction, say) clearly doesn't involve the paradoxicality or irrationality that the Existentialist programme appears to.

'*How* Is That Pleasant?'

If 'X is pleasant' does give information about X itself, what kind of information does it give?

A desirability characterization is a statement that renders it intelligible why one should want something, and which suffices as an answer to 'Why do you want that?' And there are very few statements, if any, that are *guaranteed* to play such a role. For (i) there may always be defeating considerations; and (ii) the context may render the statement itself unintelligible. As to (i): if I say, 'This is nutritious, that's why I want to eat it,' I fail to give a sufficient or adequate reason for my desire if what I propose to eat is my own arm. As to (ii): if I say, 'That would be pleasant,' I fail to be fully intelligible if what I propose to do is carry a shoe into the garden and back. There are limits on first-person authority concerning pleasure.

In this respect the concept of pleasure is like that of wanting. (See *Intention*, sec. 37.) For an activity that is not normal or natural, a reason is needed both for the activity and for wanting to go in for it, if the activity is to count as voluntary or sane. By this I mean that if no reason can be given, then we must ask, 'Why say that the person *wants* to do this at all, rather than that he is doing it compulsively or instinctively or robotically or randomly?' Statements like 'I just want it', 'I just want to', 'Just for fun', 'For the pleasure of it' and so on are not statements to which the model of infallible first-person authority can be applied (if indeed that model can be applied to anything). For all such statements there are requirements of intelligibility. And behind such requirements of intelligibility there stands the question: 'Why call this thing/activity/state of affairs something *wanted* by the person?', and related questions, such as: 'Why call this *getting* an object?' and 'Why call that *fun*?' None of these questions is properly answered by saying, 'Because the person himself calls it that.'

The statement that something is pleasant is thus subject to certain public standards of assessment, in particular as regards intelligibility. If the statement 'It's pleasant' is challenged, then sometimes the fact that the challenge is not met leaves the statement in limbo: namely, when the context renders the statement prima facie unintelligible. Hence 'X is pleasant' might or might not succeed in supplying a desirability characterization.

If I say I find some activity pleasant, and you ask me 'But how is it pleasant?', I can start describing the activity in more detail. My purpose then is to make *you* see something;

that is, my purpose is that a certain phenomenon should begin to make sense to you, the phenomenon (roughly) of a human being's freely pursuing something for its own sake. A similar case is that of finding something interesting. 'What's so interesting about biology?' is a challenge that is to be met, if it can be, by further description of biology. The person might for example say that animal organs and behaviours are amazingly well-fitted to their functions in ways that biology describes illuminatingly, or that a study of different animals' biologies shows how animals are similar to or different from us in various ways … etc. There may or may not come a point when the listener says, 'I begin to see why you find it interesting'; she may just shrug her shoulders and mutter, 'What a waste of time.' But if she *does* say, 'I begin to see why you find it interesting,' she is not thereby expressing a dawning interest in biology: my description of biology was not intended to elicit sympathetic feelings in my audience, so much as to get them to *see* the point of certain activities. Similar remarks go for explaining how some activity is pleasant.

It is important to note that in expatiating on what it is about some activity that makes it pleasant, i.e. that renders intelligible one's finding it pleasant, one need not be supplying descriptions of some end one has been aiming at. It may not be one of my reasons for going in for stamp-collecting that I want to experience a certain sort of satisfaction or excitement, for instance, even though I might mention the satisfaction of completing a set or the excitement of finding a rare stamp as examples of what makes stamp-collecting fun. 'Finding such-and-such a rare stamp will excite me' need not figure even implicitly in any practical deliberations of mine. It is true that if I mention various features of stamp-collecting in my account of the fun of the hobby, then I usually imply that I myself am drawn to stamp-collecting at least in part because it has those features – in *some* sense of 'because'. But I might mention aspects of stamp-collecting that are valued by other collectors, or even just aspects that I guess my interlocutor will see something in. This will at any rate be so when the question 'But what is the pleasure of it?' is a question primarily about the activity, and not (as it might be from the lips of one's life coach or psychoanalyst) a question primarily about the character and motives of the person of whom it is asked.

Returning to our main topic: if one says 'It's pleasant' or 'It's fun' (etc.) in answer to 'Why do you want to do that?', this answer does typically bring an end to 'Why?' questioning. But it also allows for the challenge, 'But what *is* the pleasure of it?' Of course, that question may be pointless, e.g. if the activity is well known to be the recreation of countless people. But it may not be pointless; and when that is the case, there is a sense in which questioning has not been brought to an end. Nevertheless, questions intended to elicit propositions that occurred (implicitly or explicitly) in the agent's practical reasoning *have* probably come to an end; for as we have noted, to say wherein the pleasure of something consists is not necessarily to give one's reasons for going in for it, in the sense of 'means-end' reasons for aiming at it. At the same time, a failure to give a remotely adequate answer to 'What *is* the pleasure of it?' will tend to cast retrospective doubt on the intelligibility of the claim 'X is pleasant', and so cast doubt on its capacity to bring 'Why?' questioning to an end (i.e. to be a desirability characterization).

Interpretative Motives

We are now in a position to see how 'X is pleasant' can, after all, be a desirability characterization. Let us first retrace our steps. Our main worry was that 'X is pleasant' amounts roughly to 'I like or enjoy X', and that the latter looks like a too close cousin of 'I want X'. In pursuit of an account of this statement, 'X is pleasant', we then considered the view that pleasantness can be understood in terms of going in for something just for its own sake (i.e. not as a means to anything further). On such a view, 'X is pleasant' might indeed manage to bring an end to iteration of the question 'Why?', but only in the sense in which 'For no particular reason' might also bring an end to such questioning; on this view, 'X is pleasant' could hardly be said to present an end as somehow *desirable*. But in any case, the view in question turns out to be inadequate, for two reasons: first, because one can, if unusually, pursue pleasure as a means, and second, because addictive or compulsive behaviour is also gone in for habitually and not as a means to anything further, though it may well bring no pleasure.

And at this point it will be useful to state what it is that distinguishes pleasure from mere addiction, something we are now in a position to do. The difference comes out in answers to the question 'What is the pleasure of that?' The *kinds* of thing a person can say to render intelligible his claim 'X is pleasant' are different from those things he might say if addicted to something which gives him no pleasure. They are also different from the kinds of thing one might say to explain an activity's[4] interest, or worthwhileness, or even decency. In all these cases, a desirability characterization – 'It's fun', 'It's interesting', 'It's worthwhile', etc. – points towards an account, an open-ended set of explanatory remarks, as to what *constitutes* the fun, interest, worthwhileness or whatever.

But these considerations surely indicate that a 'desirability characterization', as Anscombe defines it, need not give the description of the person's end under which he was aiming at it. You *can* aim at and pursue pleasure, but if you say 'X is pleasant' in answer to 'Why do you want to do that?', you do not thereby show that you were aiming at X as a means to something called 'pleasure'. Your answer brings an end to 'Why?' questioning because, in the typical case, you imply that in doing X you have no further end in view; but what this amounts to is this: that you indicate, without actually giving, a species of rationale, which rationale is not to be taken as entering into any means-end deliberation, but which would (if given) enable an enquirer to 'make sense' of your going in for X – by virtue of features of the activity itself. This species of rationale is what determines that *pleasure* is the relevant concept, e.g. as distinct from *interest*, *decency*, etc.; and it is what makes your answer, 'X is pleasant', a more substantial one than 'For no particular reason'.

We can now answer a question that was left hanging earlier, whether 'X is pleasant' properly speaking characterizes X itself, or the agent and her proclivities. It was because it appeared to do the latter that doubts arose as to its capacity to function as a genuine desirability characterization. The correct answer to the question seems to be: 'It does both.' For 'X is pleasant', as we said, amounts roughly to 'I enjoy X' (which gives information about the agent), while at the same time committing the speaker to the possibility of answering the challenge, 'But *how* is it pleasant?' And this challenge is to be met, if it can be, by giving a certain kind of rationale, a rationale that would typically mention features of X itself. In saying 'X is pleasant', one simultaneously points towards a kind of human phenomenon and locates oneself within a given instance of that phenomenon, as agent or patient. The range of this 'human phenomenon' is the range of human pleasures, an enormous range, whose members are linked by a host of family resemblances, including resemblances in respect of such diverse behaviours as: smiling, laughing, acting energetically, acting relaxedly – even (on occasion) moaning or screaming.

For Anscombe, the reason a person has for doing something needn't be related to some end he was aiming at; for it may relate instead to what she calls *motives*, such as the motive of revenge or the motive of patriotism. The first of these is an example of a backward-looking motive, given by some such reason as 'I killed him because he killed my brother'; while the second is an example of an 'interpretative' motive, given by some such reason as 'I joined in the singing out of love of my country'. The explanation 'I did that for fun' looks to have the same sort of function as an explanation that cites an interpretative motive. Anscombe says that to give an interpretative motive 'is to say something like "See the action in this light"'; and 'to explain one's own actions by an account indicating a motive is to put them in a certain light' (1963, 21). By 'an account', she means a fuller description of the action and its surroundings, one which is meant to enable an interlocutor to 'make sense' – a certain sort of sense – of the overall phenomenon. And this also seems to be what's going on when someone answers the question, 'What *is* the pleasure of it?'

A reason like 'Out of love of country' does not present any *end* the agent has. But we might nevertheless say that it is capable of presenting a proposed *action* as somehow desirable – that in that sense it embodies a desirability characterization. Similarly with 'It's pleasant': this statement gives a desirability characterization, as Anscombe says, but it does so (typically) in rather the same way as does a reason citing an interpretative motive. Perhaps indeed we should say that the typical force of 'It's pleasant' just is that of an interpretative motive.

What then is it to pursue pleasure? How is it possible to be a hedonist? As the word is ordinarily used, a hedonist typically aims at sensual pleasures, and in that sense aims to have various sensations, of taste, sight, touch and so on. Here is another source of the temptation to regard pleasure as itself a sensation. But presumably it is possible to pursue pleasure for pleasure's sake even where the pleasure is cerebral or social in nature. (Consider the person who loves partying, not for the sake of anything he might imbibe or ingest, but simply for the company.) The conscious pursuit of pleasure involves self-knowledge: knowledge of what one enjoys, how much one enjoys it, how to get what one enjoys. If a person devotes time and mental energy to bringing about opportunities for those activities she enjoys, conceiving of them *as* activities she enjoys, then she can be said to pursue pleasure for its own sake (or: these pleasures for their own sakes). The self-consciousness with regard to pleasure that distinguishes such a person from others may go with a lifestyle involving more occasions of pleasure – i.e. more occasions when 'For pleasure' and the like give reasons for action. But the force of this statement as a reason is the same for the hedonist as it is for others. This force, as we have seen, is akin to, if not identical with, the force of statements giving interpretative motives, such as 'I did it out of love of country'.

One who pursues pleasure can on occasion *fail* in that pursuit, for she may find only disappointment or boredom. There seems to be a disanalogy here with, e.g., doing something out of love of country: although failure is possible, it is hard to think of cases where the kind of failure is such as could be reported by the phrase, 'What I did turned out not to be patriotic after all.' And this surely relates to the fact that the concept *enjoying X* involves the agent himself, his behaviour, responses, etc. etc. Whether someone is enjoying something can very often be seen in how he is doing it. So if in answer to the question 'Why?' somebody replies 'For pleasure', his statement may be, as it were, contradicted by certain subsequent facts about *him*. The same doesn't hold of such a reason-giving statement as 'Out of patriotism' – or at any rate, it doesn't hold in quite the same way.

For there are ways in which statements giving interpretative motives *can* be undermined by subsequent facts about the agent. An example is when a person's subsequent actions lack genuineness or authenticity. Imagine that during a general strike I decide to show my respect for and solidarity with the strikers by giving a clenched fist salute to likely-looking passers-by. I find, however, that whenever I do this I feel fraudulent and silly. In answer to 'Why the clenched fist?' I would have said, 'I'm doing it out of solidarity with the workers,' thus giving an interpretative motive; but my statement is undermined rather as 'For pleasure' may be undermined, by what I find to be the case when I give my salute. What I discover has to do with me myself, and its relevance to my earlier statement has to do with the *concept* of solidarity. An expression of solidarity is only adequate if it is genuine, as opposed to contrived, stilted, half-hearted or the like, and this is in part a matter of the extent to which the agent himself can 'identify with' what he is doing. To be sure, I succeed in giving clenched fist salutes, and even in signalling solidarity with the workers; but I find that in doing these things I am not, after all, shoulder to shoulder, marching under the same banner. These metaphors fail to ring true, and since symbolic gestures depend upon such metaphorical meanings, my gesture is a flop, and hence undermines or renders futile my earlier declaration, 'I will do this out of solidarity.' There are some parallels here with pleasure, I think. One of them is the following: that in giving the salute, I was not aiming at some independently specifiable outcome, called 'solidarity'; in much the same way, a person who does something for fun isn't aiming at an outcome called 'fun', or 'pleasure'.

Pleasure as a Good

We have seen that there is a sense, albeit a modest one, in which it could be said that pleasure is a good: namely, where the notion of a 'good', as it appears in this context, is tied to that of a desirability characterization – a characterization of an action as 'somehow desirable'. And it must be admitted that, so construed, 'good' is not functioning as it does in, say, 'good knife', 'good parent' or 'good for the digestion'. Moreover, if we thus explain this use of 'good' by reference to desirability characterizations, while at the same time drawing a parallel between the motive of pleasure and interpretative motives, then (it might be objected) there is surely nothing to stop us from saying things like 'Patriotism is a good', 'Solidarity with the workers is a good' and the like. For if 'For pleasure' can bring an end to 'Why?' questioning, can't 'Out of patriotism' or 'Out of solidarity'? – And for essentially similar reasons? At any rate, given that such statements cite interpretative motives, it follows – if Anscombe's account is correct – that they don't, even implicitly, cite independently specifiable ends, as a means to which one adopts the course of action in question; so to that extent there seem to be grounds for thinking of a statement like 'I clenched my fist out of solidarity with the workers' as supplying a desirability characterization, i.e. as an answer apt to bring an end to 'Why?' questioning.

Perhaps part of the answer to this problem lies in the success or otherwise that may attend attempts to spell out what I have been calling the *rationales* associated with the relevant concepts. 'What *is* the pleasure of it?' asks for a certain kind of rationale: it asks for a description of doing X that will make sense of one's going in for it for its own sake, etc. One can similarly ask for a description of the activity of expressing solidarity with the strikers that will make sense of going in for *it*. And it may be demanded of such a rationale that (e.g.) the merits of the strikers' case be satisfactorily outlined. That is arguably a part of what is involved in 'making sense of this activity'. And just as 'For pleasure' may fail to supply a fully intelligible desirability characterization if a request for a rationale cannot be met, so 'Out of solidarity' may fail, and for similar reasons.

Still, this very parallel between pleasure and solidarity would mean that 'Pleasure is a good' and 'Solidarity is a good' belong in the same boat. And yet it seems possible that a person might want to throw doubt on the pointfulness of *any* expressions of solidarity, without thereby appearing insane. He might just regard all this chatter about solidarity as an excuse for pious strutting. Such a person would respond to the statement 'Out of solidarity', not so much by continuing the series of questions, 'But why do you want to do that?', as by denying altogether the statement's prima facie reason-giving force. Clearly, this could not sensibly be done in the case of the statement 'For pleasure'. The phenomenon of pleasure plays too large a role in human life; it is indeed essential to any recognizable form of normal human existence. It is this fact, perhaps, that serves above all as justification of the saying that pleasure is a good.

Notes

1 Desirability characterizations are introduced in Anscombe (1963, sec. 37). For a discussion of some of the issues here, see Teichmann (2008, ch. 2 sec. 3.1).
2 See Teichmann (2011, ch. 3).
3 As an idiom, 'For no particular reason' perhaps carries connotations of casualness and light-heartedness, and so is not *simply* the expression of one who performs a voluntary action but for no reason. This does not materially affect my point. For a discussion of reasonless actions, see Anscombe (1963, sec. 17, 18).
4 For simplicity, I speak here as elsewhere of 'activities', meaning to include also passive pleasures.

References

Anscombe, G. E. M. (1963), *Intention*. Oxford: Basil Blackwell, 2nd ed.
Teichmann, R. (2008), *The Philosophy of Elizabeth Anscombe*. Oxford: Oxford University Press.
———. (2011), *Nature, Reason and the Good Life*. Oxford: Oxford University Press.

Part II
ACTION

Chapter Five

THE VOLUNTARY AND THE INVOLUNTARY: THEMES FROM ANSCOMBE

Preamble

I will begin with some remarks about ordinary usage and philosophical usage. Readers who are keen to embark at once on the main argument might want to skip to the next section.

There is a strong prima facie case for being guided by ordinary usage if one is centring a philosophical discussion on certain words, such as 'voluntary' and 'involuntary'. The reasons for this are familiar, or ought to be, having to do with the fact that it is usage – *some* sort of usage – that determines linguistic meaning. In this context, ordinary usage essentially means non-technical usage. If it were some technical usage that determined the meanings of the words under discussion, a question would arise why the technical meanings should be of more interest, philosophically, than the non-technical. If no good answer could be given to this question, we should have reason to turn back to considering the ordinary use and meaning of the words.

In 'A Plea for Excuses', J. L. Austin adopts the method of looking carefully at ordinary usage, a task he executes with characteristically microscopic precision. In the course of the essay, he points out that 'the "opposite, or rather "opposites", of "voluntarily" might be "under constraint" of some sort, duress or obligation or influence: the opposite of "involuntarily" might be "deliberately" or "on purpose" or the like. Such divergences in opposites indicate that "voluntarily" and "involuntarily", in spite of their apparent connexion, are fish from very different kettles'.[1] There is, I think, some truth in this as far as ordinary usage goes, similar remarks being possible in connection with the adjectives 'voluntary' and 'involuntary'. Certain uses of these words do consequently have a queer ring to them, such as Anscombe's calling being pushed out into the river in a punt to one's delight 'voluntary'.[2] It even sounds a bit odd to say of someone's fiddling with a pencil that it is voluntary. Are such uses therefore to be deemed technical? Or have Anscombe and others simply messed up the conceptual analysis?

I doubt if Anscombe would have wanted her use of these words to be regarded as technical. She would have argued, I suspect, that Austin had only picked out some specific ways in which the words are used, and that there were other just as 'ordinary', if less everyday, uses of 'voluntary' and 'involuntary' and their associated adverbs, including the sort of use that I just called 'odd'.[3] And one may well feel that Austin is overstating the disconnection between the two words with his talk of 'very different kettles'. But I don't think it matters if Austin's account of ordinary usage is accurate, for it is surely possible that the usage to be found in the philosophical discourse on these topics (a discourse going back centuries) has a rationale or rationales, of the sort to justify a technical or semi-technical extension of ordinary language.[4] More specifically, there is an association of the voluntary with that for which a person can be held to account which makes much sense of the use by Anscombe of the term 'voluntary', and which allows consideration, among other things, of such questions as 'Can our thoughts be voluntary?', 'Can ignorance be voluntary?' and the like – questions whose status as non-pseudo-questions can be seen from the ways in which they get answered.

None of this is to claim carte blanche when it comes to using English words in philosophy. Ordinary usage is indeed a guide – only she is not a tyrant.

'Why?' and the Merely Voluntary

Anscombe famously delineates the class of intentional actions as 'ones to which a certain sense of the question "Why?" has application'.[5] This question 'Why?' can take the form 'Why are you doing X?', or 'Why did you do X?', or indeed 'Why are you going to do X?' And her notion of the *description under which* an action is intentional is connected with this way of delineating intentional actions; for if e.g. 'Why are you doing X?' receives a sincere and substantive answer from the agent of the sort that grants the applicability of the question – such as 'In order that Y should happen' – then the action is intentional under the description *doing X*.

Like intentional actions, voluntary actions are what they are only under certain descriptions: 'voluntariness is relative to description of action'.[6] But an action, e.g. fiddling with a pencil, can be voluntary without being intentional; to such an action the question 'Why?' may receive only some such answer as 'No particular reason', or 'I just felt like it.' Anscombe writes:

> I do not call an answer of this sort a rejection of the question. The question is not refused application because the answer to it says that there is *no* reason, any more than the question how much money I have in my pocket is refused application by the answer 'None'.[7]

(It was for this reason I used the phrase 'sincere and *substantive* answer' above, in characterizing her account of intentional action.)

If an action is voluntary under the description *fiddling with a pencil*, Anscombe could explain this by saying that the question 'Why are you fiddling with a pencil?' is allowed application by the agent, as e.g. 'Why are you casting a pencil-shadow on the wall?' probably would not be. But of course the agent gives, and has, no reason for fiddling with a pencil; and the 'applicability' of the question seems to be down to the fact that certain *other* kinds of answer are not given – as, 'But I'm not doing that!', or 'I can't help it, it's some sort of spasm', or 'I didn't know I was'.[8]

One might wonder in fact why Anscombe wants to deny that such an answer as 'No particular reason' rejects the question 'Why?' She says that the question 'How much money do you have in your pocket?' is not refused application by the answer 'None';

an answer that *would* refuse application would presumably be something like 'I have no pockets'. If I have a pocket, there is at least a place where money *could* be, and one might analogously venture the thought that a merely voluntary action like fiddling is an 'event in a man's history'[9] for which there *could* be a reason – i.e. fiddling is the kind of act which can be done for a reason. This might justify saying that the question 'Why?' is granted application to fiddling.

But falling over is also a kind of act which can be done for a reason. What makes Jim's falling over on a given occasion involuntary? We are looking for an answer that will distinguish involuntary falling over from voluntary fiddling: but in each case something is done without a reason, being the *sort* of act that can be done for a reason. Moreover, in both cases the agent is aware of what he's doing while he's doing it, and his awareness seems to be (as Anscombe would put it) non-observational.[10]

It might seem that we need simply to get away from considerations to do with 'Why?' and the giving of reasons, and turn to some different kind of notion, such as whether Jim could *help* doing X, or whether Jim could have done not-X instead. Some such notions are indeed of relevance to the task of delineating the voluntary; but as I hope to show, questions to do with a person's actual or possible reasons play a more significant role than do these notions, in a variety of ways.

Something Physiological?

Features of actions that are expressed by 'can be done for a reason', or 'can be commanded', are features of kinds or classes of actions. The second feature is mentioned by Anscombe as characteristic of voluntary actions,[11] and she goes on: 'If someone says "Tremble" and I tremble I am not *obeying* him – even if I tremble because he said it in a terrible voice'. The reason for this assertion must be that the verb 'tremble' carries with it the idea of involuntariness. But even if what Anscombe presumes about 'tremble' is correct, it seems that one could respond to a command – say, 'Shake all over' – in a way that left it open whether one was obeying it or not, according as one did the thing voluntarily or not. The very same thing, physically speaking, could be done either voluntarily or involuntarily, so it would seem.

Here is where it is natural to appeal to some feature of specific acts, not of kinds of acts, e.g. by saying: The person who fell over involuntarily couldn't help it. This seems to mean something like: The person couldn't have prevented it even if he had tried to (or had wanted to). But what are the grounds for such a counterfactual conditional? Jim didn't have time to try to prevent himself from falling to the ground – and yet we appear to be claiming that *had* he tried, he still would have fallen to the ground. (Presumably, 'had he tried' = 'had he tried after having tripped', or '… after having begun to fall', something which, however, is probably also true of the person who falls over on purpose.) Of course our actual evidence or grounds for saying 'He couldn't help it' on a given occasion will most likely be what Jim himself says, or how he reacts after falling over. He might, for example, utter an obscenity. If we privileged the specific reaction of his saying 'I couldn't help doing that', as allegedly supplying the crucial truth which makes for involuntariness, we should face the question how Jim could have such authoritative knowledge of what *would* have happened if he had tried to/wanted to (etc.). Does he perhaps have knowledge of causal connections, or the lack of them, 'from the inside'?[12] This seems to make little sense.

Perhaps there is some detectable physiological difference between falling over voluntarily and falling over involuntarily? If there is, we might postulate an internal mechanism whereby Jim reliably reports his physiological state, by using such a phrase as 'I could (not) help doing that'. The phrase is just a bit of idiom: voluntariness and involuntariness are in fact physiologically differentiated – so the account would go.

The idea of a physiological distinction is tempting whether or not an authority-inducing mechanism in the agent is additionally posited. But it can be shown that no such distinction will suffice for our purposes. In a discussion of Aquinas, Anscombe refers to a man's being dragged violently by others, and she considers whether such an occurrence could be 'from the man's will'. She writes:

> A movement's being 'from his will' here [i.e. in Aquinas] means the same as its being physiologically voluntary; it is of course not excluded by 'not from his will' for him to have arranged with some people in advance that they should drag him. If he had, then his being dragged would be voluntary, though not physiologically so, and the violence would be being exercised on his body, not on his will or intention.[13]

Clearly, a person can be in whatever state physiologists decide characterizes involuntary acts (or happenings) though the act (or happening) in question is voluntary – under some description. Being dragged by arrangement would be an example of this. We may even imagine that the man being dragged goes in for genuine resistance, putting up a fight, etc. Perhaps he reckons that this will make for verisimilitude; he is in fact a bank clerk in collusion with bank robbers, and has to seem to have been coerced to those who will view the CCTV footage. Since the robbers are together much stronger than him, he can safely resist them without fear of success. What does it mean to say that some shove of his is an act of resistance? Isn't an act of physical resistance a voluntary – in fact, intentional – act, whose aim is to prevent being coerced? But doesn't the man *want* to be coerced? It is natural to use Anscombe's mode of speaking and say that the resisting shove is only 'physiologically' voluntary; and indeed it seems likely that if physiologists find states which can be associated with voluntary actions, some such state will be present when the man gives his resisting shove. But the description 'resisting shove' brings with it an aim: are we then to speak of an act's being physiologically *intentional*?

We could of course avoid these difficulties by saying, 'He wasn't *really* resisting; he was only pretending to. His only aim was to be coerced by the robbers.' But he didn't just pretend to shove – he really shoved. And this was no spasm or reflex. Wasn't it intentional, in fact? It was e.g. performed so as to get Big Bruno's arm away from him. And why should he get Big Bruno's arm away, unless that is a means to an end, namely the end of resisting coercion? It looks as if a person can in some sense simultaneously pursue incompatible goals, without this indicating self-deception or deep irrationality. One of the goals, to be sure, is something the agent either expects not to be fulfilled (resisting the coercion), or at the very least doesn't care if it is or isn't fulfilled (getting Big Bruno's arm away). But I often try to do things which I don't expect will actually come about: one might as well try, as they say; and I also on occasion do things not really caring if I'm rewarded by success: quacking at a duck to get it to turn its head, for instance. What looks odd is somebody's *wanting* to fail, in the way that it seems the bank clerk wants to fail in his acts of physical resistance.

Perhaps it is this: had it not been for the prior arrangement and planning with the robbers, certain acts would have counted simply as intentional under the description *resisting coercion*, acts which – on account of that prior planning – also or instead count as intentional under the description *facilitating a bank robbery*. I say 'also or instead' because it does seem that the issue of whether the clerk is really resisting, or even really shoving, is intrinsically problematic: to say he is without qualification courts confusion, and the way to avoid such confusion is surely to use some phrase like 'doing what would be straightforward resistance were it not for the prior planning'. We can it seems also say that something which in the absence of the prior planning would have counted simply as involuntary under the description *being dragged* counts in fact as voluntary under that same description.[14]

The phrase 'had it not been for the prior arrangement' introduces a counterfactual conditional, but not of the sort that can be associated with causality. We are not saying that the prior planning with the robbers caused, or helped cause, the voluntariness of the clerk's being dragged. After all, *ex hypothesi*, the physical state of the clerk is just as it would be if he were to have been dragged involuntarily. Rather, the background to, or context of, his being dragged determines that he is being dragged voluntarily, in much the same way that a certain background determines that someone's ticking a box is her voting for some political party. 'Determines' here doesn't mean 'entails', for there are indefinitely many possible defeating circumstances – cf. 'On Brute Facts' (Anscombe 1981b). But in the absence of any such defeating circumstances (e.g. his forgetting all about his involvement in the plan) we can say that the being dragged is rendered voluntary by the prior planning. 'He was dragged voluntarily' is perhaps stilted English; we would more likely say 'He allowed himself to be dragged,' or 'He went along with being dragged.'

Now it may be objected that a passive condition like being dragged simply can't be voluntary. It isn't an action, after all! – That the *verb* is passive is indeed quite possibly the reason why 'He was dragged voluntarily' sounds odd; but if you allow yourself to be driven in a bus to London, having got into it in the normal way and knowing where it's headed, then there is no question that what you do is voluntary under the description *going to London*. It is easier to see this only because we have a way of describing the case using an active verb, the verb *to go*. But going in a bus to London is just as little the result of your ongoing efforts as is getting to a corner of a room by being dragged. It's the bus that does it, after all.[15] Maybe you got onto the bus by means of a voluntary act of stepping on; but maybe the bank clerk gets things going by a voluntary act of moving towards the alarm button.

The approach here adumbrated allows us to see in what sense acting under duress is involuntary. Acting under duress is the mirror image of allowing yourself to be acted upon by prior arrangement: for something which would in the absence of certain background conditions count as voluntary, such as giving someone your wallet, gets to count as involuntary in virtue (roughly speaking) of what led up to it – e.g. the other person's producing a gun and saying, 'Hand over your wallet.' Again, it is tempting to reach for a phrase like 'physiologically voluntary' here; but as we have seen, the physiology of what's happening isn't the real issue.[16]

Possible Prevention

What about the locution 'couldn't have prevented it'? We should first of all note that this phrase can either cover possible pre-emptive preventions or instead cover possible preventions of something while it is happening (i.e. preventing its 'completion'). Many an involuntary action could have been pre-emptively prevented by the agent: an innocent bank clerk could have prevented being dragged around by not turning up to work. So maybe what we want to say is: 'He couldn't have prevented it beforehand by an act intended to prevent it' – for presumably the innocent clerk doesn't *know* there's going to be a heist that day, so can't plan to avoid it. So does foreknowledge plus no attempt to prevent entail voluntariness? Surely not. The brave lad who goes out to meet his bullies knows he will get clobbered, but his getting clobbered is still involuntary (or counter-voluntary; see n. 14).

What of the phrase 'couldn't have prevented or stopped X while X was happening'? On its own, the phrase can't possibly characterize all and only involuntary actions: once a bus or plane has set off, you probably can't prevent yourself arriving at your destination, and yet your going to London or Vienna is typically both voluntary and intentional. And whether the bank clerk's being dragged is voluntary or not can't be down to possibilities of prevention if such possibilities are determined by the physiological facts (such as strength) – for as we have seen, physically identical happenings might be either voluntary or involuntary, depending on what went before. Even if nothing relevant went before, and the innocent clerk is simply dragged unresisting into a corner, this is surely involuntary whether or not he *could* have successfully resisted. (After all, he might actually have been strong enough to.) And conversely, where there *was* prior planning, the fact that his being dragged is voluntary is unaffected by his being unable to resist successfully, since the voluntariness is down to the prior planning.

These remarks may appear to show an agreement with the approach of Harry Frankfurt, who argues that your doing something for which you are morally responsible is not down to whether you 'could have done otherwise':[17] if we roughly equate voluntary actions with actions for which you are morally responsible, isn't the present position akin to Frankfurt's? But (i) 'could have done otherwise' is different from 'could have prevented it', and Frankfurt's discussion of such cases as that of Jones, whose brain can be interfered with by Black via a remote control, shows him using a notion of what one *does* that is very problematic – in contrast to the fairly ordinary notion of (not) preventing something which I have been assuming. The idea is that Jones couldn't have done otherwise, since if he'd been 'about to' refrain from φing, Black (realizing this) would have sent a signal to his brain which made him φ; but it's doubtful whether in that case Jones would have *done* anything at all, in the relevant sense of 'done'. Moreover, (ii) Frankfurt follows Hume in associating voluntariness with what one wants or desires, where wanting is construed as a state of the agent, somehow causally responsible for what the agent does;[18] whereas

I have been invoking the wider circumstances of an action or happening, circumstances such as the prior planning of a bank robbery. Frankfurt might see in this prior planning a 'causally efficacious' state of the bank clerk, identifiable as a *desire* of his; but what is the effect of this alleged cause? Is it other people's actions – of laying hold, dragging and so on? This seems no good. Is it then the non-resistance of the bank clerk himself? But as I have imagined things, the clerk might go in for verisimilitudinous resistance. And as for this phenomenon, it's hard to see how Frankfurt could understand it except as a case of radically contradictory desires simultaneously in play, indicative of gross irrationality in the agent. Whereas in fact this bank clerk shows a very rational, if low, cunning.

I have said that whether an agent could prevent something's happening need not determine whether what he did was voluntary. But the possibility of prevention can certainly *bear on* the question whether what was done was voluntary. Here is Anscombe again:

> Things may be voluntary which are not one's own doing at all, but which happen to one's delight [...] 'Why' it might be asked, 'did you go sliding down the hill into that party of people?' to which the answer might be 'I was pushed so that I went sliding down the bank'. But a rejoinder might be 'You didn't mind; you didn't shout, or try to roll aside, did you?'[19]

It is perhaps worth pointing out here that Anscombe is happy with the thought that there may be various kinds of voluntariness, various senses of 'voluntary'. She is surely right to be. That there are various distinguishable senses of 'voluntary' does not rule out those senses' being interconnected in various ways, so that there is still point in giving a philosophical account of this bit of conceptual terrain – something that remains true if the conceptual terrain is in part the result of technical or semi-technical extensions to the 'ordinary' sense(s) of the term (see Preamble). The notion of voluntariness now before us is different from, but related to, that of the colluding bank clerk. The notion of *possible prevention* is of interest because of such a question as 'Why didn't you shout, or try to roll aside?' The hill-roller, we may imagine, answers 'I didn't want to; I was enjoying it.' Of course enjoyment on its own isn't required for voluntariness. Other voluntary acts needn't be enjoyed: the bank clerk needn't enjoy being dragged around, nor need I enjoy fiddling with a pencil, or going to the dentist. So how exactly is enjoyment relevant here?

We can see what's at issue here by comparing the case with another in which a person is enjoying something – say going round on a merry-go-round. If you asked such a person 'Why didn't you stop? Why didn't you get off in mid-rotation?', he *might* reply 'I was enjoying it,' but is more likely to reply 'Why *should* I have stopped?' In the absence of a good reason for jumping off, the question 'Why didn't you?' has no application. Now this might be denied by a philosopher keen on certain ways of using Grice's notion of conversational implicature: such a philosopher might say that since it was obvious the person on the roundabout was enjoying himself, it was likewise obvious that his reason for not jumping off was that he was enjoying himself – so that although it is strictly true for him to say 'I didn't jump off because I was enjoying myself,' that statement could hardly give information to a normal observer, and so might be conversationally 'inappropriate' or 'odd', and the question 'Why didn't you ...?', asked by such an observer, would presumably share in this inappropriateness despite being a perfectly genuine question. But consider such a question's being asked of someone fiddling with a pencil, e.g. while on the phone: he will hardly respond to 'Why didn't you stop?' by saying 'I was enjoying it.' What he was doing was just absent-minded fiddling. But the onus is not on him to have an answer ready to such a question; the onus is on the enquirer to have a reason for asking it. The applicability of the question 'Why didn't you stop?' rests on there being some alleged reason for stopping, for example that it was irritating the other person, who had already signalled his irritation.

There is a clear reason for the hill-roller to roll aside if possible, namely to prevent something untoward – a collision with innocent persons. She could have prevented it, but didn't: her rolling, and even her rolling into those people,[20] were voluntary. But more than this, the reason for her not preventing the outcome was her enjoyment. Why is this relevant? Compare the case with another: an innocent (non-collusive) bank clerk may let himself be dragged by bank robbers, and may make no effort to prevent this untoward thing from happening, for the simple reason that he is scared to offer resistance. He may even think that he'd succeed if he attempted resistance, but be afraid of what they might do to him later on if he did. If asked 'Why didn't you stop them? You might have been able to, mightn't you?', he could reply 'I was scared to,' an explanation quite different from 'I was enjoying myself'. And so we would probably not call his being dragged, or ending up in the lumber room, voluntary. These things do not 'happen to his delight', in Anscombe's words. And this seems the right way of talking here, e.g. as compared with talking just about what the person wanted. Neither the scared bank clerk nor the hill-roller can be said to have *wanted* such-and-such to happen before it happened, and if we say that the hill-roller wants to *go on rolling* downhill, this verdict seems justifiable only by reference to her delight in doing so. As for her pitching into the party of people, it is surely false (or very probably false) that she wants to do this, though there is a strong case for saying that she does so voluntarily, if she does pitch into them – not because of the delight of the collision, but because delight (in rolling) was her reason for not preventing a collision. It is to this notion of delight or enjoyment as a *reason* that I now turn.

Conformity with the Will

'I was enjoying myself' ('It was fun', etc.) gives a reason for having done something or having continued doing something, and 'For fun' ('For pleasure', etc.) gives a reason for doing something, now or in the future. It is clearly not, or not usually, the sort of reason that appears in a piece of means-end reasoning: the agent need not have adopted some activity as a means to an independently specifiable end, *enjoying oneself*, or *feeling pleasure*. This is connected with the fact that enjoyment or pleasure is not a particular sort of sensation or quasi-sensation, accompanying the various activities an agent takes pleasure in.[21] Since 'For fun' does give a reason for action, it can in a given context be weighed as a reason; the hill-roller's 'It was fun' can, for example, be weighed against the possible counter-reason 'I'll crash into those people', and in the light of this weighing might or might not count as a good or adequate reason for rolling down the hill. The idea that enjoyment is a state of the person *causing* her to roll downhill is out of place here. Such an idea might be in play if the person said, 'I was enjoying myself too much to think of the consequences,' but even here the statement does not remove the occurrence from the space of reasons, insofar as it is still a question whether the 'cause' of the not-thinking supplies an adequate excuse. I shall return to this.

In such cases as I have been considering, the relevance of *possible prevention* appears to be this: where somebody has done something (in a wide sense of 'done') which there was a good prima facie reason *not* to do or continue doing, the question 'Why didn't you prevent or stop that?' has application, i.e. demands an answer; and what answer is given determines, or helps determine, whether the action counts as voluntary. If the answer is 'I was enjoying myself,' or 'I realized I might get into the newspapers that way,' then it was voluntary; if it is 'I was too scared to resist,' or 'I just felt fatalistic about the whole thing,' then it was not – or anyway it was not clearly so. For we should not assume a hard and fast distinction between voluntary and involuntary. There are many things people do as to which it is indeterminate whether they are voluntary or involuntary, such as making a face at a bad smell or laughing politely. That there are borderline cases does not of course throw doubt on the very distinction *voluntary/involuntary*.

Now it is not that a reason like 'I was enjoying myself' always counts as inadequate in the face of a reason not to do the thing – for enjoying yourself in that particular way may itself be a good. You could on some occasion be asked, 'Why didn't you carry on? You were clearly enjoying yourself,' and your answer might or might not be adequate. But if you continue doing something because you are enjoying yourself, or because you realize that what's happening is a good way of getting into the newspapers, then this shows a prima facie willingness to treat the event or action in question as a suitable end or means of yours. (It would be an end of yours were you to decide to go in for it for fun, i.e. 'for its own sake'.[22]) The reason 'I was too scared to resist' indicates no such prima facie willingness. These facts connect with the role of such a statement as 'I wish that hadn't happened'. Counterfactual wishes can seem highly puzzling to those in the grip of the belief/desire model of psychological states; the best analysis of our statement on offer from that model would seem to have to be something like 'My occurrent belief that X did happen causes me to feel sad' – pretty feeble. Elucidating counterfactual wishes involves, I think, seeing their connection to expressions of hope or its opposite. The bank clerk's 'I wish they hadn't dragged me around' is, as it were, the retrospective version of the hope that he *could* have expressed earlier, had it occurred to him, by saying, 'I hope no bank robbers start dragging me around.' By contrast, the hill-roller surprised by joy will not exclaim 'I wish that hadn't happened': of her it seems true that had she known what fun it would be, she might well have hoped to be pushed down the hillside, or at any rate welcomed the idea. What things or sorts of thing a person may hope for indicate what sort of person she is, or in more picturesque terms, what the general orientation of her will is. Events or actions that are in conformity with her will count prima facie as voluntary under the relevant descriptions; and the sense of the phrase 'in conformity with the will' is to be explained by reference to such things as possible answers to 'Why didn't you stop?', counterfactual wishes, etc. etc.

The picture may be very complex. It seems possible, for instance, that someone's attitude to an event or action of his should change or evolve. A person could be thoroughly enjoying himself, even racked with pleasure, but afterwards settle into a mood of regret, disgust, resentment or shame over what had happened. He might be able sincerely to answer 'Because I was enjoying myself' when asked 'Why didn't you stop?' – but he may feel alienated from his enjoyment, and also say, 'I wish that hadn't happened.' Whether we say 'voluntary' or 'involuntary' in such a case will depend on all sorts of details, including details from the person's life up to, and indeed after, the events in question – the 'wider circumstances' again.

Thus voluntariness in the sorts of case I have been considering is not down to the mere fact that the agent could have prevented or stopped the thing. But possible prevention is evidently a relevant consideration.

'It Didn't Occur to Me'

The question 'Why didn't you stop or prevent such-and-such?' is not an example of Anscombe's reason-eliciting question 'Why?' An answer to it does not typically give a description of *not stopping* φ*ing* under which it is intentional. The hill-roller does not adopt, as a means to the end of enjoying herself, the negative action of not making an effort to stop. You might as well say that when I make a pot of tea I choose *not* to drop the pot on the floor, as a means to my end. As we have seen, the salience of the hill-roller's not stopping has to do with there being a good reason to stop, rather than with any even implicit means-end reasoning. This is not to say that there aren't cases where not stopping doing something *is* intentional: a soldier might want to get confined to barracks so he can steal another soldier's cigarettes when no one's about, and so carry on talking on parade when ordered by the sergeant to stop. But the version of 'Why didn't you stop or prevent such-and-such?' which I have been considering fits into another sort of possible dialogue, answers to it yielding another sort of information.

A possible answer to 'Why didn't you stop …?' is 'It didn't occur to me; I didn't think of it.' This is a possible answer to a variety of 'Why didn't you …?' questions – such as 'Why didn't you signal before you turned left?' The applicability of the question, once again, has to do with there being a good reason to do the thing that one doesn't do. But the answer 'I didn't think of it' raises interesting issues, on account of the fact that we can often reply, 'But you ought to have thought of it!'

In discussing the idea that a failure to do X may be voluntary, Anscombe writes:

> Only if some necessary condition of [the agent's] doing [X] is lacking and the lack itself is not voluntary, will his failure be non-voluntary, like the failure of the pilot [to keep the ship afloat] when the machinery was out of order. Now an essential condition of acting is that you have an idea of doing such-and-such, and an essential condition of acting with a further intention is that you have an idea of such-and-such as your objective.

But what if you just don't *have* the idea e.g. of stopping yourself rolling into the people? What if the idea doesn't occur to you? Anscombe continues:

> Let us consider the statement that you could have and ought to have had the idea of doing such-and-such and that your failure is therefore voluntary. There is at once a contrast between this and the statement concerning the exterior act, that a man could have and ought to have done such-and-such and so that his failure was voluntary. For there, there was available one

possibility of showing that he could not have done the thing: namely that he did not have the idea of it. But even if it can sometimes be said that a man ought to have had a certain idea, here at any rate there is no such possibility. It cannot be necessary to have an idea of having an idea in order to have the latter idea. If then the voluntariness of anything necessarily involves having an idea of that act, then having an idea cannot be a voluntary thing.[23]

It could be objected against Anscombe that it is false that 'an essential condition of acting is that you have an idea of doing such-and-such', or that 'an essential condition of acting with a further intention is that you have an idea of such-and-such as your objective'. You surely don't have to think the thought 'I am walking', nor have the idea of walking before your mind, in order to walk. But by 'having an idea of doing such-and-such' Anscombe can't mean just the explicit having of thoughts/ideas prior to, or while, acting, since she goes on to say that her point is most easily seen when the case *is* one of such explicit thoughts/ideas – thus implying that the case need not be this. So in what sense is it true that in order to walk I have to have the idea of walking?

It can't be that I have to have certain linguistic abilities, such as the ability to answer the question 'What are you doing?', for animals and the languageless can act voluntarily, and indeed intentionally, as Anscombe recognizes.[24] Perhaps it is having e.g. the concept of walking, in some broad sense of 'concept' – being somehow able to show knowledge of what walking is, say. But apart from the vagueness of this idea, it seems not to be the idea which is at issue when someone says 'Such-and-such an idea didn't occur to me': the hill-roller to whom it didn't occur to try to roll aside presumably has the *concept* of rolling aside. Her failure to think of rolling aside is her failure to *use* this concept in a certain way, as we might put it.

The thought or idea of rolling aside can perhaps be said to have occurred to a hill-roller who intentionally rolled aside, simply in virtue of her having done so: her 'thought' is embodied in her action. But of course the thought of rolling aside can occur to someone and be rejected, so that they carry on rolling straight down. What does such rejection consist in? Maybe here it is necessary for the person really to have entertained the thought while rolling – though 'rejection' could consist simply in ignoring that thought, rather than in saying to oneself 'No!' However, the explanation why one pitched into the party of people which we are considering is not 'I thought of rolling aside, but rejected the idea'. It is: 'The thought of rolling aside didn't occur to me.' And if the relation between the thought of doing X and doing X (intentionally or voluntarily) is just that the thought is embodied in the action, then 'The thought didn't occur to me' looks dangerously close to 'I didn't do it' – hardly an explanation of why you didn't do it!

In fact, as the last sentence in the above quotation shows, Anscombe is not committing herself to the thesis she appears to assert, that 'an essential condition of acting is that you have an idea of doing such-and-such'. That sentence was: 'If then the voluntariness of anything necessarily involves having an idea of that act, then having an idea cannot be a voluntary thing.' Since she goes on to treat it as a real question whether our thoughts (ideas) can be voluntary, and if so in what sense, she thus appears to drop the thesis she had made as if to assert; the text shows her thinking in real time, as it were. And if we can drop the thesis, we can also reject the proposition: 'There was available one possibility of showing that he could not have done the thing: namely that he did not have the idea of it.'

So what is someone saying who says 'The idea didn't occur to me'? How is what they say relevant to the question 'Why didn't you do X?'?

I think we have here a case of our language being misleading, possibly even of its embodying a sort of mythology, in that the use of 'It didn't occur to me' as an explanation of a failure does strongly suggest that something's 'occurring to' a person is a condition of his acting – which it is not. The issue that comes to the fore is whether, and how, 'It didn't occur to me' is an *explanation* at all. What I shall propose is that statements like this have the characteristic function of describing the agent, by referring to an aspect of the agent's character or mindset, so that the failure to do X is made sense of (in particular, for an enquirer) by its place in the broader context of the practical life of the agent.

Remember that the applicability of 'Why didn't you do X?' rests upon there being an alleged reason why you should have done X, or were to be expected to have done X. The reply 'It didn't occur to me' may well acknowledge that reason as a prima facie good one,[25] while in effect saying: 'A character trait (or mood …) of mine consists in part in giving little relative weight to reasons of that sort.' For example, the hill-roller's love of excitement may involve giving priority to thrills and spills over avoiding physically discommoding other people. Giving greater weight to reason A than to reason B is embodied, on an occasion, in what the agent actually does; the agent need never consider, or manifest a consideration of, reason B at all, but simply act on reason A – which they do if they *would* answer Anscombe's question 'Why?' by invoking A as a reason. (We are ignoring subconscious reasons and motives.) In other words, we are not to think of 'having a reason', 'weighing this reason against that', etc. as describing inner processes or states, e.g. of an introspectable kind. If 'It didn't occur to me' is met with 'Why didn't it occur to you?', and the reply is 'I was enjoying the excitement of it,' then the enquirer is enlightened to the extent that he can see what *sort* of reason for not-doing-X is here to be compared, by anyone interested, with the evident objective reason to do X. That it is *this* sort of reason (e.g. excitement) that we are comparing with this other sort (e.g. not physically incommoding others) helps us to locate the phenomenon in a familiar human pattern, and so to ascribe, if only provisionally, some trait or mood or whatever to the agent. This ascription is not a psychological hypothesis put forward to explain the phenomenon, though accepting the ascription means among other things being liable to form future hypotheses about what the agent will or would do.

The statement 'It didn't occur to me' can sometimes imply 'If the thought *had* occurred to me, I would have stopped …' – a thought's thus occurring to someone being a genuine sort of event in time. The statement might thus serve as a kind of explanation of not-stopping, but not yet as an exculpation if it is appropriate for us to ask, 'But why *didn't* it occur to you?' Here Anscombe's point about not needing to have an idea of an idea in order to have the latter idea is relevant, and an answer like 'It didn't occur to me to have that thought' is clearly absurd. An answer like 'I lost consciousness for a few seconds', however, would both explain and excuse the agent's 'not having thought of it'. If no such excuse is forthcoming, and the person has to admit, 'Well, it just *didn't* occur to me, that's all,' then this may well be a case of someone's giving greater weight to one sort of practical reason than to another: for we often learn something about a person's general orientation of will if we learn that they just don't do what it takes to recognize the force of certain reasons – and 'doing what it takes' can be thinking certain thoughts. Of course if the person, having crashed into the party of people, feels genuine regret, and not just as a result of receiving obloquy, then her tearful 'It just didn't occur to me' would count as showing that she had simply been thoughtless; but even here, if it was habitual for the person to act thus thoughtlessly, we might well see the failure as conforming to a general orientation of the will, and see the person as giving greater weight to one sort of practical reason than to another.

'If the thought had occurred to me, I would have stopped ...' looks like a causal counterfactual, akin to 'If I had rolled into that small bush, I would have stopped'. This appearance is reinforced by the possibility of another's saying 'I bet you wouldn't have!', and by the fact that a degree of self-knowledge seems required for someone to have the warrant for saying 'If the thought had occurred to me, I would have stopped.' Nevertheless, there is evidently an internal relation between thinking 'I could stop' and stopping, not far removed from that between thinking 'I will stop' and stopping.[26] As to the latter, your utterance 'P' only counts as having the meaning of 'I will stop' if there is a sufficiently systematic connection between your general use of 'P' and your subsequently stopping (it is largely this that generates the internal relation); and the ability to assert that the thought 'P' did or didn't occur to you is part of your overall mastery of the use of 'P' – for when you say that the thought 'P' occurred to you, you are in a sense speaking for your former self, putting words into that self's mouth.[27] Something similar, though not identical, goes for the 'P' such that 'P' means 'I could stop'. The suitability of the thought 'I could stop' as a 'cause' of stopping is connected with such facts as: that A's saying to B 'You could φ' often functions as a form of advice or guidance. To be sure, it does this by 'causing' B to consider what he wasn't considering – but it is not just contingent that this form of words has this effect. 'It occurred to me that I could φ – whereupon I φ-ed' has the sense it has because of the broader language-game in which the advisory use of 'You could φ' is to be found; it is e.g. to be distinguished from such 'pathological' cases as Davidson's climber who has the thought 'I could let go of the rope' and subsequently lets go of the rope, the mere thought having made his fingers go weak. In the latter case, the notion of a thought's causing something is entirely at home, while in the sort of case we are considering it is only partially so. 'If the thought had occurred to me, I would have stopped ...' is therefore not the sort of 'purely' causal counterfactual exemplified by 'If you had rung that bell, you would have woken the baby'; that the thought of stopping (in the sense here meant) often results in stopping is not a contingent truth in the way in which paradigm causal generalizations are (or are typically taken to be).

This last point helps us to see what the force of 'You should have thought of it!' is *not*. The force of this statement is not to allude to a measure that the agent failed to take; thinking of stopping is not a *means* to stopping. For the connection between the two is not causal in the way in which the connection between putting salt in the potatoes and the potatoes' being tasty is causal. In saying that 'It didn't occur to me' can indicate a person's orientation of will, we are not saying that thinking of something is a voluntary action, like putting salt in the potatoes. The will manifests itself in such things as your stopping or not stopping, the orientation of the will in such things as how you weigh practical reasons against one another – and 'weighing reasons' is manifest in various ways, including in the answers you might give to certain questions.

Some Counterfactuals

There is a species of counterfactual statement we have repeatedly come across in the course of this discussion. Here are three examples:

1. NN would have said such-and-such if asked 'Why are you doing that?' [Anscombe's criterion of intention.]
2. NN would have wished that p, or welcomed the thought that p, had it occurred to him. [Connected to the sense of a later counterfactual wish, 'I wish p had been the case.']
3. NN would have stopped doing such-and-such had the thought occurred to him. [One of the criteria for a person's general orientation of will.]

It is tempting, but mistaken, to think of each of these counterfactuals as contributing to an *analysis* of some key concept, such as intention, counterfactual wishing or conformity to a will – or alternatively to think of them as proposing 'truth-makers' for propositions employing these concepts. It is clear from her discussion that Anscombe is not proposing that 'NN intentionally φ-ed' be *analysed* as meaning 'NN would have answered the question "Why are you φing?" with a substantive answer that allowed the applicability of the question', or as meaning anything of the sort. She is not interested in hunting down necessary and sufficient conditions. She aims, rather, to elucidate intentional action by elucidating the special 'reason-demanding' sense of 'Why?', which latter task involves such procedures as listing some of the kinds of 'reason-giving' (as well as 'reason-refusing') answers, contrasting these with causal statements, etc. etc. But this task of elucidation is possible because people who have the concept of intention are people who can play various interconnected language-games, such as that of giving certain sorts of answer to 'Why?' in certain kinds of situation. Anscombe follows Wittgenstein in regarding philosophical problems as typically to be dealt with by describing the workings of our language.

With these thoughts in mind, we can turn to another, instructive species of answer to 'Why didn't you do X?' – namely, an answer like 'It would have been a lot of hassle.' If this is short for a counterfactual, the counterfactual is presumably 'If I had chosen to do X, it would have involved me in a lot of hassle'. But how can it be an explanation of something's not happening to point out what would have been the case if it were to have happened? Do I explain why the doorbell didn't ring when pressed by saying that if it *had* rung, someone would have come to the door?

The answer, of course, lies in how the agent might have deliberated, had the option of doing X been presented to him. What the counterfactual is telling us is something like this: that if the agent had e.g. thought, 'I could tackle the mouse problem by putting mousetraps in every room in the house, or I could just put up with the mouse problem,' then he would have chosen the second option, and given (or been able to give) as his reason that the first option was ruled out by its entailing a lot of hassle. The interest of this, once again, lies in the relative weights which the agent would assign to two different reasons for action, something that bears upon the 'orientation of his will'. So the agent is not merely asking us to consider the possible scenario of his doing X (and suffering hassle); he is in effect asking us to consider the possible scenario of his deliberating whether to do X, and invoking hassle as a reason not to. The question 'But how do you know you would have deliberated in that way?' is inapposite: the agent is speaking for his former self, not issuing an empirical hypothesis about the past along the lines of 'If the doorbell had rung, it would have woken the neighbours' baby'. Typically, indeed, '… because it would have been a lot of hassle' expresses the agent's *present* orientation of will. He will quite probably be excusing himself, or giving his position – this 'he' being the very person who is replying to our questions. His answer invokes a counterfactual situation, one in which he figures as a deliberator rejecting one possible course of action; but the counterfactual thus invoked gives us neither part of an analysis of nor part of a truth-maker for 'I didn't do it because it would have been a hassle'.

Voluntary Ignorance

We have seen that not thinking of something can be voluntary, in the sense that (i) the question 'Why didn't you think of that?' can be apposite, and (ii) no exculpatory reason be giveable by the agent. In a similar way, not knowing something can be voluntary. There is such a thing as culpable ignorance. Here is Anscombe:

> When it was necessary and possible for the pilot to navigate and for the cook to put salt in the potatoes, the loss of the ship and the spoiling of the potatoes are ascribed to the pilot and cook as causes. (Various senses of 'possible' and of 'ascribed […] as causes' are possible here.) So when it was necessary and possible for A to know, the ignorance is ascribed to A's will as cause.[28]

Knowing, it would seem, is unlike thinking, i.e. unlike something's occurring to you. This has to do with the fact that knowing is, roughly speaking, dispositional rather than episodic; and 'You should have known!' is at least very often short for 'You should have done what it takes to acquire the knowledge'. This last statement rests upon its being *possible* for the agent to do what it takes, as in Anscombe's phrase 'necessary and possible'. She explains what she means by 'necessary' thus: 'Things are in this sense necessary when without them some good can't be got or some evil avoided.'[29]

Hence, whereas the idea of adopting a means to your thinking of something is typically absurd (as we have seen), the idea of adopting a means to your knowing something is not. (Here, 'knowing something' means 'knowing whether/who/what …', not 'knowing that p'.) We could say that if the means is within your control, so is the status of your knowledge. This justifies Anscombe's saying, 'The ignorance is ascribed to A's will as cause.' The means to acquiring relevant knowledge is often *checking*. 'When I married Jane I didn't know that my wife Mary was still alive' might well be countered with 'You should have checked', and if the man hadn't checked, he will probably count as having committed bigamy voluntarily, according to Anscombe. Certainly his not bothering to check will, unless he is intellectually subnormal, indicate his orientation of will, though of course there are many ways in which that orientation could be accounted for – hatred of Mary, passion for Jane, general selfishness, a consequentialist mindset, etc. etc.

Cases of culpable negligence frequently involve ignorance of some sort, which is why it is more natural to describe the relevant doings, non-doings and consequences as voluntary, rather than as intentional: Anscombe characterizes this sense of 'voluntary' when she says that 'one cannot intentionally, but can voluntarily, do something without knowing one is doing it'.[30] And she says also that 'sin essentially requires, not intention but voluntariness'.[31]

This remark illustrates how the notion of the voluntary which Anscombe is deploying in these contexts is tied closely to questions of responsibility, a responsibility that often cannot be shirked by such statements as 'I didn't know!', 'It didn't occur to me!' and the like. In fact her interest is largely, like Austin's, in the sorts of statement that can and can't serve as *excuses*; so despite Austin's cavils at philosophers' uses of 'voluntary' and 'involuntary', the two philosophers are in fact approaching a topic, namely that of responsibility, in somewhat similar ways. They are both, perhaps, following Aristotle's example; for as Austin says:

> Aristotle has often been chidden for talking about excuses or pleas and overlooking the 'real problem' [i.e. the problem of Freedom]: in my own case, it was when I began to see the injustice of this charge that I first became interested in excuses.[32]

Austin's thought can be expanded. For many would regard the 'real problem', when it comes to voluntariness and involuntariness, as having to do, not with actual or possible reasons for action, but with causal possibilities and powers. Some will characterize voluntariness in terms of the ability to do otherwise, or in terms of two-way powers, and so on. Others, more Humean in outlook, will characterize it in terms of the causal powers of desires, or second-order desires, or belief/desire pairs – and so on. But as I have been arguing, these various notions are less relevant to voluntariness than notions having to do with actual or possible reasons.

Thus being dragged around having arranged to be is like flying to New York having arranged to: both must count as voluntary, not on account of anything 'going on in' the agent while the thing is happening, so much as on account of the reasons the agent could sincerely give if asked 'Why did you do (or allow) that?' Whether the agent could have prevented or stopped these occurrences is irrelevant (see pp. 11–12); so is his or her brainstate at the time or in the time leading up. Of great importance is the wider context, the sort of context that includes prior actions, plans, etc., but also the sort of context that allows us to see how certain actions or occurrences fit into a person's practical life – how they reflect on his general orientation of will. Possible answers to 'Why didn't you stop or prevent that?' allow us to see how a person weighs practical reasons against one another, since the applicability of the question rests on there being good reason not to do or allow something. The same may go for 'Why didn't you think of that?' What constitutes *sincerity* in the answers people give to such questions is a deep topic, as Anscombe recognized, but one beyond the range of this chapter.[33]

Notes

1 Austin (1979, 191).
2 Anscombe (1963, 89–90).
3 'A Plea for Excuses' came out in the *Proceedings of the Aristotelian Society* for 1956–57, and the lectures on which Anscombe based *Intention* were delivered in Hilary Term 1957. It seems likely that Anscombe had heard Austin's views on 'voluntarily', etc., both philosophers being at Oxford; I suppose they might well have struck her as typical of the sort of ordinary language philosophy she felt to be misguided.
4 Extensions or adaptations of the sense(s) of '(in)voluntary' can also be expected in other 'technical' contexts, e.g. in legal judgments and in psychology – both of these cases being cited by Austin himself.
5 Anscombe (1963, 11).
6 Anscombe (1981a, 8).
7 Anscombe (1963, 25).
8 Strictly speaking, Anscombe's definition of intentional actions as 'ones to which a certain sense of the question "Why?" has application' looks better suited as a definition of voluntary actions (given what she says); and indeed in sec. 17 she allows this, writing: 'The answers to the question "Why?" which give it an application are, then, more extensive in range than the answers which give reasons for acting. This question "Why?" can now be defined as the question expecting an answer in this range. And with this we have roughly outlined the area of intentional action' (Anscombe 1963, 28). The question 'Why?' can both expect a certain kind of answer (a reason for acting) and yet 'have application' in cases where no such answer can be given.
9 Cf. Anscombe (1963, sec. 16).
10 Alternatively: the agent's awareness of what he's doing is the same sort of awareness in both cases, whether you argue that it's observational or non-observational.
11 Anscombe (1963, 33).
12 Cf. Wittgenstein's dismissal of such language at sec. 631 of the *Philosophical Investigations* (1958).
13 Anscombe (2008a, 129).
14 Anscombe uses the term 'counter-voluntary' of cases where what somebody does, or what happens to him, are contrary to his will, either through violence or through ignorance; see Anscombe (2008a, 130). We may say that the notion of the involuntary *includes* that of the counter-voluntary.
15 A philosopher might suggest that 'strictly speaking' all you do is the 'basic act', e.g. of getting on a bus, all the rest being in the lap of the gods; but insofar as *what you do* is the subject of all sorts of questions, such as questions of responsibility, wider action-descriptions than 'basic' ones must be allowed.
16 There is simultaneously a sense in which handing over the wallet will be voluntary, because intentional: if asked 'Why did you do that?' the person could reply 'So as not to get shot.'
17 See Frankfurt (1969).
18 See Frankfurt (1971). Frankfurt writes of wants or desires being 'effective', 'motivating', etc., in a way that clearly invokes causality.
19 Anscombe (1963, 89–90).
20 If, that is, she knew they were there; or indeed if she *ought* to have known they were there (as Anscombe argues).
21 For a fuller discussion of the concept of pleasure and its role in practical reasoning, see Teichmann (2011, ch. 3); also Chapter Four of the present volume.
22 This phrase is used by Anscombe in 'Will and Emotion': 'A positive act of mine is voluntary [...] because it is done by me either for its own sake or for the sake of something else' (Anscombe 1981c, 107). By 'positive act' she means, I think, to exclude both not-doings and obviously passive 'actions' such as rolling downhill having been pushed. Even so, it seems odd to say that fiddling with a pencil is done 'for its own sake'.

23 Anscombe (2008b, 110).
24 See, for example, Anscombe (1981d, esp. 209–10).
25 Though it need not. 'Why didn't you take advantage of his absence to drink the best wine from his cellar?' 'It didn't even occur to me.'
26 I am taking 'I could stop' to be the thought which, if it had occurred to me, would have made me stop, but not much hangs on this precise form of words. If there is such a thing as just *the thought of stopping*, my remarks about internal relations still hold, insofar as the thought is evidently of *me* stopping, and is deemed relevant to my actually stopping – is as it were a suggestion to myself, rather than having the content of e.g. a memory of stopping, or a fear of stopping, or …
27 'When the bottles started flying, I thought I'd better go' need not be made true by any inner events that could be said to have the content 'I'd better go', nor need you recall any such events in order to use this past-tense sentence. What happened 'within you' as you got up and began to move could just have been vague imaginings and the like.
28 Anscombe (1981a, 9).
29 Anscombe (1981a, 9). Anscombe derives this sense of 'necessary' from Aristotle, *Metaphysics* Δ. She employs it in various other places, e.g. in Anscombe (1981e, 15).
30 Anscombe (1981a, 7, n. 2).
31 Anscombe (2008a, 105).
32 Austin (1979, 180).
33 I discuss the topic of sincerity in Chapter Three of this volume.

References

Anscombe, G. E. M. (1963), *Intention*. Oxford: Blackwell, 2nd ed.

———. (1981a), 'Two Kinds of Error in Action', in *Collected Papers Vol. III: Ethics, Religion and Politics*. Oxford: Blackwell, pp. 3–9.

———. (1981b), 'On Brute Facts', in *Collected Papers Vol. III: Ethics, Religion and Politics*. Oxford: Blackwell, pp. 22–25.

———. (1981c), 'Will and Emotion', in *Collected Papers Vol. I: From Parmenides to Wittgenstein*. Oxford: Blackwell, pp. 100–107.

———. (1981d), 'Under a Description', in *Collected Papers Vol. II: Metaphysics and the Philosophy of Mind*. Oxford: Blackwell, pp. 208–19.

———. (1981e), 'On Promising and Its Justice', in *Collected Papers Vol. III: Ethics, Religion and Politics*. Oxford: Blackwell, pp. 10–21.

———. (2008a), 'Sin', in M. Geach and L. Gormally (eds), *Faith in a Hard Ground: Essays on Religion, Philosophy and Ethics by G.E.M. Anscombe*. Exeter: Imprint Academic, pp. 117–56.

———. (2008b), 'On Being in Good Faith', in M. Geach and L. Gormally (eds), *Faith in a Hard Ground: Essays on Religion, Philosophy and Ethics by G.E.M. Anscombe*. Exeter: Imprint Academic, pp. 101–12.

Austin, J. L. (1979), 'A Plea for Excuses', in J. O. Urmson and G. J. Warnock (eds), *J.L. Austin, Philosophical Papers*. Oxford: Clarendon Press, 3rd ed., pp. 175–204.

Frankfurt, H. (1969), 'Alternate Possibilities and Moral Responsibility', *Journal of Philosophy*, 66, no. 23 (4 December), 829–39.

———. (1971), 'Freedom of the Will and the Concept of a Person', *Journal of Philosophy*, 68, no. 1 (14 January), 5–20.

Teichmann, R. (2011), *Nature, Reason and the Good Life*. Oxford: Oxford University Press.

Wittgenstein, L. (1958), *Philosophical Investigations*, trans. G. E. M. Anscombe, ed. G. E. M. Anscombe and R. Rhees. Oxford: Basil Blackwell, 2nd ed.

Chapter Six

RATIONAL CHOICE THEORY AND BACKWARD-LOOKING MOTIVES

There is a well-known model of rational agency according to which a rational person's reasons for doing X will be such that doing X is either his end, or is something he takes to be a means to his end (or one of his ends). According to this model, a person has as end or goal some achievable state of affairs, such as feeling pleasure, and this goal renders certain courses of action prima facie suitable, namely those courses which would bring about the state of affairs, or would raise the likelihood of its coming to be. The person may have false beliefs about which courses of action are thus suitable for him, but this merely indicates the need for a distinction, between what he has 'objective' reason to do, and what he has 'subjective' reason to do. His practical rationality will not as such be impugned if he does something which is only 'subjectively' rational, though his theoretical rationality may be impugned, if it is the explanation for why the relevant belief of his is false.

This sketch will be familiar, as describing a model of rational choice which is standard among economists and decision theorists, its key notion being that of 'expected value', or alternatively 'expected utility'. It is a sketch only, and more detail could be added. But for present purposes, we need only look at a class of reasons for action which are inexplicable on this model of agency – namely, backward-looking reasons.

An example of a backward-looking motive is the motive of gratitude for a service done. As Elizabeth Anscombe brought out so effectively,[1] reasons and motives are alike elicited by the question 'Why?', as in 'Why are you doing that?', and if I ask you why you are sending flowers to Emily, let us suppose you reply, 'Because she drove me to hospital when I broke my arm.' On the face of it, your reason mentions a past fact, a fact of recent history. But the philosopher who adheres to the 'expected utility' model will look for a way of describing your action that makes it appear to be aiming at bringing something about, and will thus reject 'Because she drove me to hospital' as a statement of the 'real' reason. What aim or goal could be alleged in this case? Two kinds of answer suggest themselves. The first kind makes use of the key word, here 'gratitude', and inserts it into the means-end format, thus yielding the putative reason for action: 'In order to show my gratitude.' The second kind of answer relies on the notion of pleasure, as a state that is produceable by actions; we then either have the egoistic reason, 'In order to derive pleasure from my own action', or the more altruistic 'In order to give pleasure to Emily'.

Both these accounts can be shown to be mistaken, and for similar reasons. Your sending flowers to Emily may in a sense be called a means to your end, that of expressing gratitude, insofar as it is a *way* of expressing gratitude. But we have to ask, 'What is gratitude?' And any adequate answer will allude to what sort of reason for an action makes it a grateful action – namely, such a reason as 'Because she drove me to hospital'. The force of 'In order to show gratitude', in other words, here rests on the prior force of a backward-looking reason. It is no good treating the sending of flowers to Emily as your goal or desired outcome, to which means-end deliberation is indeed relevant; for this 'goal' does not in fact give your ultimate reason for action. For you can informatively answer the question, 'Why are you sending flowers to Emily?', and it is your answer to this that gives your ultimate reason. The decision theorist may allege that the reason you thus give has the function of ascribing a 'value' to the outcome of Emily's receiving your flowers, in this way insisting that your goal is after all this outcome. But this 'value' is evidently not *intrinsic* to the state of affairs in question, since it would lack that value if Emily had never taken you to hospital. How might one explain to someone what this 'value' consists in? Answer: by employing or invoking the statement, 'Because she drove me to hospital.' The other person would understand your explanation of the value of sending flowers if and only if they were familiar with the force of such a statement as a reason for action.

It is worth stressing this point about the notion of 'value', since it is a feature of decision-theoretic discourse to present the notion as if it is fairly well-understood, and then to cash it out for us in terms of hypothetical *preferences*. Thus, it may be stipulated that the value you ascribe to Emily's receiving your flowers is equivalent to the smallest sum of money you would accept in lieu of her receiving the flowers. There are already problems arising from the possibility that someone doesn't regard money as desirable in the way that the theorist wishes her to; and it is likely to be absurd to claim that if a person would accept *no* sum in lieu of Emily's receiving flowers then she must ascribe infinite value to that 'outcome'. But even if you *would* accept some lowest amount of money in preference to sending flowers to Emily, this doesn't show that your ultimate reason for action, when you do in fact send her flowers, was a forward-looking reason. For the hypothetical preference in no way removes or translates away the reason, 'Because she drove me to hospital.' All that we can say is that another (forward-looking) reason could, hypothetically, outweigh the backward-looking one, as far as your deliberations went.

I said just now that the so-called value of sending flowers to Emily would not be intrinsic to the act; but some philosophers do speak of such actions as grateful acts and promise-keepings as having intrinsic value, as also such actions as ungrateful acts and promise-breakings, these latter having intrinsic negative value. Thus John Broome writes, 'If you break a promise, one consequence will be that you have broken a promise, and the wrongness of promise breaking can be taken as a bad feature of this consequence […] In this way, the intrinsic value of acts can be absorbed into teleology.'[2] ('Teleology' is the form of utilitarianism Broome is defending.) If I keep a promise, then presumably it is under the description *keeping a promise* that my action is to be made out as having intrinsic value – for it probably won't have any intrinsic value, except accidentally, under some such description as *bringing Smith a book*. But one could argue analogously that under the description *providing for my descendants* the action of investing my money in a certain way has intrinsic value. This latter way of talking would usually be ruled out by distinguishing the value an act has in itself from the value it has on account of what happens subsequently (especially what happens as a result of the act); and similarly, one ought to distinguish the value an act has in itself from the value it has on account of what happened earlier. The crucial point to make concerning your sending flowers to Emily is just that, if we are to speak of the action's having a certain value, then that value depends on past facts, and as far as rational choice goes, it is these past facts that the agent must mention in giving her reasons for his action.

Once it is recognized that the ultimate reason for a grateful action is not given just by mentioning the action itself, the inapplicability of the expected utility model can be seen in the fact that there is no place for an assignment of *probability* in connection with the agent's ultimate reason. If sending flowers to Emily were my ultimate end, then to be sure I could assign some probability to my achieving that end, given my adoption of certain means, such as phoning Interflora. But I cannot sensibly ask, 'If I send flowers to Emily, what is the probability of my achieving my end, that of showing gratitude?' In sending the flowers I *thereby* show my gratitude. One seems forced to say that the probability of my showing gratitude is 1 – which indicates, not a special source of epistemic certainty, but the pointlessness of this way of talking. It is essential to the expected utility model that a rational agent both assign some value to a given outcome, and also assign some probability to it (given the adoption of certain means). So the expected utility model is inapplicable to actions, such as grateful ones, whose ultimate reasons are backward-looking, on account of the inapplicability of the notion of probability to those reasons.

What of the second sort of account I mentioned (five paragraphs back), the sort that relies on the notion of pleasure as a state produceable by one's actions? It can be asked what sort of pleasure it is that is allegedly being aimed at. Presumably any pleasure felt by the sender is meant to be pleasure in the fact of the recipient's pleasure. And Emily will feel pleasure on receiving flowers because flowers are lovely things; but why do you want to bring her this pleasure? If the reply is 'Because she drove me to hospital', the backward-looking reason has resurfaced. If the reply is 'To feel pleasure myself', then why choose Emily, as opposed to any other susceptible individual? Again, the obvious answer is, and must be if what we have here is gratitude, 'Because she drove me to hospital'.

A rather desperate move may be made here, that of bringing in induction, in the following sort of way: 'I have found in the past that the pleasure I get when I give pleasure to people who have helped me is greater than if I were giving pleasure to other kinds of people; so I now calculate that if I send flowers, etc. etc.' Now the idea that a type of intentional action should be *found* to produce the thing that constitutes its own rationale is clearly peculiar. This is especially true of actions not of the sort that you were trained to do in childhood: for it could be alleged that actions of the sort that you were trained to do in childhood were initially motivated by something different, namely a desire for parental approval (or perhaps indeed these early actions were cases of mere imitation, not yet fully intentional). But consider the person who for the first time in her life performs an act of vengeance, this not being the sort of thing inculcated by Mummy and Daddy. What can the aim of such an action be, on this first occasion? There is, after all, no experiential basis for predicting any particular outcome, e.g. a 'pleasure state' – so it seems as if the action must be pointless, according to the 'expected utility' model. (We might now postulate some reason like, 'I have noticed that other people get pleasure from vengeful acts, so on the assumption that I am like them, I calculate …' – evidently ludicrous.) Apart from all this, there are in any case backward-looking motives which it is quite implausible to reduce to forms of pleasure-seeking, such as motives of fidelity or loyalty that result in self-sacrifice.

All in all, then, the case for the existence of genuinely backward-looking reasons looks rather strong. Such reasons appear to falsify the 'expected utility' model of rational agency, or indeed any model which insists that rational agents always look either to the future effects of their actions or to those actions' intrinsic value. But it may now be claimed that although we do give and accept facts about the past as reasons for our actions, this very fact shows our irrationality. Maybe certain tribes have given and accepted as a reason for not doing X that X is 'taboo'; but can't we criticize that practice as irrational? Mightn't it be the same with backward-looking reasons?

When we criticize the notion of 'taboo', used as I am imagining it being used, we do so on account of the fact that the term 'taboo' fails to link up to human good or ill, in the sort of way which might make its prohibitive force intelligible. 'Why should I avoid eating that?' 'You'll be sick if you do.' This answer is quite intelligible; and the further question, 'Why should I avoid being sick?', points to an imagined need for a reason where there is none. By contrast, if the answer to 'Why should I avoid eating that?' were 'Because eating it would be taboo', then no reason would yet have been given, unless the activities listed as taboo can be made out as harmful, or bad in some way.

The intelligibility, as a reason for grateful action, of 'Because she drove me to hospital' is connected to what is good or bad for human beings, just as is the intelligibility of 'Because you'll be sick'. And this is because the phenomenon of gratitude, or returning good for good, is normal and natural for human beings (like loving your offspring and resenting injury), but additionally because a prevalence of habits of gratitude is conducive to social harmony, and this fact makes a reason for action which is expressive of gratitude fitted *as* a reason, in the context of the social language-game of asking for and giving reasons. Our concepts of what a good person is, and of what is good for human beings, are not *purely* naturalistic: their shape is partly determined by the social and empirical nature of the human practice of reason-giving. Giving reasons for what you do is giving an account of yourself, especially to others.

I spoke just now of the habit of gratitude as being conducive to social harmony; and this may seem to suggest that we do, after all, have a forward-looking rationale or justification for the human practice of accepting backward-looking reasons. The statement 'This practice is a good idea because it will (continue to) achieve social harmony' surely invokes a forward-looking reason? But, firstly, we did not *decide* to institute the practice of having backward-looking reasons, nor are we continuing with this practice for any *reason* – any more than we speak a language because of the expected benefits of doing so; secondly, even if we did have forward-looking reasons for going in for the practice, this would not show that the moves within the practice, i.e. the giving and accepting of backward-looking reasons, were after all not what they appeared.

One could perhaps argue that facts about social harmony help to explain the survival and spread of this practice among human beings; but this would not reduce the force of backward-looking reasons to that of a forward-looking one, nor would it provide a 'justification' for the practice, any more than an empirical explanation for the success and spread of an empire with its customs ipso facto provides a justification, either of the empire or of its customs.

I said above that habits of gratitude, and similar habits, are normal and natural for human beings, a fact that helps to explain why backward-looking reasons count as compelling within the language-game of asking for and giving reasons for action. However, the human phenomenon under discussion is richer than the phrase 'normal and natural' would suggest, all on its own; for part of what is at issue is our way of perceiving the world, and ourselves and our actions. This 'way of perceiving' is above all non-atomistic, and our notions of what is *significant* are typically contextual and holistic.

Understanding the significance of something often involves seeing it against the background of a larger context, a bigger picture. One instance of this truth is Frege's Context Principle, as enunciated in the Introduction to *The Foundations of Arithmetic*, where Frege enjoins us 'never to ask for the meaning [*Bedeutung*] of a word in isolation, but only in the context of a proposition'. Another instance can be found within human institutions and rule-governed practices: a piece of paper only counts as a ten pound note against a background containing banks, activities of buying and selling, etc. etc. And many events and phenomena have the significance they do because of what led up to them, or came before them. For the 'background' to an event, insofar as it is something we can know about, talk about, agree or disagree about, will typically be in the past.

Take an event within a piece of music. A cadence, a climax, a broadening out and numerous other kinds of musical events are what they are because of what has led up to them. You only hear those two chords as constituting a modulation, and so as being a harbinger of peace, or a cloud moving across the sun, or whatever, on account of what has just preceded them. Now this is not to say that what happens *after* a musical event doesn't also help determine the character of the event. Thus the point of a gradual build-up is evidently in what it builds up to. But even here there is a certain priority of past over future: for the characterization of the passage as a build-up relies on the perspective of the listener who finally hears the apotheosis, in the light of what *has already happened* – even though past musical experience may on occasion incline you to guess that what you're presently hearing is bound to be a build-up of some sort. (Rossini.) You can, after all, be cheated, and hence proven wrong, by a mischievous or incompetent composer; whereas a certain pair of chords cannot help constituting a modulation as they occur, given what has happened. What is written is written.

Analogous remarks can be made about the events of human life. Your sending flowers to Emily is a case in point: it is what it is because of what Emily has done for you in the past. Again, this is not to deny that a historical event will often assume a certain significance on account of what came after it – as with the assassination of Archduke Franz Ferdinand in 1914. But here too it is the perspective of those who recall the event which is crucial. For it is in effect they who give it its significance, which is thus a retrospective significance.

A possible partial diagnosis of why people are attracted to the expected utility model of agency suggests itself. Perhaps such people are imagining states of affairs as necessarily having some sort of intrinsic value, intrinsic significance. If they were right it would follow that the significance of a present action and a past state of affairs must be mutually independent, so that only the prospect of affecting 'overall significance' would seem to supply any reason for or against performing an action – which is to say, only the significance of the action itself, and/or the possible significance of future states of affairs, would seem to supply such a reason. But if I am right that there are species of significance that involve the broader context, and hence (in the case of events in time) that involve the past, then this notion of 'intrinsic significance' cannot be universally applicable.

It is even doubtful if it is ever applicable; for an investigation of those concepts that have, in the traditional accounts, been particularly associated with 'intrinsic value' shows, I think, that the traditional accounts have got things wrong. I am thinking especially of the concept of pleasure, which is of course the key concept for classical utilitarians, for whom the prospects of producing pleasurable states of affairs are what supply reasons for rational action. The idea that pleasure has intrinsic (positive) value goes with a picture of it as a sort of sensation or quasi-sensation, or in other words as a self-intimating episode of consciousness, with a certain duration, typically having a certain intensity, and with an intrinsic 'character' knowable authoritatively by the subject. But pleasure is no such thing; it is much more connected to the 'space of reasons' than the classical utilitarian realized. The question 'What's the pleasure in that?' is often a real one, and can receive answers embodying good, bad or unintelligible reasons.[3]

As regards the intelligibility of the reasons people give for their actions (past, present or proposed), it seems clear that one source of this intelligibility will very often be how their actions fit into a bigger picture, involving other people, other actions, other times and places – all of which contribute to an action's 'significance', as I have been calling it. This term is not meant to denote some single intuitible property à la G. E. Moore. Rather, 'significance' is a portmanteau term covering a family of ordinary but crucial action-concepts, such as gratitude, fidelity, temerity, tact, aimlessness, solidarity … And an important subclass of these action-concepts relate to backward-looking motives.

A theory of rational action and rational deliberation which ignores such motives, or presents a distorted account of them, is liable to have various ill effects, especially if it seeps into the culture at large, or becomes part of the ideology of those who govern us. For such a theory will present an impoverished picture of human beings and of human life. History comes to be regarded as at best a source of useful pointers as to how to get what we want; phenomena such as gratitude, fidelity, and justice become puzzling, and attachment to them can seem mere superstition. A picture may emerge of the human person as a repository of atomistic 'experiences', inhabiting a present from the vantage point of which his relations to past and future 'selves' are contingent, and his responsibilities and commitments correspondingly fluid. (The late Derek Parfit received praise and honour for his compendious filling-in of this picture.) And in economics, a supposedly 'neutral' account of rational choice in fact encourages and sustains a simple-minded utilitarian ethic.

Notes

1 See Anscombe (1963).
2 Broome (1995, 4).
3 For more on this topic, see Teichmann (2011 ch. 3); also Chapter Four of the present volume.

References

Anscombe, G. E. M. (1963), *Intention*. Oxford: Blackwell, 2nd ed.
Broome, J. (1995), *Weighing Goods*. Oxford: Wiley-Blackwell.
Teichmann, R. (2011), *Nature, Reason and the Good Life*. Oxford: Oxford University Press.

Chapter Seven

MEANING, UNDERSTANDING AND ACTION

Understanding Stopping and Forcing Modals

When does a child count as understanding the meaning of 'plus'? Roughly speaking, when she has sufficiently mastered the skill of addition; in other words, when she often enough uses 'plus' ('+') in the right way, where that especially means: doing correct calculations employing the symbol. 'Often enough' is of course vague. We encounter the same vagueness when faced with the question, 'When can a child play the piano?' Answer: when she sufficiently often gets things sufficiently right on the piano (playing scales, pieces, etc.).

There is a general point here about language-mastery. As Wittgenstein famously wrote: 'For a large class of cases [...] in which we employ the word "meaning" it can be defined thus: the meaning of a word is its use in the language' (*PI* 43).[1] Using a word is a form of activity. To characterize the use of a word one will often need to locate that use within a certain language-game, i.e. a rule-governed practice in which various words or expressions are used in interlocking ways. The term 'rule-governed' here points to the difference between correct and incorrect uses of words. *Understanding* a word means having the ability to use it correctly, often enough.

Although all word-use may be called 'activity', involving various kinds of action (assertion, questioning, exclamation, apology …), there are certain uses of words which are bound up with action in a very direct way. I have in mind two kinds of language-games: that involving imperatives, and that involving what Anscombe calls stopping and forcing modals. When does a child count as understanding the meaning of such imperative forms as 'Come here', 'Pass the butter' or 'Don't do that'? The natural answer is: 'When she responds appropriately often enough.' And 'responding appropriately' presumably means obeying or complying with the command or request. (Perhaps we should additionally require that she develop the ability to use imperatives herself.)

Stopping and forcing modals are linguistic cousins of imperatives. Anscombe introduces them in the course of explicating, and then jumping free of, a certain circularity that we are liable to encounter when we try to say what a promise is (see e.g. Anscombe 1981a,d). To say what a promise is, we need at least to say this: that if you promise to φ, you bring it about that you have to φ. But what does 'have to' mean? Is it this: that you have to φ, or you'll upset the other person? But you might not upset them; it could even be that they never discover that you broke the promise. Moreover, it could be that I would upset someone to whom I'd expressed an intention (to be at a meeting, say) if I changed my mind and didn't do what I said I'd do; but that fact wouldn't turn my expression of intention into a promise. How about this: you have to φ, because if you don't you'll commit a wrong? But how shall we say what the 'wrong' is, except by calling it 'breaking a promise'? (A circle.) So is it this: you have to φ, if you wish to obey the Rule of Promising? But what is the rule? Isn't it: If you promise to φ, you have to φ? (Another circle.) We still haven't explained this 'have to'.

Anscombe notes that we will be unable to solve this problem so long as we attempt to give non-circular *analyses* of such expressions as 'promise' and 'have to' (or of sentences employing them). She proposes that we instead look to how these words are used, and especially to how they are taught and learnt. This is what she does; and her investigation yields a number of findings, one of which concerns the difference between mere imperatives, such as 'Move your king', and statements like 'You have to move your king'. The meaning and function of the latter, she points out, is bound up with another kind of statement, which she calls a logos; the logos might for example be 'Your king is in check'. In the case of promising, 'You promised to do X' would give a logos for 'You have to do X', and the meanings of these two statements cannot be understood independently of one another. They must be learnt together as part of a package deal.

'Stopping/forcing modal' and 'logos' are technical terms, for which Anscombe does not give explicit definitions, reasonably enough. Should we take the characteristic just mentioned, of there being a mutual conceptual dependence between logoi and their correlative modal statements, as definitive of logoi? It seems not. For you could e.g. take some already-grasped concept and *stipulate* that, in the game you are inventing or explaining, this concept is to have the reason-giving force of a logos. 'Everyone dances around and when the music stops, you have to sit on a chair if you can.' This rule yields such statements as 'You have to sit down – the music has stopped!' Clearly, we understand the meaning of 'The music has stopped' independently of learning the rule. Nevertheless, it can be said that one learns a new *role* for 'The music has stopped', and understanding this role is indeed tied up with understanding the meaning of 'You have to sit down'.

When does a child count as understanding the meaning of the modal, 'You have to' ('You're meant to', etc.)? She needs to be able to ask or answer the question 'Why?'; if asked it, she'll need to be able to give a logos, for instance by saying, 'Your king is in check.' If 'You have to' is addressed to the child, and an appropriate logos is given, then presumably she'll need to respond appropriately often enough if she is to count as having mastered this bit of language. As with imperatives, 'responding appropriately' means *doing* the thing which she 'has to' do.

Normal adults understand imperatives and understand stopping/forcing modals. They were taught the use of these expressions as children and they have not forgotten how to use them. So if understanding is a matter of 'responding appropriately', can we infer that any normal adult will typically, or even quite often, obey authoritative commands, comply with requests, keep promises ... and generally speaking not break the rules? Would that it were so! What, then, is the *difference* between my not understanding the rules of poker and my cheating at poker? What is the difference between my failing to grasp that I should keep a promise and my simply ignoring the obligation which I have put myself under?

The significance of such questions is at once conceptual and ethical. (Philosophy and ethics are continuous.) The ethical aspect of the issue can be seen in the fact that someone's not understanding a rule will typically excuse his breaking it; in many cases we might even decide that such inadvertent rule-breaking isn't strictly speaking rule-breaking at all. I say 'typically excuse' because lack of understanding of this sort isn't always taken to be exculpatory: see, for instance, the legal principle that ignorance of the law is no defence (*ignorantia juris non excusat*). Ignorance here includes not understanding. But when the rule or rules in question go to *constitute* a practice, as chess is constituted by its rules, the 'wrong' committed by one who breaks a rule cannot be understood independently of the existence of the rule;[2] it was this fact which threatened circularity in our account of promises, a circularity Anscombe avoided by invoking the learning and use of modals and logoi. The law against murder, by contrast, forbids something which is independently wrong or wicked, and here at least the rationale for the above-mentioned legal principle is pretty clear. But the inadvertent breaking of constitutive rules is surely prima facie excusable. This is in part due to the conventionality (arbitrariness, one might say) of the *forms* specified or assumed by the rules – e.g. the shape of a given chess piece, or the actions that embody the donation of something to someone. One who is unaware, or not fully aware, of the significance of these conventional forms doesn't thereby show a bad character.

In everyday life there are straightforward criteria for determining if someone knew he was meant to φ, although he didn't φ. If he knew he was meant to φ, he of course understood the relevant formula, 'You're meant to φ'; so these criteria are also criteria for his understanding the formula. Here are some examples. If caught out, the person might admit he'd broken the rule; or if put on the spot and asked 'Now what were you meant to do?' he might just tell us. Or again, we might have witnessed him easily following the rule in other circumstances; or – often noteworthy – he might have insisted on others' following the rule, been aggrieved when they didn't do so and so on.

Equally, there are everyday criteria for someone's not understanding a rule, or not knowing about it, or not knowing that it applied here. If he is still a learner, that itself is a fact with criterial weight. If an adult, then sincere expressions of surprise when we berate him for not φ-ing will indicate lack of knowledge or understanding. Or he might have suffered a stroke with consequent amnesia. Et cetera.

With language-mastery in general, the default position is that a person above a certain age and of normal intelligence will understand the words he is using, or which others use in talking to him.[3] This default position is not something that we adopt for pragmatic or epistemic reasons; it is not, e.g., based on inductive assessments of the probability of someone's understanding something. (The past 'evidence' for such an assessment would have to include a great deal of unquestioned linguistic intercourse – unquestioned because the default position is that people know what their words mean!) Rather, the nature of this default position is similar to that described by Anscombe in her article 'On Brute Facts' (Anscombe 1981b).

In 'On Brute Facts' Anscombe discusses the move from certain premises to a conclusion like 'X owes Y £10'. (The premises could include 'X ordered potatoes from Y', 'Y delivered a sack of potatoes', etc.) For this human practice to be possible (= practicable), moves or inferences of this sort must be allowed to stand in the absence of defeating circumstances; that is to say, if certain facts hold, the *default* position is that X owes money to Y. Defeating circumstances are such circumstances as: that half the potatoes were rotten; that the bag was left two miles from X's house; that X and Y were both acting in a film. It is not possible in advance to state finitely what may *count* as defeating circumstances – again, not for 'pragmatic reasons', but rather because of the fluid and creative nature of human institutions, and because of the 'imponderable evidence' on which we so often rely in our dealings with our fellow human beings.[4]

For linguistic intercourse to be possible (= practicable), it is likewise necessary that a person is taken to be 'playing the language-game' in the absence of defeating circumstances. And this is obviously so for the sorts of language-games I've been alluding to, such as that of promising. I earlier mentioned two sets of criteria, those for determining understanding and those for determining lack of understanding, and it is in fact the second of these which is going to be more pertinent to our question, 'What is the difference between my failing to grasp that I should keep a promise and my simply ignoring the obligation which I have put myself under?' If you are an adult of normal intelligence, and you say, 'I promise I'll take you to the airport,' then your subsequent protestation that you didn't know what promises were will not be allowed any weight unless you can plausibly cite some (rather extraordinary) circumstance, capable of defeating the default assumption of linguistic competence.[5] It is not for us to invoke criteria of understanding, it is for you to invoke criteria of non-understanding.

It is tempting to 'look inwards' here in the manner of Descartes, and insist that whatever I did and said, and whatever the external circumstances, my *understanding* of my own words, or lack of it, is a purely internal – perhaps even private – matter. I will not here rehearse the critique of the Cartesian picture which we find in the later Wittgenstein, beyond saying this: insofar as the desire to 'look inwards' arises from the recognition that it can always turn out that someone *didn't* after all understand what he was saying (e.g.), this latter fact is central to, and accounted for by, the picture above adumbrated, with its reference to default positions, criteria and defeasibility.

Abilities and Inclinations

Teaching language means teaching abilities – in other words training. The bare notion of an ability or skill differs from that of an ethical virtue, in a way delineated by Aristotle (and later by Aquinas). An ethical virtue like honesty involves not just the *ability* to give a customer the correct change (say), but the desire or inclination to do so. By contrast, being good at spelling amounts, roughly, to being able to spell words correctly if you want to. For this reason, misspelling a word on purpose doesn't impugn your skill as a speller in the way that misspelling it inadvertently does; whereas walking off with another's wallet on purpose impugns your claim to be honest and walking off with it accidentally does not.

When we teach a child the use and meaning of modals like 'You have to' and 'You cannot', we aim to bring it about that the child regularly forms the *inclination* to φ when he has understood that he 'has to' φ. Indeed, as was said above, it would seem to be a criterion of his understanding the modal that he responds appropriately, i.e. voluntarily φs, often enough. Thus we are not, in teaching this bit of language, imparting a mere ability, if that means the ability to do X if one wants to (*to do X* being: to φ in response to 'You have to φ'). We are aiming to impart a readiness or inclination to do certain things. A child who *never* responds appropriately to 'You have to φ' may be said not to have mastered the language-game at all; one who responds appropriately but not often enough will either be deficient in understanding or deficient in will – which of these it is will depend on whether, and to what extent, we can appeal to the sort of criteria of (non-)understanding which I discussed earlier. What I have called deficiency in will might, depending on the case, strike us as deficiency in virtue (naughtiness), or slowness to acquire virtue, or some such. We will be more likely to talk of imperfect virtue where the case is that of the modals governing the promising language-game than where it is that of the modals governing the playing of chess. Deficiency in will as regards playing by the rules in chess would look like boredom, or contrariness, or whim. (Which is not to say that these phenomena lie outside 'the ethical'.)

In fact the teaching of language quite generally aims to instil more than just the ability to use words correctly. It is not enough that the learner can give the correct answer to 'a + b =?' when he wants to; he also needs to be someone who *does* generally want to give the correct answer, in the sense that this is his default inclination: he is not someone who quite often feels like giving an incorrect answer, for instance. Indeed, as we have seen, a person will only count as understanding the meaning of 'plus' if he often enough gives the correct answer, so that it is rather hard to coherently *depict* a child who can give the correct answer when he wants to but can't be relied on to want to. (It is somewhat easier if we are depicting an adult.) In the case of imperatives and stopping/forcing modals, however, the voluntary actions which we desire to see the language-learner performing are not just linguistic actions, i.e. uses of the very words which it's to be hoped the learner is learning – the voluntary actions we desire to see the learner performing are those ordered or required, i.e. those mentioned in the imperative or modal statement. The idea of deficiency of will has a ready application to those who don't do what they have to, or don't do what they're told: human motives for non-compliance or disobedience are often perfectly natural, flowing from our human nature.[6] *Motives* for misusing words are not in this sense humanly natural; quite a lot of scene-setting and circumstantial detail are needed to depict a scenario in which the diagnosis 'He wants to use that word wrong' has any appeal.

The person who has properly learnt the meaning and use of 'You have to φ' will be disposed to φ in response to that statement, ceteris paribus. That last phrase is intended to cover such defeaters as: recognition that the statement was a joke, recognition of pressing reasons not to φ, recognition that no suitable logos is forthcoming and so on. In the extreme case, a reflective adult may find reason to reject the very practice constituted by the rules in question. Absent such rational rejection, the person, as I have said, will be *inclined* (disposed) to act in accordance with the statement: the actions they consequently perform will be voluntary and intentional. Anscombe foregrounded an agent's actual or possible responses to 'Why?' as indicative of intention or the lack of it (see Anscombe 1963); and here the question 'Why are you φ-ing?' gets its answer courtesy of the language-game itself. For the agent will be able to reply using the relevant logos – for example, 'Because I promised to'.

The adult who has fallen into the habit of lying, cheating or breaking promises does not (as I have argued) have the excuse of non-understanding ready to hand. In the absence of defeaters, the presumption of competence stands, and our diagnosis will be one of 'deficiency of will' – which does not mean weakness of will, but rather a defective orientation of the will (a wrong ordering of priorities, weighing of practical reasons, etc.). The ordinary word for such a person is 'dishonest'. Such a person knows what 'You cannot' and 'You have to' mean; and indeed the bare ability to play the language-game may be alluded to by some such remark as 'He knows well enough how to keep an undertaking if he wishes to impress the boss'. He can do X *if he wants to*. It's just that he too often doesn't want to.

But this last fact will indicate that such linguistic training as he received in childhood did not achieve its true aim. For the aim of teaching a child the modals 'You have to', etc. is precisely to instil a standing inclination to 'respond appropriately' to them. The language-games in question, after all, have a human point, they play a real role in our lives. The aim of the teaching was not to instil a mere ability. So although we do say of the dishonest adult that he understands what it is to make a promise, answer a question truthfully, etc., we can in the same breath say that he has *not* learnt what society was, in a sense, trying to teach him.

Illusion and Confusion

This reference to what society is 'up to' should not be thought of as ruling out the possibility that society, or social groups, should themselves fall into habits of dishonesty. In a certain sense, it can become the norm – or at any rate become normal – for people to break the rules, or twist the rules, for ulterior motives, conscious or unconscious. The more this happens, however, the closer we get to a state of linguistic and practical confusion. The meanings of words become unfocused; people's accounts of what they are doing become detached from their real, more or less unconscious, aims. This kind of confusion is a species of conceptual corruption.

What shows that a prevalent use of a term or set of terms involves, not merely false beliefs, but confusion? The answer is: the tangles, dead ends, contradictions, empty statements and even plain nonsense into which such use leads people. Where the use of the terms in question is bound up with action, people's behaviour may show a corresponding incoherence: its significance will often be obscure, including to the agents themselves.

Anscombe famously argued, in 'Modern Moral Philosophy', that

> the concepts of obligation, and duty – *moral* obligation and *moral* duty, that is to say – and of what is *morally* right and wrong, and of the *moral* sense of 'ought', ought to be jettisoned if this is psychologically possible; because they are survivals, or derivatives from survivals, from an earlier conception of ethics which no longer generally survives, and are only harmful without it. (Anscombe 1981c, 26)

If she was right, a way of using the word 'moral' had become prevalent, and this way of using it should be jettisoned. But if meaning is use, how can this be? If people are prevalently using a word a certain way, the word surely has a meaning; and the only available criticism of anyone who uses the word thus will surely be that they have said something false. The use of the word can't itself be criticized. So it might be argued.

It is a natural line of argument, and it might seem to follow from the idea expressed by Wittgenstein when he wrote: 'If language is to be a means of communication there must be agreement not only in definitions but also (queer as this may sound) in judgments' (*PI* 242). But of course Wittgenstein is here stating a necessary, not a sufficient, condition of language's being a means of communication. There might be prevalent agreement that such-and-such is 'morally obligatory', although the expression 'morally obligatory' is in truth devoid of real sense, and no genuine communication is achieved by means of it. This is precisely the picture which Anscombe paints for us. The 'prevalent use' turns out to be prevalent nonsense. In virtue of what?[7]

One key aspect of the use of 'moral obligation', 'morally ought', etc., as depicted by Anscombe, is that all sorts of reasons for doing something are rejected as inadequate. Reasons that cite what is needed (e.g. for a human being's health), or that cite established rules or customs, or that cite commands – none of these, it is alleged, touch the important issue, which is: What action am I morally obliged to do? For can't I always ask, 'But *ought* I to aim for what is needed, or what is dictated by rules, or what is commanded?'? Now it is true that one often can ask some such further question, especially about commands, for instance. But a general dissatisfaction with all 'factual' reasons raises the question: What can 'I ought to φ' amount to, if there can be no substantive reasons that fully support that judgment? The result of not accepting any substantive reasons as adequate answers to 'Why ought I to do that?' is to make that question futile and empty – and also that particular use of 'ought'. I am not suggesting that every instance of the question 'Why ought I to do that?' will in fact have a substantive answer, for explanations run out somewhere, and no answer can be given to one who asks, 'Why ought I to treat matchsticks as less valuable (more dispensable) than human beings?' The criteria determining what are good, bad, intelligible or unintelligible answers to the question 'Why?', in the context of a particular kind of enquiry, cannot themselves be interrogated by that question; and the fact that enquiry is a sort of social practice involving human beings gives a clue as to why the quoted question is a senseless attempt to interrogate such criteria. And it is worth noting that nothing would be achieved – or even said – by making out that there is simply a *moral obligation* to treat matchsticks as less valuable than human beings.

'You have to give reasons why lemurs (or matchsticks) ought to be treated as less valuable than human beings: we need grounds for this alleged moral obligation'; 'You tell me that it would be dishonest to do this, but is there a moral obligation to be honest?' In such statements, as characteristically used, the phrase 'moral obligation' does no real work. We felt as if we were saying something important when in reality we were saying nothing. For we in a sense *forgot the point* of certain language-games, e.g. those in which reasons for action are asked for or given.

Anscombe's account of the prevalent use of 'moral obligation', 'morally ought', etc. was connected by her with a diagnosis: aspects of that use are explicable by reference to an earlier system of belief, one involving divine commands. Without this system of belief, she argued, an expression like 'ought' – used in the way she was depicting – had 'become a word of mere mesmeric force' (ibid., 32). But it should be noted that Anscombe's genealogical diagnosis is optional. The important thing is the futility of what people are doing with language, a futility which they themselves do not recognize.[8] To quote Wittgenstein again: 'a wheel that can be turned though nothing else moves with it, is not part of the mechanism' (*PI* 271). What is interesting is that there can be a widespread illusion that a wheel is part of the mechanism which in fact *isn't* part of the mechanism. If all this is correct, Anscombe's view does not stand or fall with the genealogical diagnosis (in terms of the earlier belief system): her description of *use* is what is crucial. And the use of these words is bound up with how people act. The problem is thus not a 'merely' theoretical one – it is also a practical one. Indeed, Anscombe's main motive for critiquing the confused use of 'moral obligation', etc., is that this use naturally leads to, or lends itself to, people's abandonment of considerations of (in)justice in favour of considerations of what is expedient, in the context of actual practical deliberations.[9]

Futility will evidently infect language-games involving stopping and forcing modals if it becomes normal to respond with indifference to 'You're meant to', 'You can't', etc. The futility might not go unrecognized, in which case the language-game in question is liable to become a shell of its former self, or simply die out. This may well be true of various forms of etiquette, for example. But we should remember that etiquette blends with morality. If the prevalent response to 'You wronged X, so you should apologise to X' (logos followed by modal statement[10]) comes to be one of indifference, i.e. if the act-type *apologizing* becomes sufficiently rarely instantiated, then the status of 'You should apologize' will approach that of the wheel that can be turned though nothing else moves with it. In the beginning is the deed, in the end is nonchalance.

Illusion that a wheel is part of the mechanism when in fact it isn't attends the situation in which 'You're meant to' comes to be used *as if* there were logoi to back it up, or (more specifically) comes to be backed up by *ersatz* logoi. The language of rights often seems to involve this species of illusion/confusion, as when 'I've a right to such-and-such' gets backed up by a more or less arbitrary logos – as it might be, 'Other people who are no better than I am have such-and-such'. The purpose of the linguistic move is to seem to be playing a trump card when one has no trump card to play. This is most likely a subconscious or unconscious purpose, however, and the person proclaiming his right might feel genuinely aggrieved if it is not respected. The continuation of this state of affairs is made possible by (among other things) the attractiveness of certain *roles*: occupier of the moral high ground; person with a complaint; person deserving of our sympathy; person to whom airtime and limelight are owed. Whether this particular phenomenon is sufficiently widespread as to merit the soubriquet 'conceptual corruption' is an empirical matter, one that is beyond the scope of this essay. But it is hard to deny that public discourse offers many instances of the sort of thing I am talking about: language being used for ulterior motives, as we might put it.

Travails of Internalism

A person who has properly learnt the meanings of stopping/forcing modals, I have argued, is someone who is not merely able, but inclined, to 'respond appropriately' to their use, ceteris paribus. The picture of human agency which emerges from this is at odds with a popular philosophical position, viz. 'internalism' about reasons for acting.[11]

For an internalist, a person can have reasons for φ-ing only if φ-ing is somehow conducive to the satisfaction of that person's desires. (Obviously this formula can be tweaked in various ways, according to the version of internalism in question.) Let's imagine that you and I are playing chess, and you threaten my king with your rook. Perhaps observing my hesitation, you say, 'You have to move your king, it's in check' – forcing modal followed by logos. According to what I've been arguing the following is true: if I have properly learnt[12] the meaning of forcing modals, know the rules of chess and see no defeating circumstances in view, then I will, unless somehow prevented, move my king. My action will be intentional – I will be ready with a reason if asked 'Why did you do that?', my reason being 'My king was threatened'. At this point an internalist may say either or both of two things: (a) neither the statement 'You have to move your king' nor the statement 'Your king is in check' nor the conjunction of the statements can, by itself, give me a reason for moving my king; (b) the circumstance that I don't *want* to move my king (or: play by the rules) is in a trivial sense a possible defeater, since if I don't want this, I have no reason to move my king.

Taking (a) first, we might start by asking 'If that isn't a reason for action, what is?' But this sort of appeal to common sense is likely to be shrugged off. A more direct attack is to ask the internalist what sort of meaning and use can be ascribed to 'You have to φ'. The answer is liable to be that such a formula is either merely factual, or merely imperatival: it is thought that each of these options leaves room for the rational agent to treat or not to treat the formula as supplying a reason, according to her own subjective preferences.

'Factual' indicates some claim along the following lines: 'You have to move your king' means 'By the rules of chess, any move here other than moving your king is not a genuine chess-move'. The claim fails for at least two reasons. First, the rules of chess do not simply state what actions shall be *called* 'moves of chess', something that can be seen in the distinction between breaking a chess-rule and doing something other than moving. By the rules of chess, scratching one's head is not called a 'move of chess', but if I scratch my head I haven't thereby broken a rule of chess.[13] Second, the rules of chess in fact include such rules as that you *have to* move or defend your king when it is threatened.[14] So the proffered explanation of 'You have to move your king' is viciously circular in virtue of its mention of 'the rules of chess'.

As for the thought that 'You have to φ' is a mere imperative, we have already seen that this is mistaken. Forcing modals differ from imperatives in being conceptually tied to logoi. And it is significant that it is a logos that I am likely to give *as my reason* when asked, 'Why did you do that?'

What about (b), above? In response to your statement 'You have to move your king, it's in check' I say: 'Ah no; you see, I don't want to move my king.' Do I mention a defeating circumstance, in the sense in which the grocer's leaving a bag of potatoes two miles from my house is a defeating circumstance relative to both 'He delivered the potatoes' and 'I owe him £10'? Clearly not. What count as 'defeating circumstances' is determined by the practicalities of the given practice and (thus) of its attendant language-game; in general – though not always – an agent's mere lack of inclination to abide by one of the rules constitutive of a practice cannot be taken as, and so is not, an adequate reason for their not abiding by it.

It is often a truism to say that someone will only do something if she wants to. If I don't want to move my king I won't do so; ditto, if I want not to move it.[15] But these truisms give no support to internalism about reasons for acting. What people do, and what people want, can after all be unreasonable, even irrational. And it is often the rules of a practice that determine what rationality and irrationality amount to.

Consider language-use itself. Language is governed by rules: you can't call that a 'fox' (it's a flamingo), you're meant to say 'Yes' (if that's the answer), you may call this shade 'blue' (or 'green'). Here are Anscombe's modals in play.[16] A philosopher says, 'I have no reason to φ unless I want to.' Being sincere, she takes herself to be saying something true. Whether it's true depends on what, e.g., the word 'want' means in her statement. Could she say: 'I want to use this word in conformity with the rules governing its use – so I will'? But how is she using the word 'want' in *that* statement? That she uses words in conformity with the rules is a presupposition of her saying anything at all; she cannot *decide* to use words correctly, since the content of any such decision will already have committed her to the 'aim' of using words correctly. And yet following rules is, for the internalist, something one only has reason to do if doing so fits in with one's desires.

Could the philosopher perhaps *think* 'I want to use the word "want" in conformity with the rules governing its use – so I will'? If she thinks the thought in English, the same argument will apply as above. If she thinks it in a private language – putting aside conceivable qualms about such a notion – she must still take it as moot whether she wants to abide by the rules of this private language, including the rule governing 'I want'. (You are to take both occurrences of (inflexions of) 'want' in the previous sentence as standing proxy for putatively private symbols.) So the same argument goes through: for her to say that she *does* want to abide by that rule involves positing a certain decision as a rational prerequisite of itself – a nonsense.

Internalism about reasons for acting, if pushed to its logical conclusion, thus appears to result in a commitment to the ineffability of a certain kind of 'mental content'. An internalist must cite the desire to follow linguistic rules as that which gives the speaker reason to follow those rules, in the sense that if he lacks such a desire his breaking the rules cannot be deemed irrational (hence subject to criticism); and the content of this desire must be regarded as being determined independently of all rule-governed meaning. For the internalist conceives of a person as 'equipped' with some standing desires, in the light of which he will have reason to do some things and not others – and these desires will have to include the desire to use 'desire' in conformity with linguistic rules, public or private. But he cannot express, to himself or to others, the content of this desire (the one with which he is already equipped). To do so, he would have to have already made the decision (to use 'desire' ...) which we are envisaging him as now rationally making. In fact, the identity of the standing desire must float free of all norms, public or private.[17]

In which case it is hard to see how it could be compatible, or incompatible, with anything at all. 'So in the end when one is doing philosophy one gets to the point where one would like just to emit an inarticulate sound' (*PI* 261). Moreover, in any actual context of philosophical debate real words must be utilized. Ineffable thoughts are not on the table.

So how *should* we think about the matter? We imagined the philosopher saying, 'I have no reason to φ unless I want to.' The question we face – that which flummoxed the internalist – is: 'Did she have a reason for using the word "want" in accordance with the linguistic rules that govern it?' In other words: 'Why did she use the word "want" in accordance with the linguistic rules that govern it?' Now the question 'Why?', in its reason-demanding sense, is susceptible of a large variety of kinds of answer. Such answers typically depend on what the person asking the question is after. Does he have in mind some reason why it would be a good idea to *break* the linguistic rules in this situation? (Perhaps he takes it that the speaker is in fact attempting to illustrate certain common misuses of words.) In the absence of some such explanation for his enquiry, it is not clear what sort of answer can be given, unless it be 'There's no reason to break the rules here'. If that is allowed as a positive answer to 'Why?' then we may say that the speaker intentionally conformed to the linguistic rules when she spoke. But it is an odd saying. The facts are: she is a normal adult and she was speaking English. *Hence* she was following certain rules.

Could the internalist say some such thing? That is, could he make out that people use language, and hence follow linguistic rules, without their having *reasons* for following these rules? The problem is that the internalist cannot do justice to the asymmetry between following rules and breaking rules. According to the internalist, if someone who does X has no reason for doing X, that'll be because he has no operative desire to do X. This might make room for 'just following' linguistic rules, but if it does, then it will at the same time make room for 'just breaking' linguistic rules: if I lack the desire not to break the rules, I cannot be deemed irrational when I break them. But misusing language for no reason at all is a paradigmatic manifestation of irrationality – while one who 'systematically' misuses language lacks an intellectual and practical capacity (so perhaps no more *misuses* language than does a gurgling baby). Conversely, ordinary fluent language-use, i.e. following the rules, is a paradigm manifestation of human rationality.

'Ceteris paribus, one has reason to follow (not break) the rules governing the uses of words' is true enough. But if there is a 'Why?' question corresponding to this truth, it is something like: 'Why go in for linguistic communication at all?' In response to *this* question, we can perhaps point to all the many benefits of having language, as we can point to the benefits of going in for promising. However, it is not as if it is an option for us to *give up* using language; so the form of the question is misleading. It would be better if it were rephrased along these lines: 'What are (some of) the benefits of having language?' – a question of about the same level of generality as 'What are (some of) the benefits of being able to move around in space?'

Conclusion

Let me give a summary of these investigations. Understanding language is manifest in using language, which is a species of human activity. In teaching a person the meanings of words, we aim to instil in them an ability, but not, typically, a mere ability: we aim in fact to instil an ability *and* an inclination – namely, to use such-and-such words correctly. (To say this need not be to impute to the learner an *intention* to use those words correctly; that way of putting it is probably an over-intellectualization.) In the specific case of stopping and forcing modals, we additionally aim to instil the inclination to do (or not do) whatever is mentioned as that which you 'have to' or 'cannot' do. The criteria for a learner's understanding the meanings of such modals include her often enough doing (or not doing) the relevant things. An adult may count as understanding what the modals mean despite having developed an erratic inclination, or even disinclination, to do what she is meant to do, etc., on account of (a) the default assumption that speakers know the meanings of the words in their language, and (b) the existence of criteria for knowing and (more significantly) for not knowing the meanings of words, or not knowing that they apply *here*. In the absence of any of these latter criteria, the 'default assumption' (defeasibly) stands.

It is possible for it to become the norm, or at least normal, for people (e.g. in some societal group) to fail to respond appropriately to stopping and/or forcing modals of one kind or another. The more this is true, the less clear the meaning of what they say and do will be. Conceptual corruption and consequent widespread forms of nonsense are humanly possible; Anscombe proposed that this picture in fact held true, at the time when she wrote and at least as regards the philosophical community, of such terms as 'moral obligation' and 'the moral *ought*'. It seems hard to deny that public discourse offers various instances of this sort of linguistic and practical vacuity.

It is natural and tempting to regard thought, will and understanding as logically independent of action. The foregoing reflections on the meaning of Anscombean modals help to undermine this notion. (They are not the only reflections to do so.) Understanding, meaning and action are here closely intertwined. An internalist about reasons for action can be seen to buy into the mistaken notion of logical independence insofar as he claims (a) that rational action can only occur when an agent has a 'motivating reason' to do something, and (b) that one only has reason to follow a rule or rules to the extent that doing so is conducive to the satisfaction of one's standing, or prior, desires. But desiring to follow the rule 'In circumstances C you have to φ' presupposes knowing the meaning of 'You have to', 'C' and 'φ'. The criteria for understanding the meaning of these terms, however, include *doing* what you 'have to'. Thus desire to follow a rule is here logically posterior to action.

In connection with the rules governing the use of words (symbols), the internalist claim founders in dramatic fashion; for it can be said to commit the internalist to the nonsensical idea that the relevant desires are independent of the doings of the agent even to the extent of those desires' having ineffable content – from which it would follow that no distinction could be made between what would, and what would not, be conducive to their satisfaction.

In using language, or in having articulate thoughts, one *thereby* follows certain rules, and in that sense can be thought of as 'responding appropriately' to the modal statements expressive of those rules. This is what constitutes the rationality of one's talk or thought; it is not constituted by any conformity of rule-following with standing desires.[18]

Notes

1. I will refer to Wittgenstein's *Philosophical Investigations* (Wittgenstein 1958) as '*PI*'; unless otherwise specified, numbers refer to the numbered sections of Part I of that work.
2. A practice like promising is necessary for the attainment of important human goods, as Anscombe argues, so the wrong involved in breaking a promise is not merely that of breaking some rule or other.
3. We should perhaps add that the person 'belongs to the linguistic community', since no one will understand what's said in an unfamiliar language. But to belong to a linguistic community is simply to understand a whole lot of words and expressions (as speaker, reader, audience …); so the 'default position' I'm referring to is not adopted *prior to* talking and listening to someone, but itself crystallizes in those moments during which one's interaction with the person enables one, through a host of contextual and other 'clues', to proceed automatically in one's dealings with them as with a speaker of English (French/Catalan/Hindi …).
4. The phrase is Wittgenstein's; see *PI*, II xi, 228.
5. As is hinted in n. 3, the term 'assumption' is not a *psychological* one. Shared 'assumptions' are manifest in human *procedures*.
6. And of course we mustn't forget the frequently imperfect behaviour of parents towards their children, including in the context of teaching or training; a child's resistance or 'naughtiness' might be a form of self-protection, or expressive of a craving for love, or any number of things – rather than straightforward 'deficiency'.
7. What follows is both a condensation and an elaboration of what Anscombe says about this in 'Modern Moral Philosophy'. (Not as paradoxical as it sounds.)
8. 'Prevalent' does not mean 'universal'. Anscombe clearly did allow that someone who calls such-and-such 'morally obligatory' *might* mean something quite intelligible – as, that not doing such-and-such would be unjust, would wrong somebody. This would come out in what further things the person said (or did), e.g. by way of explanation.
9. See Anscombe (1981c, 38–42) (from 'I will end by describing …' to the end of the article).
10. 'You wronged X' and 'You should apologize to X' are not learnt as part of a 'package deal', in the way in which 'It's mine' and 'You can't take it' are. While the concept of apology is dependent on that of wronging someone (viz. the person to whom apology is owed, typically), the reverse doesn't hold – particularly in view of the fact that 'wronged X' is an abstraction from such particular cases as 'insulted X', 'maimed X', etc. But this doesn't prevent our calling 'You wronged X' a logos. The case is like that earlier alluded to: 'The music has stopped, so you have to sit down.'
11. See e.g. Williams (1981) and Smith (1987).
12. For the sense of this phrase see the concluding paragraph of sec. 2: you won't have properly learnt the meaning and use of modals if you have failed to acquire, or have lost, a standing inclination to respond appropriately to them.
13. It might be said that the rules of chess are silent as to whether scratching one's head is called a 'chess move'. Independently existing rules of *word-use* are what forbid calling scratching one's head a 'chess move'. – The phrase 'independently existing' is suspect, since the concept *chess move* only exists once the rules of chess exist. But in any case, the rules of chess are (*pace* the position under discussion) quite generally silent about word-use. Calling a legal move of the white king a 'chess move' is not prescribed by the rules of chess. In teaching a human being the rules of chess, we do indeed introduce words, e.g. by saying, 'This [pointing] is the white king.' But (a) we are not thereby stating a rule of chess, as the presence of the demonstrative shows, and (b) we don't, and couldn't, introduce 'chess move' in such a way. You learn what 'chess move' means by learning *how to play chess* – or by learning the concept *move* in the context of other games and learning that there's a game called 'chess' in connection with which that concept is used.
14. That's to say, *if* you can do so without breaking another rule; if you can't, you're checkmated. This mention, within a rule, of other rules of the game aptly illustrates how the rules of a practice must be learnt as a 'package deal'.

15 The truism shouldn't be taken as a universal truth; after all, ordinary usage certainly allows 'I did what I had to, though I really didn't want to'.
16 A child first learns to use words correctly and only later learns the meaning of such a formula as 'You can't say that (use that word here, etc.)'. Language is rule-governed, though its speakers don't need to have such concepts as 'rule', 'have to' or 'cannot' in order to count as linguistically competent. There must, however, exist practices of correcting and confirming within a linguistic community, and a community in which articulate reflection upon such practices is possible will be one in which Anscombean modals (or equivalents) get used. What of the logoi to be used in conjunction with these modals? These are very various in kind; some enjoy a conceptual interdependence with their correlative modal statements ('You can't call him Mark, his name is Max'), and some do not.
17 An internalist who is content with a third-personal, behaviouristic conception of desire might embrace the ideas of norm-free desire and of norm-free practical rationality. A person desirous of following linguistic rules would on this account simply be, in effect, one who did in fact (often) conform to those rules, as a calculator might be said to conform to arithmetical rules. Apart from anything else, this view makes no room for that asymmetry between linguistic competence and incompetence which I go on to discuss.
18 Thanks to Richard Gipps for helpful feedback on an earlier draft of this chapter.

References

Anscombe, G. E. M. (1963), *Intention*. Oxford: Blackwell, 2nd ed.

———. (1981a), 'On Promising and Its Justice', in *Collected Papers Vol. III: Ethics, Religion and Politics*. Oxford: Blackwell, pp. 10–21.

———. (1981b), 'On Brute Facts', in *Collected Papers Vol. III: Ethics, Religion and Politics*. Oxford: Blackwell, pp. 22–25.

———. (1981c), 'Modern Moral Philosophy', in *Collected Philosophical Papers Vol. III: Ethics, Religion and Politics*. Oxford: Basil Blackwell, pp. 26–42.

———. (1981d), 'Rules, Rights and Promises', in *Collected Philosophical Papers Vol. III: Ethics, Religion and Politics*. Oxford: Basil Blackwell, pp. 97–103.

Smith, M. (1987), 'The Humean Theory of Motivation', *Mind*, 96, 36–61.

Williams, B. (1981), 'Internal and External Reasons', in *Moral Luck*. Cambridge: Cambridge University Press, pp. 101–13.

Wittgenstein, L. (1958), *Philosophical Investigations*, trans. G. E. M. Anscombe, ed. G. E. M. Anscombe and R. Rhees. Oxford: Basil Blackwell, 2nd ed.

Chapter Eight

WHY 'WHY?'? ACTION, REASONS AND LANGUAGE

Not a Heuristic Device

> What distinguishes actions that are intentional from those which are not? The answer that I shall suggest is that they are the actions to which a certain sense of the question 'Why?' is given application; the sense is of course that in which the answer, if positive, gives a reason for acting. (Anscombe 1963, 9)

This is the famous nub of Anscombe's account of intentional action. By 'the question "Why?"' she means such questions as: 'Why are you doing that?', 'Why did you do that?' and so on. Anscombe proceeds to investigate and explain *what* sense of the question 'Why?' is at issue, by contrasting it with other senses of 'Why?', by delineating the sorts of case where the question is refused application, by distinguishing certain forms of positive answer to it, etc.

We may first note that Anscombe's question 'Why?' is in the second person,[1] being addressed to the (putative) agent. This is among other things connected with a certain primacy that, according to Anscombe, is enjoyed by a person's own statement of his reasons for acting. Now it is no part of Anscombe's thesis that an action is only intentional if the agent actually *does* give the requisite sort of answer to 'Why?' – after all, it might be that nobody asks him that question. We could if we liked propose a possibly counter-factual conditional statement, 'Were the agent to be (or have been) asked "Why …?", he would/could answer (or have answered) such-and-such' – but only so long as we don't take ourselves to be giving an analysis or definition of 'intentional action'. For such an analysis or definition would be no good, for various reasons – such as that brute animals can act intentionally.

How then are we to understand the role of the question 'Why?' in Anscombe's account? I shall be proposing an answer along the following lines. Our use and grasp of the concept of the intentional, and of many of the concepts with which it is connected (*voluntary, plan, aim, for the sake of, responsible, desirability* …), have their roots in a certain pervasive language-game, that of asking for and giving reasons – reasons for action, as we come to call them. If we describe this language-game and its offshoots in sufficient detail, i.e. in the right *sort* of detail, we will cast light on at least a portion of this network of concepts. What will count as 'sufficient detail'? Answer: detail sufficient for our purposes, which in philosophy are themselves liable to be various, and in this case can come from various directions: from questions in ethics, or concerning mind and body, or our knowledge of the future, or ... In *Intention* we find a number of these questions either addressed or indicated, and of course it is very unlikely that Anscombe would have thought that her monograph represented 'the last word' on the topic, whatever that could mean.

But there are readers of Anscombe who, if unsympathetic, will regard her apparent interest in the workings of language as unphilosophical, or, if sympathetic, will prefer to see her allusions to such things as questions and their answers as a sort of heuristic device only. These latter may re-write what she says so as to conform with the 'post-linguistic turn' mode of philosophizing now generally preferred, in which the questions tackled are taken to be about *things*, and (therefore) not about words. An example of this re-writing tendency is supplied by the entry (dating from November 2011) for 'Gertrude Elizabeth Margaret Anscombe' in the online *Stanford Encyclopedia of Philosophy*, in which the author, Julia Driver, writes:

> Anscombe notes that 'intention' figures into our language in a variety of ways, through different locutions. The three she notes are:
>
> 1. A is xing intentionally. (Adverb)
> 2. A is xing with the intention of doing y. (Noun)
> 3. A intends to do y. (Verb)

These three locutions are meant to correspond to the three heads under which Anscombe introduces her topic (1963, sec. 1), and the third is meant to do duty for Anscombe's 'expressions of intention for the future' – such expressions being linguistic. It seems that linguistic expressions can't be what really interest Anscombe, so the reference to such expressions is eliminated. But apart from anything else, the expressions of intention which Anscombe goes on, immediately, to discuss (sec. 2, 3) do not even employ 'intend' or 'intention': it is rather important for her project that they are such simple future-tensed statements as 'I am going to buy some milk'. It is also important that they are not in the third person, as 'A intends to do y' is. Driver's re-writing is, I think, ill-advised. The source of this particular revision of Anscombe is probably Donald Davidson, who refers to 'the three main uses of the concept of intention distinguished by Anscombe (acting with an intention, acting intentionally, and intending to act)'.[2]

But still, when it comes to Anscombe's 'Why?', mightn't she be using it more or less as a heuristic device? Mightn't it be possible in the end to re-write what she says so as to be about things and not words? *Must* we go along with the version of the enterprise given a couple of paragraphs back, to do with a language-game of asking for and giving reasons?

There are several places where Anscombe highlights features of possible dialogues involving 'Why?', and where those features point to there being certain (more or less implicit) *purposes* had by the parties to the dialogue. The purposes will be different for the asker of the question and the giver of the answer, and typically the asker of the question, if asking it in good faith etc., can be seen as desiring an *account* of some actual or proposed action, an account which will 'make sense' of it; and the ways in which sense can be made of an action are various, relating as they do to various human interests. I have mentioned 'purposes' and 'interests'; both of these will put constraints on what could count as a legitimate or intelligible answer, and also on what could count as a legitimate or intelligible posing of the question 'Why?'

Consider the following three episodes from *Intention*:

In sec. 13, Anscombe introduces the idea of interpretative motives, or motives-in-general. Such motives are often expressed in English with phrases starting with 'out of' or 'from', such as: 'I did it out of loyalty' or 'He acted from spite'. Anscombe writes:

> To give a motive (of the sort I have labelled 'motive-in-general' [...]) is to say something like 'See the action in this light'. To explain one's own actions by an account indicating a motive is to put them in a certain light. This sort of explanation is often elicited by the question 'Why?' (1963, 21)

In sec. 15, she discusses the sometimes imprecise boundary between answers that give a reason and ones that give a cause. An imaginary dialogue goes: 'Why did you do it?' – 'Because he told me to.' Whether the answer gives a cause or a reason 'appears to depend very much on what the action was or what the circumstances were' (1963, 23). And,

> roughly speaking [...] the more the action is described as a mere response, the more inclined one would be to the word 'cause'; while the more it is described as a response to something as *having a significance* that is dwelt on by the agent in his account, or as a response surrounded with thoughts and questions, the more inclined one would be to use the word 'reason'. [...] Roughly speaking, it establishes something as a reason if one argues against it [...] in such a way as to link it up with motives and intentions: 'You did it because he told you to? But why do what he says?' Answers like 'He has done a lot for me' [etc.] give the original answer a place among reasons. (1963, 23–24)

Finally, in sec. 27, Anscombe asks in what sense it is true that 'only I know what my intention is'; and having pointed out the requirement that a person's statement of intention be sincere and truthful, something for which there can be external tests of the same sort that may be applied to a person's *later* account of what he did, Anscombe writes of such a statement of intention:

> Given that it survives all the same external tests, it comes under the same last determination: '*In the end* only you can know whether that is your intention or not'; that means only: there comes a point where a man can say 'This is my intention,' and no one else can contribute anything to settle the matter. (It does not mean that when he says 'This is my intention,' he is evincing a knowledge available only to him. I.e. here 'knows' means only 'can say'.) (1963, 47–48)

In each of these episodes the significance of an agent's reason-giving statement is tied to a certain kind of (possible) dialogue or dialogues, in which the other party is not just an Ideal Interlocutor, but rather a human being desiring specifically human enlightenment. (a) It takes a human being to be able to 'see an action in such-and-such a light' (and also to find in this a kind of *explanation*): much human background is needed to see what someone did as e.g. patriotic. (b) To understand how a response can be 'surrounded with thoughts and questions' likewise requires much human background; and the imagined counter-statement 'But why do what he says?' involves all sorts of human presuppositions and standards, and also brings to the fore the role of the *language-game*. (It is a direct response to what the agent said, in a way in which 'Are you sure he told you to?' or 'So you believe in free will, do you?' would not be.) (c) The point where 'no one else can contribute anything to settle the matter' is a point in a dialogue or discussion, one that is not (as Anscombe says) reached because the agent has access to knowledge the rest of us don't have access to, but is reached when the primary thing, the person's statement of intention, stands naked and unimpugned. We could say: this move in the game ('This is my intention') just does count as determinative.

Wittgenstein's notion of a language-game, a notion that Anscombe herself quite often makes use of in her writings, is of course a simile or metaphor. We are not talking of games that anyone has made up, or that have rules laid down somewhere, or that are participated in 'just for their own sake'. (Not that any of these is a necessary condition of gamehood; cf. *Philosophical Investigations*, 66.)[3] In speaking of the language-game of asking for and giving reasons, I mean to be driving at this: that a person's account (justification, etc.) of her actions is what it is because of its role as a possible response to others' questioning, where the specific nature of that questioning derives from background human needs and interests, these needs and interests being above all what explain (i) the existence in our language of this kind of enquiry-and-response, and (ii) the forms which this enquiry-and-response does in fact take. Part of what is involved in acquiring a mastery of language is learning the forms mentioned under (ii), i.e. learning the roles both of enquirer and of reason-giving agent.

We do of course ascribe intentions to people as well as announce our own. But there are good grounds for thinking that the first-personal expression of intention, for the future or as regards past or present action, plays a criterially central role. We see an aspect of this role alluded to in the third of the three quotations above; it is evident also in a case like the following: someone mixing cement may answer 'Why are you doing that?' with the reply, 'I'm building a wall.' If he e.g. dies before doing much more than gathering some bricks and mixing some cement, it is still true to say 'He was building a wall', for his say-so is determinative. (That this is defeasible, e.g. in pathological cases, does not detract from the determinative role of the expression of intention; the *default* position is that it has that role.) If I later say 'He was building a wall', I am obviously not e.g. making a counterfactual prediction inductively based on an observed connection between someone's saying 'I'm building a wall' and his subsequently completing the job of building a wall – or anything of the sort.[4]

Anscombe certainly regards first-personal expression of intention for the future as essential to our concept of intention; this is the conclusion of her notoriously difficult argument in sec. 20 of *Intention*. In the course of this argument she makes considerable use of the idea that our ways of drawing distinctions, classifying events, etc., are based on human *purposes*, so that if some imaginary concept (e.g. that of 'intention' minus the possibility of expressions of intention for the future) would fail to cater for the purposes catered for by our actual concept, then the two concepts are different. And these purposes are often to be looked for as embodied (or not) in the dialogues constitutive of some language-game.[5]

Voluntariness and Responsibility

I have outlined what I take to be the rationale, or part of the rationale, behind Anscombe's use of the question 'Why?' And I think that her philosophical instincts were entirely sound in this matter. If I am right, then light can be cast on many a philosophical problem to do with action by considering a context of (possible) enquiry and the human purposes and interests that lie behind it.

A good example is the sort of context in which 'Why didn't you …?' gets asked. This question *can* be a form of Anscombe's reason-eliciting 'Why?', but it very often is not. Someone might reply to the question 'Why didn't you stand up when they started playing the National Anthem?' by saying, 'So as to show my disdain for that sort of thing,' or 'Out of disdain …' (an interpretative motive); but the following sort of dialogue is evidently different: 'Why didn't you hoover up that mess?' – 'I couldn't be bothered.' A franker substitute for this answer might be 'Out of laziness', but that statement would not give a *motive*, in the sense in which disdain or patriotism can be motives. And in fact 'I couldn't be bothered' has a rather different function from 'Out of laziness': it in effect presents a (probably hypothetical) situation of deliberation, in which the agent is depicted as ruling out doing the hoovering on the grounds that it would be bothersome. His hypothetical self thus weighs one sort of reason against another – the pros of tidying up versus the pros of non-exertion – and decides that the latter outweigh the former. One who says 'I couldn't be bothered' is unlikely to do so on the basis of remembering certain facts about what he had thought or done; there may be nothing much to report there beyond some vague images or the like. Rather, he as it were puts words into the mouth of his former self (or thoughts into the mind). And he is not giving a cause or causal condition of his non-hoovering, as he would if he had said, 'I fainted' or 'My brother locked me in the coal shed.' *That* is not the sort of explanation he is proffering.

Although 'I couldn't be bothered' doesn't give a reason for (in)action, in the sense of 'reason' that is Anscombe's main quarry in *Intention*, it nevertheless belongs in the 'space of reasons'. The hypothetical deliberative scenario shows this; and so do the likely counter-responses from the other person, such as 'But you're perfectly healthy; and it was you that made the mess'. The intelligibility of 'I couldn't be bothered' as a reply to 'Why didn't you?' depends on various background facts, e.g. that there was a humanly recognizable reason to hoover. This latter fact of course also, and connectedly, supplies the ground of intelligibility for the *question*; if someone asked you as you walked down the road, 'Why didn't you stand on your head as you came level with that dustbin?', the appropriate response is likely to be 'Why should I have?' – not 'I couldn't be bothered', nor yet 'I didn't think of it'. For there is no apparent reason to stand on one's head in that circumstance.

What philosophical interest do these considerations have? Here is one line of thought arising out of them. It is sometimes said that you are responsible for the foreseen or foreseeable effects of your voluntary doings or not-doings. The lazy person above is responsible for the non-disappearance of the mess, since he voluntarily chose not to hoover it up. (This can be so independently of whether he made the mess, by the way.) But 'chose to' can suggest, what may be false, that there was a conscious decision; this 'choosing' may have simply been embodied in the (non)-action, and if we are to ascribe voluntariness here, it is really to the non-hoovering that we ascribe it. Now if I knowingly walk past a dustbin without standing on my head, do I do so voluntarily?

Someone might reply, 'Well, if choosing not to hoover can be embodied in knowingly not hoovering, won't knowingly not standing on your head likewise embody choosing not to stand on your head? Which would make that non-doing voluntary.' But this would be to lose sight of the point (or points) of the concept of voluntariness. When we say that what someone did was voluntary, we are typically saying of what she did that it was, in some sense, in conformity with the orientation of her will; and this in large part accounts for the connection between voluntariness and responsibility. Philosophers have often seen voluntariness or conformity with the will as matters of what is true of, or going on in, the agent at the time – often proposing some kind of efficacy or power as the key phenomenon (e.g. a 'two-way power', of φ-ing or not φ-ing). But this is a mistake. Something's being in conformity with the orientation of one's will is much more a matter of one's reasons for doing or not doing things, as these might be elicited by forms of the question 'Why?' Let me illustrate this with another example.

In a discussion of Aquinas, Anscombe refers to a man's being dragged violently by others, and she considers whether such an occurrence could be 'from the man's will'. She writes:

> A movement's being 'from his will' here [i.e. in Aquinas] means the same as its being physiologically voluntary; it is of course not excluded by 'not from his will' for him to have arranged with some people in advance that they should drag him. If he had, then his being dragged would be voluntary, though not physiologically so, and the violence would be being exercised on his body, not on his will or intention. (Anscombe 2008, 129)

Clearly, a person can be in whatever state physiologists decide characterizes involuntary acts (or happenings) though the act (or happening) in question is voluntary – under some description. Being dragged by arrangement would be an example of this. We may even imagine that the man being dragged goes in for resistance, putting up a fight, etc. Perhaps he reckons that this will make for verisimilitude; he is in fact a bank clerk in collusion with bank robbers, and has to seem to have been coerced to those who will view the CCTV footage. Since the robbers are together much stronger than him, he can safely resist them without fear of success. What does it mean to say that some shove of his is an act of resistance? Isn't an act of physical resistance a voluntary – in fact, intentional – act, whose aim is to prevent being coerced? But doesn't the man *want* to be coerced? It is tempting to use Anscombe's mode of speaking and say that the resisting shove is only 'physiologically' voluntary; and indeed it seems likely that if physiologists find states which can be associated with voluntary actions, some such state will be present when the man gives his resisting shove. But the description 'resisting shove' brings with it an aim: are we then to speak of an act's being physiologically *intentional*?

The solution to these difficulties lies in the wider circumstances, and in the way these show what the bank clerk's aims were. For we can say: had it not been for the prior arrangement and planning with the robbers, certain acts would have counted simply as intentional under the description *resisting coercion*, acts which – on account of that prior planning – also or instead count as intentional under the description *facilitating a bank robbery*. I say 'also or instead' because it does seem that the issue of whether the clerk is really resisting, or even really shoving, is intrinsically problematic: to avoid confusion we should probably use some phrase like 'doing what would be straightforward resistance were it not for the prior planning'. We can it seems also say that something which in the absence of the prior planning would have counted simply as involuntary under the description *being dragged* counts in fact as voluntary under that same description.[6] It would be in the light of this last fact that the bank clerk could be held responsible, not just for helping plan the robbery, but for his part in the robbery itself. The relevance to this of the answer he would (if honest) have to give to such a question as 'Why did you struggle like that?' is clear. The answer would be 'To appear convincing' – by contrast with 'To try to stop them'. The further question 'Why appear convincing, and to whom?' would yield a further answer, and the series of 'Why?' questions thus set in train would eventually uncover the overriding intention, namely *to facilitate the robbing of the bank*. (Or we could put it in terms of a third-personal aim: *that my mates X, Y and Z rob the bank*.)

Voluntariness and responsibility in this sort of case are to be determined via (possible) answers to 'Why?' Let us now return to the alternative question, 'Why didn't you …?', and to the topics of voluntariness and responsibility, as these are to be illuminated by possible answers to *that* question.

What kind of answer would be given to the question, 'Why didn't you stand on your head?'? If we can assume it would be 'Why should I have?' – or perhaps 'I had no reason to' – then it is not that not-standing-on-the-head played some even hypothetical role in the person's practical reasoning; it had no connection at all with her practical reasoning, and her inaction shows nothing about the orientation of her will, beyond the obvious fact that she appears to lack a standing desire to stand on her head near dustbins. That nothing substantive can be inferred about her orientation of will is not due to the evidential status of inaction or not-doing as such: *some* not-doings supply very good evidence of orientation of will. Rather, it is due to the fact that *there was no reason to stand on one's head* in that situation. The question 'Why didn't you stand on your head?' was absurd; it was a pretend move of a familiar language-game, not a genuine one (rather as 'Hello, my name's John Smith – pleased to meet you' would be a pretend introduction, if said facetiously by a husband to his wife of twenty years). And the statement that the person was *responsible* for not standing on her head is likewise absurd, a piece of nonsense.[7]

Thus the sorts of things that go into a description of someone's orientation of will, which is to say the sorts of things that go into a description of (aspects of) his character, are things whose salience derives from background standards of the reasonable, the normal, the needed, the humanly natural. For it is these standards that determine what there is reason to do, or not to do. 'He's the sort of person who doesn't pay his debts' is informative, something that cannot be said of 'She's the sort of person who doesn't stand on her head near dustbins' – and not just because the sort of person who does do that is so very rare. The disposition not to stand on your head near dustbins isn't a *character trait* at all.[8]

My statement 'There was no reason to stand on one's head' must be seen as being about external reasons, as they are called: reasons that are external to the particular desires and preferences both of the person asking 'Why?' and of the person being asked it. Let us imagine that the former calls out, as Sally approaches the dustbin, 'Stand on your head, would you? I would very much appreciate it.' It will still be a normal and warranted response to 'Why didn't you stand on your head?' for Sally to say, 'Why should I have?' For the other person's statement 'I want it' does not supply Sally with a reason. This point holds not only as regards giving practical reasons to others, but also as regards giving one's own reasons: an agent's statement 'I want it' supplies no reason in the context of a practical syllogism, where, as Anscombe points out, the goal of the deliberating person is shown in his drawing such-and-such a conclusion from such-and-such premises, rather than itself being stated in a premise, 'I want …'[9] (As with theoretical syllogisms, it is the premises that supply reasons to be adduced in support of the conclusion.) Conversely, if the non-hooverer responds to 'Why didn't you hoover up that mess?' by saying, 'I didn't want to', he says less than he would say with 'I couldn't be bothered': behind the latter answer, as I have argued, is an implicit weighing of reasons – the pros of hoovering versus the pros of non-exertion. The person may of course mis-weigh those reasons; but the reasons which he thus mis-weighs are not reasons simply in virtue of tying in with his own desires and preferences.

An internalist about reasons might agree that 'I want …' does not supply a practical reason, saying instead that an agent may 'value' something – non-exertion, say – and more specifically, value it more/less than certain other things, so that to 'Why didn't you …?' he may e.g. reply, 'The alternative was sitting on the sofa.' This would count as a reason, but only from the point of view of the agent (and agents like him) – that is, only because of what he happens to want or prefer. But although on this view the agent needs to say more than just 'I wanted X', all that is required of him beyond this is that he should be able to say 'I wanted X more than I wanted Y' (e.g. non-exertion more than a hoovered floor); for that, on the internalist view, states the fact in virtue of which 'The alternative to Y was X' counts as giving a reason at all. But the non-hooverer who responds to 'Why didn't you …?' with 'I wanted to relax more than I wanted the floor hoovered' has not really advanced beyond the position of saying 'I didn't want to hoover it'. He at best tells us about himself; and while this *could* be what we were after, it will not be a pertinent reply if we were after something like justification – if we want him to give an account of himself.[10] If that is what we are after, the reasons he gives us had better go beyond his personal preferences.

That practical reasons should be 'external' in this way connects with what may be called the objectivity of the language-game. The sort of enquiry-and-response we have been considering plays a particular role in human life, meets definite human needs; so what counts as a genuine, or for that matter sensible, move is not a merely subjective matter, any more than it is in actual games like chess. It is typically not up to me what shall count as a (good) reason for doing or not doing something. Of course, there are some situations where personal preference or pleasure is the point of the enterprise, so that 'I want to' (or 'I'd like it', etc.) does count as a reason. But this is not the usual case.

The above remarks have a bearing on ethics, insofar as they throw doubt on the sort of ethical subjectivism that relies upon internalism about practical reasons. That sort of subjectivism is quite often called 'Humean', and it does in fact tend to go with a view of voluntary and intentional action as *caused by* certain mental states of the agent, much as we find in Hume. The role of practical reasons gets reduced to an aspect of agent-causality, and this makes it rather difficult to construct the sort of inter-subjective (= objective) standards which, by contrast, are characteristic of the language-game of asking for and giving reasons. One might also surmise that the focus on what 'goes on in' the agent, and on what his personal preferences and desires are, finds support from the individualism that is characteristic of our culture; though, if I am right, the appeal to personal preferences which underlies internalism about reasons must involve a clash with the actual social point of the language-game, a clash which might well be called conceptual confusion.

Confusion in this area seems to infect various ideas prevailing in our culture, such as those that surround the phenomenon of taking offence. We often find here a kind of doublethink: there is (a) the recognition that a person really can, in being offended, have just cause for complaint, on account of the reasons behind his taking offence – but on top of this there is (b) a denial of the requirement that taking offence itself be justified by reference to any reasons. Given (b), the only thing to point to as the ground of your complaint is simply the painfulness of the emotion; and so the whole phenomenon is subsumed under a general utilitarian proscription on causing suffering. But it is clear that taking offence can be unreasonable, and can on that account fail to provide any reason why another should alter his or her behaviour. (I might unreasonably take offence at your declining my offer of a favourite headache cure, for instance.) Moreover, there are conceptual constraints on what can count as offence. Someone who insists that he is offended by the actions of the government of a foreign country, e.g. its passing certain laws, is like someone who says that he forgives what the Bolsheviks did to the Romanov family, when what he ought to say is that he thinks the Bolsheviks aren't to be blamed for what they did. What the first person feels may properly be called anger or disgust, but not offence. Things are not necessarily any better if he calls the foreign government's actions 'offensive', for although he need not in that case claim to feel the offence himself, he must be able to say who could, and he must also justify calling it offence.

Both kinds of error are common, that of putting offence above rational criticism, and that of describing something as offensive when offence is the wrong concept to use. These errors are not mere mistakes, however, for they have a (generally unconscious) motivation: to confer on one's moral stance both an immunity from criticism and the flavour and seriousness of an accusation.[11] But nothing can combine these two features. The language-game of accusation is one in which reasons and counter-reasons play an essential role. Without such reasons, all that you have is a kind of shout: 'Stop it!' Once again, the diagnosis we need is one that adverts to the language-game of asking for and giving reasons, and to the objectivity inherent in that language-game.

'Mental State': An Unhelpful Notion

Topics such as *intention, the voluntary, the emotion of offence* are all liable to be put in a bag called Philosophy of Mind. Philosophers of mind very often want to introduce a given topic as being about a certain mental state or process, so we might well find these topics in effect appearing under certain headings (e.g. 'intentions', 'volitions', 'emotions'), together with guiding questions of the form 'What is X?' The job of the philosopher, it is thought, is to enquire into the *nature* of intending, say, or of taking offence – these being particular kinds of mental states, states which may be ascribed to oneself, or to another, in the present, past or future tenses, etc.

On such a view, the so-called asymmetry of first-personal and third-personal uses of a psychological verb (e.g. 'I intend' vs 'She intends') is a prima facie difficulty. I can say 'I intend' without having to observe or take note of anything in my present or past, whereas I must rely on observation or perception when saying of Sarah that she intends to holiday in Morocco. And there are other differences between the two sorts of use. But if these two uses of 'intend' are so different, doesn't that mean that the word is ambiguous? But surely if I report Sarah's expression of intention by saying 'Sarah intends ...' then I am saying of her exactly what she said of herself? Surely I am ascribing *the very same mental state* to her as she ascribes to herself, in a way that rules out the word's being ambiguous? Which in turn must mean that the meaning of a word cannot after all be very closely linked with its use. Grist to the anti-Wittgensteinian mill!

The first thing to point out is that 'Does X mean the same as Y?' does not have a once-for-all Yes or No answer. For there are different possible notions of synonymy, more or less stringent, and serving different purposes. There is even a notion of sentential synonymy as phrase-by-phrase intertranslatability, such that two pieces of gibberish mean the same. (One can produce a piece of French nonsense that is a good translation of 'A half-empty square root of ducklings recurred with avuncular butter'.) With individual words, the point is if anything even clearer. Does 'in' mean the same in 'There's a nail in my shoe', 'There's a hole in my shoe', 'There's a pain in my foot', 'Alex is in pain', 'Alex is in debt', 'Alex is in a quandary' ...? How many senses of 'in' have we here? A silly question, if asked in a vacuum.

If we turn to 'intend', and ask whether it has the same or a different meaning in 'I intend ...' and 'Sarah intends ...', we may answer Yes or No, depending on how fine-grained a notion of meaning we have in mind. Now there is a fairly clear sense in which 'intend' is not (as it appears in these sentences) ambiguous in the way in which 'rose' is ambiguous in the sentences 'It rose up from the depths' and 'He gave her a rose'.[12] And it is of some interest to enquire what *sort* of synonymy is attributable to the two uses of 'intend', and what grounds it, given the differences in usage. The picture that must be rejected is one in which two occurrences of 'intend' mean the same because in each occurrence the *same state* is referred to or meant. Wittgenstein writes:

> 'The red which you imagine is surely not the same (not the same thing) as the red which you see in front of you; so how can you say that it is what you imagined?' – But haven't we an analogous case with the propositions 'Here is a red patch' and 'Here there isn't a red patch'?

The word 'red' occurs in both; so this word cannot indicate the presence of something red. (*PI*, sec. 443)

There is nothing in common to the situations of a thing's being red and another thing's not being red. So what justifies our using the same word in both situations? The answer is that nothing justifies it – just as nothing justifies our employing the sound 'red' instead of the sound 'quork'.[13] There is a *fact* – the fact that we, the members of a linguistic community, do use 'red' in a wide variety of interconnected situations, in various interconnected propositional contexts. Other examples of such interconnectedness include: that the use of 'I intend to build a wall' and 'Roger intends to build a wall' are connected in certain ways. For there are certain familiar and recurrent phenomena of human life, involving behaviours, events, human needs, etc., which make sense of our having developed a particular sort of language-game, i.e. a rule-governed practice typically involving both actions and words (words such as 'intend'). And where a language-game manifests a certain unity (which is why we pick it out as one language-game), the various uses of a given word within that language-game will very often count as meaning the same, in virtue of the interconnections between the uses. It is not that the language-game is unified in virtue of the different uses of an expression all having the same meaning ('referring to the same *state*'), but rather the other way around. For the notions *meaning* and *state* do not bring with them a single, univocal criterion of identity – any more than does the notion *thing*.

I mentioned earlier the fact that it is a criterion of X's building a wall that X says he's building a wall. So the connection between what a person does and what he says he intends to do (or just: what he says he is doing) is not purely contingent. Nevertheless, it is contingent that our accounts of what we are doing are sufficiently in harmony with our actions to enable those accounts to play the criterial role that they do play. The practice of giving an account of what one is doing depends for its continued existence on the empirical fact that people do not very often naturally and spontaneously say bizarre things about what they are up to (e.g. 'I'm writing a symphony,' said by the man with the bricks). And 'bizarreness' is here largely determined by what observers can make sense of. The account given by the person himself and the account given by other people hold one another in check. This is the social nature of the language-game; and the 'holding one another in check' by different uses of some expression ties in with that synonymy between them which arises from the unity of the language-game. There is of course the quite general formal principle: if N truly says 'I am F', then N is F – the consequent of which is equivalent to 'Another can truly say "N is F"'. This principle may be looked on as a semantic rule governing 'I'. It requires that the uses of 'I am F' and 'N is F' *be in step*; but what it *is* for them to be in step for a given 'F', and what makes that possible, are matters lying outside the principle itself.

There is reason, then, to tackle philosophical questions about e.g. intention by looking at the language-game in which 'intend' and other related expressions get used – rather than by starting with some question like 'What is an intention?', under the impression that this is a question about a particular sort of 'mental state', whose nature we wish to delineate. Any determinacy that might be available to us in the notion of a mental state will be courtesy of facts to do with the language-game, and not vice versa.

Some Implications

We can now see how wrong-headed it would be to rewrite Anscombe so as to eliminate references to questions, answers, dialogues, utterances and so on, hoping to replace these with talk about mental states, or more generally with talk about non-linguistic 'events and processes'. An example would be using Davidson's 'intending to act' in place of Anscombe's 'expression of intention for the future'. For to think that our talk simply reports, or somehow lines up with, independently conceivable states and events is naïve, and particularly so when the key concepts (e.g. that of a *reason*) are to be hunted down in certain sorts of dialogue, e.g. what I've called the enquiry-and-response dialogue involving 'Why?' Some philosophers worry that that way lies a linguistic form of idealism. It does not; and Anscombe perceived this well enough.[14]

There are many implications. One such is that the notion of causation is often inappropriate as a tool for explaining (aspects of) intentional or voluntary action. There is not a *total* dichotomy between cause and reason, and in the second of the three quotations from Anscombe I gave earlier we find a realistic depiction of a conceptual continuum between the two.[15] But if we follow Anscombe in regarding the question 'Why?' as providing the key to the concept of intentional action, and in seeing first-personal expressions of intention as criterially central, typically ungrounded, statements about past, present or future actions (as opposed to statements about current mental states), then we will find the model of intentional actions as agent-events caused by intentions (or belief/desire pairs, etc.) to be necessarily inadequate.

Thus: a person may declare her intention in sincerely answering the question 'Why are you doing that?' Her answer gives, or purports to give, a reason – e.g. 'I'm building a wall', or 'Because he killed my brother'. It may (or may not) be met with a further question or statement, such as 'Why do you want a wall *here*?', or 'But your brother was attacking him'. And so on. There is no mention in all this of any 'mental state', let alone an implication of causal relations involving such a state; and to start positing such things e.g. by saying, 'The person must be predicting her building of a wall on the basis of introspective awareness of an intention' is to impose a picture that in no way arises out of the simple facts we have stated – an alien picture, in fact.[16] And in imposing such a picture, it distracts us from the sort of enquiry which more naturally, not to mention fruitfully, investigates the nature of the dialogue we have described: its purpose or point, the role it plays in human life, the similarities and differences between it and other human interactions and so on.

Of course the imposition of the causalist picture does not arise out of a misreading of the phenomenon of enquiry and response; it arises because the philosopher has already adopted that picture, and now applies it to that phenomenon. The explanation, or diagnosis, of the philosopher's embracing of the picture must take place independently.

Another implication of our adopting an approach that looks to the language-game(s) is that we can see more clearly the connection between the topics of intention, voluntariness, etc. and such ethical topics as responsibility, means and ends, (un)reasonableness, etc. The language-game of asking for and giving reasons for action has various points in human life, and many of these evidently deserve to be called ethical; and one might go further – or sideways – and say that a fairly crucial area *within* what we call ethics has its roots in that language-game. Let us contrast our approach with that of causalism. If an intention is just one of those states of a person that produces certain outer effects, akin to blood sugar levels or epileptic seizures, then it seems natural to say, 'Well, but isn't the important thing that this person somehow produces those effects? *How* he produces them isn't so important: there are all sorts of mechanisms that could be involved, of which intending is but one.' Intentions are probably alterable by means different from those adopted to alter blood sugar levels – behavioural conditioning rather than insulin – but the basic story will be the same.

Such thoughts are perhaps most at home in a consequentialist ethical theory, of the sort that downplays the importance of intention (and also of what I earlier called someone's general orientation of will), looking instead to the 'value' or 'disvalue' of the effects of various bodily movements or non-movements. If we turn from causalism to Anscombe's account of intention, we see how the latter, by contrast, in putting the question 'Why did you do that?' centre stage, can scarcely avoid making intention the crucial component of responsibility.[17] If voluntariness is likewise to be understood in terms of a person's reasons, in the sort of way earlier adumbrated (sec. II), then the picture is further fleshed out.

It is always a good idea to take what a philosopher says at face value, if possible. This applies to Anscombe's use in *Intention* of the question 'Why?', and her references to the sorts of dialogue that contain it, and to other species of dialogue. These things are not mere heuristic devices, but point to a crucial fact about the concept of intention and related concepts: that they are embedded in the social and linguistic life of human beings.

Notes

1 Anscombe's examples are all second-person singular (I think), but the account naturally extends to the second-person plural, and would have to be so extended wherever the relevant verb was something like 'repeal that law' or 'carry out a sit-in'.
2 Davidson (1985, Introduction, xiii). Richard Moran and Martin J. Stone have pointed out this phenomenon of revision, and the exegetical and philosophical errors which it involves, dubbing the resulting straw woman 'Transformed Anscombe'. See Moran and Stone (2011).
3 *Philosophical Investigations* is hereafter referred to as '*PI*'.
4 This is of course most clearly seen when there is no non-linguistic behaviour, and where the expression of intention concerns a quite novel action, such as shaving your hair off for charity. We can still say, 'She was going to shave her hair off (but died before she could do so).' It may be said that we are relying on knowledge or justified belief as to the person's sincerity, strength of will, etc., which involve a correspondence between expressions of intention and subsequent actions; but this 'correspondence' is not what Hume might have called a natural correspondence, being rather an *internal relation*. The main reason why I can predict from Anita's statement 'I'm going to shave my head' that she will shave her head is that I know the meaning of the English phrase 'shave (my) head'.
5 I discuss the argument of sec. 20 in Teichmann (2008, ch. 2, sec. 1.1).

6 It may be alleged that a passive condition like being dragged can't be voluntary, not being an 'action'. But if you allow yourself to be driven in a bus to Cambridge, having got into it in the normal way and knowing where it's headed, then there is no question that what you do is voluntary under the description *going to Cambridge*.
7 This does not of course mean that 'NN was responsible for not standing on her head' isn't a grammatical English sentence, translatable into other languages, etc. There are various senses of the term 'nonsense'.
8 Might it become one if people started standing on their heads near dustbins in large numbers? The question is hard to answer without further detail about why and how this new activity might become prevalent. But it probably is conceivable that eschewing the activity might in certain circumstances be viewable e.g. as a species of non-conformity, indicative of character. It does not follow that in the absence of these social changes there is any character trait.
9 See Anscombe (2005b, 115–17).
10 Would his answer become more pertinent if the agent were to flesh out his self-description with a more complex picture of desires and preferences, as informed, long-standing, consistent, etc.? Perhaps so. But if so, that is because the reason *these* features of one's preferences are regarded as a plus is that the lack of them offends against the sort of objectivity that is (I am arguing) demanded in the social context of asking for and giving reasons. Why else should those features be of any interest to the enquirer?
11 I discuss this phenomenon at greater length in Chapter Sixteen of the present volume.
12 Or rather: 'rose' is ambiguous to the extent that it can occur in both these sentences; in neither sentence is the use of 'rose' itself ambiguous.
13 This of course does not mean that there aren't true and false statements of the form 'X is (not) red', and that these are true or false in virtue of the state of X – i.e. in virtue of whether X is red or not. (A truism.)
14 See her extended treatment of the whole topic, 'The Question of Linguistic Idealism' (Anscombe 1981).
15 See also Anscombe (2005a).
16 An alien picture is similarly in question in this passage from Wittgenstein:

> In what circumstances does one say 'This appliance is a brake, but it doesn't work'? That surely means: it does not fulfil its purpose. What is it for it to have this purpose? It might also be said: 'It was the *intention* that this should work as a brake.' Whose intention? Here intention as a state of mind entirely disappears from view. (1981, sec. 48)

17 The etymology of this word, as of 'accountability', may be adduced as a sort of evidence in favour of the view of the concept of intention here adumbrated. One gives a response to such a question as 'Why?', and in so doing gives an account of oneself.

References

Anscombe, G. E. M. (1963), *Intention*. Oxford: Basil Blackwell, 2nd ed.
———. (1981), 'The Question of Linguistic Idealism', in *From Parmenides to Wittgenstein: Collected Philosophical Papers of G.E.M. Anscombe Vol. I*. Oxford: Blackwell, pp. 112–33.
———. (2005a), 'The Causation of Action', in M. Geach and L. Gormally (eds), *Human Life, Action and Ethics*. Exeter: Imprint Academic, pp. 89–108.
———. (2005b), 'Practical Inference', in M. Geach and L. Gormally (eds), *Human Life, Action and Ethics*. Exeter: Imprint Academic, pp. 109–48.
———. (2008), 'Sin', in M. Geach and L. Gormally (eds), *Faith in a Hard Ground*. Exeter: Imprint Academic, pp. 117–56.
Davidson, D. (1985), *Essays on Actions and Events*. Oxford: Oxford University Press.

Moran, R. and Stone, M. J. (2011), 'Anscombe on Expression of Intention: An Exegesis', in A. Ford, J. Hornsby and F. Stoutland (eds), *Essays on Anscombe's Intention*. Harvard: Harvard University Press, pp. 33–75.

Teichmann, R. (2008), *The Philosophy of Elizabeth Anscombe*. Oxford: Oxford University Press.

Wittgenstein, L. (1958), *Philosophical Investigations*, trans. G. E. M. Anscombe, ed. G. E. M. Anscombe and R. Rhees. Oxford: Basil Blackwell, 2nd ed.

———. (1981), *Zettel*, trans. G. E. M. Anscombe, ed. G. E. M. Anscombe and G. H. von Wright. Oxford: Basil Blackwell, 2nd ed.

Part III
ETHICS

Chapter Nine

ETHICS AND PHILOSOPHY: ARISTOTLE AND WITTGENSTEIN COMPARED

Preamble

Insofar as Wittgenstein expounded any moral philosophy, what he expounded appears very far removed from Aristotle's – or Aristotelian – ethics. Wittgenstein's very notion of 'the ethical' is so distant from Aristotle's as even to suggest that they were just discussing different things; at any rate, we might think this if we have in mind his remarks on ethics in e.g. the *Tractatus* or the *Lecture on Ethics*. In these places we find him expressing such thoughts as that ethical statements are a species of nonsense, that ethics concerns the individual's relationship with the universe (roughly), that no empirical facts can possibly have a bearing on ethics and so on. Whatever these thoughts actually amount to, the concerns which they embody do not seem to come into contact with the concerns motivating Aristotle's moral philosophy.

However, when we consider Wittgenstein's later philosophy we begin to see a certain affinity between what he is doing and what Aristotle is doing in the *Nicomachean Ethics*. This affinity has various aspects, some of which are more clearly visible when we contrast the views of both philosophers with those of certain other schools or tendencies, as we shall see later. It is in any case an affinity existing at quite a deep level. Certainly, it is doubtful whether, had he read Aristotle, Wittgenstein would have felt any cousinship with the Greek. He is reported to have remarked, with more pleasure than discomfiture, that he must be the only Cambridge professor of philosophy never to have read a word of Aristotle;[1] and his *felt* intellectual affinities lay quite elsewhere.

In this brief essay I want to explore aspects of the affinity which I have alleged to exist between the later Wittgenstein and Aristotle the ethicist. One important theme that will emerge concerns the sense in which the activity of doing philosophy is itself of ethical significance.

Wisdom, Theoretical and Practical

Aristotle takes a life of contemplation to be the highest form of human flourishing, contemplation having as its aim philosophic wisdom. In the *Nicomachean Ethics* he does not say much about *what* you are meant to contemplate, and one might worry that Aristotle is in danger of having to praise any old learning, however trivial. But of course he means contemplation of higher things, and he has in mind especially the 'bigger picture': the universe, and the relationships that eternally and necessarily bind many things together into a sort of whole.

For Wittgenstein, philosophic wisdom is likewise a matter of gaining an overview of a whole and of the myriad relationships among the things comprising it, though this whole and these relationships enjoy a large measure of contingency, unlike Aristotle's.[2] The 'whole' is our language, or if you like our thought, as it is expressed or is expressible in language. But that doesn't mean that Aristotle recommends thinking about the universe while Wittgenstein recommends thinking about language instead. An overview of our language, of the sort Wittgenstein is after, *is* a sort of overview of the universe – more specifically, of those aspects of the universe concerning which philosophical puzzlement arises. This 'puzzlement' is not merely a bothersome or irritating sensation, but might be seen rather as a close relative of wonder.

Wittgenstein talks of philosophy as therapy, and of philosophical problems as having their roots in confusion. But his view of philosophy is not therefore merely negative, for if a philosophical problem has the form: 'I don't know my way about' (*Philosophical Investigations*, 123),[3] philosophical enlightenment consists in knowing your way about. And this sort of knowing your way about your own language is not simply the level of linguistic competence that suffices for being counted a speaker of a language. For one thing, that level is set as low as it is for practical reasons, to do with the smooth running of human practices of language use: induction into those practices is generally taken as established in early childhood, and a child is said to *speak English* (or French, or Italian …). This does not prevent the child from getting into knots in his talk and thought, in familiar ways. Nor does 'mastery of a language' prevent an adult from getting into knots in his talk and thought, also in familiar ways. If a philosophical mind is more immune to these problems, can philosophical aptitude be a mere negative? Health is but a relative absence of disease and disability, but it would be strange not to think it a positive thing, if we are to talk this way at all.

But there is another point to be made. Knowing your way about language is something that is positively manifest, or manifestable, in your life more generally. For, as Wittgenstein stressed, language is embedded in human life in countless ways. Thoughtfulness in speech tends to go hand in hand with thoughtfulness in deed. Similar remarks go, mutatis mutandis, for rashness, or dishonesty, or showing off … in speech or in deed. These are generalizations, of course. But they are clearly relevant to the question of whether philosophy, conceived of as Wittgenstein conceived of it, is something important in human life. Thoughtfulness, rashness, dishonesty, etc. are virtues and vices; and here we encounter another parallel between Wittgenstein and Aristotle, relating to the connection between philosophy and *character*.

Norman Malcolm tells how Wittgenstein once wrote to him, in explanation of having been 'shocked' by something Malcolm had said: 'I then thought: what is the use of studying philosophy if all that it does for you is to enable you to talk with some plausibility about some abstruse questions of logic, etc., & if it does not improve your thinking about the important questions of everyday life.'[4] That Wittgenstein himself felt his own philosophical activity to have an 'ethical' dimension is already clear from the time of the *Tractatus*, and is to be partly explained by reference to that idiosyncratic notion of the ethical which I mentioned in the first paragraph. But as the quotation from Malcolm shows, Wittgenstein also regarded the importance of philosophy as bound up with properly 'thinking about the important questions of everyday life'. If we construe 'thinking' as amounting to 'thinking and feeling', we get a rather Aristotelian picture of what the importance of philosophy is thus bound up with, for Wittgenstein. Remember that the Doctrine of the Mean is principally applied to our feelings, as they are called forth in the context of practical thought concerning (especially) problems of everyday life.[5]

Aristotle distinguished the ethical virtues from the intellectual virtues, but any distinction here doesn't amount to a separation. Some modern philosophers would insist that ethical virtue or vice can only be at issue where the subject can be held responsible for something, and that consequently what you think or feel cannot in itself manifest ethical character, since you are not responsible for what you think or feel. In their different ways, Aristotle and Wittgenstein would both reject this last thought, and the concomitant thought about character. Wittgenstein regarded philosophy itself as above all requiring will power, in contrast to intellectual acumen.[6] He especially had in mind the temptation to be seduced by false pictures, but we can surely mention additional temptations resistance to which is necessary if one is to think well philosophically, such as: the temptation not to look too closely at what might be inconvenient for your pet theory – not to go back and start again when you realize you've gone down a blind alley – to say what is fashionable or what will amaze – to focus on undermining the views of your enemies – and so on. A philosopher who succumbs to these or other temptations is not only liable to produce poor work, but shows herself to be to some extent defective in character. A severe enough case will even merit our contempt. After all, such traits as laziness, conformism, being a show-off and pugnacity will typically colour a person's behaviour generally.

The interconnectedness of the ethical and the intellectual has its most obvious embodiment, for Aristotle, in the virtue of *phronēsis*, or practical wisdom. This virtue is characterized by Aristotle as intellectual, relating as it does to the consideration of practical reasons and the weighing of them against each other, as well as to questions of means-end efficacy and the like. Its ethical aspect is seen in the fact that it governs and makes coherent the 'dictates' of the various ethical virtues (courage, honesty, temperance, etc.). One can only exhibit true courage if one can correctly assess the reasons for and against e.g. running into a particular burning building, and such assessment requires practical wisdom, which can weigh the claims of rational self-preservation against those of compassion or filial piety or professional duty or whatever.

What counts as the 'correct assessment' of reasons for and against a course of action? Aristotle famously denies that this question can be answered by reference to a calculus or algorithm, nor by reference to some list of rules or instructions. One acquires practical wisdom through training (typically in childhood) and exercise, as part and parcel of one's acquisition of the ethical virtues; and *that* some weighing of reasons counts as reasonable or 'correct' cannot be explained except in terms which only a practically wise person will fully understand. Two features of this account should remind us of Wittgenstein: first, the emphasis on training as opposed to instruction (where 'understanding instruction' would be conceived of as sufficient for going on to do the right thing); and second, the reference to a human faculty of judging such that the grounds for judgments are *not* encapsulable in a set of rules. With Wittgenstein, we find the first of these especially in what he writes concerning the learning of language, the second occurring in connection with the learning and use of language but also more generally, e.g. in connection with judging that two faces have the same expression.

Both philosophers are thus happy to acknowledge that much intelligent human activity is in a certain sense 'intuitive' – that is to say, that notions of what is reasonable/unreasonable or of what is correct/incorrect have application to such activity, despite the fact that the human agents involved are not *guided by rules*. And both philosophers have a correspondingly 'anti-systematic' attitude a level up, so to speak: Aristotle to that part of philosophy called ethics (including politics), Wittgenstein to philosophy in general. Aristotle writes:

> The same exactness must not be expected in all departments of philosophy alike, any more than in all the products of the arts and crafts. The subjects studied by political science are Moral Nobility [*ta kala*] and Justice; but these conceptions involve much difference of opinion and uncertainty [...] We must therefore be content if, in dealing with subjects and starting from premises thus uncertain, we succeed in presenting a broad outline of the truth: when our subjects and our premises are merely generalities, it is enough if we arrive at generally valid conclusions. (1934, I iii 1, 4)

Aristotle here writes of 'difference of opinion and uncertainty', whereas Wittgenstein, in regard to the unsystematic nature of philosophy, would probably have mentioned such things as context-dependence and irreducible, open-ended complexity. Nevertheless this similarity in their attitudes to ethics and philosophy respectively is worth remarking on, in part because it points to another way in which the two philosophers are alike: namely, in the realistic (non-idealizing) gaze which each philosopher bestows on human life and language.

Aristotle's ethics has for its starting point the idea of an empirically describable human nature, relative to which the key notions of flourishing (*eudaimonia*), function (*ergon*), etc. can be explicated. This sort of ethics is accordingly called Aristotelian *naturalism*, and is to be contrasted with various forms of rationalism, subjectivism, intuitionism and so on. In Wittgenstein's later work we see also a foregrounding of the empirical life of human beings, as when he writes, 'Commanding, questioning, recounting, chatting, are as much a part of our natural history as walking, eating, drinking, playing' (*PI* 25), or 'It comes to this: only of a living human being and what resembles (behaves like) a living human being can one say: it has sensations; it sees; is blind; hears; is deaf; is conscious or unconscious' (*PI* 281). What he had regarded in the *Tractatus* as beyond the proper remit of philosophy, namely empirical issues of human psychology and behaviour, have become in the *Investigations* an essential key for unlocking certain philosophical problems, even though this means that much philosophy will be in the form of 'reminders':

> What we are supplying are really remarks on the natural history of human beings; we are not contributing curiosities however, but observations which no one has doubted, but which have escaped remark only because they are always before our eyes. (*PI* 415)

Philosophy and Natural Science

If both Aristotle and Wittgenstein can be thought of as 'naturalistic' philosophers, does this mean that they see philosophy itself as continuous with science? 'Continuous with'

(Quine's phrase) is a fairly vague expression, but to the extent that the question just asked is clear, it looks as if the answers will have to be 'Yes' for Aristotle and 'No' for Wittgenstein. Aristotle's own work strays in and out of what we would now call natural science, and his general model of a body of theoretical knowledge is a deductive system based upon first principles (*archai*),[7] a model intended to apply as much to physics or biology as to metaphysics. By contrast, a theme stressed by Wittgenstein throughout his career is that of the difference in kind between the two activities of natural science and philosophy. But, as I have suggested, Aristotle's view of ethics is in fact quite close to Wittgenstein's of philosophy with regard to (non-)systematicity; and indeed he does not think of ethics as a body of theoretical knowledge at all, something which explains his warning words that 'the same exactness must not be expected in all departments of philosophy alike'.

Aristotle's model of the natural sciences as deductive systems based upon first principles is of course an ambitious one, to put it mildly. That he proposed such a model may indicate that he saw the activity of science as something which, in principle, an individual person might indulge in – rather than as an essentially communal or social activity. Once the scientific endeavour is seen as a shared one, the idea becomes much (or even) less plausible that scientific propositions should have been derived, or be derivable, from first principles available to anyone doing science. For the communal aspect of scientific activity will evidently be connected with its depending on results and observations made by some and passed on to others, on the basis of testimony; not only results and observations, indeed, but also theories.

This means that *one* contrast often drawn between science and philosophy will not have occurred to Aristotle, since the contrast in question assumes that 'science' is that ever-expanding body of knowledge built up over time by a scientific community: I mean the contrast which is expressed in the claim that there is progress in science, but no progress in philosophy. If we look at what lies behind this claim, construed as a *true* claim, we shall find that the apparent difference in the attitudes of Aristotle and Wittgenstein to the relationship between science and philosophy belies a deeper agreement.

'Progress' can mean many things. What does it mean when it is said that there is progress in the natural sciences? Does it mean, 'We know progressively more and more in scientific matters'? It does seem to mean something like that, and interpreted thus, it is surely true. But who, it might be asked, are 'we'? The claim is not, or not usually, intended as meaning that the average amount of scientific knowledge had by an adult citizen progressively rises, something that is a function of educational standards (and quite possibly false in the UK, for example). Nor is the claim even about the average amount of scientific knowledge had by a scientist. There is much division of labour in scientific research, and it is a strength of the research community that it is structured so as to allow both specialization and the pooling of results in a common pool (or pools). A result of this is that it may be possible to say, 'We know all about how mammalian endocrine systems work' when no individual person knows all about how mammalian endocrine systems work: what is being talked of is the common pool of knowledge about mammalian endocrine systems, an element of what Karl Popper would have called World Three, the world of shared theories, stories, etc.[8] The same goes for 'We know progressively more and more in scientific matters'. This means, 'The pool is getting bigger and bigger'.

What is it that makes a scientific theory common property, or that makes a pool of shared results a pool? The answer to this has to do with authority and the nature of expertise. A specialist in astronomy will justifiably accept on trust what a specialist in particle physics says or publishes, and vice versa, not because she has established the good credentials of the other scientist – which would often require her to be an expert in the same field, something only possible in a world without much specialism – but because among the practical requirements of information-sharing is the requirement that there be a rule or custom that within certain contexts one simply counts as being justified in taking another's word for something. The same goes for education of the young: education can only work at all if pupils are meant to take their teachers' words for things – if they didn't, their education couldn't even get started.

Philosophy is not like this. In philosophy, you are not in general meant to take your teacher's word for things, unless those things are non-philosophical facts, e.g. the year of publication of Hume's *Treatise*. Metaphysical and ethical theories *could* be taught as if they were scientific theories; we *could* have a set-up in which a student was simply meant to learn and repeat such theories. But if these theories were taught in this way, how would they have arisen in the first place? And how would they ever change? For them to be recognizably *philosophical* theories, they must exist in a context of rational debate – otherwise, they would be mere doctrines, or world-myths, or similar. (Perhaps some early Greek philosophy, or 'philosophy', had this status.) So in our imaginary set-up, there must at least be some context in which philosophical theories get thrashed out and debated. Maybe the custom is that you are allowed to join in philosophizing when you are old enough – thirty-five, say. But whatever the details, the subject won't be philosophy at all unless the prime mode of going in for it is by means of rational debate, rather than by repeating things learnt from authorities.

Thus the reason there is no such thing as a common pool of shared philosophical results is not that, in philosophy, everything is subjective, or a 'matter of opinion'. It is rather that in philosophy there are no practical requirements analogous to those that make sense of having a common pool in the case of natural science. For at this level, philosophy and natural science have different aims. The practicalities of the two domains depend on the nature of their aims, and the prime aim of philosophy is *individual understanding*. The reason a person goes in for philosophy is so that he or she can acquire understanding, a certain sort of understanding, roughly delineable by reference to an open-ended list of topics or questions. 'Progress in philosophy' should therefore primarily mean progress in a particular person's philosophical understanding. And such progress is certainly both possible and frequently met with.

There is also room for the notion of progress at the level of a broader philosophical culture. It makes perfectly good sense to speak of the early twentieth-century advances in logic, for example, as constituting a sort of progress in philosophy, progress in the philosophical culture, that is. Such advances will count as progress to the extent that they are taken on board by enough philosophers, where 'taking on board' involves understanding and absorbing things at the personal level. The primacy of the personal remains intact.

This primacy of the personal, of individual understanding, would surely have been recognized by both Wittgenstein and Aristotle as characteristic of philosophy. And it is connected with that intertwining of the ethical and the intellectual which I described above as underlying the fact that philosophical activity can be a manifestation of individual character. Here it should be stressed that individual understanding is also the primary aim of the activity *thinking about life*. Although you can indeed learn from those more experienced and wiser than yourself, you won't count as learning at all if you can't take on board what you hear from them. Understanding here is not manifest in what sayings you can repeat – in fact it is manifest in what you can say only in the sense that your words are among your deeds. There must be some relationship between thinking well about life and living well, and the goal of the first is typically the second.

When Wittgenstein wrote to Malcolm that doing philosophy ought to 'improve your thinking about the important questions of everyday life', he was no doubt in part invoking this parallel between thinking about life and thinking philosophically, two activities the primary aim of which is individual understanding. The scientific model, with its notion of a common pool of knowledge, does not apply naturally to these activities. And this, I suspect, will have been one of the reasons for Wittgenstein's distrust of scientism in philosophy and science worship in our culture.

For both Aristotle and Wittgenstein the primary aim of philosophical enquiry is individual understanding. This is something which evidently links up with a conception of philosophy as a form of contemplation – as opposed to a conception of it as a set of research programmes, or as a means for making the world a better place, or as a profession with a certain career structure, or simply as whatever is done by people employed by institutions that call themselves 'philosophy departments'. And both Aristotle and Wittgenstein are, I have suggested, naturalistic philosophers, in the sense that they both regard the realistic empirical description of humankind as central to philosophical enquiry. But what is called 'naturalism' in philosophy these days is very different from the sort of naturalism I have ascribed to Aristotle and Wittgenstein: the term typically denotes the invocation of natural science as authoritative, and as setting suitable goals for and constraints on philosophical activity.

Someone who has such an attitude to science will find it difficult to allow that there might be cogent philosophical objections to statements 'coming from' science, i.e. statements made by scientists or on behalf of science – first, because he will not recognize the *category* of specifically philosophical objections (philosophy being continuous with science), and secondly, because he takes scientific statements as the paradigm of authoritative (though of course fallible) statements. The resultant model of philosophical theories or viewpoints is one according to which those theories and viewpoints are to 'take as read' whatever is proposed by as-yet-unrefuted statements coming from science, just as the specialist in astronomy takes as read what is proposed by the specialist in particle physics. Now relying on testimony and authority *within science* is something with a genuine rationale, as I have argued; but to transfer that mode of reliance over to philosophy could only make sense if there were such a thing as a common and expanding pool of philosophical knowledge. The ever-changing fashions in philosophical thought ought to be enough to disabuse us of any belief in such a common pool. Perhaps 'naturalistic' philosophers would regard philosophy up to now as analogous to alchemy, and will look forward to the day when it has been superseded by philosophical chemistry. Let them dream. The human desire for individual understanding will live on, with or without philosophy departments.

Notes

1 See Monk (1990, 496).
2 Such contingency, however, co-exists with those limits to what is dubitable, or to what is conceivable, which are such an important theme in *On Certainty*, where such notions as 'bedrock' and 'hinge proposition' get adumbrated and explored.
3 *Philosophical Investigations* is hereafter referred to as '*PI*'. References are to section numbers.
4 Malcolm (1967, 93). It has to be said that Malcolm's 'shocking' reference to British national character was no more absurd, in fact rather less so, than many things Wittgenstein himself had written, e.g. concerning Jewish character; for example his remark from 1931: 'Amongst Jews, "genius" is found only in the holy man. Even the greatest of Jewish thinkers is no more than talented. (Myself for instance.)' (Wittgenstein 1980, 18e). I do not wish to argue that Wittgenstein's own thoughts about the problems of everyday life were above reproach, although I do think it is clear that those thoughts would not be as profound and thought-provoking as they so often are had he not gone in for philosophy.
5 'Practical thought' should be interpreted broadly here, so as to cover *thought about practical matters*, in the sense in which a political advisor thinks about practical matters, or in which Malcolm was thinking about practical matters when he (to Wittgenstein's disgust) invoked British national character as ruling out the likelihood of a British plan to assassinate Hitler in 1939.
6 See for example Wittgenstein (1980, 17e):

> What makes a subject hard to understand – if it's something significant and important – is not that before you can understand it you need to be specially trained in abstruse matters, but the contrast between understanding the subject and what most people *want* to see. Because of this the very things which are most obvious may become the hardest of all to understand. What has to be overcome is a difficulty having to do with the will, rather than with the intellect.

7 See especially the *Posterior Analytics*.
8 See Popper (1979).

References

Aristotle (1934), *Nicomachean Ethics*, trans. H. Rackham. London: William Heinemann.
Malcolm, N. (1967), *Ludwig Wittgenstein: A Memoir*. Oxford: Oxford University Press.
Monk, R. (1990), *Ludwig Wittgenstein: The Duty of Genius*. London: Jonathan Cape.
Popper, K. (1979), *Objective Knowledge*. Oxford: Clarendon Press.
Wittgenstein, L. (1958), *Philosophical Investigations*, trans. G. E. M. Anscombe, ed. G. E. M. Anscombe and R. Rhees. Oxford: Basil Blackwell, 2nd ed.
———. (1980), *Culture and Value*, trans. P. Winch, ed. G. H. von Wright. Oxford: Basil Blackwell.

Chapter Ten

'HOW SHOULD ONE LIVE?': WILLIAMS ON PRACTICAL DELIBERATION AND REASONS FOR ACTING

Practical Deliberation as Radically First-Personal

The starting point of Bernard Williams's *Ethics and the Limits of Philosophy* (1985) is Socrates's question: How should one live? As Williams remarks, the 'should' in this question relates to reasons for acting: '*Should* draws attention to the reasons I have for acting one way rather than another' (1985, 18). Living, of course, isn't a kind of action, but a general reflective deliberation on how to act (on what sorts of action to go in for) is at least an essential component of deliberation on how to live, and it is because of this that 'How should one live?' is a question asking after *reasons*. In Williams's words, 'Socrates' question, then, means "how has one most reason to live?"' (1985, 19).

In the chapters that follow, Williams spells out a variety of ways in which he thinks philosophers' attempts to answer Socrates's question come unstuck. And some, though by no means all, of his arguments rely for their force on Williams's own conception of practical reasons. On Williams's conception of a reason for acting, there are special difficulties faced by anyone who tries to give reasons to another person for acting in a certain way. Insofar as moral philosophers are attempting to justify certain ways of giving people reasons for acting, their task will appear daunting or even hopeless to the extent that people are free simply to rebut any practical reasons offered them. Or so it can appear on Williams's account.

Two crucial and interrelated features of Williams's conception of a practical reason are: first, his idea of practical deliberation as radically first-personal, and second, the role he assigns to the agent's desires. Let us consider these in turn.

In his criticism of Kant's argument for the impartiality of both theoretical and practical deliberation, Williams claims that the argument only works for theoretical deliberation, writing, 'It fails to apply to practical deliberation, and to impose a necessary impartiality on it, because practical deliberation is first-personal, radically so, and involves an *I* that must be more intimately the *I* of my desires than this account allows' (1985, 67). Why is practical deliberation radically first-personal? The answer is given on the next page:

> Practical deliberation is in every case first-personal [...] The action I decide on will be mine, and [...] its being mine means not just that it will be arrived at by this deliberation, but that it will involve changes in the world of which I shall be empirically the cause, and of which these desires and this deliberation itself will be, in some part, the cause. (1985, 68–69)

Of course if I am deliberating what to do, my deliberation is first-personal, at any rate in the sense that what I am wondering is expressible by the question 'What shall I do?' But what if I am deliberating what you are to do? Perhaps you have come to me for advice; or perhaps I have authority over you and am working out what you are to do, given some objective. Example: my objective is that a stockade be built around the hut. I reason: 'We first of all need wood; and to get that, some trees will need to be felled; so you should (or you must) go into that glade and chop a tree down.' Here, the action I decide on is not mine, it is or will be yours.

This, it will be said, is off topic if we are interested in Socrates' question, which we must surely read as meaning 'How am I to live?' But one consequence of Williams's account is that I cannot go about answering that question, or any of the particular practical questions relative to which Socrates' question is architectonic, by relying on or appealing to the deliberations of others. As Williams writes, 'The *I* of the reflective practical deliberation is not required to take the results of anyone else's properly conducted deliberation as a datum' (1985, 69). 'Required' here appears to mean 'rationally required'; and we might wonder how someone else's properly conducted deliberation on your behalf could *fail* to rationally require your acquiescence. The other person gives you some reasons for action, which will be good ones if her deliberation was indeed properly conducted, and yet you say, 'I don't accept that – I'm not going to do that thing.' Such a reply seems hard to justify unless amplified by mention of countervailing reasons, or unless you have reasons for not wanting to discuss the matter with that person. (A discussion is after all a human activity which there can be various reasons for or against going in for.)

But perhaps I am ignoring the phrase 'as a datum'. What I am not rationally required to do, it may be claimed, is accept the conclusion of another person's practical deliberation as a datum, i.e. without *my* seeing how it follows from the given premises. Rational autonomy requires me to make any reasoning my own before I accept it. (The thought is a very Kantian one.) However, there is much practical deliberation of which this is certainly not true, as when I rely on an authority, such as my doctor, whose conclusion that I take such-and-such a medicine I do well to heed regardless of whether I see how it was arrived at. It might be highly irrational of me to put off taking the medicine till such time as I grasp the cogency of my doctor's thinking.

Perhaps then the important phrase is 'reflective practical deliberation': considering what to do to get better doesn't count as *reflective* deliberation, something that takes place only when considering such general practical questions as that of Socrates. But Socrates' question only makes sense if answering it gives me a guide how to answer such particular questions as whether to follow doctor's orders. Part of the answer to Socrates' question will surely be that one should on occasion take the results of other people's practical deliberations as a datum. And those deliberations will of course be second- or third-personal.

Desires as Reasons

Why is Williams led to think of practical deliberation as radically first-personal? The answer, I think, has to do with the role he assigns to an agent's desires, as necessarily underpinning that agent's reasons for action. This is the second of the two features of Williams's conception of practical reason mentioned above. On Williams's account, the reasons for which somebody could act, or does act, are only reasons for him because they connect in the right sort of way with his desires, or more generally with what Williams calls his 'motivational set'. Practical deliberation consists in the summoning of reasons for or against certain possible actions; if those reasons have to be underpinned by the agent's own desires, then evidently the conclusions of bits of practical deliberation must fit in with what the agent wants, must be acceptable from the agent's point of view. Even if a bit of practical deliberation is *framed* in the second person (e.g. when functioning as advice), its cogency will depend on the (proposed) agent's having certain desires, desires expressible in the first person – 'I want …', 'I'd like it if …', etc. This view hardly justifies calling practical deliberation itself 'radically first-personal'. Be that as it may, it is a naturally tempting view, especially after Hume.

The intimacy of the connection seen by Williams as existing between practical reasons and desires can be illustrated by his statement, in chapter 1 of *Ethics and the Limits of Philosophy*, that 'desiring to do something is of course a reason for doing it' (1985, 19). How does this statement fit with the role of practical reasons in deliberation? If I am deliberating whether to φ, does the fact that I want to φ count as a reason for φ-ing? That is to say, can my desire to φ be one of the facts of the case which I am to take account of in my deliberations, a fact which may be given a certain independent weight? The problem is that in deliberating whether to φ, I am ipso facto deliberating whether to want to φ; my already wanting to φ had better not be taken as a given.

You *can* on occasion treat certain of your desires as facts of the case in the course of practical deliberation. But these will be desires with which you do not identify. Anselm Mueller gives the following illustration, in the form of a practical syllogism, of what it is to treat one's desires as facts of the case:

> Anyone who wants to kill his parents will be helped to get rid of this trouble by consulting a psychiatrist;
>
> I want to kill my parents;
>
> If I consult a psychiatrist I shall be helped to get rid of this trouble;
>
> NN is a psychiatrist;
>
> So I'll consult NN.

What this example shows, among other things, is that there is something wrong with saying that a bit of practical reasoning will point to a particular conclusion courtesy of its including reference to a relevant desire or desires of the agent. At the very least, we would need to qualify this as meaning that the reasoning includes reference to those desires of the agent with which she identifies. But which are the desires with which you identify? Answer: those which you do *not* regard simply as facts of the case in the course of deliberating what to do. The desire to kill her parents, in Mueller's syllogism, is being taken by the deliberator as one of the facts of the case – and this, crucially, is shown by what *conclusion* she arrives at. A different conclusion, e.g. 'So I'll buy a gun', would show that the agent did after all identify with her desire to kill her parents (at least for now). If the agent in fact ends up consulting a psychiatrist, and we ask, 'Why did you do that?', she might answer, 'I wanted to kill my parents', thus giving one of the reasons for her action, i.e. one of the considerations that appeared in her practical deliberation. If on the other hand she ends up killing her parents and in answer to 'Why did you do that?' just says, 'I wanted to kill them', she has not given a reason for her action at all. For we will want to know why she *wanted* to kill her parents; indeed, our original question 'Why did you kill your parents?' is in effect the same as the question 'Why did you want to kill your parents?'

Anselm Mueller[1] points out that somebody who reasons: 'Real autonomy consists in satisfying all one's desires, so I'll ...' or 'Giving in to temptation/to a strange desire is the best way to get rid of it, so I'll ...', distances himself from his desire just as much as the person in the above syllogism. That is to say, treating certain of one's desires as 'facts of the case' is compatible with acting on those desires. We should also mention the phenomenon of hunger. You can feel hungry, and hence desire to eat, and then in deliberating how to get some food treat this desire as a fact of the case, but evidently not in such a way as to prevent your 'identifying with' the desire. (I owe this point to David Cockburn.) But in fact 'I'm eating because I'm hungry' is more informative than 'I'm eating because I want to': even if hunger *involves* the desire to eat, it is not the same thing as – is not nothing more than – the desire to eat. We might say that the *reason* that hunger provides a good reason for eating has to do with its natural (though fallible) role or function, namely that of signalling the need to eat (i.e. a current need for nutrition). The phenomenon of hunger seems in fact to illustrate how natural *needs*, rather than desires, can underpin practical reasons.

Internal and External Reasons

Williams is surely wrong to say that one's desire to do something is a reason for doing it. But what of the more general thesis that reasons for action only count as such if they derive (in the right way) from the agent's motivational set? This is the thesis famously argued for in Williams's 'Internal and External Reasons', in which he coins the phrase 'motivational set'.

In practice, Williams takes the elements of a motivational set to be desires, and his model is in fact a version of that well-known beast, the belief-desire model of intentional action, according to which an action counts as intentional if and only if it is caused ('in the right way') by a suitable belief together with a suitable desire. But it may be significant that he wants to be quite liberal as to what sorts of items can appear in a motivational set, S, writing that 'S can contain such things as dispositions of evaluation, patterns of emotional reaction, personal loyalties, and various projects, as they may be abstractly called, embodying commitments of the agent' (Williams 1981b, 105). In similar vein, Davidson (1963) had in 'Actions, Reasons and Causes' bundled a number of things together under his heading of 'pro attitude': desires, urges, tastes, economic prejudices, etc. A worry arises in both cases that if an agent's reasons turn out not obviously to derive from any desires he has, the philosopher (Williams or Davidson) will recruit some other sort of state, such as a 'disposition of evaluation', in the role of proxy for a desire, taking this to confirm the original thesis about reasons for action – which it can only really do if there is a clear cousinship between the various things called 'pro attitudes' or included in

S. That there is such a cousinship does not in those two articles get argued for, and the question is evidently moot. Nevertheless, this issue is not the one I want to home in on, for I think we can locate a more clear-cut problem with the argument of 'Internal and External Reasons'.

The conclusion of that argument is that a person's reason for doing X must be 'internal', in the sense that doing X is conducive to the satisfaction of some element(s) of that person's motivational set. A putative reason for the person to act which is merely 'external', i.e. which does not connect in this sort of way with his motivational set, is not a genuine reason for him to act. To rule out various absurdities, Williams adds certain provisos – for instance, that a desire based on a false belief (e.g. that the liquid in that bottle is water, not petrol) will not count as providing an internal reason for an action under the corresponding description (e.g. 'drinking the contents of that bottle').

For Williams as for Davidson, the key thing about an element of a motivational set is that it has a productive role – it is a required causal condition of intentional action. And for Williams, this is what excludes the possibility of there being genuinely external reasons for action. The crucial sentence runs: 'Nothing can explain an agent's (intentional) actions except something that motivates him so to act' (1981b, 107).

The term 'motivate', when used as Williams uses it, is a philosopher's term, and can be explained as follows: being motivated to φ involves *both* that one see reason to φ *and* that this 'seeing reason to φ' be a potential or actual efficient cause of one's φ-ing. And the thought comes naturally that for something to be an efficient cause of a person's φ-ing it must be a state of that person, or alternatively must cause an appropriate state of that person. It cannot simply be a *fact* such as that my king is threatened by your rook. 'External' facts like these, then, cannot ever motivate you to act.

This last, however, can be allowed by one who believes in external reasons, as can the idea that the *recognition* of a reason to act may (at least sometimes) be called an efficient cause of acting. What the proponent of external reasons wants to say, or should want to say, is that an external reason can *explain* why someone did something, such as move their king. The question at issue boils down to this: whether you can only explain actions by reference to their efficient causes.

Williams argues his case in reference to the story of Owen Wingrave, whose family tried to persuade him to join the army for the putatively external reason that all his male ancestors did so. Here is the key move in the argument: 'Even if it were true (whatever that might turn out to mean) that there was a reason for Owen to join the army, that fact by itself would never explain anything that Owen did, not even his joining the army. For if it was true at all, it was true when Owen was not motivated to join the army' (1981b, 107).

This argument appears to rely on the following principle:

> If it could be the case that p without X's φ-ing, then in the case where X does φ the fact that p can't by itself explain why X φs.

Such plausibility as this principle has seems to be down to the phrase 'by itself'. Consider the principle as applied to efficient causes. Without the phrase 'by itself', the principle is surely *not* true of explanations invoking such causes. For in some cases of efficient causation the cause is a necessary, rather than a sufficient, condition of the effect's occurring, e.g. where the coming together of a sperm and an egg count as the originating cause of someone's being born. (Obviously, 'necessary' doesn't here mean 'logically necessary'.) Indeed even *with* the phrase 'by itself', the principle fails to be true for causes that are merely necessary conditions. Being only a necessary condition, such a cause cannot 'by itself' *result* in the effect; but our question is: can it *explain* it? That is to say, can one adequately explain the effect just by citing this event or fact? The answer must be Yes: for if, in order to explain some effect, you had to gather together enough conditions as would together suffice for its occurrence, then causal explanation would be much harder to come by than it actually is. Thus Williams's principle appears not to work for causal explanation. Nevertheless, the reason I think Williams finds himself relying on this principle is because he has efficient causation in mind, something that is shown in his use of the term 'motivate'.

Now it is true that if we want to explain e.g. why Owen comes to change his mind and join the army, we may well need to say, 'He came to accept the reasons given by his relatives for joining the army,' and it is this acceptance that will count, in this context, as the efficient cause or trigger of his action. But if we ask Owen why he has joined the army, his reply is likely to be 'Because all my male relatives did before me (etc.),' a reply that is not equivalent to 'Because I came to accept as a good reason that all my male relatives did before me'. Indeed, for the latter statement to be appropriate, Owen must be in the position of someone who *gives* as a reason for his action, 'Because all my male relatives did before me,' a statement which thus has explanatory priority over the one about his acceptance of the reason, either in its first-person or its third-person form. (There is an analogous point to be made about the reasons one has for one's beliefs.)

Someone who explains her action by giving a reason for it is not typically giving an efficient cause of that action, for she presents the reason as a good reason, one that we can in principle discuss and together evaluate, and none of that is true of efficient causes such as drinking too much alcohol or taking some Valium or even being in some 'mental state'. This is all very familiar territory, and in view of Williams's own critique of the tendency in utilitarianism to alienate us from our practical reasons by presenting them third-personally as 'just more causal factors', it might seem surprising that in 'Internal and External Reasons' he ends up defending a kind of causalism about reasons. But that, I think, is just what he is doing.

A further argument given by Williams is that for Owen to come to accept this reason as a reason, he must deliberate from his already existing motivations – that is, he must do so if his acceptance of the reason is to count as rational (1981b, 108–9). But can't Owen just come to see matters differently? Beforehand, other reasons, reasons for not joining the army, seemed to him stronger than those given by his relatives; now he finds the latter more compelling, relatively speaking. Why should he have *derived* this view of things from already existing motivations or beliefs or anything else? In explaining himself, he may use ideas with which he is already at home, but this modest fact hardly points to internalism.

There is in any case an unclarity in the idea of someone's *deriving* a practical conclusion from his motivations, or of his being led by 'rational deliberative processes' from existing motivations to a new motivation. If Owen starts to think 'I really ought to do this, since all my male ancestors did,' that thought itself would appear to manifest a 'disposition of evaluation', the sort of item Williams includes in a motivational set.[2] Was this disposition 'already there'? Or did it come into being? Since a little earlier Owen was *not* disposed to think or say 'I really ought to do this, etc.' we should perhaps say the second. Could this new disposition come out of already-existing dispositions by 'rational deliberative processes'? Only if the already existing dispositions could be expressed as premises of some kind; for a deliberative process is rational only if it can be expressed in the form of some sort of argument or bit of reasoning. In fact, we would surely do better to talk of the rational processes as leading from certain *thoughts* to a new thought or thoughts ('I really ought to do this ...' etc.). Perhaps these premise-like thoughts are expressible as imperatives, or *Fiats*, rather than as assertions; that could be debated. But the reference to already existing motivations made it sound as if a person's *character* was the important thing. It is, of course, in one sense, since your character is shown in the sorts of thoughts you endorse, assert, defend, etc. What we are left with is simply the truism that an agent only arrives at practical conclusions rationally if those conclusions are supported by premises (thoughts) which he endorses. Williams's statement that 'I must deliberate *from* what I am' (1985, 200) seems to be a misleading way of saying, 'I must deliberate from what I think.'[3]

And if Owen *did* derive his acceptance of the reason 'Because all my male ancestors did' from already existing motivations (whatever that amounts to), this would not mean that the force of the reason *as* a reason was, for Owen, only as good as the motivations from which he derived it. It might in fact be the other way around: that these 'motivations' can be seen as justifiable by reference to their appropriately yielding an objectively good reason for action. The 'objectivity' here, I would argue, is a species of intersubjectivity, having to do with the social nature of the practice of asking for and giving reasons; but to defend this view in detail would take me too far afield.[4]

Some philosophers wish to draw a distinction between internal and external reasons by adducing the distinct forms, 'X had (a) reason to φ' and 'There was (a) reason for X to φ', conceding *some* sort of genuine role to the latter form. Perhaps (they argue) we may be in a position to say of somebody, 'There was a reason for her to consult a psychiatrist', while having to admit e.g. that she *had* no reason to consult a psychiatrist, lacking an appropriate motivational set.[5] I will not debate the question whether these two English idioms differ in this way or not, since the point does not seem to be central. What is surely of importance is such a fact as this: that the reasons someone gives why she did or is doing or proposes to do such-and-such are (typically) on all fours with the reasons *another* might give why she should, or should not, do or have done such-and-such. The question 'Why?' elicits from an agent her practical reasons (the reasons she has or had, according to the way of speaking suggested), but that is not its only function, for the same sort of question can be asked *by the agent* – as, 'Why should I do that?', or 'Why should I have done that?'[6] An answer to this kind of question may surely mention reasons that 'there are (were)' for the agent to do such-and-such. It would be an odd sort of social delicacy that prevented you from stating such reasons; and you do not after all state them merely as tempting options – the agent might find them very untempting, given her 'motivational set'. In a dialogue between agent and interlocutor, reasons for and against will be competing; they will occupy the same logical space, so to speak, and there need be no talking at cross purposes of the sort that the alleged distinction between reasons that X has and reasons that there are would appear to entail.

It is worth pointing out also that there are some 'internal reasons' the possibility of which presupposes the genuineness of certain 'external reasons'. Let's say I want to play a game of chess, and so have an internal reason e.g. to phone my chess-playing friend. In that case, I must know what chess is: namely, a game with these and those rules. I know, for instance, that rooks move laterally, and not diagonally. But what does that mean? It means that you can move a rook laterally, and cannot move it diagonally. The 'can' and 'cannot' here are species of that sort of modal of which Elizabeth Anscombe showed the importance, calling the latter a 'stopping modal'.[7] 'A player cannot move a rook diagonally' is not a hypothetical imperative, equivalent to 'If you desire to play chess, you ought not to move your rook diagonally' – for you can neither understand nor exemplify the antecedent of this conditional unless you already know what playing chess is, i.e. that it consists in following rules such as 'A player cannot move a rook diagonally'. The attempt to cash out uses of stopping modals in terms of hypothetical imperatives of this kind thus results in a vicious circle or infinite regress.[8] And one who learns how to play chess must learn (or have already learnt) the reason-giving, action-guiding function of modals like 'can' and 'cannot'. I show my understanding of these modals by acting appropriately, as Anscombe argued. Hence desiring to play chess presupposes understanding that 'You must move your king' etc. give reasons for action that are *not* reasons because of anyone's subjective desires. If rules constitutive of practices are expressed by means of Anscombean modals, then this point will apply not only to games like chess, but also to such institutions as promising.

Human Nature and the Ethical

I have argued that there are significant problems with Williams's conception of practical reason, both as regards his claim that practical deliberation is radically first-personal, and as regards his claim that all practical reasons are internal reasons. What effect does this have on the project or projects of *Ethics and the Limits of Philosophy*?

Some of Williams's projects are *not* affected. Take chapter 9, 'Relativism and Reflection'. It is notable that in this chapter Williams is much more concerned with 'we' than with 'I', with *our* concepts and *our* ways of looking at things. Issues such as that of incommensurability between concepts of different cultures are issues that comprehend those facts about social practices and intersubjectivity which I hinted at a moment ago. The purported significance of an agent's desires plays no role in the arguments of chapter 9.

Matters are a little different when we turn to chapter 3, in which Williams criticizes philosophical attempts to locate the foundations of ethics in notions of human well-being. He distinguishes two ways of reading Socrates' question, as a question whose answer is addressed '*to* anyone' and as a question whose answer is said to hold '*for* anyone'. And he allows the Aristotelian move of prioritizing the second reading: 'How should one live?' may be answered on someone's behalf. For Aristotle, the answer will relate to that person's own well-being or *eudaimonia*, and Williams assumes that any account invoking well-being as ethically foundational will aim at providing an answer of this sort. This means that such accounts will face a well-known charge, namely that they present the virtuous person as self-concerned in a way that appears at odds with our picture of what ethical thought should look like – for such a person will apparently be aiming at *his own* well-being.

Williams discusses how this charge might be responded to, and it is in the course of this discussion (1985, 51–52) that he puts forward his reasons for being sceptical about the prospects for ethical naturalism. He begins by saying that the agent's view 'from within' of her ethical dispositions is itself expressive of those dispositions, i.e. is expressive of an ethical outlook; that is to say, even if the agent is indeed thinking of her own dispositions in the course of ethical deliberation, she will see those dispositions as aiming at good and valuable things, and as being good dispositions *because* they so aim. She thus prioritizes goods that are external to her own dispositions, and cannot be justly accused of egoism. But Williams denies what Aristotle and his philosophical descendants say, that these external goods are conceptually independent of the ethical dispositions; Williams regards the value of these aimed-at goods as in the eye of the beholder, i.e. the beholder who has those dispositions. From what he calls 'the outside view of those dispositions', we find that 'there is a sense in which they [the dispositions] are the ultimate supports of ethical value' – the value of such things as other people's welfare and the requirements of justice.

Williams then argues that whereas Aristotle thought the inside and outside views of one's dispositions of character would necessarily be in harmony if one was a virtuous person, we moderns have reason to doubt that such harmony is achievable. For the outside view tells us, what we want to deny from the inside point of view, that the exclusivity that is characteristic of our ethical dispositions (at least ideally, from the inside point of view) cannot really be justified. He writes:

> Our present understanding gives us no reason to expect that ethical dispositions can be fully harmonized with other cultural and personal aspirations that have as good a claim to represent human development. Even if we leave the door open to a psychology that might go some way in the Aristotelian direction, it is hard to believe that an account of human nature – if it is not already an ethical theory itself – will adequately determine one kind of ethical life as against others. (1985, 52)

Two points are made here, one to do with non-ethical dispositions being in competition with ethical ones, the other to do with the plurality of possible kinds of ethical life that might be determined by an account of human nature. It seems to me that neither point presents a real difficulty for an Aristotelian, and the source (or a source) of Williams's belief that there are difficulties here is, I shall suggest, his excessively 'first-personal' conception of practical reason.

The 'other cultural and personal aspirations' Williams has in mind are not, of course, things like aiming to own more Rolls Royces than your father ever owned. They are aspirations 'that have as good a claim to represent human development' as do ethical ones. What is meant by the phrase 'human development'? It is a useful and important notion; but when we begin to explain it e.g. by reference to examples, it looks very much as if we will be talking about human flourishing, where this means not only the flourishing of individuals but that of communities. As to the latter, we should remember that the natural history of human beings includes facts about the life of the group; in mentioning communities, we have not departed from the topic of human nature.

Earlier in the chapter Williams mentions creativity in the arts and sciences and 'the unhappiness and the unloveliness that may be part of creative activity' (1985, 47); and it is clear that artistic activity is meant to embody one of those cultural and personal aspirations that can allegedly conflict with ethical aspirations. The importance of a work of art, however, surely relates to its capacity to enhance human life, human thought and feeling, both in the artist and in her spectators, readers or listeners; and it is no mere cheat to say that these matters lie squarely in the domain of human well-being. That art and the creation of art are of ethical importance may be gladly admitted, and it is only those addicted to what Williams calls the morality system who will find that a hard truth to swallow. Likewise, with scientific creativity or exploration, the pursuit of knowledge or understanding is the pursuit of an important component of human flourishing, something that Aristotle himself would have stressed. There will be much messiness or indeterminacy surrounding the *ordering* of ethical goods in real life, and if there are problems of 'harmonizing', such problems will arise as much in connection with, say, justice and charity as with sociability and creativity.

Moreover, the possibility of different ways of living well and flourishing, and the fact that a person may have to choose between incompatible ways of life, are quite consistent with an account which takes well-being as ethically foundational. Such an account, admittedly unlike Aristotle's, will be pluralist. Williams's second point in the above passage assumes an unnecessary monism.

But Williams may well mean something more radical than I have so far indicated. He may mean that a person following her dream can in some sense be within her rights to respond to our question 'Why are you doing this?' by saying, 'I really want to; it is my heart's desire'; and to say this in the face of the prima facie cogent reasons we give her why she should not do the thing in question. That it is a project she holds dear, that she thinks of it as part of herself, part of her Self – these facts, I suspect, are for Williams powerful practical reasons in themselves, ones that evidently cannot be called 'ethical reasons' and which on that account will be in genuine competition with any opposing ethical reasons. And this takes us back to his claim that 'desiring to do something is of course a reason for doing it', a claim which I have argued is false.

In an interview in the *Guardian* published in 2002, Williams said that

> if there's one theme in all my work it's about authenticity and self-expression […] It's the idea that some things are in some real sense really you, or express what you [are] and others aren't […] The whole thing has been about spelling out the notion of inner necessity. That someone who [sic] has to do something, has to live in a certain way or discovers something is really him, what he belongs to, what is his destiny – I'm drawn to all that.[9]

It's clear that the terms 'authenticity' and 'self-expression' need careful explaining. And there are two directions in which an explanation might point that are equally problematic for Williams: by one explanation, authenticity and self-expression are a part of human flourishing, and hence available to an Aristotelian account of the good life, while by the other, they are as much features of the life of a Goebbels as of the life of a

Beethoven. We might try to avoid the latter possibility by stipulating that authenticity and self-expression be constrained by something like Mill's 'harm principle', but that would simply reinstate ethical priorities, as well as keeping Gauguin at home.[10] In the end, I think we must reject the picture that Williams offers and what lies behind that picture: the subordination of practical reason to subjective desire.[11]

Notes

1. In personal correspondence.
2. The thought would not be the *only* possible manifestation of this disposition: presumably Owen is now disposed to say or think other related things, such as 'Maybe my earlier stance was too self-concerned', 'One can after all take a sort of pride in one's family', 'My friend Jack did the right thing when *he* joined up' – or whatever, depending on exactly what kind of change of heart it was that Owen has undergone.
3. Even this may go too far: does the person ordered to go and chop down a tree deliberate from what he thinks, or in effect from what another thinks, concerning a matter about which the subordinate may have no opinion ('We need to build a blockade')? Asked 'Why did you chop down that tree?,' he is most likely to reply, 'Because I was ordered to,' and he need not be so reflective as to entertain any 'evaluative stance' towards his being obedient to X, a stance that might do duty as a putative 'motivation'. Unless by such a stance we just mean the trait of obedience; but that trait is manifested simply in doing things for the reason 'X ordered me to'.
4. I expound and defend this view in Teichmann (2011, esp. chapters 1 and 2).
5. This suggestion was made by both Simon Blackburn and Anthony Price during the discussion of this chapter at the original 2015 conference.
6. It is notable that both these questions can typically be rephrased as the impersonal-sounding 'Why do that?'
7. See e.g. Anscombe (1981).
8. Nor is the rule-statement equivalent to 'If you move your rook diagonally, that will not *count* as playing chess'. If you don't put one foot in front of the other alternately, what you do (e.g. hop) won't count as walking. These are at best remarks about the *linguistic* rules governing the use of 'chess' and 'walk'; our interest, however, is in the *practical* rules constitutive of activities like chess – and not of ones like walking.
9. Jeffries (2002).
10. See Williams (1981a).
11. I am grateful to David Cockburn for comments on an earlier draft of this chapter.

References

Anscombe, G. E. M. (1981), 'On Promising and Its Justice', in *Ethics, Religion and Politics: Vol. Three of the Collected Papers of G.E.M. Anscombe*. Oxford: Basil Blackwell, pp. 10–21.
Davidson, D. (1963), 'Actions, Reasons and Causes', *Journal of Philosophy*, 60, no. 23, 685–700.
Jeffries, S. (2002), 'The Quest for Truth', *The Guardian*, 30 November.
Teichmann, R. (2011), *Nature, Reason and the Good Life: Ethics for Human Beings*. Oxford: Oxford University Press.
Williams, B. A. O. (1981a), 'Moral Luck', in *Moral Luck*. Cambridge: Cambridge University Press, pp. 20–39.
———. (1981b), 'Internal and External Reasons', in *Moral Luck*. Cambridge: Cambridge University Press, pp. 101–13.
———. (1985), *Ethics and the Limits of Philosophy*. London: Fontana Press.

Chapter Eleven

'AN INCULCATED CARING': RYLE ON MORAL KNOWLEDGE

A Third Kind of Knowledge

In a number of his writings, Ryle warns us of the ill consequences of regarding knowing how as a species of knowing that. Philosophers have too often, he thinks, taken propositional knowledge as a model for the knowledge of techniques, procedures and practices. Ryle was a great anti-reductionist, a great pluralist; so it comes as no surprise to find that he did not regard knowing how and knowing that as together exhausting the types of knowledge. In 'On Forgetting the Difference between Right and Wrong' (1971), he argues that moral knowledge, or certain important species of moral knowledge, represent a third kind of knowledge, one that cannot be reduced to either or both of the other two. The reason for this is that a person who learns what Ryle summarizes as 'the difference between right and wrong' is someone who learns to care about and take seriously such things as telling the truth, resisting certain temptations and so on. And this is why, as he writes,

> it is ridiculous to say one has forgotten the difference between right and wrong. To have been taught the difference is to have been brought to appreciate the difference, and this appreciation is not just a competence to label correctly or just a capacity to do things efficiently. It includes an inculcated caring, a habit of taking certain sorts of things seriously. (Ryle 1971, 387–88)

The concept of forgetting is out of place here, Ryle suggests, because we think of forgetting as *losing* something, e.g. some 'equipment', rather than as *changing* in some way:

> If I have forgotten a date or become rusty in my Latin, I do not think of this as a change in *me*, but rather as a diminution of my equipment. In the same way, a person who becomes less or more conscientious is a somewhat changed person, not a person with an enlarged or diminished stock of anything. (1971, 388)

Ryle's point about the difference between moral knowledge and knowing how is similar to one stressed by both Aristotle and Aquinas, and embodied in a certain asymmetry as regards blame or criticism: the technical skill of one who misspells on purpose is not impugned, while that of an accidental misspeller is – but the ethical excellence of one who steals on purpose is more impugned than that of a person who accidentally goes off with someone else's wallet. An ethical virtue like honesty requires not just a capacity to do certain things, but a will to do them, and (as Ryle puts it) a habit of taking such things seriously.

Ryle argues that a 'habit of caring about' is what is learnt also when one learns to admire or enjoy wines, poems, people, landscapes, etc. And this is really *learning*; one who has learnt has acquired a kind of knowledge. 'If making a skilful tennis stroke or a skilful translation is doing something one has learned to do, i.e., is an exercise and not an effect of knowledge, why may not admiring a person for his staunchness be, in a partly similar way, an example and not an after-effect of what our study of his character has taught us?' (1971, 387).

Telling the Difference

Moral knowledge, it is natural to think, would be exemplified by such things as knowing that it would be dishonest to do such-and-such, or knowing that in such-and-such a ('morally significant') situation the agent should do X. It is a peculiarity of Ryle's discussion that he focuses on knowing the *difference* between right and wrong. How are we to understand a phrase of the form 'knowing the difference between X and Y'? Consider this statement of Ryle's: 'There seems to be a sort of incongruity in the idea of a person's knowing the difference between good and bad wine or poetry, while not caring a whit more for the one than for the other' (1971, 384–85). It appears from examples like this one that by 'knowing the difference between X and Y' Ryle primarily means 'being able to distinguish a given instance of X from a given instance of Y'. The person who knows the difference between good and bad wine is someone who can tell the two apart in a particular situation, not on the basis of their names or prices, say, but on the basis of tasting them. And one who knows the difference between good and bad poetry can distinguish a particular good poem from a particular bad poem not on the basis, say, of the authors' reputations, but on the basis of such qualities of the poems as are apparent only when one reads them.

The 'incongruity' referred to by Ryle would then seem to relate to an alleged intimate connection between a species of knowing how and a species of caring about: for the first of these would be knowing how to distinguish instances in some 'canonical' way (e.g. by tasting or by reading). Now a connoisseur of, or expert in, poetry will have powers of distinguishing that go beyond the simple epithets 'good' and 'bad'; for instance, she may be able to tell, of a poem not previously encountered, who wrote it or might well have written it, or when it was written; what figures of speech it contains, what allusions, what assonances, what structural properties; and so on and so on – these properties distinguishing it from some other poem. Indeed, if someone could make *none* of these latter sorts of judgments, is it conceivable that she could distinguish the good from the bad? I think only an extreme Moorean intuitionist could say Yes to this.

If these thoughts are along the right lines, a possible explanation suggests itself of *why* it would be (at the very least) strange if someone knew the difference between good and bad poetry while not caring more for one than for the other. Hume argued in his essay 'Of the Standard of Taste' that aesthetic merit is determined by the preferences of those with knowledge and discrimination when it comes to (say) poetry; and if he was right, then someone with the capacities that come under the heading of 'knowledge and discrimination' *will* most likely be someone who prefers what is good, since what is good is just what people like him prefer.

Will all this carry over to ethics? Can we invoke the notion of a 'moral expert', or of someone with 'moral discrimination', so as to lend substance to the idea of somebody's knowing the difference between right and wrong? Perhaps a figure like Aristotle's ideally virtuous person comes to mind. Ryle, however, does not believe in such a notion. He contrasts the honest person with the person who knows the difference between good and bad tennis strokes, or between good and bad wines, writing of these latter types: 'They have acquired special technical abilities and, therewith, special enjoyments. We others may envy them for both.' And he goes on: 'But knowledge of the difference between right and wrong is common knowledge … [the honest person] is not, *ex officio*, even a bit of an expert at anything. Nor is his life enriched by some extra relishes. He possesses nothing for us to envy' (1971, 388).

Perhaps Ryle is saying that we are all, or almost all, moral experts: that in knowing the difference between right and wrong, each of us is capable of telling, in some canonical way, whether a given course of conduct is 'more right' than some alternative course of conduct. The reference to a canonical way of telling would be needed to rule out the person who just parrots the moral lessons of an authority figure, and also to maintain the analogy with knowing the difference between good and bad wines, etc. But what could such a canonical way of telling be? Is it that each of us tells the difference between right and wrong by consulting his or her conscience? We seem to be veering towards Moorean intuitionism after all.

It is worth asking here why it is that Ryle thinks there is no room for specialization in ethics, as there is in wine tasting, nor any special pleasures associated with the moral life, nor any possibility of envying the moral capacities of another person. The answer, I think, lies in his taking the subject matter of ethics to be Right and Wrong, those thinnest of the 'thin' ethical concepts. Maybe we should broaden our remit so as to include the knowledge of the difference between honesty and dishonesty, between good and bad ways of bringing up children, between authentic and inauthentic expressions of sympathy, between just and unjust punishments of particular individuals – and so on. Knowing the difference between good and bad ways of bringing up children is surely *not* common knowledge. We certainly can and do envy those who are more patient and less bad-tempered than ourselves. And there is a characteristic pleasure to be taken in managing to forgive someone who has trespassed against you – not a 'relish', perhaps, but a pleasure, in the sense of that word which Ryle himself so successfully reclaimed from the utilitarians and others.[1]

Is there a canonical way of telling the difference between just and unjust punishments, akin to tasting the difference between good and bad wines? I do not think so; and if there is a useful role for the notion of a moral expert, I don't think it corresponds to that of the aesthetic expert in Hume's theory of the standard of taste. Hume's theory relies on an empirical generalization: that those with discrimination, judiciousness, etc. with regard to some art form (say) tend to prefer and enjoy the same things as one another. It is this consensus which supplies the 'standard' – a case of inter-subjective agreement amounting to objectivity. Now I have nothing against the idea that inter-subjective agreement in response can amount to objectivity, for reasons that are powerfully expressed in Wittgenstein's later writings. But the role in our lives of art, or of wine-making, means that the notion of a *response* has a significance quite different from that of the notion of a response to ethical situations, actions or characters.

Music, poetry, plays are all made by human beings, as is wine; and it is an aim internal to the practices of producing these things that people should respond to them in certain ways. In a fairly clear sense, artistic productions are *for* the listener, reader or spectator; and wine is *for* the drinker who has a capacity to taste it.[2] Recall that the word 'poet' comes from the Greek for 'maker', the word 'art' from the Latin for 'skill'. If we can speak at all about a practice (or practices) of morality, such a practice cannot be said to have as an internal aim the evocation of responses of certain kinds in spectators or consumers. The aims of the practice of promising relate to the harnessing of co-operation among human beings; the aims of the practice of doctoring relate to the physical health of human beings; and so on. These many and various practices are what yield opportunities for what we call moral judgments, judgments such as that X is dishonest, or caring, or negligent. These judgments do not embody responses the evocation of which is the business of any human practice.

An Inculcated Caring

All this means, I think, that it is a mistake to apply what Hume says in 'Of the Standard of Taste' to ethics, as some philosophers have tried to do. But now we must come back to the question, 'What is it that someone can do who can tell the difference e.g. between just and unjust punishment? And why is such a person to be credited with moral *knowledge*?'

To the first question, the most obvious answer may be the best one. Such a person can give *good reasons* for her judgment, can explain why the reasons proposed in favour of differing judgments aren't so good, etc. etc. So, it will be said, can the connoisseur of wine or poetry. But as I have argued, good and bad reasons in judgments of quality concerning art or wine tasting must relate at some level to a, or the, aim internal to the practices of production, namely the evocation of certain human responses. This, by the way, is not to say that music, poetry or indeed winemaking do not have a variety of functions and aims, such as enhancing religious ceremonies or providing a thirst-quenching beverage; but our concepts of the good and the bad (and allied concepts), applied in these areas, do seem to tie in with that aim which I have presented as central. Certainly when Ryle speaks of knowing the difference between good and bad poetry or wine, he has this sort of use of 'good' and 'bad' in mind. By contrast, reasons for ethical judgments, including judgments of the 'good' and the 'bad', have a different status and role, tying in with human interests in a broad sense of that term.

If this is what 'knowing the difference' amounts to in ethical matters, what grounds are there for saying, with Ryle, that there is a sort of absurdity in the idea of someone who knows the difference between (say) just and unjust punishments, but doesn't prefer one to the other?

I think Ryle is right to want to speak here of 'inculcated caring'. The typical process of learning how to give reasons why X is more just than Y no doubt involves learning to care about justice, about fairness, about the claims of other people. But there is more to be said than this. For in calling some course of action just, one is surely committed to backing this judgment up with reasons that are reasons for *doing* something – that's to say, we're not simply concerned with reasons for calling something 'just'. Example: A made a promise to help B in exchange for B's helping A – B has helped A – and there is no emergency or new information to let A off the hook. These facts supply reasons for two distinguishable, though intimately related, conclusions: (1) that it would be unjust of A not to help B as promised, and (2) that A has very good reason to help B, and no reason not to. The 'full story' behind (2) would presumably have to involve explanation of why the institution of promising is itself a good for human beings; and the explanation would include the observation that the institution of promising is characterized by the use of such modal statements as 'You *have to* do X (since you promised to)', statements whose function can only be grasped by one who recognizes them as reason-giving.[3]

Thus if I can tell that it would be unjust not to do such-and-such, then I can summon reasons *for* doing such-and-such. And there does seem to be a *kind* of incongruity in the idea that I should have no preference for a course of action which I myself can see reasons for doing, and no reasons for not doing. At any rate, if I confess that I am not moved by those reasons I myself have adduced – if I confess, in Ryle's phrase, that I don't care a whit more for one course of action than for the other – then what I say will wear its unreasonableness on its sleeve. The so-called incongruity lies in this unreasonableness.

Such unreasonableness is quite possible, is in fact a reality of human life. A well-known form of it is the phenomenon of shamelessness, embodied in such sayings as 'That man was really dumb: not for cheating, but for cheating and *getting caught*'. Could this kind of shamelessness be taught as part of a 'moral education'? Or we could put the question another way: Can we conceive of people who brought up their children to be shameless – to cheat and lie, and so on? Towards the end of his article, Ryle addresses this sort of question, and once again claims to detect a sort of incongruity; as he puts it, 'The notion of moral non-education is familiar enough, but the notion of moral miseducation has a smell of absurdity' (1971, 390).

By way of comparison, he writes of the non-absurd possibility of misinstruction in etiquette, meaning by that phrase, not teaching people to be impolite, but rather teaching them to do what is in fact impolite (e.g. remaining hatted in a lady's drawing-room), incorrectly calling it 'polite'. If an ethical analogue of 'impolite' is e.g. 'unjust', then an ethical analogue of misinstruction in etiquette would seem to be e.g. teaching someone to do things that are in fact unjust, while making out that they count as just. Now here is what Ryle writes:

> There is a difficulty in conceiving of a person's being taught to be selfish, deceitful, cruel, and lazy on principle; to be morally shocked at exhibitions of fair-mindedness; or scrupulously to make reparations for his backslidings into unselfishness. (1971, 390)

The comic effect of this passage is due to the expressions 'on principle', 'morally shocked', 'scrupulously' and 'backslidings', together with what we might call an intentional reading of such verb forms as 'taught to be' and 'morally shocked at'. Surely someone couldn't be taught to do certain things *for the reason* that they are selfish or cruel or unjust?

But it is not so clear that this last question is the one that we ought to be asking. We might put the point by saying that Ryle faces a dilemma: if 'selfish' is analogous to 'impolite', then moral miseducation will be no more absurd than misinstruction in etiquette (as characterized by Ryle), since one can be taught to do things that are in fact selfish, though not taught to do them *for the reason* that they are selfish; while if 'selfish' is analogous to 'remaining hatted in a lady's drawing-room', then surely it must stand to some 'thin' concept like 'morally wrong' as 'remaining hatted in a lady's drawing-room' stands to 'impolite' – so that once again moral miseducation looks no more absurd than misinstruction in etiquette, on account of the conceptual gap between selfishness and being morally wrong.

The dilemma, however, is a false dilemma. The analogy between 'selfish' and 'impolite' is imperfect, but not in such a way that we need to have resort to a thin ethical concept like 'morally wrong'. There is a salient difference that needs to be remarked, between ethics on the one hand, and etiquette (or legality, etc.) on the other, namely: that there's a sense in which what counts as impolite or illegal is *contingent*, having to do with the provisions of some man-made system that could easily be different, though still involving the same concepts, 'impolite', 'illegal'; whereas what counts as selfish or unjust or cruel is less contingent in this way. That is to say, it can be established fairly straightforwardly that e.g. breaking a promise in the situation I sketched above would be unjust, full stop. So there may be a kind of absurdity even in the idea of teaching someone to do things that are in fact unjust, calling them just: for, very often, the things that are 'in fact' unjust will not be contingently unjust, in the way in which it's contingently illegal to park where there are yellow lines – or indeed contingently illegal to kidnap someone (for what laws are in force is a contingent matter). Of course there will also be cases where ethical judgments can't be so straightforwardly established, where there is difficulty or indeterminacy in the issues involved. And this latter consideration indicates that the 'smell of absurdity' will be more or less strong depending on how reasonably one could argue for or against some kind of action-feature's being a *pro tanto* reason for (not) doing it.[4]

Ryle's talk of a special kind of absurdity involved in moral miseducation is thus not indefensible; but once again, the absurdity is not so much in the *notion* of moral miseducation as in the thoughts of moral miseducators. The 'absurdity' in fact is human unreasonableness, more or less extreme. In a speech to SS officers at Poznan in 1943, Heinrich Himmler, speaking of the Final Solution, said:

> Most of you will know what it means when 100 bodies lie together, when there are 500, or when there are 1000. And to have seen this through, and – with the exception of human weaknesses – to have remained decent, has made us hard and is a page of glory never mentioned and never to be mentioned.

Something that was in fact mass murder was regarded as glorious, and men were taught so to regard it. This is moral miseducation, if you like; and while the phenomenon, as exemplified here, has a strong whiff of something like insanity, the notion of moral miseducation is, alas, far from absurd.

Notes

1 See Ryle (1954).
2 A greengrocer can sell watermelons that are good or bad, though there is not exactly a practice of *making* watermelons (as there are ones of making wine or poems). But the activities of serving and eating watermelons supply the implicit aim – that food be wholesome and tasty – relative to which we can have standards of *good* and *bad* in watermelons; and the greengrocer sells watermelons to people who can be presumed to want them for serving and eating. Thanks to Constantine Sandis for pointing out this sort of case.
3 See Anscombe (1981).
4 Moreover, 'you should feel free to do this because you'd only be breaking a promise' occupies one position, and 'you should do this because you'd be breaking a promise' occupies another. So it gets quite complex.

References

Anscombe, G. E. M. (1981), 'On Promising and Its Justice', in *Ethics, Religion and Politics: Vol. Three of the Collected Papers of G.E.M. Anscombe*. Oxford: Basil Blackwell, pp. 10–21.

Ryle, G. (1954), 'Pleasure', in *Dilemmas: The Tarner Lectures*. Cambridge: Cambridge University Press, chapter 4, pp. 54–67.

———. (1971), 'On Forgetting the Difference between Right and Wrong', in *Collected Papers Vol. 2*. London: Hutchinson, pp. 381–90.

Chapter Twelve

ARE THERE ANY INTRINSICALLY UNJUST ACTS?

Preamble

In 'Modern Moral Philosophy'[1] Elizabeth Anscombe famously argued for three theses: that moral philosophy should be laid aside until we have an adequate philosophy of psychology; that the concepts of *moral* obligation and *moral* duty, and of what is *morally* right and wrong, and of the *moral* sense of 'ought', ought to be jettisoned if this is psychologically possible; and that the differences between the well-known English writers on moral philosophy from Sidgwick to the present day (i.e. 1958) are of little importance.

The reason for her third thesis relates to that trend in modern moral thought which Anscombe dubbed 'consequentialism'. Consequentialism, she argued, is incompatible both with the ethical tradition at the heart of Western culture, the Hebrew-Christian ethic, and with ancient Greek thought. In both these traditions we find the belief that certain things are ruled out absolutely – such things as killing the innocent, vicarious punishment and treachery.[2] Consequentialism abandons such ethical absolutism, an abandonment which Anscombe regarded as a disaster. Any differences between modern, consequentialist positions must therefore appear trifling in comparison with their ominous similarity; this is the purport of her third thesis.

To say that killing the innocent is absolutely ruled out is not, for Anscombe, to allege an absolute 'moral obligation' not to kill the innocent; for (as her second thesis proposes) the language of 'moral obligation' is, for various reasons, best avoided. Rather, the typical ground for saying that something is absolutely ruled out is that it is intrinsically unjust. Generally speaking, talk of moral obligation, where by such talk someone is attempting to say something worth saying, can be replaced by talk of justice and injustice.[3] And talk of absolute moral obligation is typically to be replaced by talk of intrinsic injustice.

In this essay I aim to examine what Anscombe means by 'intrinsic injustice', and what can be said for her view that there are intrinsically unjust types of act – i.e. types of act which are absolutely ruled out. I am not primarily setting out to defend some philosophical claim. I intend rather to explore a range of issues thrown up by Anscombe's discussion, including: what being a just person consists in; the nature of moral dilemmas; the relevance or irrelevance of motive to the question whether an act manifests a given virtue (e.g. justice); backward-looking reasons and practical wisdom (*phronesis*); and the idea of moral bedrock, or moral 'hinge propositions'. Some of the investigation will naturally deal with how Anscombe should be read and what her overall position looks like, but the ultimate goal is philosophical and ethical understanding. Those who would like to know the (rough) outline of the discussion to come may like to consult the final section of this chapter, which contains a synopsis.

Habitual Refusal and Exclusion from Deliberation

Anscombe distinguishes between 'the intrinsically unjust, and what is unjust given the circumstances' (*MMP* 38). Taking and using someone's property without that person's permission is typically unjust, but circumstances may render it just (or not unjust) – such as when 'you could use a machine of his to produce an explosion in which it would be destroyed, but by means of which you could divert a flood or make a gap which a fire could not jump' (*MMP* 39). By contrast, procuring the judicial execution of an innocent person is intrinsically, i.e. always and everywhere, unjust.

How shall we define or characterise justice? One way of taking this question is as one having to do with a certain virtue, a human disposition of character. While disclaiming the ability 'to do the philosophy involved', Anscombe nevertheless takes it to be 'clear that a good man is a just man; and a just man is a man who habitually refuses to commit or participate in any unjust actions for fear of any consequences, or to obtain any advantage, for himself or anyone else' (*MMP* 40). Hence, among other things, the just man will habitually refuse to procure any judicial executions of any innocent persons, for whatever reasons.

The sentence 'Smith refuses to commit any unjust actions' can be taken in two different ways, in one of which 'refuses' takes wider scope, in the other of which 'any' does. If 'any' takes wider scope, the sentence means, roughly, 'Every time Smith is faced with the possibility of committing an unjust act he refuses to do so', or 'Smith eschews every unjust option'. Adding the adverb 'habitually' to such a proposition produces a grammatical peculiarity: 'Smith habitually eschews every unjust option' – akin to 'Smith habitually never takes bribes'. The adverb 'habitually' modifies action-verbs (including inaction-verbs), and 'eschews every unjust option' is not, we might say, a proper action-verb.

That Anscombe uses 'habitually' is explained by her seeing the issue as one concerning a person's habits or dispositions, i.e. his character; but to ascribe a habit or trait of character is not to allege an exceptionless generalization about a person, and 'habitually' does not mean 'always'. In the domain of human action, 'always' is ruled out by those exceptions or failures that arise from being tempted, being terribly provoked, being drugged or hypnotized – or even undergoing a change in character. In such cases a person who habitually φs does not φ.

There are thus two reasons for interpreting 'habitually refuses to commit or participate in any unjust actions' in such a way that 'refuses' (and not 'any') takes wide scope: to avoid a logico-grammatical infelicity, and to avoid the conceptual clash between 'habitually' and 'always'.[4] We should, I suggest, read the occurrences of 'any' in Anscombe's statement as occurring in an intentional context set up by the verb 'refuses'. That is to say, we are to imagine the just man habitually saying or thinking, 'I will not commit or participate in any unjust actions for fear of any consequences (etc.)'. This would be compatible with his in fact, one day, performing an unjust action. If he does so, we may presume that one of the possibilities we have mentioned obtains – e.g. extreme hunger has driven him to snatch the bread from a fellow prisoner's hands. (Later on we will be considering another possibility: that of a just man's committing an unjust act because faced with a dilemma between two unjust courses of action.)

It is natural to think that if a habitually just man does one day commit an injustice he will (unless he is *non compos mentis* or has suffered a character-change) feel regret, remorse or the like; and that his feeling regret is in fact a criterion of his being a just man. Knowing all this, a just man aware of his own virtue might say, 'I will not commit or participate (etc.) ... but if one day I do, and have not become a different sort of person, I shall feel regret for what I have done.' His 'I will not ...' is an expression of intention, his 'I shall feel ...' is a (conditional) prediction, or as Anscombe puts it in *Intention*, estimate (1963, sec. 2–3). The difference between expressions of intention and estimates of what one will do lies especially in the different sorts of grounds one gives for the two sorts of statement, i.e. the different sorts of answer one gives to 'Why?'[5]

'If one day I do, then I shall feel regret' is only a conditional prediction. But couldn't someone have grounds for thinking that he *will* do something regrettable? He might know that extreme temptations or provocations await him; he might know he is going to be threatened with torture by people wanting him to betray his companions. Anscombe discusses this kind of situation in the final section (sec. 52) of *Intention*, writing that 'if one is considering the fact that one may not do what one is determined to do, then the right thing to say really *is* "I am going to do this ... unless I do not do it"' (1963, 93). She goes further: 'In some cases one can be as certain as possible that one will do something, and yet intend not to do it' (ibid., 94) – which would appear to warrant one's saying 'I will not do this, but I shall do it.'

Perhaps Anscombe goes too far here. Someone's being *as certain as possible* that she will do something may be thought to rule out her intending (or properly expressing the intention) not to do it. Be that as it may, it is surely humanly possible for someone who intends not to φ nevertheless to have grounds for fearing that she may (well) not be able to adhere to her intention. And her 'intention not to φ' might be the intention characteristic of the just person, viz. not to commit or participate in any unjust actions for fear of any consequences, or to obtain any advantage, for herself or anyone else.

We have seen that for intrinsically unjust acts, Anscombe's just man will have a standing intention not to φ, where 'φ-ing' is an act-description of a more specific kind than 'doing what is unjust' – e.g. 'procuring the judicial execution of an innocent person'. Anscombe indicates that such an action as procuring the judicial execution of an innocent person 'should be quite excluded from consideration' (*MMP* 40). She evidently sees such a stance of exclusion as being a part of the virtue of justice. Given the human possibilities of temptation, provocation, etc., the just man will quite exclude certain kinds of action from consideration while *not* excluding the real possibility of performing such actions.

Here it might be asked: 'So what *is* it to exclude certain types of action from consideration?' A possible answer would be: 'Consideration means deliberation; a person acting and thinking justly will, in the course of deliberating what to do, refuse to consider (as something that might have its pros and cons) an action of such-and-such type, or of such-and-such type ...' Of course the man who cracks under torture or the starving woman who snatches a fellow prisoner's bread are hardly likely to have *deliberated* what to do. Are we then to say that unjust acts must be deliberate? – that where severe temptation, provocation, etc. exclude deliberation, a person cannot act unjustly?

This would be too quick. Justice is not only put to the test in situations where the agent actually deliberates. After all, deliberation can in some sense be excluded by ordinary haste or thoughtlessness, and in such cases we can still call what is done unjust, adding only that the person *should* have thought more carefully, perhaps even *should* have deliberated. 'Should' implies 'could', it might be said; and in what sense could a hasty person have deliberated while a starving person could not? The question is a difficult one, and is among other things connected with the (in)voluntariness of (not) thinking certain thoughts.[6] But it need not detain us here, since the answer to it does not directly impinge on our topic, namely whether it is necessary for being a just person that when you *do* deliberate what to do, you habitually refuse to consider various kinds of (unjust) options.

The virtue of justice, according to this picture, involves a negative habit: the habit of not allowing certain sorts of action to figure as options on a deliberative agenda. Now one might have such a habit though one never forms the judgment 'No deliberative agenda may include such-and-such options'. An analogous possibility exists for inductive belief: a person or creature can be in the habit of forming particular expectations on the basis of particular observations or experiences, without ever forming any general judgment of the form 'Whenever p, q'. – 'But wouldn't that just show that the creature was unreflective? Shouldn't a reflective creature who has such a habit be led by reflection to form the general judgment?' The claim is dubious. I habitually sit on chairs with a confidence expressive of the belief 'This chair won't collapse under me'; but reflection does not lead me to endorse the generalization, 'No chair will ever collapse under me,' still less 'No chair will ever collapse under somebody.'

It seems that a reflective person might have the negative habit belonging to the virtue of justice without forming a corresponding general judgment. But it still might be thought that the negative habit is not enough, and that a just person *ought* to say or think, 'No deliberative agenda may include such-and-such options.' Anscombe's characterization of the just person does not entail this. But as the above discussion of 'habitually' and 'any' indicates, her just man *will* say or think 'I will not commit or participate in any unjust actions for fear of any consequences (etc.)'; and as regards *intrinsically* unjust acts, it might naturally be supposed that he will not only think such a thought, but also the thought 'I will not allow any such actions to figure among the options on my deliberative agendas' – a commitment tantamount to 'May no deliberative agenda of mine ever include such options'.

However, 'May no deliberative agenda of mine include …' differs from 'No deliberative agenda of mine may include …' The first is an optative or third-person imperative; the second uses 'may' as a modal verb, and the whole sentence can be read as containing a 'stopping modal', being equivalent to 'Deliberative agendas of mine must not include …'[7] The first statement can be rephrased in the first person as 'May I not/never include on any deliberative agendas …' This shows why it expresses the same commitment as the expression of intention, 'I will not …', so that it too may be attributed (as a possible thought or utterance) to the just person. Nothing that has been said so far warrants our attributing to the just person the 'stopping modal' judgment. The paradigm use of stopping modals is within rule-governed practices, such as games, where a 'must not' is backed up by what Anscombe calls a *logos* (e.g. 'my queen is attacking your king', or 'that bicycle isn't yours'). The *logos* is partly what distinguishes the stopping modal from a mere imperative. No *logos* appears forthcoming to back up the statement 'No deliberative agenda of mine may include …'[8] One might respond to such a statement, 'Why not? According to what rule?' A Kantian will perhaps look for a principle of reason to answer that question, but Anscombe is not one to follow the Kantian here – and nor do I.

Moral Dilemmas

As we saw above, cases where a just person does commit an injustice will, for Anscombe, be ones where she *fails* – where for some reason she has not the strength to adhere to her overriding intention not to commit or participate in unjust actions. She is then likely to feel regret for what she has done. These two features of the situation – failure ('coercion of will', etc.) and regret – are absent from the situation in which a person decides to adopt an unjust choice as 'the best thing to do', especially on the basis of a calculation of consequences.

Anscombe is famously critical of consequentialist reasoning about whether to commit injustices. And her aversion to such reasoning carries over to an aversion to framing hypothetical extreme scenarios in which a blanket refusal to consider doing what's intrinsically unjust is put under pressure. In 'Modern Moral Philosophy' she writes: 'The point of considering hypothetical situations, perhaps very improbable ones, *seems* to be to elicit from yourself or someone else a hypothetical decision to do something of a bad kind' (*MMP* 37). A bit later in the article she states her objection more directly, in a footnote:

> In discussion when this paper was read, as was perhaps to be expected, this case was produced: a government is required to have an innocent man tried, sentenced and executed under threat of a 'hydrogen bomb war'. It would seem strange to me to have much hope of so diverting a war threatened by such men as made this demand. But the most important thing about the way in which cases like this are invented in discussions, is the assumption that only two courses are open: here, compliance and open defiance. No one can say in advance of such a situation what the possibilities are going to be – e.g. that there is none of stalling by a feigned willingness to comply, accompanied by a skilfully arranged 'escape' of the victim. (*MMP* 40, footnote 6)

It is clearly a real objection to say: 'A case like this needs to be spelt out *in detail* if we are to know what the best course of action would be; and to arrive at a conclusion about that in advance of looking at any such details is wrong-headed: practically wrong-headed if you find yourself in such a situation, and philosophically wrong-headed if you are thinking about it hypothetically.' But if 'no one can say in advance of such a situation what the possibilities are going to be', then no one can say in advance that there will *be* any possibilities of stalling, feigning or of similar ruses. The details of a case surely might rule out all such possibilities. We need not conclude that in that case only the 'weighing of consequences' can help us; the situation might instead wear the guise of a genuine dilemma, maybe even a dilemma between two courses of action each of them unjust – or at any rate prima facie unjust.

In an unpublished and undated typescript which appeared posthumously under the title 'Two Moral Theologians', Anscombe (2008) addresses the topic of moral dilemmas.[9] She writes: 'That if you can see no possibility except to give some information you must not give, or to lie, you will do better to lie than, say, to betray the unjustly persecuted fugitive – this is sufficiently obvious' (2008, 163). But she takes the fact that a person can't *see* a way out of such dilemmas as indicating his imperfection; for it remains true that to lie is sinful. Of the question whether in such cases it is possible to 'avoid any sin at all', she says: 'The truth is: you might not be good enough to do that.'

Perhaps a moral dilemma is a situation where whatever you do you end up spoiling your life, leaving a blot on it. But it isn't so clear that being, or acting, in such a situation implies any imperfection of character: why must it be a question of a person's not being *good* enough to see how to avoid sin? That goodness of character need not be at issue seems to come out in what Anscombe herself writes a bit later on: 'If you *cannot* see any alternative to committing one sin or another, you act better if you choose the lesser sin. And you may not have time or cleverness to find out a better possibility' (2008, 164). Lack of time or cleverness can hardly be taken as indicative of defect of character, particularly lack of time. And the same must surely be said of an inability to see (= think of) practical routes available in what could, after all, be a situation both novel and surrounded by constraints.

It would also need arguing that even where one cannot *see* a way out of a moral dilemma there will always be such a way. At Corinthians 10.13, St Paul says, 'But God is faithful; He will not suffer you to be tempted beyond that which ye are able to bear, but with the temptation will also make a way to escape, that ye may be able to bear it.' Could a Christian interpret 'a way to escape' as pointing to such ruses as stalling and feigning? The passage surely suggests, rather, that Paul has in mind situations in which what is put to the test is someone's strength of will, their ability to withstand the force of certain temptations. So this passage, at any rate, seems not to be one which, as a Christian, Anscombe would have reason to quote in her defence.

It seems to me impossible to maintain that in every moral dilemma of the sort we are considering there will in fact be a 'way out' for a just person. This indeed appears to be a consequence of the fact mentioned by Anscombe herself, that 'no one can say in advance of such a situation what the possibilities are going to be'. But if I am right about that, it does not follow that the virtue of justice cannot be seen as Anscombe sees it, as involving the standing intention not 'to commit or participate in any unjust actions for fear of any consequences, or to obtain any advantage, for himself or anyone else'. It is true that things will begin to look worrying if insoluble dilemmas *between unjust courses of action* are conceivable. If such dilemmas are possible, then the just man who finds himself facing one will be unable to abide by his intention; and in grasping one horn of the dilemma, he will presumably be opening himself up to regret or something like it. A dilemma like that between taking another's property and diverting a flood will not be of *this* sort, since in such a case, if Anscombe is right, an act-description which typically entails injustice does not do so (i.e. the act-description 'taking another's property without his permission'). Nor are we thinking of dilemmas where each horn is prima facie unjust and where it is *indeterminate* which one represents the best option, such indeterminacy resulting from the non-algorithmic nature of practical wisdom; for unless each prima facie injustice is an intrinsic injustice (in which case the phrase 'prima facie' is out of place), the person who chooses one horn of the dilemma may surely point to the other horn as constituting a circumstance analogous to that of the need to divert a flood – i.e. as nullifying the description of what he does as 'unjust'.

Thus if there are insoluble dilemmas between unjust courses of action, they are dilemmas between *intrinsically* unjust courses of action. Now the difficulties surrounding this idea are fairly obvious. Philippa Foot agrees with Anscombe that some kinds of action are absolutely prohibited (i.e. that their performance will always be vicious, necessarily detracting from the agent's goodness as a human being). But she argues against the thesis

> that two absolute moral prohibitions, which will relate to intentional actions, could conflict. For however terrible the inescapable choices that people have to make, they will never be between two intentional actions, as, for instance, torturing X and torturing Y, but only between torturing X and *not preventing* another from torturing Y, or from bringing about some other horrible result. (Foot 2002, 188)

For Foot, intrinsically unjust actions will be intentional *actions*; they will not be nonpreventions. Anscombe's example of the unjustly persecuted fugitive appears to show, by contrast, that she thinks that *not preventing* unjust pursuers from finding a fugitive might count as betrayal, and hence as unjust; but the passage in question is not entirely clear on this point, since Anscombe describes one horn of the dilemma as 'giving some information you must not give' (a type of intentional action). If the dilemma could be avoided simply by doing nothing, then it would seem strange for Anscombe to dwell on the phenomenon of a person's seeing no possible way out, given that doing nothing is always an obvious option. Hence I am inclined to think that she did believe in the conceivability of dilemmas between intrinsically unjust courses of action, at least at the time of writing 'Two Moral Theologians'. She did not, however, think of these dilemmas as insoluble, since she took it that there would have to be some 'way out', such as a feint or a ruse. This thought, I have argued, lacks justification, and indeed credibility; but without it, the claim that such 'tragic' dilemmas are conceivable leads to the conclusion that even a perfectly just and wise person can end up doing 'the wrong thing'. And as Foot writes,

> If we want to accept 'wrong if you do, wrong if you don't' as an intelligible possibility, and still keep [the] negative relation between doing what is wrong and personal goodness, we have to revamp the latter notion to make that goodness vulnerable to the 'taint' of involvement in a horrifying, humiliating, or tragic situation, or to the hatred of the gods; and then say that a choice that involves such *badness* is 'wrong'. (2002, 188)

(Ir)relevance of Motive

Two questions face us. First, why should it be thought a virtue to have these two characteristics: (a) maintaining a standing intention not to commit or participate in any unjust actions (etc.), and (b) being someone who quite excludes certain types of action (viz. intrinsically unjust ones) from consideration? Second, why should we think there *are* any intrinsically unjust types of action?

It could be argued that a person who is temperate in her eating has a standing intention not to go in for any gluttonous actions, for whatever reasons. She might on some occasion choose to eat an enormous amount, for instance if the customs of the country she is in make it likely that her hosts (who have piled her plate with sweetmeats) will strongly resent her leaving any food untouched. But in this scenario her eating will not count as gluttony: for her motive is not foodie bliss, but avoidance of conflict. So she has abided by her standing intention.

We might sum this up by saying that there are no 'intrinsically gluttonous' acts; but seemingly this can only be true if there is a limit on how *detailed* the descriptions of types of act can be – for a sufficiently detailed description of an act of eating, one that includes description of the surroundings, the lead-up to the act, etc., may in practice rule out any motive *other* than foodie bliss. I say 'in practice', since it is arguable that the list of possible defeating conditions (conditions which would defeat the verdict 'gluttonous') is an open-ended list, of the sort described by Anscombe in 'On Brute Facts'.[10] If we do say that about the list of possible defeating conditions, we shall be able to stick to 'There are no intrinsically gluttonous acts'. And for similar reasons we may, following Anscombe, say, 'There are no intrinsically larcenous acts.'[11] In what follows I will assume that these are things we *do* want to say.

The fact that there are no intrinsically gluttonous types of act is what enables us to claim that a person who is temperate in her eating has a standing intention not to go in for any gluttonous actions, for whatever reasons. The trick pulled here will not work for any virtue-concept, however. It works for temperance because of the importance of *motive* for deciding whether something counts as gluttonous. The concept of tidiness, for example, looks rather different. Consider a habitually tidy person who is enrolled by the secret service, and is one day required to leave his flat in a complete mess to make it seem as if he is an alcoholic going off the rails (hence appearing to be easy prey for the other side's agents). He has certainly left his flat untidy – has in fact failed to *be* tidy. He has been deliberately untidy. Here motive is irrelevant. Some courses of action just are intrinsically untidy, and motive has nothing to do with it.

The difference between temperance and Anscombe's version of justice lies (in part) in the non-existence of intrinsically gluttonous kinds of act and the existence of intrinsically unjust kinds of act. We saw that whether eating a huge amount counts as gluttonous depends on the motive with which it is done, and something similar seems to go for those sorts of act which can be sometimes unjust, sometimes just: it is the motive *that the flood be diverted*, e.g., which turns what would otherwise be an unjust use of someone else's machine into a just use of it. And it might be now asked: why may not the motive behind judicially executing an innocent man be relevant to whether *it* counts as just?

Anscombe writes:

> No circumstances, and no expected consequences, which do *not* modify the description of the procedure as one of judicially punishing a man for what he is known not to have done can modify the

description of it as unjust. Someone who attempted to dispute this would only be pretending not to know what 'unjust' means: for this is a paradigm case of injustice. (*MMP* 39)

Paradigm cases lie at the centre of concepts: where a person's very mastery of a given concept, F, involves knowing (or: being able to say) '*This* is an F, if anything is', the 'this' in question counts as a paradigm case. Hence denying that a paradigm case of an F is an F shows either that you are not master of the concept, or that you are 'only pretending not to know what "F" means'.

Anscombe's argument appears to run: 'The concept "just" is such that X is a paradigm case of injustice; so X is always and everywhere an injustice; so what motive a person has cannot prevent an instance of X from being an injustice.' The term 'X' here denotes a *kind* of act, or course of action: here, judicially executing an innocent person.

Roasting a chicken is a paradigm case of preparing food, but not every case of chicken-roasting is a case of preparing food. One might roast a chicken so that it can sit on a table as a realistic prop in a play. 'Well, that *particular* chicken-roasting wasn't a paradigm case of preparing food, then.' What follows if we agree to that statement? Surely not: roasting a chicken is *not* a paradigm case of preparing food. The lesson of 'On Brute Facts' is once again relevant; the list of defeating conditions on whether some action is a case of food-preparation is indefinitely open-ended. If we insist on talking of all instances, we shall have to say that every chicken-roasting performed in normal (ordinary) circumstances is a case of preparing food, and the open-endedness is now simply embodied in the concept *normal*.

Where there is an *analytic* connection between the concept F and the concept G, Gs being paradigm cases of Fs, then for sure, every G must be an F. Tomcats are paradigm cats; and every tomcat is a cat. But this is because of the definitional connection of 'tomcat' and 'cat'. Anscombe cannot, I think, be alleging *that* sort of connection as holding between 'judicially executing an innocent person' and 'unjust'.

Well, maybe the move from 'The concept "just" is such that judicially executing an innocent person is a paradigm case of injustice' to 'Judicially executing an innocent person is always and everywhere an injustice' is not as it stands quite safe. But surely what Anscombe is really saying is: doing this is going to count as unjust *regardless of the agent's motive*? And that sort of thing can be said elsewhere, after all, as we saw in the case of untidiness. Intentionally or voluntarily leaving your flat in a mess is being untidy, whatever your motives.

But that very fact about untidiness is what makes it seem wrong to claim that the tidy person quite excludes untidy types of action from consideration. A tidy person can easily (and properly) allow that untidiness might on a given occasion be acceptable, even required. If certain sorts of action simply have injustice written into them, so to speak, how can we claim that it is a *virtue* to exclude those types of action from all consideration? – a vice not to exclude them? (I assume that to lack justice is to be to that extent vicious.) It cannot just be that questions of justice and injustice are much more important than questions of tidiness and untidiness, for importance can often outweigh importance, as when one takes someone's expensive machine and uses and destroys it in the course of diverting a flood. One does not do such a thing lightly – but still, one does it.

The Nature of Practical Wisdom

To make headway with this problem we should turn to the motives behind actions that are performed *from* justice – actions that are just in a sense that goes beyond being 'not unjust'. (Here, 'actions' include not-doings.)

A major reason why calculation of consequences often looks out of place in deliberative situations to which considerations of justice are relevant is this: the virtue of justice relates especially to reasons for action that arise from present or past facts. An important subclass of these are those institutional (i.e. practice-based) facts that are paradigmatically expressed using stopping and forcing modals – 'You can't take that, it's not yours', 'He didn't do it, so you can't punish him for it', 'She should do it since she promised to'. Again, the just person who has erred against justice will feel called upon to express regret or remorse in such terms as 'I am sorry; I lied to you', and behind this utterance lies the thought, 'I did such-and-such: I must apologise'. Justice itself requires our apology, and the 'must' belongs to a human practice, that of making apology.

An institutional 'must' or 'cannot' may be overridden by facts having to do with consequences. 'You cannot take another's property without his permission' may be overridden by 'Only by doing so in this situation can we divert the flood'. But one who decides to act against the 'cannot' won't have done so by calculating or estimating the badnesses of two outcomes and choosing the lesser. The badness of ignoring the rule about property doesn't reside in any *consequences* of doing so, in the sense of 'effects brought about by doing so'. Nor does it if we expand the sense of 'consequences' to include what might be naively called 'the act itself'.[12] Talk of 'badness' here is indeed clumsy; what is true is that understanding 'You cannot take another's property without his permission' involves taking it as a reason against φing that if you φ, you take another's property without his permission.[13] How then do I weigh the reason for not taking another's property against the reason in favour of diverting a flood?

The answer to this need not – cannot, I would say – advert to any calculus or currency, any single 'scale of value'. For the two reasons for action are of radically distinct types. After all, even consequential or forward-looking reasons can be incommensurable. In the marketplace you are asked to pay £60 for a rug; you say 'I'll give you £45'; the vendor says '£50' – whereupon you say, 'OK … or I could invite you to be a guest at my daughter's wedding.' A classical utilitarian will insist that the vendor must now calculate the amounts of something, e.g. pleasure, available to him from each choice, if he is to decide on anything. But *this* 'must' is the 'must' expressive of enchantment by a philosophical picture. What the utilitarian claims is a truth neither of reason nor of experience, as Hume might have put it. So what *does* go on in the mind of the vendor? Perhaps he spends a moment imagining being at a wedding; if he knows who else is likely to be there he can imagine it in more detail, of course. He may ask himself whether the offer made him is an affront, or insincere. Or he may just laugh and repeat his offer of £50. Nothing more need happen. To say that something else *must* happen, maybe subconsciously, is simply to express adherence to the above-mentioned picture (one that was pretty thoroughly exploded by Wittgenstein in his later writings, by the way).

The vendor's possible reasons for action are all of them to do with consequences: they are forward-looking. In situations where one of the reasons in play is forward-looking and the other is backward-looking, e.g. relating to a promise made, the notion of a quantitative calculation is even more out of place. Now an expected-utility decision-theorist may stipulate that the value ascribed by Mary to keeping her promise has a precise quantity, being equivalent to the smallest sum of money she would accept in lieu of keeping it. (And if she'd accept no sum, then she ascribes infinite value to keeping it.) Insofar as the point of the stipulation is to allow for interpersonal comparisons of 'utility', it assumes that everyone ascribes the same, positive, value to money – after all, everyone knows that money is exchangeable for anything you want! (Thinking that money is the root of all evil must be radically confused.) But more pertinently to our topic: such a manoeuvre could only show that, for Mary, a certain forward-looking reason could, hypothetically, override the backward-looking one. This we already knew to be possible. The question is how Mary arrives at her decision. That she one day opts for the money doesn't mean that she is operating with a single scale or calculus; that she *would* do so, hypothetically, even if there is a fact of the matter about that at all, shows even less.

If it is possible for human beings to decide between conflicting reasons for action (i.e. reasons for incompatible courses of action) without their employing a single scale of value, how do they do it? This question is rather like: how do human beings hear the direction from which a sound comes? Typically you do not employ a *method* for detecting where a sound comes from, and if asked 'How did you do that?' would have to reject the question – or interpret it as a question not about methods but about your constitution, your faculties. If you are knowledgeable, you will advert to the slight temporal difference between when a sound reaches one ear and when it reaches the other. No *physiological* answer can be given to the question at the head of this paragraph, of course. But we can also take that question as asking about our faculties. Taken as a question about methods it can only be met by an entirely uninformative answer, along the lines of 'By thinking carefully about the salient issues – sometimes'. Taken as a question about our faculties, the answer – also hardly informative – will be: human beings have common sense, or practical wisdom. (Those are not synonyms, by the way.)

The faculty of practical wisdom differs from that of directional hearing in that there is an independent test for where a sound is coming from – independent, that is, from verdicts made on the basis of where we *hear* it as coming from. There is not in that sense an independent test for whether it would indeed be right to choose to divert the flood rather than avoid using another's property. It does not follow that such a choice is merely subjective – that there's no such thing as going wrong. Here, roughly speaking, objectivity arises from the twin phenomena of intersubjective agreement and a social practice of giving and comparing reasons. Such an account of objectivity will be familiar, having been explored and spelt out for a variety of discourses, not least ethical ones. I will not dwell on it here, but will rather return to the question: What is to rule out a just person's taking certain e.g. consequential reasons as overriding the reason 'He did not commit the crime' (when deliberating whether to punish someone)?

Practical wisdom is the faculty, among other things, of knowing when one reason for action overrides another, and this can include cases of a forward-looking reason's overriding a backward-looking one, as we have seen. Now Aristotle was surely right to think that practical wisdom (*phronesis*) cannot be taught by means of instruction, e.g. in rules: a person must acquire, through experience of life and reflection on it, a kind of sensibility, or rather kinds of sensibilities, enabling him to know when a concept like 'lying' truly applies, for example. So when someone asks, 'Why is it sufficient reason to take his machine that you can thereby divert a flood?,' nothing like a proof or demonstration is going to be available, and such remarks as can be given by way of reply will only persuade someone who himself has an adequate degree of practical wisdom. This means that it is open to Anscombe to say that 'Why can't we punish this innocent man to avert a riot?' (e.g.) can only be answered with 'reminder-like' remarks whose force will appear adequate only to those with practical wisdom.

Bedrock

The problem is that Anscombe is committed to a blanket assertion: that there *can* be no practical reason that could override 'The man is innocent' so as to favour the conclusion 'Let us punish him'.[14] So far, practical wisdom has been invoked only as the faculty enabling us to 'weigh' particular reasons against each other; can it also be credited with seeing in advance that no such weighing could ever lead to a certain practical conclusion?

We have seen that Anscombe regards it as possible that someone should be in a situation where he faces two choices, each of them unjust. It was of such a situation that she wrote: 'That if you can see no possibility except to give some information you must not give, or to lie, you will do better to lie than, say, to betray the unjustly persecuted fugitive – this is sufficiently obvious.' I suggested above that there seems no good reason to suppose that in every case where you cannot *see* a way out of a moral dilemma, there must nevertheless *be* one; and, in addition, that one's not being able to see a way out (even where there is one) needn't betoken a defect of character – neither a defect in justice nor a defect in practical wisdom.[15] If I am right, there may in principle be a dilemma between two courses of prima facie unjust action, one horn of which is *judicially executing an innocent man*, such that one who cannot see a 'way out' is not therefore to be counted an unjust person – where 'ways out' are ways of jumping between the horns of the dilemma (by adopting feints, ruses, etc.). But of course it might, for all that's been said, still be 'sufficiently obvious' that one must not execute the innocent man.

The issue seems to be one of onus of proof. Is it for Anscombe to show us why there can be no practical reason that could override 'The man is innocent', or for her opponent to show us that there *can* be such a reason? On the face of it, it would look more reasonable to require the second, not the first, if only because the truth of a negative generalization is harder to demonstrate than that of an existential statement. One might of course decline to pass judgment either way in the absence of persuasive grounds. It seems in any case clear that Anscombe regards as morally (not just intellectually) beyond the pale the philosopher who, *without showing why or how*, claims that there can be a practical reason that could override 'The man is innocent'. Indeed, she goes further than this, describing as 'corrupt' the philosopher who, without showing why or how, claims that *it is an open question* whether there could be a practical reason that could override 'The man is innocent':

> But if someone really thinks, *in advance*, that it is open to question whether such an action as procuring the judicial execution of the innocent should be quite excluded from consideration – I do not want to argue with him; he shows a corrupt mind. (*MMP* 40)

Is the alleged corruption to be understood as a failure to have adopted the stance of the just man, as embodied in the two characteristics mentioned earlier: (a) maintaining a standing intention not to commit or participate in any unjust actions (etc.), and (b) being someone who quite excludes certain types of action from consideration?

It is characteristic (b) which is more immediately relevant. If I am right that 'consideration' means 'deliberation', then Anscombe's just person habitually excludes certain kinds of act (intrinsically unjust ones) from her deliberative agendas, and can be credited with the thought 'I will not allow any such actions to figure among the options on my deliberative agendas' – an expression of intention. Since these are general remarks about what it is to be just, one may conclude 'No just person will, when deliberating justly, allow such actions onto her deliberative agendas.' 'A good man is a just man,' according to Anscombe – i.e. only just men are good men. So to think that it is open to question whether such-and-such an action *should* (always) be excluded from consideration is the same as thinking it open to question whether such-and-such an action *would* (always) be excluded from consideration by a just person deliberating justly (i.e. abiding by her standing intentions); for in this context, 'should' can only mean 'should, given the aim of being a good person'. But given that such-and-such an action is intrinsically unjust, it *cannot* be open to question whether it would (always) be excluded from consideration by a just person deliberating justly. To say that it is open to question is to be in the dark either about what justice is, or about the (putative) fact that such-and-such an action is intrinsically unjust, or it is to pretend to be in the dark about these things. Leaving the third case to one side, it *might* be argued that the other two forms of 'darkness' are symptoms of injustice or less than perfect justice; although the alternative diagnosis, of philosophical darkness, appears to have its attractions. Perhaps moral darkness and philosophical darkness cannot always be disentangled from one another.

'But isn't the question whether procuring the judicial execution of the innocent *is* intrinsically unjust? The arguments of the previous paragraph are quite ineffective if the answer to that is no.' That is right. And the passage quoted from Anscombe does not contribute anything to that question. I think, in fact, that the 'corruption' Anscombe has in mind is not just a case of 'being in the dark', as described in the last paragraph – something which, in any case, might seem to embody philosophical rather than moral failure. Her complaint comes out in the italicized phrase '*in advance*'.[16] Merely saying 'It is an open question whether …' is not what bothers her – it is saying 'It is an open question whether …' in advance of any details of possible cases being given. Perhaps someone might come up with a hypothetical (or real) scenario and say, pointing to it: 'You see; it's an open question whether certain practical reasons might not outweigh the reason

"He didn't commit the crime".' Anscombe believes that he will have gone wrong – but at least he will have taken the issue seriously enough to see that the onus is on him to give grounds. Now someone who has come up with such a hypothetical (or real) scenario would not in fact need to speak as tentatively as I have imagined. He could instead say, 'You see; on occasion certain practical reasons would outweigh the reason "He didn't commit the crime".' Hence it appears pointless for Anscombe to have directed her ire at the philosopher who 'really thinks, *in advance*, that it is open to question whether ...' She would have done better to refer to the person who thinks, in advance, that such an action as procuring the judicial execution of the innocent *certainly shouldn't be* quite excluded from consideration.

We might here wonder why the best course is not that of simply declining to pass judgment on the question whether any practical reason could outweigh 'The man is innocent', in the absence of persuasive grounds either way. For Anscombe's opponent, such grounds would most naturally take the form of detailed descriptions of cases. Anscombe's grounds can evidently not take that form. What form could they take?

Perhaps it is sufficient for Anscombe (a) to go through a number of candidate cases in which it might be made out that there were adequate grounds for executing an innocent man, in each case rebutting the claim; (b) to insist that the onus of proof must (now) be met by her opponent. How else, after all, is one to argue for what seems to one to be a clearly true negative generalization? How would you argue for the thesis that no one in America has in fact been abducted and later returned to earth by aliens? Those liable to deny that thesis will probably not have the sort of common sense that would enable them to hear your 'reminder-like' remarks as having any force; and no doubt Anscombe feels herself to be facing a similarly deaf opposition when it comes to the issue of executing innocent people.

It is often useful to note the parallels existing between the practical and the theoretical. And it is surely a part of theoretical wisdom – or if you like, of common sense – to say such things as 'Nothing will induce me to believe that anyone in America has been abducted and later returned to earth by aliens.' The epistemic virtue in question here is flanked by the two vices of excess and defect, called gullibility and scepticism. 'Only a gullible person would believe such-and-such,' we say; and it is an essential feature of the language-game that we should be warranted, sometimes, in refusing to consider various claims at all. Something similar goes for 'Only an excessively sceptical person would disbelieve such-and-such (e.g. that invisible bacteria cause diseases)': we will often be warranted in refusing to take certain doubts seriously.

What is the status of the blanket assertion 'Nothing will induce me to believe that ...'? Well, common sense is acquired not through learning specific facts or rules, but through experience and reflection, as was said above. Hence it is in the nature of the case that *grounds* for such a blanket assertion cannot be given, beyond those paralleling (a) and (b), two paragraphs back. These are facts to which Anscombe can appeal.

It is worth noting that one who says, 'Nothing will induce me to believe that p' is not committed to calling 'p' a necessary truth – a logical or conceptual truth, for example. We are evidently in the domain of those propositions discussed by Wittgenstein in *On Certainty*, especially those dubbed by commentators 'hinge propositions', after

Wittgenstein's remark that 'the questions that we raise and our doubts depend on the fact that some propositions are exempt from doubt, are as it were like hinges on which those turn' (1969 sec. 341). Although exempt from doubt, hinge propositions could 'in principle' be overturned, abandoned – but not, it would seem, in ways that we can *now* spell out as conceivable. When we do attempt to spell out situations where we would be justified in abandoning hinge propositions we either face the riposte 'But what gets judged by what?'[17] or describe situations where the standards of enquiry – within history, say – themselves start to crumble.

Conclusion

It is time to summarize the argument of this chapter.

Anscombe characterizes the virtue of justice by reference to two features of the just person: (a) that of having a standing intention not 'to commit or participate in any unjust actions for fear of any consequences, or to obtain any advantage, for himself or anyone else'; and (b) that of being someone who 'quite excludes' certain types of action from consideration (viz. intrinsically unjust ones). 'Consideration' means or amounts to 'deliberation'.

As to (a), it seems that an analogous feature can be imputed to the temperate person, this being possible because of the relevance of *motive* for what shall count e.g. as gluttonous. The point is a conceptual one, and does not, for example, carry over to the concept of tidiness. For Anscombe, motive is sometimes relevant to whether some act shall count as unjust (e.g. in connection with using another's property) – but sometimes it is irrelevant (e.g. in connection with procuring the judicial execution of the innocent). This might be said to make the concept of justice an interesting hybrid.

Those kinds of acts which are unjust regardless of motive (and indeed of any other circumstances) are 'intrinsically unjust'. Their intrinsic injustice fits them to be quite excluded by the just person from her deliberative agendas. This exclusion amounts to a negative habit, but also, presumably, involves a standing intention. There are however no grounds for imputing to the just person the thought 'No deliberative agenda may include such-and-such options', involving as it does a general stopping modal.

The question arises why certain kinds of act are to be deemed intrinsically (always and everywhere) unjust. This question becomes particularly pressing if we allow, as Anscombe does, the possibility of dilemmas between courses of action each of them unjust. Anscombe seems to address the question by allusion to 'paradigm cases'; but if so, her inference from 'Fs are a paradigm case of unjust acts' to 'All Fs are unjust' appears dubious. I argued that a better route to investigating the question was by starting with the observation that justice and injustice frequently, perhaps typically, supervene on past or present facts, e.g. institutional facts of various sorts. This means that there will typically be no 'scale of value' available to the person deliberating what to do, when reasons in favour of one course of action relate to such past or present facts. The only answer to 'How then do people decide what to do when there is a conflict of reasons?' is: 'By using practical wisdom or common sense'. As Aristotle said, practical wisdom is acquired not via instruction but through experience and reflection, and it involves a kind of case-by-case use of reasons.

Practical wisdom, characterized as the virtue employed in the 'weighing of reasons', may allow someone to see, e.g., that there is sufficient reason to take another's machine without his consent if one can thereby divert a flood. But we must ask: can practical wisdom also be credited with enabling someone to see, in advance, that *no* proper 'weighing of reasons' could ever lead to the practical conclusion 'Execute this innocent man'?

Anscombe could reply affirmatively to this latter question by drawing an analogy between practical and theoretical assertions of the form 'Nothing will induce me to think that p', and also between 'Only a corrupt mind would think …' and 'Only a very gullible/sceptical person would think …' Whether the analogies thus drawn are persuasive is something I have not here gone into (although I myself do find them persuasive). If the status of 'p' in 'Nothing will induce me to think that p' is that, roughly, of a hinge proposition, then we might indeed have to say that the claim that justice requires us always and everywhere to exclude from consideration the judicial execution of the innocent is one which – in principle – could one day be abandoned, without this abandonment being a symptom of unwisdom. But the sense of 'in principle' here means that such a 'concession' is compatible with our reasonably ignoring the person who claims, in advance, that there *must* be reasons (already available from within our rational armoury, so to speak) that could outweigh 'The man is innocent'.

Notes

1 Anscombe (1981b, 26–42). 'Modern Moral Philosophy' will henceforth be referred to as *MMP* in this chapter.
2 See *MMP* 34, 41.
3 *MMP* 38–41.
4 The logico-grammatical infelicity is independent of the conceptual clash, as can be seen from the fact that it is also found in the sentence 'Smith habitually eschews almost every unjust option'.
5 The obvious answer to 'Why will you feel regret if you do that?' will in fact give a reason, in the sense of 'reason' which is at the centre of Anscombe's account of intentional action: for it will be something like 'Because doing such a thing is unjust'. But this is the reason for the predicted *regret*, i.e. the answer that might later be given to the question 'Why do you feel regret?' The reason for the man's prediction, i.e. for his *belief*, is not this, but has to do with his view of his own character.
6 For a discussion of the voluntariness of thoughts, see Chapter Five of this volume.
7 For Anscombe's terminology of 'stopping modals', see e.g. her 'Rules, Rights and Promises' (Anscombe 1981b, 97–103).
8 The phrase 'of mine' is odd, of course. The point made here applies equally to 'No deliberative agenda may include …'
9 The essay discusses the writings of Arthur Vermeersch and Bruno Schüller. Since in it Anscombe uses the term 'consequentialist', which she had first introduced in *MMP*, we may infer that this article was written later than *MMP*.
10 Anscombe (1981b, 22–5).
11 'Thievish', if you prefer.

12 John Broome writes, 'If you break a promise, one consequence will be that you have broken a promise, and the wrongness of promise breaking can be taken as a bad feature of this consequence [...] In this way, the intrinsic value of acts can be absorbed into teleology' (1995, 4). 'Teleology' is the form of utilitarianism Broome is defending. – If I keep a promise, then it must be under the description *keeping a promise* that my action is to be made out as having intrinsic value; for it probably won't have any intrinsic value, except accidentally, under some such description *as bringing Smith a book*. But one could argue analogously that under the description *providing for my descendants* the action of investing my money in a certain way has intrinsic value. This latter way of talking would usually be ruled out by distinguishing the value an act has in itself from the value it has on account of what happens subsequently (especially what happens as a result of the act); and similarly, one ought to distinguish the value an act has in itself from the value it has on account of what happened earlier.
13 In the background is the fact that it is good for human beings to have and abide by the institution of property – better than not having it (at least 'in the nearest possible world'). But *this* good, consequent upon there existing the institution, does not and cannot play a part in any consequential deliberating by an individual agent.
14 Anscombe of course refers to the judicial *execution* of the innocent. She is not, evidently, against execution per se; nevertheless there is a question whether she would absolutely rule out judicial *punishment* of the innocent. For present purposes, we do best to put to one side the question whether execution per se can ever be justified.
15 Whether Anscombe is right to attach the importance she does to the rule against lying is a further question.
16 The importance of this phrase in the argument of *MMP* has been pointed out by Sabina Lovibond (see Lovibond 2004).
17 Cf. 'Hume and Julius Caesar' (Anscombe 1981a, 86–92, 89).

References

Anscombe, G. E. M. (1963), *Intention*. Oxford: Blackwell, 2nd ed.
———. (1981a), *From Parmenides to Wittgenstein: Vol. One of the Collected Philosophical Papers of G.E.M. Anscombe*. Oxford: Basil Blackwell.
———. (1981b), *Ethics, Religion and Politics: Vol. Three of the Collected Papers of G.E.M. Anscombe*. Oxford: Basil Blackwell.
———. ([2008] 2012), 'Two Moral Theologians', in M. Geach and L. Gormally (eds), *Faith in a Hard Ground: Essays on Religion, Philosophy and Ethics*. Exeter: Imprint Academic, pp. 157–69.
Broome, J. (1995), *Weighing Goods*. Oxford: Wiley-Blackwell.
Foot, P. (2002), 'Moral Dilemmas Revisited', in *Moral Dilemmas*. Oxford: Oxford University Press, pp. 175–88.
Lovibond, S. (2004), 'Absolute Prohibitions without Divine Promises', in A. O'Hear (ed.), *Modern Moral Philosophy*. Cambridge: Cambridge University Press, pp. 141–58.
Wittgenstein, L. (1969), *On Certainty*, ed. G. E. M. Anscombe and G. H. von Wright, trans. D. Paul and G. E. M. Anscombe. Oxford: Basil Blackwell.

Part IV
LANGUAGE

Chapter Thirteen

THE IDENTITY OF A WORD

Words in Context

Does the word 'rat' occur in the sentence 'Socrates loved Plato'? There is *one* way of taking this question such that the answer to it is Yes, namely the one whereby the answer is No when we replace 'rat' by 'sausage'. But there is another way of taking it such that the answer is No, and where we would say, 'Only three words occur in that sentence: "Socrates", "loved" and "Plato".'

According to this second reading of the question, and of similar questions, how shall we answer the following: Does the word 'Plato' occur in 'Plato loved if'? Of course the letters p-l-a-t-o occur in that order, but that can't be enough, given that we are denying the occurrence of 'rat' in 'Socrates loved Plato'. There is a gap after 'Plato', if we are speaking of the written sentence (or 'sentence'); but what if our enquiry concerns speech, rather than writing? – Well, if you say those sounds, someone writing down what you say is likely to write 'Plato loved if', with just those gaps between the words. But their doing so appears a matter of decision on their part, maybe influenced by precise vocal inflexions. For why not write down 'Play toe loved if'?

It's tempting to put the question here, 'Did you *mean* "Plato" or "play toe" when you said it?' But what would it be for me to have meant 'Plato'? 'Plato loved if' is after all meaningless. Is the issue one of whether the word, or the man, came before my mind as I spoke? In *that* sense I might mean 'rat' when I say 'Socrates loved Plato'. But we are meant to be construing 'Does X occur in …?' in such a way that 'rat' does not occur in 'Socrates loved Plato'. Moreover, nothing relevant may come before my mind when I say 'Plato loved if'; or I might have both 'Plato' and 'play toe' in mind, e.g. if discussing this very question.

I might of course say 'Plato loved if' – or rather 'Plato, loved, if' – if I am reading out answers to crossword clues, or saying what the first words on pp. 1, 2 and 3 of a book are. In that case I can be said to have meant the word 'Plato', in the sense of knowingly and intentionally uttering that word, the name of a Greek philosopher. And if somebody (over)hears me say 'Plato loved if', he may well take me to be uttering the three words in some kind of list, the truth-value of his surmise depending on what procedure it was I was actually engaged in. By contrast, if a parrot began calling out what sounded like 'Plato loved if', one could not claim that it was saying 'Plato' rather than 'play toe'.

If the question is whether 'Plato loved if' can count as an English sentence, in which the words collaborate and are not simply thrown together, it seems we can answer by reference to inferential relations. 'Plato loved Socrates' is inferentially related to various other sentences, such as 'Plato loved somebody', 'Somebody loved Socrates', 'Either

Plato loved Socrates or I'm a Dutchman' and so on. And this is not true of 'Plato loved if'. It does not, for example, entail 'Plato loved if or snow is white'. We can discuss the sentence 'Plato loved Socrates' and its inferential relations without considering any actual assertive use of it, though in saying that it e.g. entails some other proposition, we are in part saying what an assertive use of it *would* commit the speaker to, etc. And we assume that the speaker, if asked 'What do you mean by that first word?', would be the one who replies, 'I mean the Greek philosopher, Plato' – rather than the one who replies, 'It's the answer to 7 down: "Plato"; and the answer to 8 down is "loved" …' When we said above that 'rat' does not occur in 'Socrates loved Plato', we made a similar assumption as to what would count as an assertive use of that string of letters or sounds.

Someone might still insist that the name 'Plato' occurs in the written string 'Plato loved if', regardless of any background activity or practice (such as listing answers to clues). For haven't we put gaps between the words to show what they are? But the rule 'Put gaps around all words, and only words, when writing' requires that we *already* discern and distinguish words. The rule can after all be broken, e.g. if I write 'Every day language is not always perspicuous'. My *decision* to put a gap between 'every' and 'day' does not result in there being two words, and no such decision will all by itself make it true that there are three words in 'Plato loved if'. For us to discern the word 'Plato' in 'Plato loved if' requires justification. Now is it a justification to point out that one who wrote out this string would be likely to know that there exist the three words in question, and to have some purpose in writing them down? We could call that a justification if we wanted to; but this notion of justification would not really go beyond the facts cited (that one who wrote the string would be likely to know, etc.), and would moreover differ significantly from that given for saying that 'Plato' occurs in 'Socrates loved Plato'.

Consider now the following:

(PC) 'Plato is the cube root of some rose.'

We had to justify saying that 'Plato' occurs in the string 'Plato loved if'; do we not also need to justify saying that 'Plato' occurs in PC? Someone might argue that PC differs from 'Plato loved if', for either or both of the following reasons: (i) no special story about a 'background activity' (such as listing crossword answers) is needed to justify the claim that 'Plato' occurs in PC; (ii) 'Plato' is not just an element in some list in PC: it is working in collaboration with the other words, as it does in 'Socrates loved Plato' – working as the name of a person.

These two claims are likely to be themselves justified by the observation that PC is at any rate a *grammatical* sentence. But what are the 'rules of grammar' it is meant to conform to? Any such rules will pick out certain categories of expression, such as verb, adjective, noun – and it will be alleged that a grammatical sentence is one in which expressions are combined 'in the right way', as determined solely by their grammatical categories. Two problems now arise. First, there is more than one way of delineating grammatical categories; to some extent, delineation is stipulation. Secondly, if we take PC to be grammatical, we are assuming that 'rose' occurs as a noun in it, rather than as the past tense of the verb 'rise'; and what could justify this assumption?

Taking the second problem first, the only available answer seems to be something like 'It *has* to be the noun if the sentence is to be grammatical'. After all, won't we say some such thing if asked whether 'rose' is a noun or a verb in 'He gave her a red rose'? Perhaps there is a sort of circularity involved in calling the latter sentence grammatical: for to do so, we have to assume that 'rose' occurs as a noun, not a verb, and this assumption is apparently based on the requirement of taking the sentence to be grammatical. But the circularity is not vicious. For it is a practical necessity involved in language use that someone who has achieved linguistic mastery take a sentence in the most natural way, where this involves both assuming (if possible) that it's grammatical, and being generally in (actual or potential) agreement with others in the linguistic community as to how to understand it. The training that leads to this results in a person's being able to take a sentence or word a certain way without calculation or reasons.[1] If reasons *were* required, the circularity above mentioned would arise and would indeed be vicious, and language use could not get off the ground.

A moment ago I mentioned agreement in how to understand a sentence. Will there be such agreement in connection with PC? Well, understanding a sentence means in part being able to make inferences to and from it, and can't I and others e.g. infer 'Plato is a cube root' from PC? It may be asked why this inference is any better than the inference of 'Plato loved if or snow is white' from 'Plato loved if'; each 'inference' seems to be a purely formal manoeuvre. Of course, 'cube root' is a noun phrase, and 'if' is a conjunction. And it will be said that our rules of inference are framed in terms of grammatical, or logico-grammatical, categories, so that the inference of 'Plato is a cube root' from PC is akin to the inference of 'Plato is an author' from 'Plato is the author of the *Cratylus*', both 'author' and 'cube root' being nouns/noun phrases.

This brings us to the first problem I mentioned, namely that there are different possible grammars. In one sort of grammar, the word 'three', in 'I have three cats', counts as an adjective, belonging in the same category as 'red', 'big' and 'non-existent'. But if adjectives get explained as words that describe things, we have good reason to exclude 'three' (which as Frege showed does not describe any cats, in 'I have three cats', nor yet in 'My cats are three [in number]'). And there are further reasons for putting numerals into a separate grammatical category, such as that they only 'go with' count-nouns – obviously – 'There are three heats' being ill-formed. Reasons can also be given for putting 'big' in a different category from, say, 'red': for 'big' functions as an attributive adjective (in Geach's sense[2]), so that from 'Tim is a big mouse' you cannot infer a self-standing proposition 'Tim is big'. For 'Tim is a small mammal' is also true, and if the inference to 'Tim is big' worked, so would an inference to 'Tim is small', and we would get a contradiction.

In 'A Theory of Language?' Elizabeth Anscombe discusses this issue, writing: 'The difference of opinion about what belongs to grammar arises from belief in and practice of a "formal" science of grammar on the one hand, and a study of what a given use of words amounts to or achieves or tells us on the other'.[3] The philosopher who would insist that PC is grammatical has in mind the idea of a formal science of grammar, concerned only with 'structure' and 'form'. It is a formal rule that you can't put a finite verb after 'the'. But why not say that it is likewise a formal rule that you can't attach a numerical concept to a personal name, as in 'Plato is a cube root'? It would seem to beg the question to reply that *numerical concept* is not a grammatical category.

The fact is that the first of the two notions of grammar alluded to by Anscombe cannot be kept utterly distinct from the second. Relatedly, it seems impossible to define 'grammatical' in terms of formal rules governing independently graspable categories of expression: the delineation of those categories itself depends to some extent on what we are inclined to call 'grammatical' or 'ungrammatical', the latter being a close cousin of 'nonsensical'. Isn't 'There were three heats in the house' ungrammatical? How about 'London's half-heavy pertinence is buttery'? If the answer is Yes, then there is a case for saying such things as that 'pertinence' belongs to a different grammatical category from 'horse' (not that simply substituting 'horse' for 'pertinence' cures that particular sentence). The interdependence between the notion of the grammatical, on the one hand, and the rationale(s) for proposing certain grammatical categories, on the other, is related to that interdependence mentioned above, between the question whether S is grammatical and the question what grammatical category some constituent of S belongs to. (E.g. with regard to 'He gave her a red rose' and 'rose'.)

Given all this, shall we say that the name 'Plato' occurs in PC? We can say Yes, on the view I've been considering, so long as PC is grammatical. But in that case we can say Yes or No, depending on how fine-grained our grammar is; for evidently there is a case for having a grammar in which *numerical expression* is a grammatical category, with attendant rules about which expressions can properly be attached to a numerical expression – such a case as we saw hinted at in relation to 'three'. This does not go for 'Plato loved Socrates', since there is no degree of fine-grainedness of grammatical categorization which would justify calling the sentence ungrammatical.

I said that a choice of a grammar depends to some extent on what we are inclined to call grammatical sentences. The sort of inclination I have in mind is one that would be backed up by considerations of 'what a given use of words amounts to or achieves or tells us', in Anscombe's words. And our data here include such things as that an assertion of 'Plato is the cube root of some rose' would achieve or tell us nothing, in the relevant sense – though it could have various effects on listeners and even aim at such effects. This datum is connected with the fact that we cannot identify the use of 'Plato' in this sentence with its use in such a sentence as 'Socrates loved Plato': the two sentences do not belong together in a unified or unitary linguistic practice.

The foregoing remarks relate to the question whether a certain word occurs in a given sentence, or 'sentence'. And of course a word can occur without occurring in a sentence. I can look a word up in a dictionary and find the entry for it, at the head of which occurs the word itself. Assertive uses and inferential relations have nothing to do with this mode of occurrence. But why do we say that e.g. the word 'rebarbative' occurs on p. 607 of the Oxford English Dictionary, and is the *same* word that occurs in 'Henry was being rebarbative'? The answer is that there is a *connection* between these uses, these linguistic phenomena: the first phenomenon is an instance of a convention, a convention with a point or purpose (or points, purposes) – by which e.g. someone who encounters 'rebarbative' in a sentence like 'Henry is rebarbative' and finds it unfamiliar can read something likely to enable him to understand the sentence, produce similar sentences himself, etc. The convention itself rests on certain background conventions, notably those of spelling and of an alphabetical order.

The fact that 'if' occurs in the dictionary unbuttressed by other words, as the head of an entry, is not enough to show that it occurs in similar unbuttressed fashion in 'Plato loved if'. To repeat our earlier point, what would be needed to show that 'if' occurred in some written or spoken production of 'Plato loved if' would be a reference to some background activity, practice or convention, sufficiently determinate in its rules for there to be answers to such questions as 'What word is that [e.g. pointing to a string of letters]?', where such questions are *not* like 'What word did that parrot's squawk remind you of?' Examples of such activities and practices are: reading out quiz answers, listing your favourite words … and also writing in code. If there were a code in which 'if' meant 'Socrates', then not only would the string 'Plato loved if' include an occurrence of 'Plato', but that occurrence would be the same sort of occurrence as the occurrence in 'Plato loved Socrates': i.e. as the name of a man about whom one is saying something.

A Theory of Language?

In 'A Theory of Language?' Anscombe's main goal is to consider two questions: whether it is in principle possible to construct a theory of language, where this means a 'micro-reductionist' account of what it is for a sound (or written shape, etc.) to be meaningful; and more specifically, whether Wittgenstein can be read in the *Philosophical Investigations* (hereafter *PI*)[4] as proposing, or pointing towards, such a theory – the nub of the theory being expressed in the statement 'A sound is an expression only in a particular language-game'. (This is a fragment of a longer sentence occurring in *PI* 261.)[5] Her answer to the question about Wittgenstein is No, and it seems likely it would be No to the more general question also. Anscombe's argument is difficult and obscure; but one important strand in it is the challenge, for a 'micro-reductionist' theory of language, of specifying what it is for the same expression to occur in different contexts.

The basic case we will have in mind is where the same sound occurring in two different contexts counts as the same expression.[6] And we will want to say, as above, that the sound 'rat' in 'Socrates loved Plato' is *not* the same expression as the same sound in 'There's a rat in the attic'. Anscombe focuses on 'Slab', which is of course one of the few words that together comprise the primitive language-game described by Wittgenstein in *PI* 2. We can imagine that language-game being added to and expanded in a variety of ways, and to any extent. If it is so expanded as to include the phrase 'This lab work', understood as we understand it, then the word 'slab' will not occur in that phrase, any more than did 'rat' in 'Socrates loved Plato'. Anscombe writes:

> Whatever 'language-game' you may introduce 'This lab work' into, if this is the familiar phrase, the concatenation of the S phoneme with the cluster l-a-b isn't morphemic. – But now, of course, we want to know the criterion for morphemic as opposed to phonemic concatenation.[7]

The reason why this last question is difficult is that it is unclear what the difference is between 'mattering for the meaning' and 'making a meaning-contribution'.

> Shall we say: by itself the phoneme S does not have the kind of role we mean, the role of the sound in the language-game, but only when combined with other phonemes to make the sound 'slab'? Only the sequence has that role, and the single phoneme's contribution is that it is part of that sequence. To be sure the individual phoneme matters, witness the difference between 'slab' and 'slat'; we can't deny that it 'matters for the meaning'.

We would like to say of cases such as 'slab' vs. 'slat' that a single phoneme, e.g. B, may 'matter for the meaning', but will *not* 'make a meaning-contribution'; and Anscombe's challenge (which she goes on to articulate) is for us to explain and justify this distinction. A 'micro-reductionist' theory of the English language will have failed if it classifies the phoneme B as an expression; but how is it to avoid doing so, given that B does often matter for the meaning, make a difference to the meaning? How is the sound B to be denied a 'role in the language-game'?

Anscombe's use of the notions of morphemic and phonemic concatenation is worth remarking upon. It is no doubt motivated in part by the fact that her enquiry cannot be conducted using the simple notions of morpheme and phoneme, as these are usually defined. In particular, the way 'morpheme' is usually defined makes it unfit for our purposes. The *OED* definition is: 'A minimal and indivisible morphological unit that cannot be analysed into smaller units.' 'Morphology' in linguistics is defined in the *OED* thus: 'The structure, form, or variation in form (including formation, change, and inflection) of a word or words in a language'; and the general notion of *form* or *structure* will not, unaided, allow us to deny that the 'rat' in 'Socrates' is a morpheme – for it is certainly a structural part of the word 'Socrates'. (One sort of word-structure, among many, is syllabic structure.) Hence a more useful definition would seem to be *Merriam-Webster*'s: 'a word or a part of a word that has a meaning and that contains no smaller part that has a meaning'. But again, 'rat' has a meaning. What we want to say is that it does not have meaning *as it occurs in 'Socrates'*. And the standard definitions of 'morpheme' do not help us with this idea of 'meaning something (or: meaning X) when occurring in such-and-such a context'.

Returning to Anscombe: could we perhaps distinguish the word 'slab' from the same sound in 'this lab work' by reference to those 'connections' between uses of language which I discussed earlier, exemplified by inferences, by dictionary entries, by crossword clues and so on? Could we not say that there will be no such suitable connections between uses of 'this lab work' and uses of the word 'slab'? – But this would be to presuppose that we can already identify *uses of the word 'slab'*, i.e. occurrences of that sound in morphemic combinations. And doesn't this mean that we would be taking the identities of words as given, something which would undermine micro-reductionist goals?

However, in the basic case, identifying uses of the word 'slab' is the same as identifying utterances of the sound 'slab' in certain sorts of situations, involving certain human interactions (the bringing of slabs and so on). An explanation of the meaning of 'slab' would consist in showing how that sound is used in such situations. Hence, were we to

THE IDENTITY OF A WORD

advert to 'connections between uses of language', with the aim of distinguishing the word 'slab' from the same sound in 'this lab work', we need not be illicitly presupposing a criterion (or criteria) of word-identity. We need only presuppose the ability to see certain situations as belonging together: that in which A utters 'Slab!' in the presence of B, who then picks up *this* thing and carries it over to A – that in which B utters 'Slab!' in the presence of C, who then picks up *that* thing and carries it over to B – etc. And we will claim that a normal human being with this ability will *not* see as belonging with those situations one in which 'this lab work' gets uttered (e.g. by someone holding a sheaf of papers, having earlier written on those papers after doing things with test tubes …). The idea of a normal human being is here playing the sort of role which is indicated by Wittgenstein's phrase 'form of life'.

But now consider those earlier-mentioned additions to and developments of the original language-game involving 'slab'. Wittgenstein imagines two developments: (1) the addition of 'here' and 'there', used with pointing gestures, and (2) the addition of 'a', 'b', 'c' and 'd', which are used in (as we should say) *counting* slabs, pillars, etc. Does the sound 'slab' in 'd slab there' mean the same – is it the same word – as the sound 'slab' which was being used before the introduction of the new symbols? The uses of the latter sound were utterances of it in certain sorts of situation, situations which a normal human being would see as 'belonging together'. The sort of situation in which 'd slab there' gets uttered are ones e.g. where A utters it in the presence of B, who then carries four slabs, one after the other, to a spot at a distance from A (A's having pointed his finger at that spot). Surely this looks like quite a *new* sort of situation?

Anscombe regards the statement that the same word 'slab' is being used both before and after the introduction of the new symbols as a *stipulation*. It is Wittgenstein's describing matters thus that determines that it is so, just as it is Shakespeare's saying that 'Horatio' is the name of Hamlet's friend that determines that *that* is so. But it is a permissible stipulation, because of what Wittgenstein's aims are in the opening paragraphs of *PI*. Anscombe sums these up thus:

> The 'clear and simple language-games' are offered as objects of comparison, not models – to give us the idea of the possible functioning of a word in use, without even invoking that of meaning. For 'it [the idea of meaning] surrounds our considerations with a fog'.[8]

It is this contrast between objects of comparison and models that is important for Anscombe's case that Wittgenstein is not in the business of presenting us with a theory of language. Were he offering his 'clear and simple language-games' as models of language in general, his remarks about those language-games would appear to point towards a general account of language. But in that context, his statement e.g. that the same word 'slab' is being used both before and after the introduction of the new symbols would be 'positively fraudulent'[9], because question-begging.

And yet we surely *can* say that a normal human being would, or could, see the new developments of the builders' language *as* developments of it – and not as a distinct set of proceedings. They are still evidently putting up buildings, they are still co-operating in characteristic ways (perhaps they have a foreman with authority over the others), it is still slabs and pillars they are carrying around and placing here and there ... It need not even be the same set of builders who are employing what I have called the new symbols; a person coming across a case of the more developed language-game would surely be inclined to see it as a more sophisticated version of the less developed language-game, on account of the human activities in which the two are embedded. And on that account he would surely be within his rights to say that the same word 'slab' occurred in both language-games. That verdict need not be *compulsory*, since the idea of one language-game's being a development of another supplies a permissive, rather than a compelling, reason. But the verdict 'same word' would be a perfectly natural and intelligible one. If asked 'What *determines* the sameness here?' we could reply, 'The natural response (= judgment) of the normal human being.'

Hence I think Anscombe may be mistaken to speak here of mere stipulation on Wittgenstein's part. Her description of what he is aiming at in the opening paragraphs of *PI* might well, on the other hand, be perfectly accurate. Anscombe could however raise the following awkward question: if it is all right to say that the same word 'slab' occurs both in the original language-game and in the more sophisticated one, and is thus the same expression, *what category of expression is it?* We surely cannot talk of 'same expression' without being in a position to say 'same verb', 'same noun', 'same imperative' or whatever. But in the context of the 'developed' language-game, it is easily imaginable that the utterance of 'Slab!' will produce puzzlement, in roughly the way in which an English-speaker's shouting 'Slabs!' on a building site might. The utterance may force such questions as 'How many do you want?' and 'Where do you want them?', something that was not the case in the original language-game; and in fact it would not be at all clear that the sound 'slab', uttered thus in the developed language-game, had any function at all, on its own – let alone the function of an imperative, as we might have hoped. At any rate, it would be unclear that it had any function on its own in the case where the builders *no longer* utter 'Slab!' on its own and as tantamount to 'Bring me a slab'.

There is however much to be said against the statement made a moment ago, that we cannot talk of 'same expression' without being in a position to say 'same verb', 'same noun', 'same imperative' or whatever. The notion *same expression* is extremely versatile, even protean. In Anscombe's words:

> Language and human capacity are so complex that e.g. different words can come to be counted as in some way the same word. Cf. different *inflections*, as we call them. Or it might be that one used a different sound the next time: 'Slab', 'Tink', 'Noffle' might all be the 'same word' – you say 'Tink' if *last* time you said 'Slab', etc. but otherwise the role is the same. I don't know of any language in which that happens, but it *might*.[10]

'Slab' and 'Tink' are evidently the same imperative (if either is to be called an imperative, that is). But consider 'She is going', 'She goes' and 'She will go'. These involve different inflections (different tenses) of the same verb, it is usual to say. Does that mean that the words 'going' and 'go' in the first and third sentences are *not* the same expression as 'goes' in the second sentence? For e.g. the future-tensed verb in the third sentence is not 'go' – it is 'will go'. The 'go' in the third sentence we might call an infinitive, and an infinitive verb is surely not the very same expression as a corresponding finite verb. Meanwhile, 'going' appears to be an adjective – unless we take it to be simply a fragment of 'is going', not belonging to any part of speech itself.[11] But there surely *is* a sense in which 'goes', going' and 'go' are all the same expression – or if you like, forms of the same expression?

For certain purposes we may call 'goes', 'going' and 'go' the same expression, while *for certain other purposes* we may call them different expressions. And in the first case, whether we also speak of the same verb, or the same anything, will likewise depend on what purposes we have, i.e. on what use it would be to us to say so.[12] All this, I think, goes also for 'slab' as spoken in the original builders' language-game and as spoken in the developed builders' language-game.

A 'micro-reductionist' theory of language inspired by the opening paragraphs of the *Philosophical Investigations* will contain statements of the form: 'Sound S is meaningful (is an expression of the language) in virtue of its playing such-and-such a role in the language-game.' The character of the normal human being, analogous to that of the reasonable person as referred to in legal judgments, is on hand to guarantee that situations in which the expression 'slab' is used do not belong with ones in which 'this lab work' is used, and that the various situation-groups in which uses of 'this lab work' are to be found do not show the sound 'slab' as playing a distinctive role. Other sounds occurring in those situation-groups *will* play such distinctive roles, e.g. 'lab'; and this is connected with the fact that explanations of meaning can be derived from consideration of the uses of those sounds, but no explanation of meaning for the sound 'slab' can be thus derived. The notion of a role in the language-game appears, in this account, to be in the eye of the beholder, the beholder being 'the normal human being' – but this should be no objection against the micro-reductionist theory of language, given the Wittgensteinian equivalence between inter-subjectivity and objectivity (to put the matter briefly). The normal human being does provide a standard, and if this standard does not yield concepts with sharp edges, it is no worse for that.

But will the normal human being judge that the original 'slab' plays the same role as the sound 'slab' in the new sentence 'd slab there'? Will she judge that 'goes' plays the same role as 'going'? What about the English word 'in', as it appears in 'I have a pain in my foot', 'Smith has written a commentary in this book', 'They are in a muddle', 'They are in a huddle', 'John is in London' …? How many roles are played by the sound 'in' in such cases? (We could add 'in such cases'.) This last question is evidently void for uncertainty, the uncertainty arising from the fact that no *purposes* are specified or understood, relative to which the applications of 'same role' and 'same expression' might be justified in a given case. The normal human being will be powerless to judge how many roles a sound is playing in the absence of any purpose that might be served by the adoption of one criterion of role-sameness as against another.

And this does seem to spell trouble for our micro-reductionist theory of language. For the theory states that we could in principle proceed as follows: first, detect and classify those sounds which appear repeatedly in contexts of language use; secondly, determine which of those sounds play some role in a language-game. The second task would be the same as: determining which situations, of those in which certain sounds repeatedly occur, a normal human being would see as belonging together in the sort of way that meant that an explanation of the meaning of those sounds could be derived. (Such 'derivation' is of course not to be thought of as *proof*-like.) There are two problems: (a) there are indefinitely many different ways of 'taking situations as belonging together in the sort of way that means that an explanation of the meaning of the sounds can be derived'; and (b) an explanation of meaning, even if in some sense derived from (consideration of) a certain group of situations, does not on that account delimit what situations in which the sound appears count as ones in which it appears with that meaning.

Problem (b) can be illustrated as follows. An explanation of the meaning of the original word 'slab' that works by showing how it gets used on the building site will not determine for us *in advance* whether the use of 'slab' in 'd slab there' counts as the same use, or a new one; and indeed either verdict could be given, depending on what our purposes were in adopting the given criterion of sameness.[13] For certain purposes (and here problem (a) becomes relevant), we can take the *totality* of situations, original and later, involving the sound 'slab', and see *them* as belonging together in the sort of way that means that an explanation of the meaning of 'slab' can be derived. To be sure, the explanation would *look* different from the one we imagined in connection with the original word 'slab'; but this is compatible with our regarding the two explanations as explanations of the same word with the same meaning. Remember that explanations of meaning come in all sorts of guises, as Wittgenstein stressed so effectively; cf. the explanation of 'game' in *PI* 69: 'How should we explain to someone what a game is? I imagine that we should describe [sc. specific] *games* to him, and we might add: "This *and similar things* are called 'games'"'. For the sake of the interlocutor who thinks there must be such a thing as *the* ('complete') definition of any expression, he adds: 'And do we know any more about it ourselves? Is it only other people whom we cannot tell exactly what a game is?'

Some Recent Attempts

Anscombe's denial of the possibility of a micro-reductionist theory of language inspired by the opening paragraphs of *PI* thus seems to be right. What about other kinds of micro-reductionist theory of language? All such theories will need to be able to explain why the word 'slab' does not occur in 'this lab work'. And they will face Anscombe's challenge of distinguishing between 'mattering for the meaning' and 'making a meaning-contribution': they will need to be equipped to say, when it comes to 'slab' versus 'slat', that a single phoneme, e.g. B, matters for the meaning, but does not make a meaning-contribution. Finally, they will need to give some sort of account of when two sounds[14] uttered in different contexts count as the same expression, with the same meaning. Such an account may allow for some indeterminacy, some fuzzy cases, etc., but an account there must be.[15]

Jeff Speaks, the author of the online *Stanford Encyclopedia of Philosophy* entry for 'Theories of Meaning', writes that there are basically two kinds of theories of meaning, which should not be confused:

> One sort of theory of meaning – a *semantic theory* – is a specification of the meanings of the words and sentences of some symbol system. Semantic theories thus answer the question, 'What is the meaning of this or that expression?' A distinct sort of theory – a *foundational theory*

of meaning – tries to explain what about some person or group gives the symbols of their language the meanings that they have.

The first sort of theory of meaning, as described, would be tantamount to a dictionary. Is a dictionary a theory? In fact, what Speaks has in mind turns out more to resemble general theories *about* symbol systems, and about types of symbol; hence his taking semantic theories to address such questions as 'What sorts of things are contents?' and 'What is the relationship between content and reference?' Be all that as it may, the sort of micro-reductionist theory of language we have been discussing would I suppose be classified by Speaks as a foundational theory of meaning. He divides such theories into mentalist and non-mentalist varieties, the latter including causal theories, regularity theories and social norms theories. An illustration of the sort of thing on offer is the following description of a proposal of David Lewis:

> His idea was that the assignment of contents to expressions of our language is fixed, not just by the constraint that the right interpretation will maximize the truth of our utterances, but by picking the interpretation which does best at jointly satisfying the constraints of truth-maximization and the constraint that the referents of our terms should, as much as possible, be 'the ones that respect the objective joints in nature'.[16]

Lewis is considering what 'interpretation' of linguistic phenomena would give the right answer, e.g., to 'What does "slab" mean in this community?' The answer would 'assign content' to that expression. What would such an answer look like? Perhaps it would take the form 'The word "slab" has the content C'.[17] The expression 'C' would presumably be a synonym of 'slab'; we are evidently in the (putatively) lexicographical domain of 'semantic theories of meaning'. Of course even dictionaries do not only assign contents to words by giving synonyms or analyses, as is indeed impossible for vast numbers of words ('the', 'akimbo', 'sky', 'every', 'number', 'hello', 'in' …). But Lewis can hardly allow for a healthy liberalism as to what shall count as an adequate content-assignment, given that the imagined 'right interpretation' must involve our really *pinpointing* the meanings of expressions. 'A variety of dog' would be no good, for instance.

All is not lost, however, so long as we 'pick the interpretation which does best at jointly satisfying the constraints of truth-maximization and the constraint that the referents of our terms should, as much as possible, be "the ones that respect the objective joints in nature"'. It is to be supposed that most – or most of the important – expressions in our language are referring terms. And the meanings of these building blocks may be best assigned by assuming that they 'respect the objective joints in nature'. (We presumably already know ourselves what the objective joints in nature are, having – at some point – perfected our science.) We should like 'rabbit' to line up with a certain species of animal, rather than with some weird disjunction of properties. The question will arise *how* 'rabbit' comes to line up with the first and not the second.

A popular answer to this last question invokes causal origin: if the causal origin of a use (or uses) of 'rabbit' is perception of or interaction with actual rabbits, then 'rabbit' refers to that natural kind, and not to some weird disjunction of properties. It is suggested that the linguistic theories originally adumbrated by Kripke and Putnam can be extended from the cases of proper names and natural kind terms to the rest of language, or to a sufficiently large chunk of it. How would a causal theory of meaning address some of the questions raised earlier in this chapter?

The word 'rat' does not appear in 'Socrates loved Plato'. Let us assume that the meaning of some utterance of the word 'rat' is down to the causal origins of that utterance; if there is a (non-deviant) causal connection between rats and a given utterance of 'rat', then and only then will 'rat' mean what it means in 'There's a rat in that cage'. But what if, in my utterance of 'Socrates loved Plato', my production of 'rat' is as a matter of fact the effect of previous interaction with rats? This is surely not logically impossible. The philosopher could bite the bullet and say, 'In that case you do mean the animal.' But this would have to be retracted if my explanation of my words was along the lines of: 'I mean that the famous Greek philosopher Socrates, associated with the dialectical method, loved his pupil Plato, author of the *Cratylus*.' The philosopher might now allege that since this was my explanation, the causal connection with rats must have been 'deviant'. But that just shows he is admitting as primary the connection between what a person means and the phenomenon of explanation of meaning (verbal, ostensive or what have you).[18] A causal connection is not in itself deviant or non-deviant. And hand-waving about 'the intention to refer to the same thing as the people you learnt the word from' will not help matters.

Of course to interpret 'Socrates loved Plato' as involving the name of the animal is anyway ruled out on account of that interpretation's leaving the whole sentence in the lurch. We would have to ask: What then do 'Soc', 'es', 'loved', 'Plato' mean here? Perhaps causal origins can be found for all these uttered sounds. But evidently a little holism is necessary: among other things, we do need to be able to point to other situations in which the same sounds occur, with a view to finding those in which the sounds mean the same as in our first situation. The hopeful theorist who claims, in advance, that we'd be able to find (not that we'd ever be able to make the investigation) that what we *want* to call the 'same expressions' all do have the same (sorts of?) causal origins invites the Humean query: 'And is this a truth of reason? – of experience? – Or is it a product of the imagination?'

Part of the diagnosis of the problem is surely to be found in the phrase which Speaks uses in the above quotation: 'the assignment of contents to expressions of our language'. There is a strong suspicion that the 'theorist' has already got a list of the expressions of a language, and now wants to determine what they mean. But how would one have sorted out, from the jumble of noises and inscriptions that constitute a language, what the expressions of that language are? The expressions are the meaningful bits; is it that we could know that a certain sound was meaningful without knowing its meaning? This might be conceivable for a particular sound, but it seems inconceivable as applied to all the sounds discerned prior to the task of 'interpretation'. Of course Speaks could respond, for Lewis, that he is indeed assuming that he has a list of meaningful expressions, and that it is no part of his task to sort out, from the jumble of noises and inscriptions that constitute a language, what its expressions are. He takes *that* task as having been done. In other words, the hoped-for foundational theory is not intended as micro-reductionist. This would certainly explain the apparent lack of interest in such questions as whether 'this lab work' contains the word 'slab'; but it is worth noting that what is referred to as a 'foundational theory' turns out to presuppose its own underlying foundations.

Philosophy of Language and Beyond

What, then, can we say about what it is for one sound to be the same expression as another sound, uttered in a different context?

In the first section I emphasized how specific forms of this question might be answered by appeal to such *connections* between the uses of the sounds as are exemplified by inferences, by crosswords, by dictionary entries, by codes and in general by appeal to what can be called *background human practices and activities*. The terminology is obviously, and benignly, vague. By considering the different species of 'connections' that we count as such, a philosopher comes to see how extremely versatile and variable is the notion of 'the same expression'. This is something of which Anscombe is evidently aware, and in the second section we saw how problems with the notion of 'the same expression' are connected by her with difficulties in explaining the difference between morphemic and phonemic concatenation, and with correlative obstacles to the construction of what she calls micro-reductionist theories of language. She also brings to our attention the interdependence between what we are inclined to take as grammatical categories and what sentences we are inclined to take for nonsense – an interdependence that, once again, constitutes an obstacle for reductionism, in the form of 'bottom up' theories of grammar.

The lessons to be learnt are not only in the philosophy of language. You very often hear, in some philosophical discussion, an objection to a line of thought that can be summed up thus: 'If you adopt that line, then you're committed to saying that such-and-such expression is *just ambiguous*. But my/our intuition is that it isn't ambiguous. So that line of thought is unpromising.' The 'intuition' that an expression isn't ambiguous, but has a single sense, should not be allowed to play this sort of judicial role. For the adoption of a given criterion of synonymy, among a plurality of such criteria, is something that depends on a variety of issues, issues that should be brought out into the open. Our intuitions are, or ought to be, quite helpless when faced with such a question as: How many senses does 'in' have in 'I have a pain in my foot', 'Smith has written a commentary in this book', etc. etc.?

One application of this point is to be found in the philosophy of psychology. Consider: Does 'intend' mean the same in 'I intend to go' as in 'She intends to go'? Are 'intend' and 'intends' (forms of) the same expression? These questions concern what is often referred to as the problem of the first-/third-person asymmetry of psychological verbs. The problem arises especially because 'I intend …' (e.g.) is typically uttered without grounds and without the need for observation of the person (oneself), and because such an utterance has a special weight or authority – all this being in contrast to 'He/she/NN intends …' (These facts are in this context assumed to rule out those brands of behaviourism which allege that observation of behaviour is as necessary for 'I intend …' as for 'He/she/NN intends …') If the meaning of a word is determined by, or is correlative with, the way the word is *used*, then given the radical difference in how the first-person and third-person verbs are used, doesn't it look as if they must mean something different?

On what might be called a Cartesian view, 'I intend ...' is a report of a privately known inner state, while 'She intends ...' must be a report of something else, such as bodily behaviour.[19] On a more Wittgensteinian view, 'I intend ...' is not a report at all, being more like a declaration, while 'She intends ...' is a report, where the notion of a *mistake* is applicable to reports but not to declarations. On either sort of view, the uses or functions of the first- and third-person forms of the verb appear very different.

But our intuitions tell us that 'intend' and 'intends' mean the same, are the same expression! So either the idea of some deep first-/third-person asymmetry was illusory, or the picture of meaning as use looks unpromising – or both.

The argument is of course hopelessly swift. The proper philosophical task would be to investigate the ways in which it is *true* that 'intend' and 'intends' mean the same, and the ways in which it is *false* – relative to different criteria of synonymy and (thus) different purposes. We can certainly say: there are multiple connections between the first- and third-person uses of 'intend', connections which allow one to speak of a unified or unitary language-game. The unity of meaning of 'intend' is grounded in the unity of that language-game.[20] Against the background of that language-game the point of saying that 'intend' and 'intends' have the same sense is clear; while if our concern is to highlight the above-mentioned differences in the use of these words – e.g. to show up the implausibility of behaviourism – then the point of saying 'different in sense' is likewise clear.

These are remarks about philosophical method, backed up by considerations in the philosophy of language, considerations to do with criteria of identity and difference for *expressions*. This might pique philosophers who wish that the 'linguistic turn' had never happened; but that can't be helped. Meanwhile, the non-occurrence of 'rat' in 'Socrates' proves to be a trickier and profounder business than might at first have been thought.

Notes

1 This connects with the fact, as Cora Diamond (speaking for Frege) puts it, that:

> the rules of the language are in a sense permissions, though conditional ones: to make sense of a sentence is to apply such rules, but it is still a *making* sense, and not a mere recognition of what the pieces are and how they are combined, plus a following of the directions-for-use that have been determined for the individual pieces and their mode of combination. (1991, 111)

2 See Geach (1956).
3 Anscombe (2011, 201).
4 Wittgenstein (1958).
5 Anscombe (2011, 193).
6 The term 'expression' includes words, phrases, exclamations, sentences ...
7 Anscombe (2011, 196).
8 Anscombe (2011, 199).
9 Anscombe (2011, 198).
10 Anscombe (2011, 195).
11 It of course belongs to the part of speech *present participle*. But although that concept appears in grammar books, someone might still say, 'But (here) it only functions as a fragment of the genuine grammatical unit, "is going". After all, in French that would just be "va".' The issues

here evidently tie in with those mentioned earlier, to do with differences of opinion about what to count as grammatical categories.
12 A relevant concept here, it might be said, is that of the verb stem. 'Goes', 'going' and 'go' all share a verb stem, viz. 'go'. But even if the purport of this statement is quite clear, it does not dictate an answer to 'Same expression or different expressions?'
13 Thus the present point does not have to do with 'rule-scepticism', of the sort associated with Kripke's Wittgenstein; it concerns rather an indeterminacy that is consequent upon *theoretical abstraction* – the doing without reference to those concrete human purposes which alone could provide any determinacy.
14 Here as elsewhere, 'sounds' is an abbreviation of 'sounds, inscriptions, etc'.
15 David Kaplan proposes a criterion of word-identity that focuses on the speaker's or writer's intention, writing:

'The identification of word uttered or inscribed with one heard or read is not a matter of resemblance between the two physical embodiments (the two utterances, the two inscriptions, or the one utterance and one inscription). Rather it is a matter of intrapersonal continuity, a matter of intention: Was it *repetition*?' [I.e. Did the person intend to repeat a word, however incompetently?] It is not wholly clear, but it looks as if Kaplan might have to say that if I intend to refer to a sort of animal when I utter the 'rat' in 'Socrates loved Plato', then I do refer to that animal. (1990, 104)

16 Lewis (1984, 227).
17 It might e.g. read: 'The word "slab" has the content *noffle*'. See p. 178.
18 There is no supreme first-person authority in such explanations. I can't sensibly explain my utterance of 'Socrates loved Plato' by saying, 'I mean that causalism is a philosophical dead end'; or rather, I can't in the absence of some background practice or game, such as a prearranged code. For the default background practice is that of English language-use. The lack of supreme first-person authority here also means that you do not establish the occurrence of the name 'Plato' in PC just by laying it down that you would (or could) explain your use of 'Plato' in the usual way, i.e. as the name of a Greek philosopher, etc. Despite all this, a person's non-frivolous and sincere explanation of what she means or meant evidently has a default weight.
19 On this view, I do not have *grounds* for my belief that I intend to do X, since I am immediately aware of that intention. A Cartesian could attempt to assimilate the first- and third-person uses of 'intend' by taking the latter to involve ascription of *the same state* as is reported by 'I intend'; the third-personal judgment would then be a species of (unverifiable) inference, from outer behaviour to inner state. Wittgenstein's remarks about 'It's five o'clock on the sun' are relevant here; see *PI* 350–51.
20 I elaborate this thought further in Teichmann (2015, 40–46, 114–19).

References

Anscombe, G. E. M. (2011), 'A Theory of Language?' in M. Geach and L. Gormally (eds), *From Plato to Wittgenstein: Essays by G.E.M. Anscombe*. Exeter: Imprint Academic, pp. 193–203.
Diamond, C. (1991), 'What Nonsense Might Be', in *The Realistic Spirit*. Cambridge, MA: MIT Press, pp. 95–114.
Geach, P. T. (1956), 'Good and Evil', *Analysis*, 17, 32–42.
Kaplan, D. (1990), 'Words', *Aristotelian Society Supplementary Volume*. 64, 93–119.
Lewis, D. (1984), 'Putnam's Paradox', *Australasian Journal of Philosophy*, 62, no. 3, 221–36.
Teichmann, R. (2015), *Wittgenstein on Thought and Will*. New York: Routledge.
Wittgenstein, L. (1958), *Philosophical Investigations*, trans. G. E. M. Anscombe, ed. G. E. M. Anscombe and R. Rhees. Oxford: Basil Blackwell, 2nd ed.

Chapter Fourteen
RYLE ON HYPOTHETICALS

Hypotheticals and Inference Precepts

In 'General Propositions and Causality', F. P. Ramsey argued that for a large class of general propositions of the form 'All Fs are Gs', any such proposition amounts to a sort of rule: 'If I meet an F, I shall regard it as a G'.[1] For Ramsey, to express a rule of this sort is the same as expressing or reporting a psychological 'habit'. That wouldn't rule out genuine disagreement between somebody who uttered the quoted rule and somebody who e.g. uttered the rule 'If I meet an F, I shall regard it as a non-G', on account of its being possible for one to be proved right in what he believes (e.g. 'This F is a G') and the other wrong. Still, it would arguably be an improvement on Ramsey to infuse proper objectivity into the rule corresponding to 'All Fs are Gs' by rephrasing it more impersonally as: 'If one meets an F, one should regard it as a G.'

Ramsey adopted this account of such general propositions especially because of problems connected with the view of them which he and Wittgenstein (in the *Tractatus*) had earlier maintained: the view according to which any general proposition is equivalent to the conjunction of all its instantiating propositions, so that 'Everything is green' amounts to 'a is green and b is green and ...' A proposition 'All Fs are Gs' turns out to be a conjunction of propositions of the form 'If x is an F, then x is a G'. The main difficulty Ramsey saw for this view was that it implied the existence of infinite conjunctions when the relevant domain is infinite, which would be the case where the domain is that of the natural numbers, assuming one can 'quantify over' numbers – but also, apparently, where the domain is the universal domain, as it is alleged to be for many propositions of the form 'All Fs are Gs'. The notion of an infinite conjunction seemed to Ramsey to be a fudge, and at odds with the principle enunciated in the *Tractatus* that whatever can be said at all can be said clearly. If our domain is finite, then all well and good, 'All Fs are Gs' may be looked upon as a conjunction, true or false;[2] but if it is infinite, we have what Ramsey called a 'variable hypothetical', and this sort of statement is to be understood as expressing a preparedness to move from 'This is an F' to 'This is a G', or a 'habit' of so moving, as Ramsey put it.

Ramsey summed up his dissatisfaction with his and Wittgenstein's earlier account with what became a well-known quip: 'But what we can't say we can't say, and we can't whistle it either'.[3] As Cora Diamond (2011) has pointed out, it is ironic that this quip has come to be thought of as expressing Ramsey's doubts about Wittgenstein's ideas concerning unsayability, as embodied in the famous last words of the *Tractatus*, 'Whereof one cannot speak, thereof one must be silent'; for the quip was made in connection with a worry about general propositions, namely that if they amounted to infinite conjunctions they would violate *Tractatus*-style constraints on *sayability*.[4]

Ramsey's account of variable hypotheticals was a characteristically bold and imaginative proposal, but one which his early death prevented him from developing. A philosopher who subsequently put forward an account similar to Ramsey's was Gilbert Ryle, in his paper, ' "If", "So", and "Because" '.[5] Ramsey's phrase 'variable hypothetical' pointed to the connection between general propositions and hypothetical ones: 'Every F is a G' amounts to 'If anything is an F, then it is a G' (leaving to one side the question whether the former commits one to the existence of Fs). Ryle in his paper looks at hypotheticals in general, mentioning variable hypotheticals as a species. But his account of hypotheticals is obviously similar to Ramsey's of variable hypotheticals.

Ryle writes:

> If we ask what is the point of learning '*if p, then q*', or what is the evidence that someone has learned it, part of the answer would be a reference to the learner's ability and readiness to infer from '*p*' to '*q*' and from '*not-q*' to '*not-p*', to acquiesce in the corresponding arguments of others, to reject affiliated invalid arguments, and so on. But we should also expect him on certain, perhaps rare, occasions to *tell* his hearers or readers '*if p, then q*'.... Making a hypothetical statement is sometimes giving an inference precept; and the first object of giving this precept is that the recipient shall make appropriate inferences. A posterior object of giving him this precept is, perhaps, that he shall in his turn give this inference precept to others, again with the same primary object, that they shall learn to perform the appropriate inferential operations. (1971, 239)

Ryle does not lead up to his view as Ramsey did, via a rejection of a truth-functional account of the statements under scrutiny. He does so by an examination of the nature of arguments ('p, so q'), and their relationship to the corresponding hypotheticals ('If p, then q'). In particular, he criticizes the following views:[6] (a) that the hypothetical is entailed by the argument (Ryle points out that an argument, not being a proposition at all, can't entail anything); (b) that the argument is equivalent to a conjunction of the hypothetical with its antecedent, 'p' (again, an argument isn't a proposition); (c) that the hypothetical is the same as the argument, just 'misleadingly worded'; (d) that an argument 'p, so q' is always invalid unless 'If p, then q' is among the premises, along with 'p'.

It is especially through a consideration of (d) that Ryle arrives at his 'inference precept' account of hypotheticals. Now there is a pedantic sort of way in which (d) can be faulted, namely by coming up with such cases as: 'p' means 'q', or is an appropriate truth-function of 'q' – or 'q' is a necessary truth – or whatever. We can ignore such cases. The more interesting problem with (d), as Ryle points out, is that if it were true it would generate the infinite regress to which Achilles succumbed at the hands (or feet) of Lewis Carroll's Tortoise. For in the case where 'p' is equivalent to 'r, and (if r, then q)', we should according to (d) have to add a further premise, 'If (r and [if r, then q]), then q' ... and so on.[7] The argument 'r and (if r, then q), so q' must be fine as it stands. What's wrong with (d), it seems, is the word 'always'.

The main lesson of Carroll's Tortoise is that a rule of inference (e.g. *modus ponens*) shouldn't be thought of as a sort of (background) premise. To treat it as a premise is to generate the infinite regress. But Ryle goes further: he wants to say a similar thing of statements of the form 'If p, then q'. He considers the argument 'Today is Monday, so tomorrow is Tuesday', and says that its validity does not require us to add the additional premise, 'If today is Monday, tomorrow is Tuesday' (1971, 238). Rather, he says, the argument is an *application* of the hypothetical, much as a given *modus ponens* argument is an application of a rule of inference. It is to the notion of an application that he then turns.

Evidently things have gone too far. We should start by noting that Ryle's example is a bad one, since the validity of 'Today is Monday, so tomorrow is Tuesday' rests on the conceptual or linguistic connection between 'Monday' and 'Tuesday'; and it is for *that* reason that addition of the corresponding hypothetical is unnecessary. We have an inference precept, or set of such precepts, just by virtue of knowing our days of the week – a form of linguistic competence. The same doesn't go e.g. for 'The kettle has been on for ten minutes, so the water will have boiled'. If validity is what's in question, then this last argument is, as it stands, invalid, and to render it valid we would probably reach for an additional premise in the form of a corresponding hypothetical.[8]

I say 'probably' because of course one could 'render the argument valid' in various ways – such as by adding the premise 'It's not true that the water won't have boiled'. The reason why a hypothetical premise ('If the kettle has been on for ten minutes, then the water will have boiled') seems the natural addition is precisely because it adds much less, as it were, than do other candidate premises. It doesn't do violence to the original argument in the way other premises do. But what does that mean? It seems to mean something like this: a (rational) person who argued 'p, so q' would, ipso facto, *be* someone who believed that if p, then q. So if we've said they've argued thus, we don't need to attribute any further beliefs to them, on top of 'p' (and 'q'). And this is presumably what Ryle is getting at.

It might be objected that for a rational person to argue 'p, so q' they must already have the belief 'If p, then q'. But if that means they must have consciously entertained the thought 'If p, then q', then it seems false: no such mental episode need have taken place. Might the 'belief' in question be something other than a conscious mental episode? If it is there 'already', it looks very much as if it will be either (i) an unconscious episode or state, or (ii) a disposition. In general, postulations of unconscious events or states don't sit well with the prefix 'It must be that …' And as for a disposition, we seem now to be back with Ryle, since the disposition in question will surely be none other than the disposition to infer 'q' from 'p', 'not-p' from 'not-q', etc.

It appears we can maintain two things which have a look of mutual inconsistency, but which are in fact consistent:

A. An argument 'p, so q' will be invalid without the addition of a corresponding hypothetical *premise* (assuming that 'p' is neither a truth-function of 'q' nor conceptually connected with it, that neither 'p' nor 'q' is necessarily false/true, and that quantifiers are not involved);

B. A person may rationally argue 'p, so q' without having any *beliefs* other than 'p', from which to infer 'q' (even where 'p' is neither a truth-function of 'q' nor conceptually connected with it, neither 'p' nor 'q' is necessarily false/true, and quantifiers are not involved).

Ryle's mistake, I think, is to argue from B to a denial of A, which he does because he takes premises of arguments to express certain beliefs of persons who argue using those arguments, namely the beliefs from which they derive their conclusions. This eventually leads him on to some curious claims, as that 'p' doesn't occur in 'If p, then q' in the way that it does occur in 'p and q' – indeed, cannot really be said to occur in the hypothetical statement at all. (I shall be looking at this part of Ryle's account later on.)

But if the premises of arguments don't necessarily express the beliefs from which people who use those arguments derive conclusions, what do they do? To answer this question, we need to say more about what an argument is.

What Is an Argument?

I can produce an argument, e.g. as a logic exercise, without believing the premises I set forth. But can the same be true if I *argue* using the argument? Here we need to distinguish three sorts of cases. First, the case where an argument is produced (e.g. written down), the production being used to get to, or show, the truth of some matter, as one might use a diagram; second, the case where someone explains a belief he has by adverting to reasons, presenting his explanation in the form of a produced argument with the reasons appearing as premises; third, the case where other people explain someone's belief by adverting to reasons, presenting the explanation in the form of a produced argument with the reasons appearing as premises.

Each of these cases involves arguments as productions: that is, as embodied in written or spoken or inwardly thought *symbols*. It is that sense of argument that was at stake when we said that one can produce an argument as a mere logic exercise. We can, of course, take an argument in English to be 'the same as' a certain argument in French, the one being a translation of the other; but this no more commits us to some Platonic argument-form than the statement 'It's the same time in Glasgow as in Manchester' commits us to Platonic times o'clock. The point to hang on to is that in giving an example of an argument, or in presenting or using an argument, one has recourse to symbols. In fact this is true regardless of the merits or otherwise of Platonism about arguments.

In the first of the three sorts of cases just outlined, where the argument serves as a kind of aid, the person may well derive a conclusion from beliefs she has, those beliefs being expressed in premise form. But it needn't be like this. For you might want to see what follows from certain premises, being prepared to jettison them if they yield absurd conclusions. (You may be wondering *whether* to believe the premise propositions.) Or you might want to show the truth of a belief by means of a *reductio ad absurdum*, one of whose premises you will actually disbelieve. This could be done, NB, using our *modus ponens* argument: 'If p, then q – and p; therefore q. But q is false. So not-p.'

In the second of the three cases, the important point is that giving reasons for a belief is not the same thing as mentioning some beliefs of yours as the ones which led to your adopting the belief in question. The same goes, mutatis mutandis, for the third sort of case. Essentially this is because of the gulf first insisted on by Frege, between the logical and the psychological. It may be that my acquiring belief B led me to acquire belief

B*; but if I am to *justify* my belief B*, I must give proper reasons for it, and B will only embody a reason if it stands in the right sort of logical or evidential relationship to B*. The fact that the one belief led to or produced the other is neither necessary nor sufficient for that relationship to hold. Against this it might be insisted that for me to have reasons for a belief, I must have *derived* it from those reasons – and won't those reasons then have to be *my* reasons, in the sense of being believed by me to be true?

But this need not be the case. For the reasons you can give for some belief needn't be things from which the belief was derived, if that verb carries the chronological implication: first the reasons, then the belief. In part, this has to do with the social nature of the language-game of giving and receiving reasons. If I ask you for your reason for thinking p, I am typically asking for a reason why *I* should think that p, alias a reason *to* think that p. You will, of course, typically believe the reasons that you give for thinking that p, since after all you think that p, and (we may assume) are happy to explain to me why p is the thing to think. But your *belief* in the reasons you give me may have effectively come into being along with your giving of the reasons. The reasons, in the form you give them to me, need not have occurred to you on some previous occasion.

And even if they did occur to you, we must ask: in virtue of what did you take these thoughts *as* reasons for the belief in question? A thought may occur to you without your even believing it. It may occur to you, and you may 'inwardly assent', whatever that means; but you may fail to see that it is a reason to think that p. What is it to see that it is a reason to think that p? 'Seeing the logical/evidential relationship' between r and p doesn't appear to be enough – don't you have to *draw* the conclusion, p? But what is that? Is it a further psychological process?

There is a useful parallel that can be drawn with cases of practical reasoning. Elizabeth Anscombe argues that when representing the (first-personal) reasons for an action in the form of a practical syllogism, we ought not to insert as a premise 'I want X', X being the goal or end. 'I want X', if it does occur among the premises, will be just one of the facts of the case – as in the following argument:

> Anyone who wants to kill his parents will be helped to get rid of this trouble by consulting a psychiatrist.
> I want to kill my parents.
> If I consult a psychiatrist I shall be helped to get rid of this trouble.
> *NN* is a psychiatrist.
> So I'll consult *NN*.[9]

(Anscombe says she owes the point and the example to Anselm Mueller.)

If the operative want doesn't occur among the premises, how is it operating? The person decides to visit the psychiatrist *NN*. Anscombe writes: 'The decision, if I reach it on these grounds [i.e. on the basis of the given premises], *shews* that I *want* to get rid of the trouble' (2005, 115–16). My going off to visit *NN*, it might be said, is a criterion, in these circumstances, of my wanting to get rid of the trouble. This is what it *is* to 'draw a conclusion', a practical conclusion, from certain premises.

I have spoken of my going off to visit *NN* as showing what it is I want. After all, if I just *said* 'So I'll consult *NN*,' that wouldn't yet show anything – I might be joking, or trying to get you to dissuade me (we're both terrified of psychiatrists), etc. I have to, as it were, endorse my own conclusion. I have to be able sincerely to declare 'So I'll consult *NN*,' and sincerity here would consist in my attempting at some point to visit *NN* (unless I change my mind or am prevented).

Can something similar be said about drawing a theoretical conclusion? Yes; for a person's arriving at 'p' on the basis of the premises 'r' and 'If r, then p' *shows* that he reasons in a certain way (i.e. according to the rule of inference, *modus ponens*); and in similar vein, Ryle would claim that a person's arriving at 'p' on the basis of the premise 'r' *shows* that he believes 'If r, then p'. It is for that reason that we don't need to attribute the belief 'If r, then p' in addition to the belief 'r', as beliefs from which the person rationally infers 'p'. It is not a complete accident that a similar point can be made about dispositions – thus you don't need to cite the water solubility of a sugar lump *in addition to* its having been put in water (plus its having a certain molecular structure, if you like), in order to explain why the lump has dissolved. A sugar lump's dissolving in water shows, is a manifestation of, its being water soluble.

The objection may now be made that *all* beliefs are dispositions, so that if disposition-ascriptions can't function as (elements in) explanations, then not only the belief that if p then q, but also the simple belief that p, will be unavailable for explaining actions – an absurd result. The objection is of particular relevance insofar as Ryle himself regards beliefs as dispositions, but it is of more than ad hominem interest. The most natural answer to the objection relies on distinguishing disposition-terms that semantically imply disposition-manifestations from ones that don't. 'x is soluble in water' is semantically related to 'x dissolves in water'. 'x believes it's raining' is not in the same way semantically related to 'x picks up what he takes for an umbrella'. (In *The Concept of Mind*, Ryle registers this by calling the second sort of disposition-term 'determinable'.[10]) If 'x believes that if p then q' is to be regarded as the ascription of a disposition, then there is a pretty good case for likening it to 'x is soluble in water', since, as Ryle says, a person who has been told 'If p, then q' can be expected to do certain things involving 'p' and 'q', such as infer the second from the first. There will then be a semantic connection between disposition-term and manifestation-statements, so long as (i) 'p' really occurs in belief-ascriptions, 'X believes that … p …' and (ii) 'p' really occurs in 'If p, then q'. Ryle, as we shall see, actually denies (ii), but, as I shall argue, he shouldn't.

Whether beliefs are to be thought of as a species of disposition is a delicate question, raising among other things tricky issues of normativity. The sorts of consideration in favour of agreeing with Ryle that a person who rationally argues 'p, so q' need not be credited with the extra belief 'If p, then q' are not considerations that require the truth of a dispositional view of beliefs; my discussion of that view has been something of a diversion.

I said above that the following appears true: a person's arriving at 'p' on the basis of the premises 'r' and 'If r, then p' *shows* that he reasons according to *modus ponens* – and if Ryle is right, a person's arriving at 'p' on the basis of the premise 'r' *shows* that he believes 'If r, then p'. Two phrases that need examining are 'on the basis of' and 'arrives at'. In the practical case, my drawing a practical conclusion on the basis of the premises means something like my being disposed to give those premises as reasons if asked, 'Why have you decided to do that?', at least in the paradigm situation. We can say something similar in the theoretical case: if asked why I believe that p, I can give as my reasons, 'r – and if r, then p' (or I may just say 'r', Ryle will insist). But my simply *saying* 'p' doesn't show that I have really drawn it as a conclusion, any more than my saying 'So I'll consult *NN*' shows I've drawn *it* as a conclusion. For me to arrive at 'p' on the basis of the premises requires more than my saying 'p' (for I might be joking, etc.) – it requires that I say 'p' sincerely, i.e. believing it to be true. The criterion of sincerity in the practical case was action – going off to see the psychiatrist. And that's hardly surprising, since it was a practical syllogism we were dealing with. What criterion of sincerity is on offer for the theoretical case?

In many instances, the answer will be, or will include, action – just as for the practical case. If I sincerely say 'That telephone doesn't work,' then when I want to make a call I will not (except from forgetfulness) use the phone in question. But of course many beliefs are not straightforwardly manifestable in action, if that means non-linguistic action – such as the belief that Marco Polo probably got stung by a bee at some point in his life. We will have to include linguistic actions if we are to use action as a criterion of sincerity, and Ryle's account of beliefs as determinable dispositions quite properly includes dispositions to say things.[11] 'You mean, to say them *sincerely*', will come the rejoinder; and the threat of circularity can only be avoided by (i) including further manifestations of (in)sincerity in our account, such as facial expressions or tones of voice, many of these manifestations being 'imponderable', as Wittgenstein puts it,[12] (ii) being pretty 'holistic' in our attributions of beliefs (the bigger picture to include (i)-type facts as well as actions and other beliefs) and (iii) being content with a non-reductive sort of philosophical account, one which would elucidate the concept of belief rather than giving necessary and sufficient conditions for 'S believes that p'.

The fact that the criteria for beliefs are or include actions allows us to see what is at stake in Chrysippus's famous example of a dog reasoning logically.[13] In pursuit of a rabbit, the dog comes to a point where the road splits into three. Assuming for some reason that the rabbit will stick to a road and not flee across country (perhaps the rabbit is on a motor bike), the dog sniffs two of the three roads for rabbit scent, and *without bothering to sniff the third road* dashes down it. Chrysippus suggests that such a dog would evidently be reasoning as follows: P or Q or R; but not-P & not-Q; so R.

An argument, I have said, is a production using symbols, and we do not need to postulate that the dog produces this argument inwardly. Rather, *we* produce the argument, e.g. in schematic form as I have just done, when giving the reasons why the dog believed R ('R' = 'The rabbit went down road No. 3') – or alternatively when giving the dog's reasons for dashing down the road. What we have is an example of the third sort of case of a person's (or dog's) 'going by' an argument, mentioned above (p. x).

Now there is in fact an independent question whether one can attribute reasons, for beliefs or for actions, to animals, given the impossibility of an animal's answering the question 'Why?' It may well be that we often *can* do so, and in a way that is compatible with the primacy of the case of a person's giving a reason (i.e. giving an answer to 'Why?'). But when we attribute reasons or intentions to animals, it is because some animal behaviour strikes us as describable in this sort of way; it is not that we form a *hypothesis* about the animal along the lines of 'It must have reasoned thus ...' Many philosophers have, I think, taken Chrysippus's example as suggesting to us a (plausible) hypothesis of this sort. And that is because those philosophers think that where there is rationality there is reasoning, and the latter must be an inner process – a view of whose problems we have had a glimpse, and which Ryle among others very effectively combated.

Truth and Truth-Functionality

I suggested above (p. x) that the claims A and B were compatible, despite having an appearance of incompatibility. And I have endeavoured to show how this is so by making out that the premise of an argument is not, qua premise of an argument, the expression of a belief from which one who goes by that argument derives the conclusion of the argument. An argument can be used in various ways; arguments can even be used in describing the actions of dumb brutes.

None of this, however, actually supports Ryle's account of hypothetical statements as inference precepts. At best it merely saves him from having to draw some of the unpalatable conclusions which he does draw from his account. The most that I have said in support of Ryle's account is that there seems to be some reason to say that a person who argues 'p, so q' is ipso facto a person who thinks that if p, then q. No extra belief, on top of 'p' and 'q', is really attributed to such a person. The linguistic form, 'If p, then q', is therefore not needed in order to represent any such belief. What then *is* the function of the linguistic form? Ryle says it functions as an inference precept; but what does that mean exactly?

Well, we have an idea of what Ryle means from the above quotation (p. x). One question that is raised by what Ryle says there is: Can a hypothetical proposition be called true or false? Now in fact Ryle himself is happy to say Yes to this, e.g. when he writes, 'In some way the validity of the argument ["p, so q"] requires the truth of the hypothetical statement ["If p, then q"]'.[14] But there are a couple of lines of thought that seem to throw doubt on this.

The first line of thought appeals to a correspondence account of truth, or something like it. What is it, it might be asked, that makes 'If p, then q' true, if that statement is an inference precept? What state of affairs ('out there', as philosophers like to say) could possibly make a *precept* true? Surely no state of affairs could do that. To say this, however, will likely involve us in a vicious circle, since the decision that there is (or is not) some state of affairs, or fact, ready and willing to make some statement true is a decision that typically waits upon the prior decision to allow (or not to allow) truth-aptness to that sort of statement – rather than vice versa. This indeed is one of the problems faced by correspondence theories of truth. So this line of thought doesn't really manage to throw doubt on the claim that inference precepts might be true or false. (There is a metaphysically innocent sense of the question 'What if anything makes a hypothetical statement true?', the answer to which *does* throw some light on our topic. I will be turning to this a little later on.)

The second line of thought is similar to the first, but does without any dubious correspondence account of truth. It appeals to the idea that a precept must be, or must be akin to, an imperative of some kind – and surely an imperative cannot be true or false? At this point we should clear things up a bit, taking note of the distinction between the modals 'may' and 'must'. Ryle speaks as if a hypothetical statement tells one that one *may* go from 'p' to 'q', e.g. where he compares such a statement to a railway ticket, and uses the phrase 'inference warrant' (1971, 239), and where he writes: 'When I learn "*if p, then q*", I am learning that I am authorised to argue "*p, so q*", *provided that I get my premise "p"*' (1971, 244). And 'may' can indeed look preferable to 'must' here, to the extent that, after all, even if you've learnt that if p then q, you might just want to say 'p' and then shut up – surely you can't be faulted for not coming out with 'q'? Similarly, you surely can't be faulted if you simply fail to move straight from the belief that p to the belief that q. What you can be faulted for is coming out with 'not-q', or alternatively, believing that not-q (having said or come to believe 'p'). But then we might say that 'If p, then q' does issue a 'must' after all, specifically a 'must not': 'You must not, if you say or believe that p, also say or believe that not-q.' Ryle alludes to this aspect of things when he says that 'If p, then q' can be reworded as 'It cannot be that p and not that q' (1971, 245). And these facts bring home why it is that in many cases 'If p, then q' is required in addition to 'p', if 'q' is to be validly inferred; for although a merely *reasonable* inference, 'p, so q', may allow for the possibility that p and not-q (e.g. if the premise 'p' states defeasible criteria), the addition of 'If p, then q', by ruling out that possibility, renders the argument deductively valid.[15]

However we distribute the 'mays' and 'musts', we seem to have modal statements, akin to imperatives or permissions, which because of that kinship (so the second line of thought goes) appear not to be truth-apt. Ryle's assertions that hypothetical statements are true/false is then most naturally defended by taking a fairly 'grammatical' approach to truth-ascription, and saying that, since 'If p, then q' is a normal indicative sentence, the 'correctness' of any given utterance of such a sentence just *is* its truth. That is what truth amounts to here. And we might well want to say something along these lines of such rule-statements as 'The bishop in chess moves diagonally': the statement is true, though naturally taken as tantamount to a sort of imperative (at any rate, in the context of teaching someone chess).

The 'grammatical' approach to truth-ascription I have mentioned shouldn't be overgeneralized, since there are indicative sentences 'correct' utterances of which cannot properly be called true – such as 'I promise to pay you back'. (Of course, if Jones said this in the right circumstances, 'Jones promised to pay X back' would be true – but that is another matter.) Nevertheless, I think that Ryle probably can maintain his inference precept account of hypotheticals while calling such hypotheticals truth-apt, by invoking a basically 'grammatical' notion of truth. Hypotheticals differ from promises, declarations and the like, on account of such things as their being susceptible of the same sort of justification or criticism as applies to paradigmatically truth-apt utterances: 'Why do you say/think that if p then q?' will typically make good sense, the same sort of sense as is made by 'Why do you say/think that p?' In both cases, an answer will typically give what we would call *evidence* for the assertion or belief.

What in that case distinguishes a hypothetical statement from e.g. a conjunctive one? Both sorts of statement are truth-apt, and both sorts of statement are useable as premises in arguments (whatever Ryle says). Ryle refers to the inferential operations that one who has been told 'If p, then q' will be prepared to make, the permissibility or mandatoriness of which operations he can convey to others by saying 'If p, then q'; but somewhat similar things can be said about 'p and q'. A rational person who learns the truth of 'p and q' will infer 'p', will be prepared to infer 'r' if he gets the premise 'If q, then r' – and so on. As to the last mentioned sort of inference, it would be difficult to maintain that the person's preparedness is *really* grounded in his learning 'If q, then r', not in his learning 'p and q', given that for such a person both acquisitions are necessary. It should be noted that 'preparedness to infer' can be associated with propositions none of which is a hypothetical: for instance, if you believe the truth of 'p or q', you will be prepared to infer 'p' from 'not-q'.

What then *is* the big difference between hypotheticals on the one hand, and conjunctions or disjunctions on the other? For Ryle, the big difference seems to be that a hypothetical is not 'a resultant, product, or truth function of any incorporated statements' (1971, 245). You can explicate a conjunction or a disjunction by means of a truth-table, thus showing how the proposition in question is a truth function of its incorporated (constituent) propositions. You cannot, Ryle thinks, do this for a hypothetical proposition.

The view that hypotheticals are non-truth-functional is familiar, and used to be backed up by reference to the so-called paradoxes of material implication, some of which arise from the apparent oddity of ascribing any truth-value at all to 'If p, then q' in cases such as that in which both 'p' and 'q' are false.[16] But Ryle is not thinking of the paradoxes of material implication. Unfortunately, his thoughts at this point involve, it seems to me, a fair amount of confusion. He not only denies that 'If p, then q' is a truth function of 'p' and 'q' – he wishes to say that the statements 'p' and 'q' *in no way* appear in, or are constituents of, the statement 'If p, then q'. If by 'statement' he means 'assertion', all well and good, since it is true that in saying 'If p, then q' one does not assert that p, nor assert that q. But Ryle also objects to our saying that 'p' and 'q' occur unasserted in 'If p, then q' (1971, 246–47). His reason is that it is the job of a statement to be asserted, so that an unasserted statement is not a statement at all. 'A statement bereft of its employment is not a statement' (1971, 247). If this argument worked, we should have to say a similar thing about disjunctions, for in asserting 'p or q' one does not assert that p. But it would be odd to say that 'p' doesn't occur in 'p or q'. For that matter, we do not assert 'p' when we say 'Not p' – nevertheless, as Wittgenstein put it, 'if I falsely say that something is *red*, then, for all that, it isn't *red*' (*PI*, sec. 429): it is, and must be, the same expression (predicate or sentence) that occurs after a negation sign as can occur on its own.

Ryle's mistake arises from a too simplistic conception of *similarity of function*. He writes that 'what tempts people to say this sort of thing [sc. that "p" and "q" occur unasserted in the hypothetical] [...] is the patent similarity between protasis expressions and apodosis expressions (as commonly worded) on the one hand and statements on the other.' Here he means 'similarity in appearance', or something like that. A little earlier he has told us what he regards as the *functional* difference between e.g. protasis expressions and 'statements': 'What the hypothetical statement does embody is not statements but statement specifications or statement indents – bills for statements that statements could fill' (1971, 245). So in 'If today is Monday, then tomorrow is Tuesday', the words 'today is Monday' are just a statement-shaped hole, with no genuine (logical) similarity to the statement 'Today is Monday'. And Ryle backs up his claim with a characteristic metaphor: 'In many ordinary cases there is no similarity whatsoever between bills and what fills them. The specification of a consignment of bicycles is not in the slightest degree like a consignment of bicycles' (1971, 247).

The response to all this, in brief, is to reject the question: Does 'p' have the same function, or a different one, as it occurs when simply asserted and as it occurs in 'If p, then q'? The function of a proposition 'p', it might be said, is manifold – it includes both the sorts of occurrences mentioned by the question. The two occurrences are very different in one way, and yet very similar in another, insofar as they both belong to a unified package of possible occurrences, that package effectively constituting the sense of 'p'. 'The same or different?' presents a false dichotomy.

Truth-Conditions versus Use

And yet when it comes to truth-functionality, Ryle may be on to something when he contrasts conjunctions with hypotheticals, something that can be brought out by invoking the notion of 'making true'. The truth-table for 'p and q' enables us to specify the way in which 'p and q' can be *made true*, namely, by its being the case that p and its being the case that q. Similarly, the truth-table for 'p or q' enables us to specify ways in which that proposition can be made true, namely, by the fact that p, or by the fact that q, or by both facts together. This notion of 'making true' is unmysterious, being innocent of any metaphysical commitments of the sort that typically go with correspondence accounts of truth. It is a notion to be explained by means of examples, such as the example of how 'p or q' can be made true – rather different from the way in which, say, 'Jim broke the law' can be made true by 'Jim forged his employer's signature'. So when we turn to 'If p, then q', it is going to be an open question whether it makes sense to say that a given statement of that form is (if true) made true by anything.[17] And indeed it seems that we cannot use the phrase 'make true' in connection with hypotheticals, taking that phrase in anything like the way it is to be taken in connection with conjunctions or disjunctions. Let us allow for the sake of argument that a truth-table can be given for 'If p, then q' that includes at least one line where 'If p, then q' is true (perhaps Grice is right that the truth-table should in fact just be that of material implication). Still, it would evidently be wrong-headed to infer from the truth-table that a given statement 'If p, then q' was made true e.g. by the fact that p together with the fact that q. Someone says 'If the wind blew last night, there'll be leaves on the path'. The wind did blow last night, and someone carrying a bag of leaves emptied them onto the path. If we decide on this basis to call the hypothetical statement 'true', we will be employing a fairly minimal notion of truth, similar to the notion of innocence as embodied in the dictum, 'Innocent until proved guilty'. There is then no point in referring to the events that occurred as having *made* the statement true; you might as well say that the cat's being on the sofa makes true the statement 'The cat is not on the mat'. (Why not say the cat's being on a green sun-dappled item of furniture makes it true, or the cat's being three yards away from the mat, or ...?) If we ask, 'But what *more* is there to the hypothetical than can be specified by reference to facts that could make it true?,' there is a ready answer: a hypothetical statement is an inference precept.[18]

We are back with Ramsey, who in presenting his account of variable hypotheticals pointed to the contrast between that account and one framed in terms of truth-conditions, the latter being inadequate for reasons to do with infinite conjunctions. There are in fact two different models of propositional sense now before us, one reliant on the giving of truth-conditions, the other reliant on depicting a kind of *use*. The Ramsey/Ryle model of the sense of (variable) hypotheticals, in eschewing truth-conditions, stresses instead a kind of use, and each philosopher effectively characterizes that kind of use by comparing the propositions in question to other species of statement – precepts, rules, imperatives and the like.[19] 'Comparing to' is the right phrase here, rather than 'classifying as'. Hypotheticals are *like* precepts – but they are also (obviously) unlike them in certain respects. But drawing attention to the respects in which the two species of statement are similar is what brings philosophical enlightenment.

As often in philosophy, the switch of attention from truth-conditions (or possible truth-makers) to aspects of use neutralizes a certain metaphysical urge. The question 'What makes a hypothetical statement true?' all too often leads to a metaphysical search, though what is 'discovered' will of course simply be an excogitation. Ryle is well aware of this feature of his topic. He writes:

> Fascinated by the model of simple, singular, affirmative, attributive, or relational statements, theorists are apt to ask 'What exactly do hypothetical statements assert to characterise what?'… or, more generally, 'What do such statements describe?' or 'What matters of fact do they report?' And they are apt to toy with verbally accommodating replies about Necessary Connections between Facts, or Internal Relations between Universals, and the like. (1971, 243)

Remember that he was writing in 1950. David Armstrong's theory of laws of nature as necessary relations between universals was yet to be published.[20] There is nothing new under the sun. Ryle's therapeutic method in '"If", "So" and "Because"' is to emphasize the relationship between hypotheticals and arguments, and what he would say to Armstrong can be gleaned from this passage:

> Hume might be doctored into saying: 'Causality is not a relation; for "p, so q" is an inference and not a statement, and so is not the statement of a relation. "So" is not a relation word, or a relational predicate, or a predicate of any sort. For "p, so q" is not a subject-predicate statement since it is not a statement at all. Predicting an event from another event is not describing a bond, for it is not describing.' (1971, 243)

Armstrong and his followers would probably respond by asserting the priority of 'If p, then q' over 'p, so q', and armed with an indicative sentence would then hunt for its truth-maker. Ryle's claim that the priority is the other way around points us into rather dense thickets in the philosophy of language, where metaphysicians usually prefer not to roam, lacking suitable clothing; but the assertion that a true hypothetical must have a truth-maker can anyway be questioned, by putting pressure on the allegedly general notion of 'making true', as Anscombe does (see n. 17). One can only imagine what Ryle or Ramsey would have made of subsequent attempts to posit truth-makers for *subjunctive* hypotheticals, such as counterfactual statements. Infinite conjunctions and relations between Universals look like small beer beside 'the plurality of worlds'.[21]

Notes

1 Ramsey (1929, 149). In fact, Ramsey calls the general proposition 'a rule *for judging* "If I meet a φ, I shall regard it as a ψ"' (my italics); but nothing much seems to hang on this way of putting it.
2 Ramsey allows this for 'Everyone in Cambridge voted', writing: 'the variable here is, of course, not people in Cambridge, but a limited region of space' (1929, 145). By 'variable' he clearly means something determining a domain.
3 Ramsey (1929, 146).
4 Diamond (2011). The irrelevant comparison of Ramsey's quip with the last proposition of the *Tractatus* is even made by authors who must have known of the quip's original context, e.g. by D. H. Mellor in his Introduction to Ramsey (1929, xvi). Mellor goes so far as to state that the quip 'sums up a deep objection to the whole of the *Tractatus*', when in fact it expresses endorsement of one of the main claims of that work.
5 Ryle (1971). Basically the same account is found in *The Concept of Mind*, from the previous year (Ryle 1963, 116–18).
6 Ryle (1971, 237–8).
7 See Carroll (1895).
8 In the last paragraph of '"If", "So", and "Because"', Ryle says that there are inferences the validity of which requires to be vouched for by observation and experiment, and this may seem to suggest that it is the 'informal validity' (reasonableness) of arguments that he chiefly has in mind, not their formal validity. But his claim that an inference in no way needs a hypothetical to back it up is not simply the observation that a hypothetical is only needed for *formal* validity, and not for informal validity; for he clearly thinks the role of a hypothetical is closely analogous to that of a rule of inference, e.g. *modus ponens*, and that in both cases it is redundant (at least) to insert the hypothetical/rule as a premise, regardless of whether we have formal or informal validity in mind. Hence his talk of an argument's being an *application* of a hypothetical.
9 Anscombe (2005, 115).
10 Ryle (1963, 114).
11 See e.g. Ryle (1963, 129).
12 See Wittgenstein (1958, Bk II, 228).
13 Mentioned, for example, by Aquinas in *Summa Theologiae* 1a1 1ae.
14 Ryle (1971, 237). NB: Ryle is not here saying that the hypothetical is needed as a true *premise* in the argument, in order for it to be valid; as we have seen, he denies that.
15 That is to say, 'If p, then q' rules out the possibility 'p and not-q' within the context of the argument – it need not rule it out tout court, if that means alleging logical impossibility or the like.
16 Remember that we are not talking of *subjunctive* hypotheticals, such as 'If the Spitfire hadn't been invented, the Germans would have achieved air supremacy'. There's no problem with having a false antecedent and false consequent for these.
17 In 'Making True', Anscombe discusses the ordinary notion of making true, and argues, as I have done, that from such cases as disjunctive and existential statements no quite general concept of making true can be derived. To say of a given statement that it was made true by something may be to say nothing, and there is in general no necessity that anything should fulfil the role of 'truth-maker' for some species of proposition. See Anscombe (2000).
18 There are in fact good reasons for denying that the sense of, say, 'p or q' is *given* by its truth-table. There is more to a disjunction than its truth-conditions. See Anscombe (2000) and Teichmann (2008, ch. 6 sec. 1.2).

19 For Ramsey, it is the use to which a variable hypothetical is *put* (by the individual) that matters. Variable hypotheticals together 'form the system with which the speaker meets the future' (Ramsey 1929, 149).
20 See Armstrong (1983). Once again, Ramsey's opinion is worth quoting: 'But may there not be something which might be called real connections of universals? I cannot deny it, for I can understand nothing by such a phrase; what we call causal laws I find to be nothing of the sort' (Ramsey 1929, 160).
21 See Lewis (1986). Interestingly, Ramsey does apply his theory about variable hypotheticals to counterfactual statements (see Ramsey 1929, 161).

References

Anscombe, G. E. M. (2000), 'Making True', in R. Teichmann (ed.), *Logic, Cause and Action*. Cambridge: Cambridge University Press, pp. 1–8.
———. (2005), 'Practical Inference', in M. Geach and L. Gormally (eds), *Human Life, Action and Ethics*. Exeter: Imprint Academic, pp. 109–47.
Armstrong, D. M. (1983), *What Is a Law of Nature?* Cambridge: Cambridge University Press.
Carroll, L. (1895), 'What the Tortoise Said to Achilles', *Mind*, 4, no. 14, 278–80.
Diamond, C. (2011), '"We can't whistle it either": Legend and Reality', *European Journal of Philosophy*, 19, no. 3, 335–56.
Lewis, D. (1986), *On the Plurality of Worlds*. Oxford: Basil Blackwell.
Ramsey, F. P. (1929), 'General Propositions and Causality', in D. H. Mellor (ed.), *F.P. Ramsey: Philosophical Papers*. Cambridge: Cambridge University Press, pp. 145–63.
Ryle, G. (1963), *The Concept of Mind*. London: Penguin.
———. (1971), '"If", "So", and "Because"', in *Collected Papers Vol. II*. London: Hutchinson, pp. 234–49.
Teichmann, R. (2008), *The Philosophy of Elizabeth Anscombe*. Oxford: Oxford University Press.
Wittgenstein, L. (1958), *Philosophical Investigations*, trans. G. E. M. Anscombe, ed. G. E. M. Anscombe and R. Rhees. Oxford: Basil Blackwell, 2nd ed.

Chapter Fifteen

METAPHYSICS AND MODALS

Metaphysics – Hume and Wittgenstein

Metaphysics as traditionally conceived is concerned with what has to be the case, and also (therefore) with what cannot be the case. An object cannot be in two different places at the same time; a cause must occur before its effect; a pain cannot be felt by more than one person; you cannot access other possible worlds; I must know what I'm thinking about.

Philosophers asserting such things have always faced the question, 'How do you know?' Hume's scepticism as to whether good answers were forthcoming to (various instances of) that question characteristically led him to *diagnose* the propensity to make metaphysical claims – e.g. as a tendency to project our felt psychological impulses onto the world; or as he put it, the mind's tendency to 'spread itself on external objects'.[1] Metaphysics, for Hume, should be replaced by psychology. Volumes of unreconstructed metaphysics may be consigned to the flames.[2] Insofar as we are left with any unexceptionable necessity-claims, these can either be taken as dressed-up expressions of psychological impulse, or as harmless statements of the relations of ideas (what later got called 'analytic statements').

Wittgenstein, in both his earlier and later work, likewise rejected the pretensions of metaphysical philosophy. He too was diagnostic in his approach, at any rate in his later writings. To speak in very broad-brush terms, where Hume's psychological diagnosis had invoked our tendency to project, Wittgenstein's invoked our tendency to be in the grip of a picture; and where Hume talked of relations of ideas, Wittgenstein mentioned 'grammar', as when he wrote 'Essence is expressed by grammar'.(*Philosophical Investigations*[3] 371).

These broad similarities or analogies don't of course mean that there aren't crucial dissimilarities. Hume would often approach some claim of necessity by asking, 'Can't I imagine the opposite?' – construing that question as a psychological one, an issue to be settled by going in for some introspection. But Wittgenstein writes:

> What does it mean when we say 'I can't imagine the opposite of this' or 'What would it be like, if it were otherwise?' – For example, when someone has said that only I myself can know whether I am feeling pain, and similar things.

Of course, here 'I can't imagine the opposite' doesn't mean: my powers of imagination are unequal to the task. These words are a defence against something whose form makes it look like an empirical proposition, but which is really a grammatical one. (*PI* 251)
He gives an example of a grammatical proposition:

'Every rod has a length.' That means something like: we call something (or *this*) 'the length of a rod' – but nothing 'the length of a sphere'.

If Hume proposed substituting imaginability for metaphysical possibility, Wittgenstein, we might say, proposed substituting grammar or logic for *both* metaphysical possibility *and* imaginability.

The main problems with imaginability as a proxy for possibility are: (a) if 'I can imagine ...', qua psychological statement, enjoys first-person authority (in the way Hume must think it does), then nothing can block a person's sincere statement 'I can imagine going back in time / turning into stone and feeling pain / becoming the Universe / etc.' – (b) the criteria for 'success' in imagining X (i) are not in fact down to any 'introspectible representational qualities' in one's imaginings, (ii) nor could they be. For (i) I can imagine Plato talking to Socrates, although in some sense all I imagine is a couple of bearded chaps in conversation, and (ii) *any* picture, external or internal, has multiple capacities for (incompatible) representations, on account of there being different possible 'methods of projection' (see *PI* 139–41). It follows from all this that if someone says e.g. 'I can imagine going back in time', we can either take it as possibly true, and as corresponding to some story that might be given, where 'stories' may be incoherent (as accounts of dreams often are) – or take it as involving commitment to there being a coherent description of 'going back in time', where *coherence* is not a subjective matter. In neither case can possibility be derived from imaginability.

Anscombe saw a deep kinship between ancient philosophers like Plato and Parmenides, on the one hand, and Wittgenstein on the other, when it came to issues of possibility and necessity. She wrote:

> It was left to moderns to deduce what could be from what could hold of thought, as we see Hume to have done. This trend is still strong. But the ancients had the better approach, arguing only that a thought was impossible because the thing was impossible, or, as the *Tractatus* puts it, 'Was man nicht denken kann, das kann man nicht denken': an *impossible* thought is an impossible *thought*. (Anscombe 1981a, Introduction, xi)[4]

'The thing is impossible' looks a bit like the form of a metaphysical claim. But as her citing of the *Tractatus* shows, Anscombe intends the phrase to point us in the direction of logic – or of grammar, to use the later Wittgenstein's term.

Grammar and Modals

'We call something "the length of a rod", but nothing "the length of a sphere"' – *alias* 'Every rod has a length' – is a grammatical proposition. It has to do with our use of words, and more specifically with the rules governing that use. You'd be breaking one of those rules if you said, 'The length of that sphere is more than a metre.'[5] We might state the rule thus: You can't say of a sphere that it has length.

The word 'can't' in that last statement is what Anscombe calls a stopping modal. It belongs to a family of modals; there is also 'have to', which she calls a forcing modal. These terms she introduces in the course of explicating, and then jumping free of, a certain circularity that we are liable to encounter when we try to say what a promise is.[6] To say what a promise is, we need at least to say this: that if you promise to φ, you bring it about that you have to φ. 'Have to, lest what?' it might be asked. Is it this: you have to, lest you commit a wrong? But how say what the 'wrong' is, except by calling it 'breaking a promise'? So is it this: you have to φ, if you wish to obey the Rule of Promising? But what is the rule? Isn't it: If you promise to φ, you *have to* φ? We still haven't explained this 'have to'.

Anscombe's way with this problem involves considering how one might teach someone the use of modals like 'you have to' and 'you can't', as these appear in such statements as 'You promised to, so you have to'. This approach of course shows Wittgenstein's influence, and the rationale for it is, in large part, that the meaning of a word is what is known by someone who has learnt how to use it. We can imagine a child's learning the modal expressions as part of learning a game, e.g. the one in which several players pile their hands on top of one another, the hand at the bottom to move to the top, repeatedly. 'You have to put your hand on top' will be among the statements used when teaching the game, alongside appropriate actions – e.g. if the child doesn't move her hand, gently moving it for her. The use of these modals is intertwined with action; that is an essential part of the game, and of the language-game.

How does 'You have to move your hand' differ from a mere command 'Move your hand'? The important difference, Anscombe argues, is that the modal statement goes with another kind of statement, which she calls a logos – e.g. 'It's your turn'. In fact, you won't understand (know how to use) a modal statement until you can also use a logos, by way of 'justifying' the modal statement. That word 'until' suggests that you *first* need to learn the use of logoi, and then … But modal statement and logos belong to a package deal, just as the concepts 'white king' and 'black king' belong to a package deal in chess: in a sense, you have to learn the whole game before you know about any part of it. In the case of promising, 'You promised to do X' would give a logos for 'You have to do X'; these two statements must also be learnt as part of a package deal. In fact the concept of a promise isn't learnable independently of understanding the modal 'You have to'.

We need not, by the way, take *this* degree of mutual conceptual dependence between logoi and their correlative modal statements as definitive of logoi. For it is possible to take some already grasped concept and *stipulate* that this concept is to have the reason-giving force of a logos in the game you're inventing or explaining. 'Everyone dances around and when the music stops, you have to sit on a chair if you can.' This rule yields such statements as 'You have to sit down – the music has stopped!' Clearly, we understand the meaning of 'The music has stopped' independently of learning the rule. Nevertheless, it can be said that one learns a new role for 'The music has stopped', and understanding this role is indeed tied up with understanding the meaning of 'You have to sit down'. The role is that of logos.

Now there are two ways in which a modal like 'can't' appears in those statements that underlie the rule-governed nature of a practice such as a game: for a statement can either express a rule, or cite one. 'Knights can't move diagonally' expresses a rule; 'You can't move it there, it's a knight' cites that same rule.[7] In the second statement, 'it's a knight' gives the logos. But no logos is required to 'justify' the first statement; and if someone on hearing it asked, 'Why not?' the question would show a misunderstanding. ('Because that's the rule' says no more than 'Because they can't', and would only have the form of an answer, being in fact a rejection of the question.)

That language is rule-governed is these days a very familiar idea, and what Wittgenstein had to say about rules and rule-following has been discussed possibly more than has any other aspect of his philosophy. It should be surprising to us that so little of that discussion has adverted to stopping and forcing modals, whose relevance to the concept of a rule was highlighted by Anscombe. The expression of a linguistic rule typically employs an Anscombean modal, as we see from the example already given: You can't say of a sphere that it has length, i.e. you can't use 'length' in application to spheres. And aspects of Anscombe's discussion of modals usefully carry over to a discussion of Wittgenstein's 'grammatical remarks'. Thus, the question 'Why not?' is best rejected in connection with 'You can't use "length" in application to spheres' – but can be answered, using a logos, if it is the question, 'Why not say this is a metre long?' (answer: It's a sphere).

The metaphysician who anticipates that these modal expressions are going to be used to defuse his metaphysical claims might now jump in with the objection: 'To say that a knight can't move diagonally must be quite different from saying that the past can't be altered, say; for it is physically possible for me to move a knight diagonally, but *altogether* impossible to alter the past.' The reply to this is that the intended analogue of a knight is a word, one that is used interconnectedly with other words within a certain language-game ('past', 'happened', 'when?' etc.). There is nothing to stop me, physically, from saying, 'By wiggling my fingers thus, I will reverse the result of last year's election.' But I will misuse language in a certain way if I do.

Surely what I say will be *grammatical*, however? Why call it a misuse? I haven't space here to go into Wittgenstein's reasons for employing the term 'grammar' as he does.[8] His use of the term links it with the notions of a misuse of language and of nonsense, and these are the notions that are needed here. The thought is persistent among philosophers that a sentence which is grammatical by the standards of traditional grammar books will make perfectly good sense. Given the idiosyncratic way prepositions are used in English, a good way of countering this thought is by taking a sentence involving one and replacing the preposition by another one, thus preserving surface grammaticality: 'I put the money into my bank account' becomes 'I put the money under my bank account', say. Insisting that this is not nonsense, merely false, shows, I think, an entrenched mentality.[9]

The *way* in which statements about changing the past involve a misuse of language, and are consequently nonsensical, is illuminated in Anscombe's early paper 'The Reality of the Past'.[10] The argument of this paper is difficult and intricate – the following resumé will have to suffice. Anscombe points out that if the past could be changed, it would be possible to say e.g. that the Battle of Hastings used to be in 1066, but since last November it was in 1068. But whereas the question 'When was the Battle of Hastings?' has a use and a sense, the question 'When was the Battle of Hastings in 1066?' (*not* 'When in 1066 was the Battle of Hastings?') has no use and no sense. We could of course give it a sense. But we will only have succeeded in giving the question a sense if there is such a thing as teaching and learning the sense. The same goes for any putative answer to the question. It is not enough that the learner should be taught to *say the words*, 'Since last November, the Battle of Hastings was in 1068'; there must be criteria for the correct use of that sentence. And it is an illusion to think that we already have the sense we want ('in our minds'), so merely need to 'attach' it to this sentence, this form of words. Indeed, our opening supposition, 'If the past could be changed, it would be possible to say ... (etc.)' itself turns out not to have expressed any determinate sense.

Possible Worlds

The distinction was made above between physical possibility and rule-related possibility, i.e. between two senses of 'can'. In the one sense I can move my knight diagonally, in the other sense I can't. And there are on the face of it various species of modality (necessity and possibility). Latter-day metaphysics makes room for some such variety, but within a unified machinery: the machinery of 'possible worlds'.

I began with a characterization of metaphysical questions as typically concerned with necessity. Latter-day metaphysicians will translate 'An object cannot be in two different places at the same time' (assuming that to be a metaphysical claim) thus: 'In every metaphysically possible world, no object is in two different places at the same time.' Whether metaphysically possible worlds exhaust all the possible worlds is an issue within possible worlds theory. Physically possible worlds obviously constitute a subset.

The nature of possible worlds is itself a metaphysical matter; so we have a sort of metaphysical club sandwich, in place of the metaphysical bread and butter of former times. This means that we face some enjoyably meta-metaphysical questions, like 'Is it necessarily true (true in every possible world) that no access exists between one possible world and another?'

Now our latter-day metaphysician is likely to take any talk of language and 'grammar' to be a distraction. Metaphysical necessity is bigger and bolder than *that*. Let us then examine this alternative approach.

If something's possibility consists in what is the case in another possible world, then whenever we assert something to be possible we face the old question 'How do you know?' It will be obscure why facts about the actual world should provide an 'inductive base' for inferences about inaccessible other worlds. Those other worlds will apparently occupy the same sort of position as that occupied by the world beyond the Veil of Perception for representative realists like Locke.

In fact the question 'How do you know?' is liable to be answered (if any attention is paid to it) by appeal to the person's intuitions. The *capo di capi* of possible worlds theory, David Lewis, was lucky enough to have a good supply of these: his imaginary case of 'mad pain' involves a creature in whom the typical symptoms of pain are doing mental arithmetic while crossing the legs and snapping the fingers, and of this scenario Lewis writes simply: 'my opinion that this is a possible case seems pretty firm'.[11] It sounds like an introspective report. Indeed it sounds rather like an attempt to 'deduce what could be from what could hold of thought'. As Anscombe said, this trend is still strong.

There is an interesting argument for the reality of possible worlds, and it goes like this. There are various forms of inference involving modal terms; these include 'p, therefore it's possible that p', 'It's necessary that p, therefore it's not possible that not-p' and so on. These might just exemplify a sui generis species of validity; but it would be more economical if we could explain these inferences by reference to other well-established forms of inference. We can achieve such an explanation by equating 'It's possible that p' with 'There exists a possible world in which p': the various inferences now go through courtesy of classical predicate logic. So we should make this equation. Following Quine's dictum that existence is expressed by the existential quantifier, plus his claims about the ontological commitments of theories, we find that whenever we say 'It's possible that such-and-such' we are in fact asserting the existence of possible worlds.

Many things could be said about this argument. I want here to consider how the argument looks in the light of the phenomenon of Anscombean modals. As is to be expected, some at least of the above-mentioned modal inferences have versions which involve stopping modals and their kin; for instance, 'You *may* move your pawn, therefore it's not the case that you *cannot* move it' (analogous to 'Possibly p, therefore not necessarily not-p').[12] Can Anscombean modality then be subsumed within the machinery of possible worlds? Is 'You cannot move your knight from A to B' to be translated: 'In every chessically possible world, you do not move your knight from A to B'? Well, *this* world is a chessically possible world, and what if I *do* move my knight from A to B? That's illegal, we're assuming; but does that mean I didn't do it?

It has sometimes been said that the rules of a game state, or imply, what *counts* as a move – the same holding, mutatis mutandis, of 'moves' in other rule-governed practices, like paying a debt. The thought might lead us to conclude that you can never make an illegal move, can never (for example) cheat at something; for we won't call it a move at all if it breaks the rules. A so-called illegal move in chess will be akin to any action a player might perform *not* as part of the game, e.g. scratching her nose.

But if I move my knight from A to B, you could after all say to me, 'You can't do that!' Do what? Move my knight from A to B, of course, which is what you saw me do (hence your protest). I must have done it for you to see me do it. And you wouldn't say 'You can't do that!' if I had merely scratched my nose. Concessively, we might say that in one sense I moved the knight, in another sense I didn't. The statement 'In every chessically possible world, you do not move your knight from A to B' will then have to rely on the second sense of 'move', tantamount to 'legal move'. But distinguishing a 'physical move' from a 'legal move' can only be done by reference to chess rules, i.e. by appeal to such facts as that you can't move a knight diagonally. You can't distinguish the two kinds of moves just by looking. In other words, in describing our chessically possible worlds we are forced to use modal vocabulary, which it was the point of the possible worlds machinery to eliminate, or allow us to do without.

Hence Anscombean modality cannot be subsumed within the machinery of possible worlds. This, however, means that we are left with sui generis inferences, such as 'You may move your pawn, therefore it's not the case that you cannot move it'. That would perhaps be merely a shame, were it not for the striking kinship between some of these sui generis inferences and inferences involving other species of modality (e.g. physical possibility). It looks very much as if modal inference should be treated as a relatively unitary phenomenon. Quinean economy might even require it. But then we should treat all modal inference as, in the relevant sense, sui generis, which will defeat the argument

I spelt out earlier for the reality of possible worlds. We could of course use the machinery of possible worlds for some kinds of modality, e.g. physical, while eschewing it for Anscombean modality; but that would leave the evident kinships between Anscombean and non-Anscombean modalities hanging, in all their 'disturbingly' sui generis surdness, not to mention the Anscombean-modal inferences themselves.[13]

The Sorites Paradox

If Wittgenstein is right, many a so-called metaphysical necessity boils down to a grammatical remark, one that embodies a linguistic rule. Such linguistic rules are expressible using Anscombe's modals. As well as stopping and forcing modals, there are permissive modals, as in 'You may move your pawn'. Such modals express *possibility*. It is in fact a feature of rule-governed practices that all three modals have work to do, and language is no exception. This fact enables us to make headway in dissolving a notorious paradox: the Sorites. The dissolution of that paradox will among other things highlight the important truth that assertion is a species of action. I said earlier that the use of Anscombean modals is intertwined with action, and that goes for those actions which are called 'assertions'.

Alex, with a friend, visits his sister Beatrice, who has just bought some new curtains. 'What lovely green curtains!' he exclaims. His eyesight, by the way, is perfectly normal. 'Green?' Beatrice responds. 'I'd have called them blue.' Note that Beatrice is not one of those people who in such a situation says, 'Green? They're not green – they're blue!' That's to say, she is not a child or childish; nor is she merely contrary, nor solipsistic. She is a mature person and a competent speaker.

Alex's friend now pipes up. His name is Timothy. 'If they're green, they can't also be blue, can they?' he points out. 'One of you must be mistaken.' But of course neither Alex nor Beatrice is mistaken. The colour of the curtains occupies that grey area – as it were – between blue and green, or if you like between definite blue and definite green. Of this colour it would be correct to say: 'You may call it blue; and you may call it green.' This employs the permissive modal and is analogous to: 'You may move your king here; and you may move your bishop there.' The latter doesn't entail 'You may move your king here *and* move your bishop there' – this would be a scope fallacy, and would also permit moving twice, which is illegal. Similarly, 'You may call it blue, and you may call it green' doesn't entail 'You may call it blue *and* call it green'. Language use is often more easy-going than chess, and calling the curtains blue, then green, might only count as changing your mind: or better, as *following a different inclination*. Nevertheless, it is useful to note the non-entailment.

When Beatrice says, 'I'd have called them blue,' she expresses her inclination to call the curtains blue. Where did she get that inclination? Did she arrive at it by some process of reasoning, or of inner comparison with memories of blue things? *Unconscious* comparison, of course, since no doubt she doesn't notice any such inner process going on. Inner processes like these, however, could not explain anything even if they had gone on; see Wittgenstein's discussion of 'Fetch me a red flower' in the *Blue Book* (1969, 3). We need not go into any of this here, though, since whatever happens in Beatrice's inner life, she is certainly a competent speaker of English – as is Alex. That is all we need. And the best answer to 'Where did she get that inclination?' is in fact something like, 'She learnt English as a child.'

Let's turn now to the Sorites paradox. Premise 1: a ripe tomato is red. True. Premise 2: if X is almost the same colour as a red thing, then X is red also. True ... but what does it mean? It means: if it's OK to call X red, then it's OK to call something which is almost the same colour as X red.[14] – But haven't I substituted a proposition about language for one about redness? That's right: what looks like a metaphysical claim (about colour) turns out to be a grammatical remark. The payoffs from this manoeuvre will become clear presently.

Here is a scenario from the Sorites research lab. I am repeatedly asked 'Is this red?' while a series of swatches passes before me, moving gradually from definite red all the way to definite orange (or yellow, or green). What will I do? What *should* I do? Perceiving that I can't go on saying 'Yes' forever, I realize that I had better at some point switch to 'No' – these two responses (let's assume) being the only ones I'm allowed, by the rules of the 'experiment'.[15] At *which* point shall I switch? There is no 'right point'; somewhere within the grey zone I decide to switch. The situation is exactly parallel to that in which I take leave of my hosts of an evening. One shouldn't do this too early, nor hang around and leave when it's too late. 10.30 would be fine, say – but so would 10.35. How do I decide? As Wittgenstein would say, the question contains a mistake.

I've just called a swatch lying within the grey area 'red' and now call an almost indistinguishable swatch 'not red'. I didn't have to do that, for I could have called the second one 'red'; the linguistic rules here are permissive: you may call it red, and you may call it not-red. Alex's friend Timothy will protest that it *can't be both*. But at best that exclamation invokes a rule: 'You cannot call this red and not-red', which might indeed be correct, for all that I've said. Yesterday, perhaps, I called the very same swatch red which I have just now called not-red. Haven't I called it red and not-red? No; for these were two moves in a game, not one. They did not belong to a single stretch of assertion. (See below.)

There will be stopping modals in play as well as permissive modals. Of the ripe tomato we might say, 'You can't call that orange.' Regarding the forcing modal, it isn't strictly true that I *have to* call it red if I call it anything, for I might call it scarlet; questions perhaps arise as to whether I *have to* agree if someone else calls it red. (Though why not just give them an enigmatic look?) But to focus on stopping modals: when, it might be asked, does the rule 'You can't call that orange' cease to be applicable? In connection with which swatch, that is? The answer is: there is no 'right point' at which to switch from 'You can't call that orange' to 'You may call that orange'. This fact corresponds to the phenomenon often referred to as 'higher-order vagueness'.

We are not, however, facing an unpleasant infinite regress, because what is at stake *here* is simply the vagueness in the concepts of word-meaning and of linguistic competence. Our use of words relies on agreement in judgment – you call this red, so do I, so does Beatrice ... but *how much* agreement there has to be in the usage of a word for it to count as having a particular meaning is a vague matter.[16] Likewise, how much I have to be in agreement with others in order to count as using words correctly, or to count as using these words correctly, is a vague matter. The status of a linguistic rule such as 'You can't call that orange' will be correspondingly vague, and this for two reasons. First, insofar as this rule is to be read off, as it were, from the general usage of 'orange', including people's responses to one another's uses (e.g. puzzlement, attempts to correct, etc.), it is vague what is going to suffice to underpin 'You can't call that orange'. Second, a modal formula like this is itself a linguistic tool, one used in the teaching of language and in the conduct of language-games (especially in face of what might be called conflicting inclinations); and a situation in which one person asserts the formula while another asserts its negation may be like that in which Alex says 'Green' while Beatrice demurs. Neither party need be mistaken.

But what about truth? If truth is the aim of assertion, won't an assertion only be successful if it is true? If it was OK for me to call that swatch not-red, then my assertion was presumably successful. So it was true. But if it was also OK for me to call it red, then that assertion would have been successful, i.e. true – and if someone else did call it red, her assertion *was* successful and true. But if *P* is true and *not-P* is true, then *P & not-P* is true, which is absurd. Timothy appears vindicated.

'Is it true that X is red?' means the same as 'Is X red?' In connection with the swatch in the grey area, permissible answers to that question include 'Yes' and also 'No'. To repeat, this does not entail that a permissible answer is 'Yes and no'. It doesn't *entail* it, I said; but note how idiomatic an answer that would in fact be. I don't think that all this threatens the foundations of classical logic. As will be discussed in the next section, rules of logic are expressible by means of Anscombean modals, and this applies to the introduction-rule for 'and', viz. 'From *P* and *Q*, infer *P & Q*'. It was this rule which was invoked a moment ago so as to land us with *P & not-P*. But of course the rule can only apply to such assertions ('P' and 'Q') as are made in the course of a single stretch of assertion: if yesterday I said 'It's raining' and today say 'It's not raining', these assertions are not made in the course of a single stretch of assertion, and I have not contradicted myself. We do not need to stipulate (as Frege did) that my two utterances were not really 'P' and 'Not P'; the stipulation is only made in the interest of abstraction *from* what I am calling stretches of assertion. And an attempt to lock the assertions of Alex and Beatrice together with the clamp of the introduction-rule for 'and' would evidently be wrong-headed.

As for truth, the purport of the term 'true' in 'P is true' is not independent of the character, meaning, and use of 'P'. For example, any doubts or hesitations we have when faced with the question whether certain grammatically indicative sentences can aptly be called 'true' or 'false' will turn out to stem from, and be resoluble only by reference to, the characteristic use made of those sentences. Such doubts can't be addressed by wielding some topic-neutral notion of truth; if anything, *that* picture gets things the wrong way round: the notion of truth gets applied or withheld only after the doubts have been dispelled. Consider performative sentences ('I name this ship *The Enterprise*'), future-tensed sentences, statements of the form 'Students are to arrive punctually', metaphors and clichés like 'Time flies', or 'emotive' statements like 'This is yummy!' True or false? One thing is clear: you won't find out by looking for a correspondence-relation with a fact at the other end.

Returning to 'This swatch is red': the question whether such a statement is true or not on some occasion should be approached via a delineation of the way the sentence is used and of the role the statement would play for us, in the imagined (or actual) scenario. The question cannot be approached via the inchoate thought that it's just the *business* of a proposition to be true.

In this way the Sorites paradox can be disposed of.[17] We felt as if logic itself were forcing us against our will towards self-contradiction and absurdity. This was an illusion; but it showed, among other things, how in awe we are of the logical 'must'. It is to the logical 'must' that I now turn.

Logic

In 'The Question of Linguistic Idealism' Anscombe writes:

> Valid inference, not logical truths, is the subject matter of logic; and a conclusion is justified, not by rules of logic but, in some cases by the truth of its premises, in some by the steps taken in reaching it, such as making a supposition or drawing a diagram or constructing a table. If someone invents variant rules, e.g. a system with more than two truth values, there is the question whether these rules have been followed in some exercise. According to what rules is the deduction, the transition, made from given rules to particular practice? Always there is the logical *must*: you 'can't' have this *and* that; you can't do that if you are going by this rule; you must grant this in face of that. And just as 'You can't move your king' is the more basic expression for one learning chess, since it lies at the bottom of his learning the concept of the game and its rules, so these 'You must's' and 'You can't's' are the more basic expressions in logical thinking. (1981a, 121)

This passage raises the question whether some basic logical 'must' will have to *underlie* our use of any rule. For if I am playing some game, a game which is governed (defined) by certain rules, the situation may arise which justifies your saying, 'You can't do that if you are going by this rule.' Let's say the rule is that one can't move knights diagonally; then if I do move my knight diagonally, you say, 'You can't do that if you are going by this rule,' which evidently involves a different 'can't' from the one in the formula 'You can't move knights diagonally'. 'You can't do that if you are going by this rule' doesn't itself appear to be the rule of some further game or practice, not even one called Logic. For if it were just another rule, the question might arise whether I was following it in a given case; and if I seemed not to be, you'd have to say, once again, 'You can't do *that* if you are going by this rule.' We must surely avoid setting off on this regress, and we can only do so by denying that the logical 'must' is just another stopping modal. So it might be thought.

In an ordinary chess game, you would no doubt just say, 'You can't move knights diagonally.' So let us imagine that there are two variants of chess, one in which you can, the other in which you can't, move knights diagonally – and you and I have agreed to play the second variant. I move my knight diagonally; you say, 'I thought we were playing Variant Two chess'; I say, 'We *are*'; you say, 'Well, you can't do that if you are going by the Variant Two rule.' Maybe I had forgotten the rule, in which case you will in effect be reminding me: 'You can't move knights diagonally.' No meta-rule comes into play. But if I stare blankly and say, 'I wasn't moving my knight diagonally', what then? Our bone of contention becomes the word 'diagonally', and again it will either be a case of your reminding, or even instructing, me what that words means – or a case of fundamental collision, of the sort Wittgenstein might seem to be inviting us to conceive as possible in the course of his 'rule-following considerations'.

The apparently conceivable collision comes about with the deviant party protesting 'But I *am* following the rule (doing the same thing, etc.).' We want to say: you have misinterpreted the rule. We then provide the correct interpretation. How? By giving a perspicuous formulation of it; that is the only way. But the new formulation can in turn be misinterpreted.

Wittgenstein's cure works by pointing out that 'there is a way of grasping a rule which is *not* an *interpretation*, but which is exhibited in what we call "obeying the rule" and "going against it" in actual cases' (*PI* 201). My inability to play by the rule 'You can't move knights diagonally' is just that – an inability. If explanations bounce off me, that doesn't show that there's no ground under our feet, only that I am not of normal intelligence. The phrase is Anscombe's: having described the use of stopping and forcing modals, not only in games but in 'logical thinking', she writes of such modals that 'they are understood by those of normal intelligence as they are trained in the practices of reasoning' (1981a, 121). She is, in effect, indicating the point where (in this enquiry) our spade is turned – the point where our question 'But how?' is forced to accept something that doesn't look like an Ultimate Justification at all, but which instead has the quotidian appearance of the humanly obvious.

A logical rule might run: 'You cannot assert *not-Q*, having asserted *If P, then Q* and *P*. Going against the rule in an actual case would be asserting (propositions of the form) *If P, then Q; P*, and *not-Q*. These assertions will be actions. To say this is implicitly to invoke some action-descriptions as against others; we are not, for example, concerned with the sounds a person makes (pitch, volume, sibilants, vowels ...). We are concerned with what sentences he utters, a sentence being something with a certain meaning – obviously. The meaning of an utterance is not down to what accompanies it in the hidden realm of the person's mind, any more than is the significance of a chess move which he makes. It is a matter of how the components of the sentence are generally used, very roughly.[18] The action is what it is in virtue of its *surroundings*, to use a Wittgensteinian notion, just as is a move in chess.

The logical 'must' thus manifests itself in human actions. Drawing a conclusion is an action; so is jettisoning a supposition.[19] Perhaps there can be inner forms of such actions – mental concludings and jettisonings. But for these too, what an action *means* is not and cannot be determined by 'intrinsic features' of the action, only by the surroundings, the background. If a person goes wrong, i.e. reasons wrong, we use the formula, 'You can't say that'. Or we might say 'You can't think that.' Either way, we use Anscombe's stopping modal, a species of social tool.

As I put it above, Wittgenstein (we might say) proposed substituting grammar or logic for both metaphysical possibility and imaginability. The term 'substituting' is appropriate insofar as there is philosophical error or confusion requiring treatment. 'The work you want done cannot be done by what you are calling metaphysical possibility and imaginability; it can only be done by invoking grammatical rules.' Grammatical or logical rules, we can now add, are embodied in human action.

Where is the *necessity* in merely human actions? it might be asked. If you want a locus for this necessity, let it be in those linguistic instruments, the modals *can't* and *must*, whose use is intertwined with human action, linguistic and non-linguistic.

I earlier discussed two philosophical hot topics, possible worlds and the Sorites paradox. The status of logic came to the fore in the discussion of each topic: the argument for realism about possible worlds relied on the thought that appeal to classical predicate logic allows us to explain modal inferences economically – while worries about the Sorites concerned especially the perceived threat that the Law of Non-contradiction might be violated. Both the argument for modal realism and standard worries about the Sorites embody wrong notions concerning the nature of logic. Let us look at each in turn.

The thought that a principle of *economy* might require us to explain certain inferences by appeal to predicate logic is a Quinean thought: the economy in question is the sort one encounters in inference to the best explanation, where explanation is done by theories and the better theories are the well-confirmed ones. Predicate logic is a very well-confirmed theory, on this picture – even better confirmed than atomic physics. But it is a theory in the same sense as is atomic physics.

I quoted Anscombe as saying that the subject matter of logic is 'valid inference, not logical truths'.[20] By 'logic' she means the study of arguments, a study one of whose tools is a symbolic calculus, such as predicate calculus. If we call predicate calculus itself (a form of) logic, we are using 'logic' in a different sense. Predicate calculus cannot be said to have a subject matter at all. As Anscombe says, it involves the use of rules, not of logical truths: valid inference within the calculus (as in ordinary language) is inference according to certain rules, those rules being expressible in the form 'You have to φ' or 'You cannot φ'. Inference, in fact, is a kind of action. Insofar as all this is true, predicate logic is more akin to chess than to atomic physics; and chess is not a theory.

The phenomenon of Anscombean modals plays havoc with modal realism. As we saw, Anscombean modality itself cannot be given a possible worlds reduction, since for such a reduction to work, Anscombean modals would have to appear in the descriptions of the possible worlds themselves. This fact leaves the 'economy' argument in a mess. Moreover, the nature of predicate logic, whose authoritative status is appealed to in the realist argument, must itself be understood by reference to Anscombean modals, as we have just noted. It thus makes no sense to invoke economy, or inference to the best explanation, in connection with it.

In the case of the Sorites paradox, the worry about the Law of Non-contradiction arises in particular because of the apparent urgency of the question, 'But is such-and-such a statement *true*?' Truth and falsity are conceived of as things which a meaningful statement will incur willy-nilly. On this picture, to say that it is OK for Beatrice to call X green can only mean that if she says that, then what she says is *true*. It is notable that much effort is usually expended by anyone proposing a theory of vagueness to give us a semantics of vague terms, where that means offering us a suitable 'model' of truth, one which 'our logic' can swallow without too much indigestion. But as I argued above, questions of truth are often if not typically posterior to ones about meaning and use; and as for logic, what needs emphasizing – again – is that logical rules are expressed by means of Anscombean modals governing certain *actions*, such as assertions. That goes for the introduction-rule for 'and', as we saw. And a description of how we use terms like 'green' and 'blue' reveals the role played by the permissive modal, as in 'You may call this green; and you may call it blue'. To understand this role we don't need to (and therefore shouldn't) appeal to Truth. Hence we can resist the Sorites paradox without worrying about the Law of Non-contradiction.

Latter-day metaphysics continues to cater to the human appetite which metaphysics has always catered to, the appetite for marvels and wonders. We listen wide-eyed as we are told that there are infinitely many worlds in addition to this one, worlds in which near-replicas of you and me are walking around. With equal amazement we learn, as it might be, that there is a particular age, specifiable to the second, at which a person becomes old – although no one knows when it is.[21] These theories are like brightly coloured toys or delightful holograms – or like shadows on the wall of a cave, to wield Plato's simile against him. Real human life, action and language, as well as being *real*, are richer than these. This richness is referred to in the following passage from Anscombe:[22]

> The things which Wittgenstein attacks – these are impediments to a true conception, or to true conceptions. It is an impediment to looking at [a] picture, if you are struck with the conviction that you must either extract the picture from the description of the colour of each colour patch in a fine grid laid upon it [reductionism], or that you must have a theory of what the picture *is* apart from what that description describes [Platonism]. If you forswear both inclinations you may get to look at the picture, and doing so you may find yourself full of amazement. Or, as Wittgenstein once put it, you may find yourself 'walking on a mountain of wonders'.[23]

Notes

1 E.g. *Treatise of Human Nature*, 1.3.14.25.
2 *Enquiry Concerning Human Understanding*, Section 12: Of the Academical or Sceptical Philosophy Pt. 3.
3 *Philosophical Investigations*, hereafter referred to as *PI*.
4 Anscombe is freely quoting *Tractatus* 5.61: 'Was wir nicht denken können, das können wir nicht denken.'
5 Which isn't to say that we might not see what someone was 'getting at' if they said such a thing; e.g. that the sphere's diameter was more than a metre.
6 See especially 'On Promising and its Justice' (1981c, 10–21) and 'Rules, Rights and Promises' (1981c, 97–103).
7 These uses of 'express' and 'cite' are simply for ease of exposition; what they amount to should be clear from how I'm using them.
8 See Anscombe (2011a); also Chapter Thirteen of this volume.
9 The recognition that the sentence is (a mild sort of) nonsense might indeed lead one to adopt a more 'fine-grained' grammar for English, such that e.g. 'put into a bank account' counts as a single verb. It wouldn't be enough to count 'put into' as a single verb, for so must 'put under' be, since it occurs in 'I put the book under the bed'; and as we see from my example, 'put into' and 'put under' are not quite generally intersubstitutable *salva congruitate*. I discuss the symbiotic relationship between the concepts *grammatical category* and *nonsense* in Chapter Thirteen of this volume.
10 Anscombe (1981b, 103–19).
11 Lewis (1980, 216).
12 We also have the validity of 'You must move your pawn, therefore you may move it' (analogous to 'Necessarily p, therefore possibly p'), and the invalidity of 'You may move your pawn, therefore you must move it' (analogous to 'Possibly p, therefore necessarily p').
13 Sui generis inferences are meant to be disturbing qua logical tufts that need shaving with Occam's Razor. Insofar as the point of the Razor has to do with 'inference to the best

explanation' and allied notions, we are faced with a conception of logic as a kind of *theory*, a conception rebutted in the last section of this chapter.
14 I am, as is customary, ignoring complications arising from contextuality and from English idiom; e.g. someone's red *hair* will typically be closer in colour to that orangey-brown swatch than this red one.
15 Other rules are of course possible, e.g. that a third response, 'Not sure', is allowed. This will not alter the nature of the task facing me.
16 And, of course, the concept of agreement is itself pretty open-textured: 'calling the same things X' won't capture all cases of agreement, e.g. where X is the word 'but'.
17 The approach I'm recommending here has affinities with the 'multi-range' account of vagueness, with its notion of 'permissible stopping places' (see Raffman 2014). A permissible stopping place is a place where it'd be OK to switch from 'red' to 'not red', for instance. Raffman stipulates that a permissible stopping place gives the (precise) boundary of a 'range', and she solves the paradox by making out that its major premise is false relative to every *range* of the predicate – the major premise being e.g. '(For all x) if x is almost the same colour as a red thing, then x is red'. Although I applaud Raffman's appeal to 'permissible stopping places', her talk of 'truth relative to a range' indicates, I think, the bloated role being assigned to the notion of truth in her account.
18 This mention of 'components' does not point to any reductive account whereby we might say that a given linguistic expression was a sound (shape, etc.) with such-and-such (use-based) semantic features. See Anscombe (2011a).
19 A person's concluding something might only be *shown* in what they do or say. Discussion of this important complication would take us too far afield, however.
20 'Logical truths' cannot be required to justify or ground valid inferences, as the encounter between Achilles and the Tortoise demonstrated. See Carroll (1895).
21 The view of 'epistemicists' about vagueness.
22 Anscombe (2011b, 186).
23 Thanks to Richard Gipps for helpful feedback on an earlier draft of this chapter.

References

Anscombe, G. E. M. (1981a), *Collected Papers Vol. I: From Parmenides to Wittgenstein*. Oxford: Blackwell.
———. (1981b), *Collected Papers Vol. II: Metaphysics and the Philosophy of Mind*. Oxford: Blackwell.
———. (1981c), *Collected Papers Vol. III: Ethics, Religion and Politics*. Oxford: Blackwell.
———. (2011a), 'A Theory of Language?', in M. Geach and L. Gormally (eds), *From Plato to Wittgenstein: Essays by G.E.M. Anscombe*. Exeter: Imprint Academic, pp. 193–203.
———. (2011b), 'Wittgenstein's "Two Cuts" in the History of Philosophy', in M. Geach and L. Gormally (eds), *From Plato to Wittgenstein: Essays by G.E.M. Anscombe*. Exeter: Imprint Academic, pp. 181–86.
Carroll, L. (1895), 'What the Tortoise Said to Achilles', *Mind* 4, no. 14 (April), 278–80.
Hume, D. *A Treatise of Human Nature*.
———. *An Enquiry Concerning Human Understanding*.
Lewis, D. (1980), 'Mad Pain and Martian Pain', in N. Block (ed.), *Readings in Philosophy of Psychology, Vol. I*. Cambridge, MA: Harvard University Press, pp. 216–22.
Raffman, D. (2014), *Unruly Words: A Study of Vague Language*. Oxford: Oxford University Press.
Wittgenstein, L. (1958), *Philosophical Investigations*, trans. G. E. M. Anscombe, ed. G. E. M. Anscombe and R. Rhees. Oxford: Basil Blackwell, 2nd ed.
———. (1969), *The Blue Book and Brown Books*. Oxford: Wiley-Blackwell, 2nd ed.

Chapter Sixteen

CONCEPTUAL CORRUPTION

Concept Loss

Concepts can persist, can evolve, can change beyond recognition. But can they simply disappear? Can we lose our concepts?

The idea that it's possible for us to lose our concepts might be backed up by reference to a concept like *phlogiston*. 'Phlogiston' was the name given to the substance hypothesized by eighteenth-century chemists as existing in all combustible bodies, and released in combustion. This theory of combustion proving to be unsustainable, there was then no use for the term 'phlogiston' – other than in such sentences as 'There is no such thing as phlogiston'.

But doesn't that last sentence show that the concept did *not* disappear? We surely couldn't frame the sentence at all if the concept (as expressed by the word) had disappeared. To this we might respond by pointing out that the role intended for the word 'phlogiston' is one which it now does not and cannot fulfil, and that insofar as a word is (meant to be) a tool, any meaning it might possess – any concept it might express – would have to *be* its role, or function. The counter-response is that the word never *could* have fulfilled any such role, given that the role related to its use in (good, adequate) explanations of phenomena of combustion; and in that case, we should seem to have to say, not so much that the concept has disappeared, as that it never got off the ground in the first place. But surely 'phlogiston' was not a meaningless noise?

We might try interpreting 'phlogiston' as 'the substance released in combustion (etc.)', adopting a Russellian approach to the definite description, and construing sentences about phlogiston as 'Ramsey sentences'.[1] If that tactic worked, the statements of the eighteenth-century chemists would come out false (not senseless), and the still-with-us concept of phlogiston would be on a par with that of a unicorn – roughly speaking. But various questions arise about the general motivation for such a manoeuvre. Shall we, for example, attempt a parallel, Ramsey-sentence-involving account of the meaning of the word 'water'? The word 'water' is used in scientific discourse, to be sure, but it is also used in everyday life; and only if we have a picture of *the* function of common nouns as being simply to 'classify things', determine a particular 'extension', etc., will we be tempted to regard an account looking like that as adequate to all our needs. This is not to rule out the possible usefulness of the imagined interpretation of 'phlogiston'. The notion of meaning may be sufficiently flexible for our adoption of such an interpretation to have a purely pragmatic, context-dependent justification.

This is not an article about chemistry. I have used the example of phlogiston to highlight some of the issues which we will be encountering in what follows. Some of the sorts of difficulties I have raised in connection with phlogiston arise also in connection with more complex and profound cases of (alleged or putative) concept-disappearance. These other cases have a kind of significance lacking in the case of phlogiston, a significance having to do with the fact that the concepts in question are, or were, more deeply entangled with human life, activity and experience.

In a richly exploratory paper, 'Losing Your Concepts',[2] Cora Diamond discusses the possibility of the disappearance of moral concepts from our lives. By moral concepts (or 'concepts central to moral life'[3]) she does not mean concepts expressed by a special 'moral' vocabulary or mode of discourse; indeed, her view, more fully expressed elsewhere,[4] is that the moral/ethical is not to be understood by reference to characteristic vocabulary, linguistic forms, or subject matter, at all. For Diamond, almost any concept might be or become a moral one, in virtue of the use or uses to which it is put. Some concepts play central parts in much of human life and thought, and when they are doing so they count as moral concepts. Among these will be, e.g., *human being, parent, lust, nation* – all of which come under scrutiny in 'Losing Your Concepts'.

In her article Diamond raises the question what it means to say that our having (using, living with) certain concepts is a good, i.e. is a good for us, in such a way that the loss of those concepts might be seen as regrettable. She evidently believes that this does make sense, and I think she is right about that. There is a correlative possibility: that our having certain concepts is an ill, something to be regretted. Diamond alludes to this possibility in another article:

> There are concepts, there are samples and paradigms and measures; there are metaphors, stories, and other things, through which we think, through which we understand ourselves and our world, and what we can and cannot do, and what we are doing; and some of these concepts, metaphors, stories, and other things are (reality being what it is) enormously useful, while others we could well do without, others may be disastrous, as elements in our lives.[5]

Diamond does not in this article further examine the idea of our having disastrous concepts: that is not her theme. It will be one of my themes in what follows. I will be arguing that one route to our having disastrous (or regrettable) concepts is through confusion in the, or a, prevalent use of certain words and phrases, a confusion amounting to futility. With regard to these words and phrases the question 'Are they meaningful?' doesn't admit of a determinate answer. This is the picture presented by Anscombe in her well-known critique of the concept of 'moral obligation'.

Anscombe on 'Moral Obligation'

The second of the three theses put forward by Elizabeth Anscombe in 'Modern Moral Philosophy' is the thesis

> that the concepts of obligation, and duty – *moral* obligation and *moral* duty, that is to say – and of what is *morally* right and wrong, and of the *moral* sense of 'ought', ought to be jettisoned if this is psychologically possible; because they are survivals, or derivatives from survivals, from

an earlier conception of ethics which no longer generally survives, and are only harmful without it.⁶

Here Anscombe is speaking about certain of our present concepts, recommending that we jettison them. ('Present', it should be borne in mind, refers to 1958, when the article was published.) On the face of it, she is not saying that 'moral obligation', for example, is a phrase without a meaning. In fact she suggests an account of how the 'ordinary (and quite indispensable) terms "should", "needs", "ought", "must" – acquired this special sense' – the 'special sense' being the sense expressed by (a certain use of) the word 'moral'. Her suggestion is that the ordinary words came to be 'equated in the relevant contexts with "is obliged" [...] in the sense in which one can be obliged or bound by law, or something can be required by law'.⁷

But the 'equation' mentioned in that last sentence is clearly regarded by Anscombe as in a certain sense impossible, or at any rate problematic; and it seems that she is drawn to a way of putting things that is in conflict with her earlier ascription to 'ought' etc. of a 'special sense' – a way of putting things according to which 'morally ought' et al. must, given their present mode of use, *fail* to express any concepts, fail to have any meaning worth the name. Thus, in ironic endorsement of Hume's claim that an 'ought' cannot be inferred from an 'is', she writes that 'this word "ought", having become a word of mere mesmeric force, could not, in the character of having that force, be inferred from anything whatever'.⁸

Diamond discusses Anscombe's view, and her version of it follows the 'no meaning' interpretation rather than the 'special meaning' interpretation:

> She [Anscombe] claimed that the background of a divine law conception of morality was required for the notion of the moral 'ought' (or of moral obligation) to have any content. What we have nowadays is the survival of the terms 'moral ought', 'moral obligation', with a sort of atmosphere clinging to them, but no meaning, since they are used without the necessary background.⁹

Diamond takes it that the picture presented by Anscombe is not exactly one of concept-loss:

> The argument is not directly that we have lost concepts [...] [rather] we go on using the old words, but the words can no longer carry their old significance.

Shall we then regard Anscombe as positing words with a special meaning or words without a meaning?

The two interpretations are compatible. If asked whether 'moral obligation', used as the phrase tends to be used, conveys any meaning or not, Anscombe would, I think, reply 'Yes and no,' or 'In one sense yes, in another no.' Insofar as meaning is use, what we have is a confused sort of use, a use that among other things involves conceptual idling – so that we perhaps have a case of 'confused meaning'. It would be inappropriate to resist this conclusion by e.g. attempting an analysis of 'moral obligation' that yielded Ramsey sentences, as scouted above for 'phlogiston' – i.e. an analysis in which 'moral obligation' is equivalent to 'the species of obligation such that so-and-so', there just happening to *be* no such species of obligation. For it is not as if we have a perfectly good understanding of the terms that would appear in the analysis ('obligation', etc.); or rather, we do have an understanding of such terms as they appear in many particular contexts, but cannot rely on the naïve move 'I am just using "obligation" in my analysis *with the same meaning* as that which it has in these other, ordinary contexts'.[10]

What shows that a prevalent use of a term or set of terms involves, not merely false beliefs, but confusion? The answer is: the tangles, dead ends, contradictions, empty statements and even plain nonsense into which such use leads people. Now one key aspect of the use of 'moral obligation', 'morally ought', etc., as depicted by Anscombe, is that all sorts of reasons for doing something get rejected as inadequate. Reasons that cite what is needed (e.g. for a human being's health), or that cite established rules or customs, or that cite commands – none of these, it is alleged, touch the important issue, which is: What action am I morally obliged to do? For can't I always ask, 'But *ought* I to aim for what is needed, or what is dictated by rules, or what is commanded?'[11]

It is true that you often can ask some such further question, especially about commands, for instance. (Your commanding officer might have gone mad.) But a general dissatisfaction with all 'factual' reasons raises the question: What can 'I ought to φ' amount to, if there can be no substantive reasons that fully support that judgment – nor, of course, reasons that count conclusively against it? The result of not accepting any substantive reasons as adequate answers to 'Why ought I to do that?' is to make that question futile and empty – and also that particular use of 'ought'.

We felt as if we were saying something important ('You tell me that it would be dishonest to do this; but is there a moral obligation to be honest?'), when in reality we were saying nothing. For we in a sense *forgot the point* of certain language-games, e.g. those in which reasons for action are asked for or given.

Where does such confusion lead moral philosophers? Anscombe's own contemporaries were often led to endorse some form of subjectivism, according to which moral statements simply express personal preferences, sentiments or whatever. These days one might instead find philosophers reaching for their 'intuitions'. The question 'What am I morally obliged to do?' might be answered by someone who finds it 'intuitive' to say something or other – 'maximize happiness', say, or 'discourage racism'. For their intuitions tell them that happiness has 'positive value', racism has 'negative value'. But as Anscombe argued, the function of the phrase 'moral obligation' in this context appears to be simply to allow the speaker or writer to insist on an indeterminate but overriding reason why you should do certain things, and to give putative grounds (indeterminate but overriding) for blaming those who do not. The mesmeric force lives on.

The Autonomy of Grammar

If Anscombe's account of 'moral obligation' is correct, then we could say that our having certain moral concepts is a bad thing, something to be regretted. The ill in question is – at least – that of confusion or emptiness of thought; but there is arguably more to it than that. Alasdair MacIntyre picks up Anscombe's critique of modern moral thinking and extends it, among other things, to those Bloomsburyite intellectuals who in the early part of the twentieth century embraced G. E. Moore's theory of goodness as a simple, non-natural property. And MacIntyre sees in the Bloomsburyite ideology a kind of *bad faith* which he takes to be characteristic of corruption in our moral concepts, writing:

> An acute observer at the time [...] might well have put matters thus: these people take themselves to be identifying the presence of a non-natural property, which they call 'good'; but there is in fact no such property and they are doing no more and no other than expressing their feelings and attitudes, disguising the expression of preference and whim by an interpretation of their own utterance and behaviour which confers upon it an objectivity that it does not in fact possess.[12]

This sort of critique is evidently not 'merely intellectual'. It has a moral dimension, relating to human relationships, to people's self-image, to the (perhaps disguised) tendency to present 'I want' and 'I like' as if they were reasons for doing things.

MacIntyre's critique did not stop short at the Bloomsburyites. The acute observer mentioned in the above passage becomes, in MacIntyre's version of events, the emotivist philosopher – the theorist who claims that all moral discourse is and must be like this: a mode of talk in which people express their feelings and attitudes in forms of language which appear to confer upon their talk 'an objectivity that it does not in fact possess'. And general changes in modern culture make it the case that emotivism is true, as applied to prevalent moral discourse. People generally *are* just emoting when they go in for moral talk, according to MacIntyre. But the terms they use once had real point in our life, given earlier social and cultural arrangements. This leads him to say that emotivism is a correct theory of use, but an incorrect theory of meaning.[13]

That way of putting things invites an obvious objection. One needn't go as far as to *identify* meaning with use for it to seem paradoxical to claim that an account of how various terms are used in a linguistic community might be a correct account, while the parallel account of what those terms mean would be an incorrect one. Surely MacIntyre would do better to say that those terms once had an unexceptionable meaning, but have now lost it? As now used (if he is right), those terms surely either have no meaning, or have a 'confused meaning' – the choice here being non-exclusive in the way it was argued to be above when we looked at Anscombe's views.

However, the connection between meaning and use which I have just mentioned is such as to suggest a deeper and more wide-ranging objection, one that would apply as much to an Anscombean as to a MacIntyrean account of moral discourse. The Wittgensteinian slogan suitable for *this* objection might be 'the autonomy of grammar'.

By what standards are we to criticize the human goings-on that constitute a given discourse? From where are the criteria to come, according to which uses and usages get to count as 'confused' or 'corrupt'? Not from within the discourse (our autonomist avers); but if from outside, from some other discourse, then won't those criteria in fact be intended for application to the human goings-on that constitute that other discourse? It will be as if we invoked the criteria for right and wrong, allowed and disallowed, which hold sway within golf, in the hope of advancing criticisms of moves made in chess.

The philosophical strategy here is a familiar one. It has been made use of in connection with a variety of discourses or language-games, including religious discourse and inductive reasoning. I mentioned earlier the distinction between describing a situation as one in which certain terms fail to express any concepts and describing a situation as one in which those terms express confused or corrupt concepts; and the 'autonomy of grammar' move appears to pose a threat to the latter in particular. But if Diamond is right that loss of concepts can be regrettable on account of its being a good to us that we have those concepts, then one might think that room must be made for the thought that having certain concepts should be an ill for us. Such concepts, and the practices which embody them, will surely be subject to bona fide critique.

The proponent of the autonomy of grammar might respond:

> But the 'good' of our having certain concepts will itself only be thinkable from within the language-game; the criteria for this good must surely be tied up with those very concepts. Through the lens of these concepts we cannot but see life without them as impoverished. The claim that having certain concepts is a good is thus a sort of grammatical note – or, if you like, a transcendental truth (in Kant's sense). The statement that having certain concepts is an ill for us, by contrast, can be sustained by no grammar, nor by anything else.

The opening assertion ('But the "good" …') might well be true in particular cases. I think it is probably true, or largely true, of concepts like *funny* and *witty*. The idea of a language-game, however, is not and was never meant to provide (or promise) anything like a taxonomy; one cannot divide our thought and talk up into a set number of language-games, nor depend on there being determinate answers to such questions as 'Does such-and-such lie inside or outside language-game L?' The occurrences of 'will' and 'must' in that opening assertion ought to provoke the caution: 'Don't think, but *look*.'

The idea that concepts are above criticism goes naturally with a quite different picture of language, according to which the sole or main function of common nouns and predicates is that of classifying things (determining a particular extension, etc.).[14] If the function of a common noun or predicate were simply to divide logical space in two, it would indeed seem futile to criticize our employing a given such expression, except perhaps for the sorts of reasons for which Frege held certain expressions of ordinary language to account: vagueness, ambiguity and the like. Strictly speaking, it might be said, one cannot criticize the concept *phlogiston* – only the theory of combustion in which it was used. An empty concept is still a perfectly workable concept; we can truly say, 'There is no phlogiston,' for instance. A false theory is ipso facto not workable.

The picture of language just described is of course *at odds* with that associated with the 'autonomy of grammar'. But once we start to flesh out the thought that there is more to common nouns etc. than extension-determination, we find that the complex, concrete and active aspects of human language use confound, rather than support, the picture of discourses as logically sealed or 'autonomous'.

Authenticity and Dishonesty

An important role played by many moral concepts (in a broad sense of 'moral') has to do with enabling people to express themselves and describe their experiences in ways that are genuine or authentic. In her paper, Diamond discusses that species of inarticulateness which is arguably suffered by those who have lost certain concepts, concepts which would have enabled them to talk about their own experience in an authentic way. She quotes the author John Berger:

> There are large sections of the English working and middle class who are inarticulate as the result of wholesale cultural deprivation. They are deprived of the means of translating what they know into thoughts which they can think. They have no examples to follow in which words clarify experience. Their spoken proverbial traditions have long been destroyed: and, although they are literate in the strictly technical sense, they have not had the opportunity of discovering the existence of a written cultural heritage.[15]

Berger describes many English people of his time as suffering from a conceptual lack. Would this lack have been describable by those people? It seems not. The vocabulary with which to describe *what* is missing from their expressive life is *ex hypothesi* unavailable to them; it belongs to a 'discourse' which might be said to be external to, or detached from, those discourses in which they are active participants. The privative ill that Berger is alleging of the language which is used by the people he writes about is not, on the face of it, an ill that is describable in that language.[16]

Of course, the task of showing that a given community suffers from expressive privation of the sort sketched by Berger would be considerable, and would surely belong as much to empirical sociology as to philosophy of language or moral philosophy. So it is not clear whether we have yet delineated a possible problem for the 'autonomy of grammar' view (or the version of it to which I've been alluding). However, the task suggested by the thoughts adumbrated in the previous two sections of this chapter would be a different one: that of showing that a given community suffers from corruption in thought and expression. This task is more particularly threatened by the 'autonomy of grammar' move, but it is also one which, if it can be tackled at all, can be tackled just by investigating concepts, as it might be put – always remembering that investigating a concept often involves looking at the lives of those who use it.

I said above that one of the roles played by moral concepts is that of enabling people to express themselves and describe their experiences in ways that are genuine or authentic. Let us expand this so as to include also 'enabling people to relate to one another in ways that are genuine and authentic'. Our question now is: With what are the terms 'genuine' and 'authentic' being contrasted? To what do these adjectives stand in opposition?

The key idea is something like *honesty*. Modes of thought and expression which lack authenticity include, for example, ones that are fake, sentimental, disingenuous, self-dramatizing, pretentious, hypocritical or moralistic. These are forms of dishonesty. Of course the idea of dishonesty in play here is not simply that of knowingly saying things that are false, in the sense of 'false' that is encapsulated in Aristotle's phrase, 'saying of what is that it is not, or saying of what is not that it is'. That the needed notion of dishonesty doesn't simply make use of Aristotle's definition of the false is connected with the fact that there is more to the role of concepts than extension-determination. After all, the moralizing pundit who describes Westerners who wear sarongs as guilty of cultural appropriation might not be best criticized on the grounds that wearing sarongs *isn't* cultural appropriation – in other words that sarong-wearing *lies outside* the extension of 'cultural appropriations'. What may be needed, rather, is a criticism aimed at the concept *cultural appropriation* itself.

If such a criticism is to involve the idea of dishonesty, it looks as if it will amount to, or generate, claims of the form 'People who (habitually) use concept C are liable to be dishonest (fake, sentimental, self-dramatizing …)'. It would probably be better to refer, not to concept C in isolation, but to some cluster of concepts to which C belongs; but for simplicity's sake I will take the claim in the form as I have given it. Now there is a way of taking claims of that form such that they purport to highlight an internal relation, between use-of-concept-C and being dishonest. That is to say, a ground for such a claim will be that saying such-and-such (in such-and-such circumstances) *is* – *counts as* – a manifestation of dishonesty.[17] By contrast, the person who presents a claim of that form as an empirical one, i.e. as one which asserts an *external* relation between use-of-concept-C and being dishonest, would seem to have to rely on evidential grounds, i.e. evidence of people's dishonesty that is logically distinct from their use of the concept C.

When MacIntyre's 'acute observer' imputed bad faith to those Bloomsburyites who invoked Moorean 'goodness', was he asserting an internal relation or an external relation? Was he taking their utterances as themselves being forms of bad faith, or was he hypothesizing (the psychological phenomenon of?) bad faith as the cause of their utterances?

Neither account is quite right; or, if you prefer, there is some truth in each. The imagined observer will surely have listened to and considered what was said, but have found it impossible to hear what was said *as* exemplifying the ('normal') practice of assertion – that practice being characterizable in terms of reasons, counter-reasons, truth, falsity and so on. Perhaps (but not necessarily) motivated by this inability-to-hear-as-assertion, he will have come to perceive what was going on *as* something else: as human beings posing or strutting, or putting others down, or …[18] But this alternative way of perceiving things was only possible because of the words uttered – because of what they meant, that is. (It was not as if the acute observer gave up on making sense of what he heard and turned instead to the gestures and facial expressions of Strachey et al.) And 'what they meant' *here* amounts to something like 'the nonsense which they meant': we are back with the two possible ways of reading Anscombe's second thesis – as invoking senselessness or as invoking a 'special sense', a 'confused meaning'.

We can say, if we like, that the relation between the Bloomsburyite utterances and the diagnosis of bad faith is (assuming MacIntyre is right) an internal relation. Those words, insofar as they meant what they did, counted as – embodied – bad faith in the speakers. But one could only *see* this if one had a lot of background knowledge of human nature and human life, of the ways people go on. That, of course, is empirical knowledge; and there could be detailed and subtle debate between different observers as to what the behaviour of the Bloomsburyites signified or amounted to.

It is essential to this kind of critique that one looks at or listens to the words used, and to how they are used – *then* teases apart the confusions, exposes the emptiness, derives the nonsense – after which it may be possible to present the phenomenon under the aspect of hypocrisy, or pretentiousness, or Nietzsche's *ressentiment*, or whatever. There is a well-known kind of critique of concepts which proceeds differently: by taking the use of certain expressions as ipso facto a sign of bad character, regardless of any further facts about how and in what circumstances they are used. The language in which that species of critique is typically couched is often a good candidate for the first kind of critique. (Who knows what the findings might be of an acute observer set to study the use of terms like 'safe space'.)

Returning to the phenomenon described by John Berger: those whom cultural deprivation has rendered inarticulate could simply suffer from an inability to express themselves; their predicament could resemble that of people who are emotionally repressed or terribly shy. But there is another possibility: the culture might (start to) offer them *ersatz* relief, in the form of modes of speech which can be taken up as one takes up slogans and catch-phrases. Indeed, the modes of speech in question very often *are* slogans and catch-phrases. To many of these forms of language MacIntyre's 'emotive theory of use' will be readily applicable. Loss of concepts, in short, may lead to a psychological vacuum, a vacuum which ends up being filled by the badges and banners of a pseudo-morality.

The reason why the 'autonomy of grammar' move fails to show such a description of things to be suspect is just that people adopt ways of talking for all sorts of reasons, including what might be called ulterior motives. When the adoption of certain ways of talking counts as conceptual corruption, this will be primarily evident from its being impossible to make full sense of what people are doing in terms of assertion, enquiry, debate, etc. It is thus a philosophical or conceptual task that faces the social critic here, namely the task of showing that such-and-such utterances have no meaning, or have a special ('confused') meaning – and on the back of that, of showing (or suggesting) that there is another aspect under which to see these human behaviours, notably that of dishonesty or bad faith.[19]

Ethics and Philosophy

The type of critique I have described bears obvious similarities to Wittgensteinian critiques of philosophical claims and positions. A Wittgensteinian critique can often be thought of as proceeding through two stages. First comes the detailed interrogation of modes of expression, resulting perhaps in a transition from disguised to patent nonsense.[20] Then (or perhaps in parallel) comes diagnosis, e.g. in such terms as 'being in the grip of a picture', 'being misled by surface linguistic forms', 'craving generality', etc. (It is not impossible, indeed, that a diagnosis of 'intellectual dishonesty' should on occasion suggest itself, in full parallel with the MacIntyrean critique.)

No autonomy of grammar protects the victim of philosophical error and confusion. A devotee of 'inner processes' cannot claim immunity from criticism on the ground that there is a raft of technical terms – 'sense data', 'qualia', 'subjective viewpoint', 'zombies' – which go to make up a distinct discourse or language-game, the rules governing which are internal to the practice. For one can ask 'What do you mean?' of a person's use even of so-called technical terms – perhaps particularly of these. And if 'sense-datum' is a technical term in this context, so are 'cultural appropriation', 'expected utility', 'productivity'[21] and other moral concepts, in the broad sense of 'moral'. It is the enquiry generated by 'What do you mean?' which will supply grounds, if grounds there be, for the sorts of conclusions arrived at by Anscombe and MacIntyre; and that question is also often the first step in a critique of a philosophical position.

One can draw a kind of general analogy between ethics and philosophy. At the start of this chapter, when I contrasted the loss of concepts like *phlogiston* with that of moral concepts, I described the latter sort of (putative) concept-loss as enjoying a significance arising from the fact that the concepts in question are more deeply entangled with human life, activity and experience. And Diamond's view of the 'moral' I characterized as involving the idea that concepts which are found to play certain crucial roles in human life and thought count to that extent as moral concepts, as 'concepts central to moral life'. But phrases such as these, relating to human life and thought, are surely well-suited to another job: that of characterizing philosophical problems and questions. Philosophical questions are ones like 'What is knowledge?', 'Is the future less real than the past?' and 'Can I imagine another person's pain?' – and *not* like 'How do you make a jet engine?', 'What is the visual cortex?' and 'Did Hitler ever meet Churchill?' For concepts like *knows*, *past* and *pain* are 'more deeply entangled with human life, activity and experience' than ones like *jet engine*, *visual cortex* and *meeting between Hitler and Churchill*. The pervasiveness and relevance to so much of our lives of a concept like *the past* explains, or is a large part of the reason, why our thoughts about it quickly become dizzyingly labyrinthine in the way characteristic of distinctively philosophical puzzlement.[22]

There are two consequences of this account of the nature of philosophical questions. First, a question's being a philosophical one is a matter of degree: for it is a matter of degree how deeply embedded in our lives and thought a given concept (or concept-cluster) will be, and a matter of degree how far into the labyrinths we will go when we start reflecting. Second, the range of 'deeply embedded' concepts is not unified in subject matter, and for that reason Wittgenstein was surely right to see philosophy as having no proprietary subject matter. In the sense in which there is a subject matter uniting *molecule, oxygen, combustion, distillation, gas, acid*, there is no subject matter uniting *knowledge, time, sensation, causation, truth, happiness*. Could we perhaps say that the subject matter of philosophy is 'deeply embedded concepts'? Maybe, but the assertion has something misleading about it, insofar as it suggests that we are after a taxonomy, when what we are (or ought to be) after is clarification, enlightenment, wisdom. Moreover, the dichotomy 'concepts vs. things' is a false dichotomy; it needs to be stressed that in talking about concepts one is very often thereby talking about things.

If these two consequences hold of philosophical questions, won't analogous consequences follow from the fact that *moral* concepts are also ones which 'are more deeply entangled with human life, activity and experience'? That's to say: first, won't it be a matter of degree whether an issue is a moral issue, and second, won't there, as Diamond says, be no such thing as the subject matter of morality?

The first of these two claims seems to me clearly true. Charles has been getting more and more unpunctual of late, and I say it's because he's fallen in love and hence is extremely distracted. Is what I say a moral criticism? It surely doesn't just depend on whether I'm annoyed by his behaviour, nor on whether I 'intend' my criticism to be a moral one. Certainly, one can imagine a further account of the facts which strikes us as clearly moving into the domain of the moral; but one can equally imagine a further account which leaves the 'moral or not?' question unsettled, as correlative with such theoretical and practical questions as 'vice or foible?' and 'condemnation or sympathy?' (An *unsettled* question is often appropriately answered with 'Say what you like' – and if practical, with 'Do what you like'.)

The question whether morality, or better, ethics, has a subject matter seems less straightforward. The reasons sketched above for saying that philosophy has no subject matter alluded to the way in which many of our concepts are pervasive in, and relevant to, much of our life and thought. But although our human nature determines our interests and proclivities, and hence helps determine what concepts we have and what shapes they take, it doesn't follow that all our thought is of ourselves. The objects of our enquiries are infinitely various, and this variety is to some extent reflected in the range of concepts with which philosophy explicitly or implicitly deals. The pervasiveness and relevance to our lives of moral concepts, on the other hand, surely has to do with the fact that those concepts operate especially within enquiries, debates, parables, etc. that are *about* human life and welfare (= faring well). An enquiry or debate or parable can be 'about human life and welfare' without having a proprietary vocabulary; it might be the *locus of use* of a concept, i.e. within such an enquiry/debate/parable, which earns it the title of 'moral concept' – as I think Diamond would suggest. For all that, the pervasiveness and relevance to our lives of moral concepts has a different explanation from the parallel explanation regarding what may be called philosophically-charged concepts. The question whether an effect can precede its cause is not a question in ethics, despite the fact that *cause* and *effect* are among the concepts most deeply embedded in our thinking. For it is not as such, and in the relevant sense, a question about human life and welfare.

The sense in which ethics does or does not have a subject matter is, however, not my main concern in this paper, and to discuss it properly I would have to give it more attention than I am able to here. I will conclude instead with some remarks about the two non-exclusive alternatives I mentioned earlier, of describing what people say as senseless and of describing what they say as having a special (e.g. confused) sense. This will initially involve jumping to an apparently altogether different topic; but it is a topic which will be very familiar to readers of Diamond.

Special Sense or No Sense?

A well-known debate about how to read Wittgenstein's *Tractatus* centres on the dilemma 'Special sense or no sense?' In the penultimate section of the book, 6.54, Wittgenstein declares that 'my propositions are elucidatory in this way: he who understands me finally recognizes them as nonsensical'. Examples of such 'nonsensical propositions' are 'The world is all that is the case' (1) and 'Objects are simple' (2.02). If such propositions are both nonsensical and elucidatory, it is tempting to think they are somehow 'getting at' truths which cannot be expressed in language – ineffable truths.

Diamond has persuasively argued that it was no part of Wittgenstein's aim to invoke ineffable truths. Rather, she says, he wants us to realize that 'Objects are simple' is *plain nonsense*; there is nothing 'hidden behind' it, as it were.[23] Crucial to her argument is the lack of any ground for saying that *this* symbol, occurring in *this* well-formed proposition, may be discerned occurring also in *that* ill-formed proposition.[24] It is uncontroversial that the word 'rat' (the one which occurs in 'There's a rat in my garden') does not occur in 'Socrates loves Plato', despite the occurrence of the letter-group r-a-t. But by the same token, we ought to say that the word 'object' (the one which occurs in 'There's at least one object that growls', alias 'For some x, x growls') does not occur in 'Objects are simple', or in 'Henry is an object'.[25] Maybe 'object' as it occurs in 'Henry is an object' has, or can be given, some meaning *other than* that which it has in 'There's at least one object that growls'; but it cannot be given, or stipulated to have, meaning just by pointing to the latter proposition and saying, 'I intend it to have the same meaning that it has there.' The concomitant lesson concerning nonsense is this: if we have a piece of nonsense in the form of a proposition it won't be nonsense because in it we find symbols – the same ones as occur legitimately over there – being made to play roles 'in violation of their proper use'. For a symbol not doing its job is not a symbol at all. (I.e. 'symbol not doing its job' is an oxymoron.)

This line of thought is very powerful and can be of great use e.g. when showing that an alleged 'metaphysical impossibility' dissolves into a rule of grammar – also in situations where disguised nonsense is being brought out into the open. But does it rule out our *ever* saying, 'The word W occurs in this nonsensical statement'? If it did, that would seem to cast doubt on my description of those who use 'corrupt concepts' as really *using concepts*: as meaning certain kinds of nonsense by their words.

To make headway with this problem we might consider the phenomenon of secondary sense.[26] If I say that Wednesday is fat, whereas Tuesday is lean, I am not using 'fat' and 'lean' in the normal way, the way I was first taught to use them. But nor am I using them as metaphors, in the sense of 'metaphor' according to which one can set about explaining or elucidating a metaphor by reference to features of the subject. Tuesday has no *features* which I would allude to in explanation of my inclination to call it lean.[27] I just find it natural to say that, and to reach for that word. Which word? The word 'lean'. What do I mean by that word? Well … thin, not fat. But how *can* I mean 'lean', 'thin' or 'not fat' if what I'm saying is 'Tuesday is …'?

The use of 'lean' made by one who says 'Tuesday is lean' is clearly different from the use made of it in 'Yon Cassius has a lean and hungry look'. The latter is, of course, a rather different use from the one we get in 'Those are lean cattle'; but explanations of the meanings of the 'Cassius' and 'cattle' sentences will be closely related, whereas an explanation of 'Tuesday is lean' will in the end rely on something like the speaker's inclination to say it. If meaning were closely tied to use we should have to say that 'lean' in 'Tuesday is lean' means something quite different from 'lean' in 'Those are lean cattle' – or that it means nothing at all. The latter verdict, indeed, looks quite attractive. And yet the 'secondary sense game' is one which we do play, and of course it has many forms beside the one to do with days of the week, some of them of considerable importance in our thinking. Reflection on the phenomenon of secondary sense in fact helps one to see that talk of meaning is not always assimilable to talk of use.[28]

Still, when we ask the person who says 'Tuesday is lean' what she means by 'lean', her reply (we imagined) is 'Thin, not fat'. And isn't that as if, when asked what I mean by 'frog' in the statement 'I intend to dream two frogs under my breath', I were to reply 'a short-bodied, tailless amphibian of the order *Anura*'? My saying that that's what I mean is surely not a guarantor of my meaning it, any more than is my saying that by the syllable 'rat', occurring in the statement 'Socrates loved Plato', I mean 'medium-sized, long-tailed rodent in the superfamily *Muroidea*'. Such a self-explanation falls in the same category as the form of explanation 'I just mean here what I meant by this word over there'. It's not that such an explanation can never work, but that it cannot quite generally constitute, nor guarantee, sameness of meaning – in particular where the sense of the whole statement is already in doubt.

The sense of 'Tuesday is lean', we might say, is its role in a certain game, in a rather obvious sense of 'game'. Asked for elucidation, we can only point to the game, noting such features of it as that one 'helps oneself' to words that have a bona fide primary sense. That it *is* the word 'lean' I am reaching for and using is down to my citing it (in effect citing bona fide sentences containing it), and doing so *in the context of this game*. Let us imagine a detached and acute observer of people playing the game. Such an observer will quickly reject 'normal assertion' as a description of what they are up to and, like the acute observer of the Bloomsburyites, will move to another description – not one invoking bad faith or disguised motivation, however, but one invoking *fun* or *whimsy*.

Are those who play the days-of-the-week game talking nonsense or not? Yes and no. In the context of the game, 'Tuesday is lean' is a different move from 'Tuesday is fat', and an incompatible one, i.e. you'd not be playing correctly if you said both without qualification. (Actually, one can imagine that rule being dropped and there still being *a* game to play.) These are distinct moves in a language-game played by real human beings; in that sense, they're meaningful. But attempts to understand the meaning of the players' utterances in the same way that one would attempt to understand primary uses of (what the players are calling) the words they've chosen – such attempts lead nowhere. In that sense, their utterances are nonsense. Even so, the *kind* of nonsense that is at issue is determined by the nature and point of the game, and, more fundamentally, by those 'general facts of (human) nature' which underlie our *finding* a point in the game.

So the statement 'The word W occurs in this nonsensical statement' can on occasion be justified. A lot of work would be needed to show that, pace Diamond, the word 'object' occurs in the (putatively) nonsensical statement 'Henry is an object'; her arguments cannot be rebutted by mere appeal to the possible truth of 'The word W occurs in this nonsensical statement'. Still, it would also be unsafe to rely on a rigid sense/nonsense dichotomy of the sort espoused by Wittgenstein in the *Tractatus*, for reasons flowing naturally from the ideas of the later Wittgenstein.

Returning to our main topic, it is now possible to see what a critique of corrupt concepts – or one such critique – will involve. It will involve, first: showing that the, or a, prevalent use of a concept cannot be taken (interpreted) as straightforward assertion, on account of the kinds of tangles and dead ends into which it leads, or would lead, those who use it (e.g. when quizzed about what they're saying). It will involve, second: suggesting an aspect under which the given concept-use may consequently be seen, an aspect which shows that something is wrong. The aspect may be that of dishonesty, in one of its many forms – in contradistinction to, say, whimsy. The idea of *something's being wrong* cannot here be undermined by appeal to 'the autonomy of grammar'. Nor can the idea of people's *meaning a certain kind of nonsense by their statements* be undermined by appeal to the sorts of consideration used by Diamond in her rejection of the 'ineffability' reading of the *Tractatus*.

Notes

1. Ramsey sentences translate (or replace) sentences which employ 'theoretical' predicates by ones which employ existential quantifiers, variables and (esp. 'observational') predicates. The name derives from Ramsey (1929).
2. Diamond (1988).
3. Ibid., 256.
4. See e.g. Diamond (1996). In this paper Diamond is more concerned to establish the view's tenability than its truth.
5. Diamond (2019, 212).
6. Anscombe (1981a, 26).
7. Ibid., 29–30.
8. Ibid., 32. The qualification 'in the character of having that force' might appear to make room for the thought that 'in the character of having semantic content S' (or something along those lines) 'ought'-statements *could* be inferred from 'is'-statements. Anscombe does indeed think that the ordinary 'uncorrupt' concept *ought* allows us to make inferences like that: see her comparison of 'ought' and 'owes' in Anscombe (1981b). But the remark I have quoted concerns the 'ought' which has, in the mouths of moderns, 'become a word of mere mesmeric force' – 'ought' as '*morally* ought'.
9. Diamond (1988, 256–7).
10. For more on this move, see the final section of this chapter. The move is often highlighted and undermined by Wittgenstein in his later writings; see for example Wittgenstein (1958, sec. 350).
11. That one can always reject substantive reasons for a moral judgment is the gist of Moore's Open Question Argument, said to supply the test for whether a 'naturalistic fallacy' has been committed.
12. MacIntyre (1981, 16).
13. Ibid., 13, 17.
14. Diamond highlights the distorting effect of this idea in her paper; see the discussion of the concept *human being* (1988, 264–6). In particular, she stresses that one cannot correct the philosophical picture just by adding a second 'function' (for common nouns) to that of extension-determination, namely 'evaluation'. The difference between 'human being' and '*Homo Sapiens*' is not that the former expression carries some 'evaluative' connotation not carried by the latter.
15. Berger (1982, 98–9).
16. As Berger's reference to proverbial traditions indicates, the privation he is discussing is not simply a matter of size of vocabulary: even a relatively small stock of words can yield a multitude of phrases, sayings, jokes, metaphors, all capable of embodying human wisdom.
17. A claim construed thus will typically be defeasible – hence the use of 'are liable' after 'People who (habitually) use concept C …' What we have are constitutive but defeasible grounds, *alias* 'criteria'.

18 Might he not put the tangles and empty statements down to straightforward dimness or common-or-garden irrationality? To be able to do so, the observer would need to see in the Bloomsburyites' conversations on other (relatively intellectual) subjects a similar degree of dimness. Moreover, the *kinds* of non sequitur, abrupt subject-shift, question-begging, etc. which manifest ordinary dimness differ from those which embody *motivated* nonsense. One of the differences lies indeed in the resort to a favoured vocabulary ('morally ought', 'elitist', 'best practice' …).
19 There is a parallel here with those causal explanations of a person's behaviour which are resorted to when the *reasons* they give for what they do strike us as inadequate (without being consciously deceitful).
20 See Wittgenstein (1958, sec. 464).
21 As in 'NHS productivity'.
22 In talking of concepts I am of course talking, roughly, of words and their uses; some of the *items* mentioned – people's visual cortices, for example – obviously play an enormously prevalent and important part in human life.
23 More recently, Diamond has argued that a proposition of the *Tractatus* might (come to) have a use as a 'solo proposition', or 'thinkable-with-no-alternative' – specifically, might (come to) have a use as indicating a path in thought *not* to be taken (see Diamond 2019, 199). And if it is 'part of the business of thinking to guide, or help put back on track, the business of thinking' (2019, 227), and if Aristotle was right to say that 'for theoretical thinking, the "well and badly" are truth and falsehood' (2019, 162), then a solo proposition, e.g a path-blocker, might after all be counted true. Diamond doesn't, though she surely could, apply this conclusion directly to such *Tractatus* propositions as have taken on the role of path-blocker (say). These will have 'taken on' that role only for those who can *use* them as such, i.e. who have 'seen through' their apparent substantialness. In *that* role, 'The world is the totality of facts, not of things' could perhaps be counted true – but not in the (non-)sense that it expresses an ineffable truth.
24 See the discussion of 'Socrates is identical' in Diamond (1991a, 196–97).
25 See *Tractatus* 4.1272.
26 The term is Wittgenstein's; see Wittgenstein (1969, 136–39) and Wittgenstein (1958, Part II, 216). See also Diamond (1991b, 225–42).
27 An empirical hypothesis as to why I have that inclination might conceivably be true – as, that the 'oo' sound in 'Tuesday' stimulates, via audition, certain neurons in my brain adjacent to ones which … None of that, of course, would indicate that 'lean' functions as a metaphor (or as anything else).
28 See Diamond (1991b, 240). Interestingly, Diamond in this article raises the question whether the phrase targeted by Anscombe, 'morally ought', could be regarded as a 'secondary sense' extension of an ordinary, primary-sense 'ought'. See Diamond (1991b, 237).

References

Anscombe, G. E. M. (1981a), 'Modern Moral Philosophy', in *Collected Papers Vol. III: Ethics, Religion and Politics*. Oxford: Blackwell, pp. 26–42.

———. (1981b), 'On Brute Facts', in *Collected Papers Vol. III: Ethics, Religion and Politics*. Oxford: Blackwell, pp. 22–25.

Berger, J. (1982), *A Fortunate Man*, photography by J. Mohr. New York: Pantheon Books.

Diamond, C. (1988), 'Losing Your Concepts', *Ethics* (January), 255–77.

———. (1991a), 'Throwing Away the Ladder', in *The Realistic Spirit*. Cambridge, MA: MIT Press, pp. 179–204.

———. (1991b), 'Secondary Sense', in *The Realistic Spirit*. Cambridge, MA: MIT Press, pp. 225–42.

———. (1996), 'Wittgenstein, Mathematics and Ethics', in H. Sluga, D. G. Stern (eds), *The Cambridge Companion to Wittgenstein*. Cambridge: Cambridge University Press, pp. 226–60.

———. (2019), *Reading Wittgenstein with Anscombe, Going on to Ethics*. Cambridge, MA: Harvard University Press.
MacIntyre, A. (1981), *After Virtue*. London: Duckworth.
Ramsey, F. P. (1929), 'Theories', in R. B. Braithwaite (ed.), *The Foundations of Mathematics and Other Logical Essays*. Paterson, NJ: Littlefield and Adams, pp. 212–36.
Wittgenstein, L. (1958), *Philosophical Investigations*, trans. G. E. M. Anscombe, ed. G. E. M. Anscombe and R. Rhees. Oxford: Basil Blackwell, 2nd ed.
———. (1969), *The Blue Book and Brown Books*. Oxford: Wiley-Blackwell, 2nd ed.

SOURCES

'Are There Any Intrinsically Unjust Acts?', in *Zeitschrift für Ethik und Moralphilosophie*, October 2018.
'Conceptual Corruption', in *Cora Diamond on Ethics* (ed. Balaska), Palgrave, 2021.
'Ethics and Philosophy: Aristotle and Wittgenstein Compared', in *Aristotelian Naturalism: A Research Companion* (ed. Hähnel), Springer, 2019.
'The Functionalist's Inner State', in *Wittgenstein and Contemporary Philosophy of Mind* (ed. Schroeder), Palgrave, 2000.
'How Should One Live? Williams on Practical Deliberation and Reasons for Acting', in *Ethics beyond the Limits* (ed. Chappell, van Ackeren), Routledge, 2019.
'The Identity of a Word', in *American Catholic Philosophical Quarterly*, February 2016.
'"An Inculcated Caring": Ryle on Moral Knowledge', contribution to *Ryle: Intelligence, Practice, Skill*, Åbo Akademi University, Finland, June 2015.
'Is Pleasure a Good?', originally published as 'Le plaisir est-il un bien?', in *Elizabeth Anscombe et le Philosophie Contemporaine* (ed. Pavlopoulos, Aucouturier), Paris: Publications de la Sorbonne, 2014.
'Meaning, Understanding and Action', in *Enrahonar, An International Journal of Theoretical and Practical Reason*, 2020.
'Metaphysics and Modals', in *The Anscombean Mind* (ed. Haddock, Wiseman), Routledge, 2022.
'"Not a Something"', in *Nordic Wittgenstein Review*, 6, no. 1, June 2017.
'Rational Choice Theory and Backward-Looking Motives', in *Economic Objects and the Objects of Economics* (ed. Rona, Zsolnai), Springer, 2018.
'Ryle on Hypotheticals', in *Ryle on Mind and Language* (ed. Dolby), Palgrave Macmillan, 2014.
'Sincerity in Thought', in *The Moral Philosophy of Elizabeth Anscombe* (ed. Gormally, Jones, Teichmann), Imprint Academic, 2016.
'The Voluntary and the Involuntary', in *American Catholic Philosophical Quarterly*, Summer 2014.
'Why "Why?"? Action, Reasons and Language', in *Philosophical Investigations*, January 2015.

INDEX

addiction 55, 58
Anscombe, G.E.M. 1–2, 39n.3, 41, 42, 44–45, 46–47, 48–49, 53–54, 59, 65–67, 68, 71, 81n.22, 74–76, 78, 79–80, 83, 91–92, 93–94, 96, 98, 105–8, 110, 116, 117, 151–59, 162–66, 173–74, 175–79, 199n.17-18, 202–3, 204–5, 210, 211, 212, 213, 216–18
Aquinas 68
arguments 188–90
Aristotle 48, 82n.29, 123–30, 138–40, 161–62, 221–22
Armstrong, D. 198
Augustine 7
Austin, J.L. 65–66, 80
'average' 6–8

backward-looking motives 59, 83–88, 161
behaviourism 17, 20
beliefs 190–93, *see also* thoughts
Berger, J. 221
Broome, J. 84–85, 167n.12

Carroll, L. 188–89, 214n.20
chess 29–31, 33–34, 99–100, 138, 203–4, 206, 210–11
Child, W. 27
Chrysippus's dog 193–94
Cockburn, D. 134
conceptual corruption 96, 98, 102, 216–28
consequentialism 12, 117, 151, 155
context 28, 37, 87–88, 110–11, 171
counterfactual conditionals 32, 69, 77, 78
cultural appropriation 221–22

Davidson, D. 106, 134–35
deliberation 131–34, 153–55, 160–62
desirability characterizations 2, 53–54, 55, 56, 58, 60–61
desires 132–35
Diamond, C. 187–88, 216, 217, 228n.14, 221, 224, 226, 226n.26, 229n.26, 229n.28

doubtfulness (of thought) 42, 44
Driver, J. 106

economics 13, 83, 88
emotion 9
enjoyment 71–74, *see also* pleasure

feeling *see* emotion
Foot, P. 12, 157
forcing modals *see* modals
Frankfurt, H. 70
Frege, G. 28, 87
fun *see* pleasure

Geach, P.T. 173
Gellner, E. 4
Gipps, R. 13n.16
gluttony 158
good 11–12, 53, 60–61
grammar 172–74, 202, 211
gratitude 83–87
Gustafsson, M. 30

hate crime 10–11
hedonism 54–55, 59–60
Hume, D. 113, 144–46, 201
hypocrisy *see* insincerity

individualism 9–13
injustice 98, 151–60, 162–66
inner (state, process) 17, 22–23, 28–29
insincerity *see* sincerity
intellectual virtues *see* virtues
internalism about reasons 11, 99, 112–13, 134–38
interpretative motives 59, 60, 107

justice 146–47, *see also* injustice

Kaplan, D. 185n.15
Kripke, S. 8, 185n.13

Leibniz's Law 30–31
Lewis, D. 18, 20, 22, 181, 200n.21, 205
logoi *see* modals
Lovibond, S. 167n.16

MacIntyre, A. 218–19
Malcolm 124–25
McDowell, J. 27–28
Mellor, D.H. 199n.4
mind-brain identity 18, 33, 36–37
modals 2, 91–93, 94–96, 99–100, 101–2, 138, 160, 194–95, 202–13
Moore, G.E. 12, 228n.11, 218–19
moral dilemmas 155, 162
moral obligation 96–98, 151, 216
morphemes *see* phonemes
motivational set 134–35
motives *see* backward-looking motives, interpretative motives
Mueller, A. 47–48, 133–34, 191

'Noffle' *see* 'Tink'
nonsense 97, 111, 114, 174, 222–23, 225–28

offence 9–10

pain 18–19, 20–22, 27–28, 37–38, *see also* sensations
paradigm cases 159
philosophy 2–4, 123–25, 126–30, 223
phlogiston 215–16, 220
phonemes 176
physicalism *see* mind-brain identity
pleasure 11–12, 53–61, 85–86, 88
Popper, K. 127
practical deliberation *see* deliberation
promises 84–85, 91–92, 94, 146–47, 202–3
Putnam, H. 20–21, 22

Raffman, D. 214n.17
Ramsey, F.P. 187–88, 198, 200n.20, 200n.21, 228n.1
rationale 58–59, 61
Ryle, G. 143–48, 188–99

St Paul 156
Sandis, C. 149n.2
secondary sense 226–27
sensations 27–28, 37 *see also* pain
Shewmon D.A. 25n.1
sincerity 41–50, 192–93
'Slab' 175–77, 178–80
Smith, M. 103n.11
Speaks, J. 180–81
Specht, E.K. 27
stopping modals *see* modals
Strawson, P.F. 24–25,

thinking *see* thoughts
thoughts 31, 41–42, 44–45, *see also* beliefs
'Tink' *see* 'Slab'
Tolstoy, L. 46

vices *see* virtues
virtues 44, 94–95, 96, 124–26
voluntariness 48–50, 65–80, 109–11

wanting 54, 56, 191–92, *see also* desires, voluntariness
'Why?' 2, 44, 53–54, 55, 58, 66–67, 73–74, 76, 78, 83–84, 105–12, 116–17, 193–94
Williams, B. 103n.11, 131–40
wine and poetry 144–45, 146
Wittgenstein, L. 1, 3–4, 7, 18–19, 21, 23–24, 27–29, 31–32, 34, 35, 37, 38, 50n.1, 50n.2, 81n.12, 91, 97, 98, 100–1, 108, 114–15, 118n.15, 123–30, 164–65, 175, 177–78, 180, 185n.19, 187–88, 196, 201, 204, 207–8, 211, 213, 228n.10, 223, 225–26, 229n.26, 227

www.ingramcontent.com/pod-product-compliance
Lightning Source LLC
Chambersburg PA
CBHW021140230426
43667CB00005B/192